DOG'S
BEST FRIEND

ALSO BY MARK DERR

Some Kind of Paradise
The Frontiersman
Over Florida
(with Cameron Davidson)

MARK DERR

DOG'S
BEST FRIEND

Annals of the Dog-Human Relationship

With a new Preface

The University of Chicago Press
Chicago and London

The University of Chicago Press, Chicago 60637
Copyright © 1997, 2004 by Mark Derr
All rights reserved.
First published in 1997 by Henry Holt and Company, Inc.
University of Chicago Press edition 2004
Printed in the United States of America

Portions of this book appeared in different form in the following publications:
"The Politics of Dogs," *Atlantic Monthly*, March 1990; "The Perilous Iditarod,"
Atlantic Monthly, March 1995: "Marathon Mutts," *Natural History*, March 1996;
"Common Scents," *Scientific American*, September 1995.

13 12 11 10 09 08 07 06 05 04   1 2 3 4 5
ISBN: 0-226-14280-9 (paper)

Library of Congress Cataloging-in-Publication Data

Derr, Mark.
    Dog's best friend : annals of the dog-human relationship / Mark Derr.
      p.   cm.
    Originally published: New York : H. Holt, 1997. With new pref.
    Includes bibliographical references and index.
    ISBN 0-226-14280-9 (paper : alk. paper)
    1. Dogs—Behavior. 2. Dogs. 3. Dogs—History. 4. Human-animal relationships.
I. Title.

SF433 .D47 2004
636.7—dc22

                                                            2003057036

To David Byer and Bob Singer

CONTENTS

PREFACE

Publication of this paperback edition of *Dog's Best Friend* gives me the opportunity to reflect once again on the complex interplay of continuity and change, tradition and innovation, that defines what I have called the "culture of the dog," which, perforce, includes people. It also leads me to ask anew why an animal beloved by so many people, who often depend on it for their survival, can be reviled by so many others. I believe the answer is in part that the dog straddles the "natural" and "human" worlds, is itself domestic, devoted, and loyal, yet capable of turning "wild" or savage—of literally biting the hand that feeds it. By their presence, dogs, even to some degree those fancy toy breeds that breeders have attempted to turn into virtual dolls, force us outside the confines of ourselves and our constructed world to face another consciousness.

The dog's natural abilities and senses have always complemented and extended those of its human companions, whether they be hunters and gatherers living in small bands, herders and farmers, city dwellers, or suburbanites roving in their cars. In our urban/suburban society, many of the dog's traditional tasks are continually morphing into new activities, like field and herding trials, sled dog racing, Frisbee chasing, flyball, agility and other athletic competitions, scent detection work, assisting people with disabilities, tracking down endangered species for scientific study, not slaughter, and the new ecochallenges, those rugged cross-country adventure races. Yet the majority of the nation's 65 million dogs—up from 57 million in 1996, according to the 2003–2004 National Pet Owners Survey of the American Pet Products Manufacturers Association—are expected to be both well-behaved companions and protective guardians. In our densely settled world, those roles, among the dog's earliest, frequently collide, with results that can be disastrous for people and dogs.

Nor do all dogs manage psychologically or emotionally in a latchkey world. Aggression, anxiety, excessive barking, biting, and other behavioral problems still land several million dogs a year in shelters or new homes. Others are exiled to the yard, a store room, or a crate, because they chew or run around or have become inconvenient. The steady expansion of no-kill shelters has improved the lot of unwanted dogs in many areas, but an unacceptable number are still put down for lack of homes. So, too, a steep decline in the number of dogs bought from pet stores, along with continuing public relations campaigns by animal welfare groups, has put pressure on puppy mills—a major source of dogs with genetic and behavior problems—although not enough to shut them down.

Over the past decade a growing number of unwanted dogs have found employment as detector dogs, sniffing out everything from toxic chemicals to explosives. In fact, demand for those dogs has become so great in the United States and elsewhere in the wake of the September 11, 2001, terrorist attacks that government agencies are having a difficult time finding enough animals to meet their needs. Some agencies are pursuing their own breeding programs—a difficult undertaking that ideally should spur research into genetics and behavior. But experts observe that research into the dog's olfactory abilities and into the interaction between handler and dog that could lead to improvements in their training, use, and reliability has lagged far behind their deployment in the field. These trainers and behaviorists also worry that the rush to produce more detector dogs has put an unknown but not insignificant number of poorly trained, error-prone dogs and handlers in the field. Several well-publicized failures could jeopardize detector dog programs and reinforce the bias in many agencies in favor of machines over dogs, even though the machines are not nearly as efficient or accurate.

The gap within many breeds between animals bred for work—retrieving, herding, and hunting, for example—and those bred for the show ring, without regard to their ability to perform, has also continued to grow. While breeders everywhere strive to produce purebred dogs of physical, mental, and emotional soundness, far too many continue to breed dogs with genetic defects, many of which can be avoided. Some breed clubs and the American Kennel Club have offered limited backing in recent years to the Dog Genome Project, often tied to the hunt for the genes for a breed-specific disease, but they have failed to develop comprehensive policies. By the summer of 2004, the Whitehead Institute for Biomedical Research is expected to have sequenced the full genome of a highly inbred boxer, which should speed the search for genes that cause disabilities, as well as help scientists begin to unravel the genetics of behavior. But geneticists caution that biological organisms are considerably more than their genes. Understanding how genes work, as well as how the environment and other factors affect them, will doubtless take many more years.

Controversial genetic research has also cast new light on the origins of the dog that in some respects supports the general outline of my own speculation in the opening chapter. Shortly after *Dog's Best Friend* was released in 1997, evolutionary biologist Robert K. Wayne and his colleagues at the University of California at Los Angeles published a paper in *Science* magazine (June 13, 1997), suggesting that the dog split from the wolf perhaps as early as 135,000 years ago. Wayne and his colleagues wrote that domestication appeared to have occurred no more than four times and perhaps only once, although they were unable to pin down those locations or even identify the wolf subspecies from which the dog arose, beyond observing that it was a gray wolf, *Canis lupus*. Many archaeologists, but not all, flatly refused to accept the date, claiming that the earliest identifiable dog in the fossil record dated only to about 15,000 years ago. They rejected the notion that the "protodog," as Wayne called it, could have existed for tens of thousands of years without becoming physically distinguishable from the wolf. The debate took another turn on November 22, 2002, when *Science* printed an article by Peter Savolainen of the Royal Institute of Technology in Stockholm, Sweden, one of Wayne's original collaborators. Savolainen and his colleagues argued, based on genetic evidence, that the dog originated around 15,000 years ago in East Asia. Wayne has not accepted that revision, so the debate over the origins of the dog continues. The early date suggests that modern humans and dogs co-evolved—an intriguing notion that, if true, should temper our anthropocentrism.

Recent scientific research has also begun to document ways in which the dog has evolved—through what Darwin called conscious and unconscious artificial selection—to employ its intelligence not only to survive but to flourish as a working partner in human society. So, too, a growing number of people have come to see themselves not as "owners" of their dogs but as "companions" to them, a long overdue conceptual change. Reward-based training methods have also expanded rapidly, especially that of using "clickers," pioneered by Karen Pryor and Gary Wilkes in 1992. While we can hope that reward-based training will relegate punitive methods to the scrap heap of history, judging from the sale of prong collars and of electric collars and fences designed to deliver a jolt to straying dogs, that day remains in the unforeseeable future.

The years since the first appearance of *Dog's Best Friend* have also brought profound changes to my own household. Clio and Marlow, the intrepid Catahoula leopard dogs who had been with my wife and me since puppydom, died within eight months of each other in 2001 and 2002, at thirteen and fourteen respectively. We had to make the hard choice in each case of ending their lives—a decision that never becomes easier. We now have a little kelpie, Katie, renowned for her acrobatics in tracking and catching tennis balls on the fly or while leaping into the pool. She swims like a retriever, although her small size puts her at a disadvantage when the surf is up. Katie also teaches visitors how to play ball with her, first depositing the ball at their feet and then, if they fail to respond, dropping it in their laps or engineering it onto their chairs in such a way that it touches some part of their anatomy and is also guaranteed to roll off, helped only by gravity. Once the ball hits the floor, the game is on because the human has technically touched it.

Several older dogs who frequented our neighborhood dog park also died, seemingly within a couple of years of each other, and new puppies and adopted dogs arrived. Construction within the park of an appropriately named "bark park" brought a flood of people and dogs from outside the neighborhood and new conflicts between dogs and their human companions—the sorts of disputes over proper behavior that the small, unwelcoming enclosure was supposed to forestall. A few of us who had walked our dogs in the park for years protested the initial plan for the enclosure, arguing instead for unpublicized off-leash hours. That would have legitimized the status quo and kept the small park from being over-whelmed. But the decision had been made, just as it has increasingly been made in cities and suburbs throughout the county, into Canada, and doubtless wherever growing numbers of dogs and people are forced to share what little open space can be found. Often the bark parks are too small and overcrowded for dogs to get proper exercise, and some of them become flea- and tick-laden. Bark parks are canine ghettos, but to park managers and politicians, they present the illusion of compromise in increasingly bitter land-use battles between people who share their lives with dogs and those who do not. The challenge to all dog lovers re-mains to find ways for their dogs to exercise their natural talents, free of unnecessary constraint, and in so doing to fully enjoy the company of their canine companions.

August 2003

ACKNOWLEDGMENTS

Many people and dogs contributed their time and knowledge to the making of this book. For teaching me about the way of huskies, I wish to thank Susan Butcher and David Monson, Gareth Wright, George Attla, Earl and Natalie Norris, Doug Swingley, and especially Martin Buser and Kathy Chapoton, who welcomed me into their home. Hal Black took me to the Navajo Reservation to observe the little sheepdogs and spent many hours discussing them with me. George Cauley and the folks at the American Treeing Feist Association gave me a primer on squirrel hunting with those little dogs. Sandy Seward and Lourdes Edlin allowed me to watch the training of the Beagle Brigade and introduced me to the world of Frisbee dogs. Kit Jenkins and Rick Collard of the Humane Society of Greater Miami helped put the work of local animal shelters in perspective. Jeff McDaniel taught me about cow hunting with dogs and horses. Eve McNanamy and Rory showed me something of the world of guide dogs. Leida Jones welcomed me to her kennel and farm to observe a sheepdog trial. Ethel Conrad talked to me for hours about border collies. For information on detection and search-and-rescue dogs, I am indebted to Bill Whitstine, Carl Newcombe, Skip Fernandez, and Larry Myers. Phil Hoelcher provided perspective on Schutzhund and protection-dog training. Ed and Cheryl Richardson, Sally Sullivan, and Greg Oyer welcomed me to the Ducks Unlimited Hunting Trial and gave me a glimpse of the sport of bird hunting over dogs. Robert Milner shared his knowledge of Labrador retrievers.

Among the veterinarians and researchers who discussed their findings with me are: Jasper Rine, Joe W. Templeton, Stanley J. Olsen,

Arleigh Reynolds, Karin Schmidt, Ken Hinchcliff, Eliot Stetzer, Mark Steele, John Blake, Peter Borchelt, Robert K. Wayne, Andrew Rowan, and Franklin M. Loew. Merritt Clifton shared his knowledge of the humane movement, while Bob Baker taught me about puppy mills. Daniel Suman proved what a person dedicated to raising well-socialized puppies can do. Charles Fergus provided introductions and insight. Cameron Davidson offered moral support and amusing photographs.

I would also like to thank C. Michael Curtis, William Whitworth, and the *Atlantic Monthly* for its support in several of my investigations, as well as Bruce Stutz at *Natural History*. This book would not have been possible without the unflagging encouragement of my agent, Barney Karpfinger, and my editor at Henry Holt, Allen Peacock. My wife, Gina Maranto, did more than provide support; she lived this book. Whatever virtue and truth lie in this book derive from these men and women and their dogs. The errors of omission and commission are my own.

DOG'S
BEST FRIEND

PROLOGUE

The evening before Max died, we found him lying in the front yard, waiting in the fading light for us to return from work. Without rising, he slowly wagged his tail, and we greeted him with a single voice that asked, "What's wrong?" We had left him inside when we went to catch the train to New York City that morning, and although a quick look confirmed that no doors or windows were open, there he was outside, unable to move. I carried him through the front door and laid his arthritic body on a mattress my wife, Gina, had thrown on the living-room floor for him. We offered him his favorite snack, a chocolate chip cookie, but, for the first time in his life, he refused it. Max, the Chesapeake Bay retriever who had pirated a bag of chocolate kisses when a puppy, levitated butter, sweet rolls, and bread from the far reaches of kitchen counters, opened an oven door to steal a quiche, picked a plate of barbecue ribs from the table at our wedding reception, and never turned down a chance to bury his head in an empty ice cream container, trash the garbage, or slurp beer, would neither eat nor drink. His every action underscored the message he had delivered with his impossible escape and patient wait for our return: it was time to go.

The veterinarian's office was closed that night, and since Max had gone to sleep on the mattress, we decided to take him the next morning for what we knew would be his final ride. As we prepared to leave, a mild temblor rattled southern Connecticut, as if the earth had decided to mime our state of emotional instability. At the vet's, we held Max while the sodium pentothal took effect and the pain that had overwhelmed him vanished—I would like to think before he died, but who can say? Gina swore that she could feel Max's spirit looking down

1

at us as we drove away. I remember yellow autumnal leaves rustling in the dead air, and ten years later, with two wonderful dogs in the house, we still reminisce about Max breaking ice on a frozen pond; diving for river rocks as big as softballs and building, with those he retrieved, a pyramid on the shore; swimming with all his considerable power against a current running so fast he could only hold his position; being swept through rapids without a trace of panic; crashing surf; playing hide-and-seek with a beaver; fetching sticks, Frisbees, or balls by the hour, as long as they were thrown in the water.

But his most prodigious effort was made on land: One day, as we walked along the tow path of the C & O Canal in Washington, D.C., Max decided to pick up a log measuring ten feet in length, six inches in diameter, and weighing close to fifteen pounds. He fretted and barked until he got the thing balanced in his mouth and then pushed his way past us, so he could walk in front with his prize. Astonished hikers pointed and laughed. A few wondered whether he was insane. Max occasionally stopped to rebalance his log, but having learned at the start that he could not easily pluck it from the ground, he would rest one end on a stump. Tail wagging, possessed by the "fever," he carried that log for a mile, triumphant.

He had belonged first to a family that gave him away when he was nine months old because he had bitten a child while they were playing and the family wanted to avoid a lawsuit. His next set of owners found him "too difficult," so they placed him with a veterinarian for killing— euphemistically referred to as being "put down." Indeed, he would jump and kill rabbits and once dispatched a kitten who trod too close to his food. In his spare time, he practiced dissecting his kill by chewing the hard covers off golf balls he and our German shorthaired pointer fetched from a water hazard outside the door of a little two-room house in Kansas my first wife and I rented. Throughout his life, he had a stubborn streak when it came to obeying commands that did not interest him, and I suspect it was that which had landed him on death row. Some people should not have high-energy dogs intent on being boss.

My first wife and I rescued him when he was ten months old. After we divorced four years later, he lived with her a few months, then with me, and finally with Gina and me. He introduced Gina to his way of life on their first extended walk by rolling in particularly ripe excrement while I ran a twenty-mile race through the hills north of Baltimore. In his first ten months, he had been in four homes and one kennel. Over the next eleven years, he lived in four states and thirteen houses, which he protected by his sheer presence. What intruder wanted to test the mettle of a ninety-pound chocolate-brown retriever with gold eyes, a broad head, and booming bark? That was Max, a dog no one had wanted, who became an integral part of our lives and a decade after his death continues to loom large in our memories.

Everyone who has had a dog has experienced the sorrow of its death from natural or unnatural causes. One afternoon in 1995, I was visiting Martin Buser, two-time winner of the Iditarod Trail International Sled Dog Race, and his wife, Kathy Chapoton, at their home in Big Lake, Alaska, listening while they talked about Stafford, the female leader who had died on the trail six years earlier, the only dog he had lost during more than a dozen Iditarods. Noticing that she had begun to struggle, Buser, one of the most humane mushers in the sport, stopped midrace, loaded her onto his sled, and carried her to a checkpoint, where she died from internal bleeding in the arms of a race veterinarian. Her death resulted from a freak rupture of a blood vessel under the foreleg that allowed blood to drain into her abdomen without any outward swelling. It could have happened anywhere, anytime. It was, Buser said, while Chapoton wiped tears from her eyes, the worst thing that had happened to him in any race.

Not every dog death elicits such a response. Annually, there are hundreds of thousands of dog owners who kill their charges through cruelty or neglect; they are unfit for human or canine society. And, callous though it might seem, the death of those dogs who are deformed, demented, destructive, misbegotten, or vicious is often a blessing. But when dogs die who have become part of our lives, who have kept us company, hunted for us, literally and figuratively pulled us through heavy weather, excelled with us in competitions, protected us, asking nothing in return but food and affection, their passing is cause for mourning.

Though modern commentators occasionally deride dog owners who memorialize their lost companions through formal burial—the United States alone has close to 500 pet cemeteries—through taxidermy or literature or art, the practice is as old as the relationship between the two species. Mummified dogs dating as far back as 12,000 years have been found scattered throughout the Northern Hemisphere, as have their representations in art. Poets throughout the ages have eulogized their dogs, often in memorable verse. Criticized as anthropomorphism, the practice seems to me to spring from deeper roots—a recognition of the fundamental interconnectedness of life and of the inherent virtue of the dog.

By most reliable surveys, 38 percent of the households in the United States have one or more dogs—estimated at 50 to 57 million— while only 35 percent have children. In much of Europe, in Australia and Canada, the average is often well above 20 percent, while in Japan, at 12 percent, dog ownership is growing faster than anywhere else in the world. Since many dogs are pariahs foraging through streets and fields, and therefore uncounted, the actual census worldwide must run in the hundreds of millions, a far cry from 5.7-billion tallied people but nonetheless a significant number. Dogs live more intimately with humans than perhaps any other species—cats and birds notwithstanding.

The variety of uses to which we have put these animals is astounding. From an early date, they were a valued food source, which they remain in many Asian and Oceanic cultures; sentinels and guardians; hunters of game and humans; fishers; draft animals; guides; competitors in various sports; camp scavengers; entertainers; and companions. Today, they are also used to detect everything from explosives to contraband and lost souls; to assist people with disabilities; to improve the morale of the old and infirm; and to pursue such diverse activities as playing with Frisbees, scuba diving, and performing in movies. If there is something people do, there is probably a person who has tried to train a dog to do it as well—and often succeeded.

In close to fifty years, I have never been without a dog, and although I pledge occasionally to swear off them, because of the time required to care for them properly, I know I will not. They provide for me a certain calm, a connection to the broader world we call nature, a world beyond human control. They remind me that the human way of viewing reality is circumscribed by our senses, our bipedalism, our brains. They daily teach me that kindness, consistency, patience, and understanding succeed much better than intimidation. Susan Butcher, four-time winner of the Iditarod, tells the story of how for two and one-half years she tried to give away a young husky named Granite because he was a bad eater and slow learner. She failed, and Granite became the leader of her team in three of her victories. In an age demanding instant gratification, such dogs provide a necessary corrective.

Like most people today, I do not work professionally with dogs, but I do train ours somewhat and exercise them for nearly two hours a day. I expect our dogs to come when called, to sit and stay, not to beg for food or jump on guests, and not to fight with other dogs or people unless physically threatened, and then I expect them to perform according to their nature, which they do. Just before dawn, one day in 1993, an intruder climbed through an open window on the ground floor of our house. We figured later that he had watched me drive away and assumed no one was home. But Gina was asleep upstairs, unfortunately for him, with the dogs, who heard the window screen rip. Our female leopard dog, Clio, who seldom barks and is one of the sweetest dogs I have ever known, raced downstairs, saw the man, and charged him while raising an alarm. Our male leopard dog, Marlow, who barks at every stranger, first positioned himself between Gina and the bedroom door, then answered his running mate's cry. The intruder fled. They earned their keep that morning.

My dog stories are about average for people who have lived with these animals all of their lives. The mushers, ranchers, hunters, and shepherds, the trainers who work daily with dogs often have much more dramatic tales than I, a number of which are included in the pages that follow. Susan Butcher, for example, tells of the time her lead dog, Tekla, for whom her daughter is named, pulled her from freezing water after she had fallen from her sled through thin ice. Realizing something was wrong, Tekla circled the team back, grabbed her drowning mistress by her snowsuit, and pulled her to safety. That same dog would sit on her dog box at night and howl, calling wolves into the dog yard from the Alaska tundra, where they moved freely among the staked dogs, like shadows. To their credit, they killed none of the huskies.

I am a fan of dogs, a collector of dog anecdotes. Like many dog people, I have a bias, although mine is directed not toward particular breeds; rather, I prefer medium to large dogs with a somewhat assertive (not vicious) temperament and the ability to think for themselves. I consider myself the guardian of my dogs, someone who has entered into an agreement to provide them food, shelter, health care, which includes keeping them physically fit, in exchange for their protection and companionship. I will exercise my judgment in the realms in which I am expert, and I expect them to do the same.

I do not subscribe to fashionable arguments that dogs are slaves—although legally, of course, people do own their animals and within the bounds of defined cruelty possess the power of life and death over them—nor do I believe them to be surrogate children or toys for my amusement. Those descriptions are categorically incorrect, poor metaphors that at best reflect the attitudes and behavior of certain people toward their animals. Dogs cannot be slaves or children or royalty. They can only be dogs. The people who are most successful in training, handling, even breeding dogs today—and I suspect throughout time—are those who recognize that reality.

But what precisely are dogs? How was our relationship with them formed? How have we used them over the years? How do we use them now? What are our responsibilities to them? How can we expect them to adapt to an urban-suburban existence that even drives many of us mad? How can we preserve traditional uses of dogs in a technologically changing world? How can we stop producing animals for profit and vanity that we know suffer physically and mentally because of our breeding practices? How can science help us produce more mentally and physically healthy dogs? What is a breed? Are dogs really so specialized that only certain of those breeds can perform specific functions? Finally, how do we emphasize what is positive and enduring in our relationship with dogs, while ridding ourselves of the negative, which does not always involve actual abuse and abandonment?

I began to raise these questions in an article I wrote for the March 1990 *Atlantic Monthly*, which focused on the overbreeding of dogs for the show ring and for profit under the auspices of the American Kennel Club, the largest and richest registry for purebred dogs in the world. In essence, the inbreeding of animals for appearance alone and the mass production of puppies to feed consumer demand have led to an epidemic of genetic disorders and the loss of temperamental soundness and working ability in most purebred dogs recognized by the AKC. Today, despite a flood of articles and special television reports documenting the same abuses, human greed and vanity continue to do incalculable damage not only to dogs but also to our conception of them. The failure of the AKC and its member organizations to clean up the mess and produce healthy, intelligent, good-tempered dogs leads to the inescapable conclusion that the single greatest problem with dogs is people. The largest proportion of those problematic people are in the "fancy," the name by which the show world knows itself. Given that show dogs are bred to conform to a standard invented by humans and the histories of particular breeds are largely fictional, the name "fancy" seems especially ironic. The dogs are judged by how close they come to an imagined ideal, a fancy.

I revisit those issues in *Dog's Best Friend*, but I have tried more particularly to explore what we know about the origins, genetic makeup, and behavior of the dog, to look more deeply at how we can discard outmoded notions of purity to define quality in a dog, to examine more closely the ways in which we have worked with dogs over the millennia and continue to use them today.

The nature of that relationship between dogs and humans—what I call the culture of the dog—is the subject of this book. That culture includes not only training and breeding but the entire emotional, intellectual, and physical atmosphere in which the animal is born and lives. That culture encompasses many different human societies: hunter-gatherers who first accepted wolves into their lives and from them created dogs; conquistadors who used them to seize a continent; mushers in Alaska who breed and race huskies; Navajo ranchers whose mongrel sheepdogs are born and reared with the animals they protect; squirrel hunters with their little feist dogs; cowmen who count on dogs to round up their herds; wealthy sports enthusiasts who fire thousand-dollar shotguns over pointers handled by hired kennel hands; fire-fighters with dogs trained to sniff out arson; people who rely on the unquestioning love of their pet; dog fanciers who want a show champion; people with disabilities who turn their lives over to their guide dogs. The culture also includes those men and women who work to ensure the health of dogs both as practicing veterinarians and as researchers into canine genetics and behavior. Too often, their findings and advice are ignored.

On the surface, that appears a curious statement. The dog business in the United States alone approaches $10 billion a year. Dog books, dog art, dog movies and television programs, dog shows and competitions draw millions of participants annually. People love to talk about their dogs, to tell stories about them. Some of those are amusing; many are of heroic acts. The number of books on dogs alone can fill a large library. Paradoxically, the amount of accurate information in those volumes might fill a shelf. The rest consists of received wisdom, fictions and legends, many of them quite fine. A few of these are classics of the human-meets-dog genre, memoirs, and elegies.

In many ways, those genre books provide more information on how to get along with a dog than do the tomes of "professionals," especially those dealing with the origins of breeds and training. Even finding accurate information on dog food is difficult, as every manufacturer pushes its own version of the perfect diet. That said, there is a growing body of serious work on the genetics, behavior, nutrition, training, and evolution of the dog, and I have drawn upon that research, as well as conversations I have had with scientists and veterinarians. In so doing, I have attempted to screen out material that is inaccurate. Experts accustomed to academic debate might find that disappointing, but I do not want to burden the reader. For example, much of the scholarly (and popular) material talking about inherited behavior and the nature of the dog is speculative, often citing as proof other theories, and I mention only those that are part of the public legend of the dog and therefore in need of correction.

That we know so little about this animal should not be surprising. After all, we know little about our own motivation and behavior. Unfortunately, with dogs, our incomprehension often leads us to commit grave harm—producing and sustaining mutants, breeding dogs with genetic defects, misrepresenting to ourselves the nature of this animal and then behaving toward it accordingly. The people who work daily with dogs probably know them the best, yet they often are least inclined to write down their knowledge. The result is a larger than usual gap between what the real experts and the laboratory experts purport. I can attempt to bridge that chasm only by excluding the more outrageous and unsustainable theories.

No one can deny that ours is a unique relationship, with both positive and negative aspects. There is a long and bloody history of our use of dogs in war to hunt down, maim, and kill the enemy, to brutalize and terrorize civilian populations and captives; but we have also used dogs to protect lives, carry messages, and rescue the wounded. There are within many of the world's cultures, including our own, strong biases against dogs, which have periodically led to their slaughter. The current drive to outlaw "vicious" breeds falls within that tradition, as does genetic manipulation that causes dogs to suffer from disabling and sometimes fatal congenital defects.

Thus, throughout *Dog's Best Friend* I make recommendations that I feel can improve the lot of dogs and our relationship with them. Several of those have to do with breeding practices and the need to understand the genetic structure of the dog in general, its talents and disabilities in particular. Others pertain to the need to rescue vanishing breeds; to end commercial exploitation; to curb abuse whether in the laboratory, kennel, or home; to reform the show world; to establish and enforce strict standards for the training and use of dogs in law enforcement.

The point is that an obsession with pedigree can lead, paradoxically, to elevating false differences between types of dogs while obscuring true distinctions. It also can blind us to the unique talents of individual dogs and their trainers. That finally is the theme that informs this book: the people who succeed best with their dogs are those who have what they themselves universally and independently refer to as an ability to get inside the heads of their dogs. Like all people involved with these animals, they may disagree on techniques, definitions, even the nature of the beast, but by talent, training, and long practice, they have learned to understand "dog." It is one of many paradoxes that define the relationship. Whether masters of Schutz-hund (the German protection-dog sport), competitive mushers, train-ers or handlers of working detection or search-and-rescue dogs, or simply keepers of dogs, they communicate directly with their animals. And the dogs respond by performing what appear to be incredible feats. That is why we have celebrated our dogs for millennia.

Chapter One

A WOLF IN DOG'S CLOTHING

Tracks of Ages

Emerging from the deep shade of a sandstone outcropping that shelters their flock, three skinny black-and-white dogs warily approach pieces of cantaloupe rind thrown to entice them into the open, sniff, then begin eating, their eyes fixed on the strange Anglos talking with their Navajo owner. I am amazed at how much they resemble a photograph I recently saw of the Basketmaker dog, a rare, complete mummy dating from the time of Christ that was found at White Dog Cave, not far from this hogan, in 1921 and resides at the Peabody Museum, Harvard University. Traveling through the Navajo Reservation with Hal Black, a zoologist from Brigham Young University, I will observe a dozen more of the dogs, some with buff coats and gray muzzles but of the same physical type as the 2,000-year-old mummy, as if in this country of wind-blasted sandstone mesas there is no divide between the quick and the dead.

Bred to no particular purpose, the Navajo dogs, who range from fifteen to sixty pounds, live with flocks of sheep and goats they protect from coyotes, other dogs, horses, mules, even strange people who come too close. Most are born among the sheep and goats they accept as members of their own pack, but others are adopted as barely weaned puppies from the ranks of feral dogs (who have severed their bond to humans and grown to fear and avoid them) living around the reservation's garbage dumps or found on the roadside. I recognize many of them as mutts from modern breeds and dismiss them, not because they are less good as sheep guards but because I am fascinated by the

11

ancient ones. The latter remind me of the feists and curs of the American South, who are generally believed to descend from the dogs of Native Americans mixed with those of seventeenth- and eighteenth-century colonists. It seems incredible that the type could persist for so long without change despite exposure to countless other dogs, and I would like to believe that my eyes have deceived me, the way I know when my male Catahoula leopard dog sleeps on his back in a contorted pose resembling the dog from Pompeii zapped in the ash of Vesuvius that the relationship is purely visual.

Back home in Miami Beach, I check with Stanley J. Olsen of the University of Arizona, one of the world's foremost experts on canine paleontology and a man given to skepticism regarding claims that certain dogs represent ancient breeds. "Oh, yes," he says, "those little dogs on the reservation—they look just like the Basketmaker mummy." He agrees that a comparative study would be interesting, but for now the techniques of genetic analysis are not refined enough to determine whether the sheepdogs are heir to the animals of people who lived in that land of buttes and mesas before the Navajo themselves arrived.

Around the world, there are dogs who have apparently remained unchanged for thousands of years—bred true to type—often on islands where ancient wanderers dropped them, in jungles, parts of the Arctic, or relatively remote desert environments like that of the American Southwest where for long periods they would have come into contact with other dogs rarely, if at all, but also in regions where people have retained a strong tradition of using certain kinds of dog. Some researchers even speculate that many of these dogs are derived from an ur-dog domesticated 10,000 or more years ago from the Indian wolf and carried around the world with migrating bands of people, mixing along the way with indigenous wolves.

In its effort to account for the affinities in behavior and appearance among these unique dogs, this theory oversimplifies the process of domestication and dispersal. Foremost among them and closest to the wolf in appearance and behavior is the dingo, who first appeared in Australia some 4,000 years ago when seafarers from Indonesia or Southeast Asia beached their dugouts to trade with the Aborigines and lost some of the dogs they carried for companionship and food. The dogs reverted to the wild and became the top carnivore, next to humans, on that island continent, joined over the centuries by other travelers who went walkabout. Although some Aboriginal tribes tamed puppies and kept them as hunting aides and camp guardians, as well as food in times of famine, the dogs bred in the wild and in general behaved so differently from those of European explorers arriving in the eighteenth century that they were called dingoes and declared a separate species.

The New Guinea singing dog, now nearly extinct on its home island, is said to be a dingo of sorts, as are the pariahs, the ownerless dogs who live around towns and villages in Southeast Asia, and even some of the Native American dogs. A number of Middle Eastern and African dogs are similar in appearance but probably domesticated from different subspecies of wolf. The Canaan dog from Palestine was a pariah used to guard and herd sheep until the 1930s, when Rudolphina Menzel, an expert on dogs who had fled Hitler's Germany with her husband, Rudolph, consolidated it into a breed for use as a messenger, tracker, search-and-rescue dog, and guide dog. Among the !Kung San bushmen of the Kalahari Desert, those who hunt with dogs—medium-sized buff or piebald animals—bring home 75 percent of the animal protein their band consumes. Pygmies use little hounds (refined by English and American breeders, they are called basenjis) to hunt birds and other game. On Sicily and in Portugal are graceful prick-eared hounds who appear to have changed little for several millennia.

In fact, dogs like these are sought by collectors in increasing numbers because they are deemed "primitive"—more quintessentially canine in their abilities and demeanor than the "refined" European and English breeds: pointers, retrievers, toys, terriers, and other denizens of the show ring. Even the various curs and feists of the American South and the Arctic sled dogs are often called "primitive." Despite all the rationalizations and examples used to support the distinction, it primarily refers to dogs who are more generalist in their talents, independent in their habits, and relatively free of disabling genetic defects compared with those selectively bred for specific traits,

size, color, and specialized talents like pointing. Since many are
country dogs, they are deemed exotic, or rare, when taken as pets.

I prefer the word "basic" to "primitive" because it bears less cultural baggage. It also recognizes that types like the Alaskan husky and
curs have over the years received infusions of new blood without losing
their distinguishing characteristics. Huskies retain their tough feet,
somewhat wolfish appearance, and habits as sled dogs despite the presence in their midst of individuals with lop ears and thinnish coats.
Coming in a range of sizes and colors, curs are identified by their
ability as herders, hunters who trail and tree, occasional pointers, and
guardians, as well as by their general deep-chested build.

In Australia, dingoes are currently hybridizing freely with domestic
dogs, raising concerns that they will become extinct. Hybridization
occurs most frequently in areas where human predation has created a
shortage of available dingo mates, meaning humans can help reverse
the process by ending the senseless slaughter. But to the dingo,
hybridization has always offered life, not extinction. In the centuries
before Anglo settlement, it interbred, especially along the coast, with
dogs arriving, as its forebears had, with Southeast Asian and Indone-
sian traders. Like those early hybrids, many of the ones produced today
are virtually indistinguishable from dingoes into whose society they are
born. The dingo phenotype and culture prevail, leading me to conclude that the obsession with curbing interbreeding has less to do with
preserving the dingo than with maintaining old notions of blood
purity. Such a view is heretical in the world of wildlife protection, but
the dingo is a dog who went wild because of the circumstances in
which humans left it. If it changes in relationship to new human-made
conditions, it is simply being a dog.

Whatever terms we use, the attempt to draw clear distinctions
between basic and pedigreed show dogs, or even between breeds,
reflects our continuing attempts to understand the animal who shares
our lives more intimately than any other. Underfunded and assigned
low priority by paleontologists, archaeologists, and evolutionary biologists, whose efforts are directed more toward examining issues relating
to humans, extinct and endangered species, those efforts proceed in fits
and starts, like a dog trying to fix on a cold trail.

Whether read on cuneiform tablets, scrolls, bas-reliefs, paintings, books, film, or the flickering pixels of cyberspace, divined from bones or mummified flesh, deciphered from the genes, what we know remains an unstable mixture of fact and received wisdom, which is too often accepted as revealed truth. As biologists decipher the dog genome—the genetic blueprint that makes it unique—archaeologists open new sites, and behaviorists deepen their knowledge of dog and wolf behavior, the story will doubtless become, paradoxically, more clear and complex. On a practical level, I hope that this knowledge will lead to a revolution in breeding that will bring an end to the production of mutant animals fit only to serve human vanity and create animals of good health and temperament, sound minds, and abundant talent. Bred to type, like the sheep guards of the Navajo, the curs, and huskies, these dogs would show considerably more variability than is allowed in the narrowly prescribed physical standards of show dogs, like the Pekingese, malamute, or any of the other 140 or so pure breeds recognized by the American Kennel Club.

Enough has been learned over the past three decades to allow concerned breeders and trainers to make dramatic improvements. But more must be done. The chief drawback to that reform, one expert told me, lies in inadequate dissemination of the information at hand and continued reliance on folk wisdom that views inheritance and behavior in overly simplistic terms. I would add to that list an unwillingness among many people involved with dogs to change their ways.

Defining Dog

What we know is this: the dog is a subspecies of the wolf altered over more than fifteen millennia by selective breeding. Analyses of mitochondrial DNA, which is inherited only from the mother, have shown no distinctive differences between wolf and dog or even between breeds of dog, no matter their shape and size. (DNA fingerprinting does allow scientists to identify individual dogs but not their breed or type.) The New Guinea singing dog and dingo appear to have one or two distinctive genetic markers, perhaps due to thousands of years of island isolation, but they are not significant enough to distinguish them as separate species. Contrary to theories set forth in the past and still repeated in some quarters, no contributions were made by jackals, coyotes, foxes, otters, or bears, nor were there any ur-dogs who appeared suddenly on the earth and then vanished into the bosom of domesticity, like a canine Adam and Eve. Our dog is formally *Canis lupus familiaris*.

Canis means "dog" in Latin, so the dog is technically a domesticated wolf, which is a wild dog. *Canis lupus* is one of thirty-four living species grouped in Canidae (the dog family) of the order Carnivora, which also includes Ursidae (bears), Mustelidae (weasels), Procyonidae (raccoons), Ailuropoda (pandas), Otariidae (sea lions), Odobenidae (walruses), Phocidae (seals), Felidae (cats), Viverridae (civets), and Hyaenidae (hyenas).

Collectively the carnivores are intelligent animals that care for their young and possess relatively large canines for killing, carnassials—the first molar on the lower jaw and last premolar on the upper—for rending flesh, and molars for crushing bones. They have four to five toes with claws that are retractable in the cats, except the cheetah, and not in the others. All lack the opposable thumb, even those with five digits. In dogs, the fifth toe of the fore and hind feet has become a dewclaw, although some breeds have no rear dewclaws while others, especially among the French sheepdogs and some yellow blackmouth curs, have two on each foot. Dogs and cats walk on their toes; bears on their heels and soles. Classification being a less than exact science, some of these carnivores are omnivores and one, the panda, eats bamboo. Still, among this group are the top terrestrial predators, next to humans—the only natural enemy of many of them.

Canids—members of the dog family—began to distinguish themselves from other mammalian carnivores some 50 to 60 million years ago, almost immediately upon their first appearance following extinction of the dinosaurs. These animals were miacids—ferret- to fox-size creatures with a longer body than legs, tails, and those mashing and cutting teeth. Miacids gave way to larger creodants with five distinctive toes. Around 15 million years ago in the Western Hemisphere, another foxlike animal, *Hesperocyon*, appeared, walking on its toes. From there the line passes through *Leptocyon*, believed the common ancestor of wolves and foxes. *Canis lepophagus*, whose remains were found in Texas and dated to the Pliocene some 5 million years ago, might be the forerunner of the wolflike canids. From their origins in what is now North America, early canids migrated to Eurasia, Africa, and South America.

By the best current estimates, 7 to 10 million years ago the dog family began to divide into the broad groupings we see today: the wolflike canids, South American canids, red foxes, and miscellaneous. The foxes, miscellaneous, and South American canids have different numbers of chromosomes from the wolflike canids and do not figure in the evolution of the wolf, although the South American bushdog (*Speothos venaticus*), which dives under water, has been domesticated occasionally.

The wolflike canids have seventy-eight chromosomes and could conceivably all be classed as *Canis*, but two are not: *Lyacon pictus*, the African wild dog, with four toes front and back and the highly variable markings usually associated with domestic dogs; and *Cuon alpinus*, the dhole or red "dog," native to Asia and India. Those grouped in *Canis* are the wolf (*lupus*); golden jackal (*aureus*); side-striped jackal (*adustus*); black-backed jackal (*mesomelas*); Simien jackal or Ethiopian wolf (*simensis*); coyote (*latrans*); and red wolf (*rufus*). The huge dire wolf (*Canis dirus*) rose and fell during the Pleistocene, while its cousin, the gray wolf, flourished.

Although the wolf, coyote, and golden jackal probably diverged 3 to 4 million years ago, they can mate and produce fertile offspring. Largely because of its geographic isolation in eastern and southern Africa, the African wild dog (also known as the Cape hunting dog) went its separate way about the same time. All of these canids have strong jaws and the relatively big teeth typical of carnivores, as Little Red Riding Hood discovered. Their legs are adapted for loping or trotting long distances, with the exception of the mutant domestic dog breeds, and running for shorter periods with bursts of speed. As a general rule, they show a marked propensity toward pack or group behavior. They also communicate vocally through a variety of calls, physical posturing, and scent marking. Their olfactory abilities are superb, as is their hearing. They have excellent peripheral and night vision, as well as high sensitivity to light and movement. Dogs and wolves, and perhaps other canids, see fairly well at a distance and discern colors, although not as acutely as humans.

Observers have long argued that wolves and dogs possess some sort of extrasensory perception that allows them to sense the moods of humans or prey, to locate someone at a distance, to anticipate the arrival of a master, pack member, or quarry, to discern when they are nearing their destination, even if riding in a closed car. Of particular fascination to a number of experts is "psi trailing," the apparent ability of an animal to find its owners after they have left it and moved to a place it has never been before. ESP is, of course, a term humans use for any psychic phenomenon beyond their explanation, and so its use with canids is probably irrelevant. It is more fair to say that canids live in a perceptual universe far different from ours and that we are unaware of many of the olfactory and auditory signals they detect. Both dogs and wolves respond to higher frequencies than humans, and wolves reportedly can hear sounds on the Alaska tundra from a distance up to ten miles.

No one knows how many subspecies of *Canis lupus* have existed. Estimates range from twenty to forty. Part of the difficulty, as with defining breeds of dogs, is that wolves are highly variable in size, coloration, and behavior. Also, heavy human predation has seriously diminished their numbers worldwide, making it difficult even to determine with accuracy what has been lost. Due primarily to heat and parasites, wolves tend to be smaller in southern than in northern latitudes, so that the little Arabian wolf and the red wolf are in the forty-five-pound range while the Arctic gray wolf regularly exceeds one hundred pounds. The Arabian wolf seems to howl rarely and generally hunts alone or in small groups. Indeed, many of these subspecies have been studied little; more than a few cannot be examined at all, except in their remains. Thus, we will probably never know how the behavior of specific wolves is reflected in the dogs derived from them millennia ago.

Taming Wolf

Fossil evidence from Zhoukoudian, China, shows *Homo erectus pekinensis*, the elusive Peking or Beijing man, was sharing time and space, food and shelter with wolves (generally classed as *Canis lupus variabilis*) at least 500,000 years ago. Remains of *Homo erectus* and wolves have also turned up in Boxgrove in Kent, England, dated to 400,000 years ago, and Lazeret in the south of France, 150,000 years ago. It is more likely that throughout the Northern Hemisphere these precursors of modern humans and wolves lived and hunted in close proximity than that these three sites represent an accidental accumulation of old bones. Beyond that, we have only questions and surmise, especially since we know less about our prehistoric forebears than we do about wolves.

Relatively short, with slightly smaller brains, flatter skulls, more prominent brow ridges, and a noticeably more protruding jaw holding larger teeth than we, these hominids were probably seminomadic hunter-gatherers who colonized much of the world. They had stone tools to help them butcher their kill for cooking. The fossils found at Zhoukoudian indicate that the brains of their compatriots—or competitors—made up at least part of their diet. But in the main, early hominids were omnivores, deriving an estimated 60 to 80 percent of their calories and protein from nuts and vegetables.

Although even estimated dates are in dispute, it seems fair to say that sometime around 200,000 years ago archaic humans, *Homo sapiens*, emerged in Africa. They possessed significantly larger brains than *Homo erectus*, whom they supplanted, and made superior stone weapons with which they hunted big game. Whether Neanderthals, who emerged around 100,000 years ago and vanished 70,000 years later, were a separate human species or a stocky, heavy-browed, big-brained cousin of *Homo sapiens*—the way the dog is a subspecies of wolf—is not yet clear, but these powerful Ice Age hunters were also found throughout Europe, Asia, and Africa. Around 40,000 to 50,000 years ago, slightly different beings arose, modern humans (*Homo sapiens sapiens*) with brains wired for invention and the drive to remake the world. More precisely, our ancestors showed up with a more highly developed and enlarged basal neocortex (believed to be involved in ethical and social behavior, as well as formation of personality) than their predecessors.

As humans colonized the world, some of them became—especially in the Arctic, Patagonia, the Great Plains of North America, and steppes of Asia—predominately carnivorous in response to ecological conditions. (The polar bear, which evolved as a separate species 20,000 to 40,000 years ago, shows a similar adaptation, becoming the only solely carnivorous and semiaquatic bear.) But in the main, they moved in small bands of approximately twenty-five men, women, and children, taking most of their calories from plants and nuts.

From my childhood in the 1950s and 1960s, I remember portrayals of early humans as people terrified of the world and its animals, living a marginal existence on the edge of death by starvation, exposure, or assault. Since then, we have come increasingly to perceive those ancient hunters and gatherers as having had a rich culture and diet. They moved through their world as easily as we navigate ours, only in that world the boundary between human camps and nature was highly porous.

Hunter-gatherers viewed animals as beings with their own habits, cultures, and souls, making of many of them totemic figures, the way we invest material objects like cars and houses or famous humans with special status, not to mention God in his various guises. Early humans tamed nearly every animal they came into contact with, and that impulse to collect animals has remained as strong as the related impulse to hunt them; in fact, it is no mistake that some of the most ardent conservationists have been hunters, which is not the same as saying that all hunters are conservationists—far too many of them are not.

Even with weapons, hominids and early humans were not natural hunters, and so they would have scavenged carnivores' kills and also looked to them for guidance on how to bring down their own meat. They turned not to the bear, another omnivore, nor to the cats, but to animals—wolves and African wild dogs—that, like them, hunted in packs to bring down game much larger than themselves. Humans wanted those heavy animals for the same reasons wolves did: they provided enough meat to feed the group for days.

Wolves and humans do not talk the same language—I assume, as do many enlightened naturalists, that all animals possess language, defined here as the ability to communicate through verbal or visual signs—but they understand each other to a remarkable degree. By the look on their faces, the tilt of their ears, position of their tails and bodies, wolves convey a great deal about their mood and intent that humans can interpret. Like humans, wolves possess associative minds and wanderlust. The social structure of their packs and their habits of nurturing and educating their young parallel those of human groups.

People adopted wolf puppies who were orphaned or whom they or their children lifted from dens during explorations. Women nursed the youngest of those puppies the way they suckled their own children. Not surprisingly, some of those hand-raised wolves hung around their adoptive family, becoming companions to the children or even the young men who played with them and learned to hunt with them. The tamed wolf took to the village as its home, alerting people to danger, the way it warned its own kind if a stranger approached the den—by barking. In some regions—for this process was occurring in many parts of the world—when food got scarce or if a spirit needed to be propitiated, people sacrificed and ate the wolf. If it proved a foul-tempered ingrate, it was driven off or killed.

The wolves who became the tamest and lingered around the camps were those who were in personality the most social and least fearful. Mating with each other and free-ranging animals living near the camps, the tamed wolves produced over time a population with a high overall level of sociability, a group of fellow-traveling wolves. Under no breeding pressure from humans, allowed to come and go as they wished, they retained their wolfish look and demeanor.

Becoming Dog

Near the end of the Paleolithic (Old Stone) Age, our direct forebears developed better, sharper stone blades, the atlatl for throwing spears, and, around 18,000 to 20,000 years ago, the boomerang (subsequently isolated in Australia) and the bow and arrow. These weapons allowed hunters to kill larger animals with greater ease from a longer range. Around the same time, in many parts of the world humans took up fishing and established semipermanent villages with populations larger than their traditional bands, constructing their homes of the materials at hand: wood, earth, stone, skins, mammoth tusks. They developed better ways to carry water, food, firewood, and pelts back to camp: baskets, ceramic pots, sledges, toboggans, and travois. Boats extended the distances they could travel in search of food and in trade for furs or tools or ceramics. These humans also turned the tamed wolf into a dog, the first fully domesticated animal, meaning its evolution and breeding became directed more by humans than by nature.

The circumstances in which our forebears found themselves changed dramatically—in part because of their activities—between the last glacial advance, which peaked around 18,000 years ago, and the end of the Pleistocene some 8,000 years later. At their maximum, glaciers in eastern North America extended south over what are now the Middle Atlantic states and in the west covered Alaska, western Canada, Idaho, Washington, and Montana. In Europe, Scandinavia, Denmark, most of Great Britain, Poland, Germany, and Russia were under ice. Glaciers embraced the Alps and Dolomites, covering what are now Switzerland and sections of Austria, France, and Italy. Bordering the ice sheets were dry steppes and grasslands supporting herds of animals, including mammoths, reindeer, and giant bison. Among the predators hunting them were saber-toothed tigers, scimitar cats, dire wolves, gray wolves, and humans with their wolfdogs. In some areas, the wolfdogs resembled short-faced wolves—that is, they were barely distinguishable from dogs.

As glaciers retreated, the earth warmed and sea levels rose, reconfiguring shorelines, flooding the Bering land bridge between the Americas and Eurasia. Established ecosystems collapsed while new ones emerged. Heavy rains turned solid land to marsh, lakes dried up, steppes and grasslands turned to forests, and the great inland sea of North America, with its lush marshes, became a high desert, the Great Plains. As many as forty species of mammals vanished, especially of the huge predators and prey, among them mammoths, mastodons, great-horned bison, giant rhinoceroses, giant sloths, cave bears, dire wolves, all the saber-toothed cats, and the armadillo-like glyptodonts. Others, like the horse and camel, disappeared from North America, finding refuge in Eurasia or the Southern Hemisphere.

To a degree we cannot yet determine, paleo-hunters contributed to the extinction of some of those large animals, like the mammoths, giant bison and rhinos, with hunting techniques that included driving them off cliffs or into bogs where they were slaughtered, baying them up with wolfdogs so they could be filled with arrows. In turn, their demise hastened that of the giant predators who fed on them. But many of those animals, especially the predators, also appear to have reached an evolutionary dead end because they were unable to adapt to a world that had turned suddenly warmer and, in some cases, to the loss of their preferred food. Their populations stressed, they were pushed over the brink by human activities, but we must not overestimate the force behind the shove. Humans with bows and arrows and atlatls, no matter how skilled, cannot drive a vibrant population to extinction, as we can see by observing how little impact the Plains Indians of North America had on the bison herds during the centuries they hunted them without horses and guns—and that is just one example. Even with those weapons, the bison endured until white commercial and sport hunters slaughtered them by the thousand for their skins. (Curiously, the Plains Indians do not seem to have used dogs in hunting bison, although they kept hundreds in their villages and donned wolf pelts while stalking their prey.)

The animals that survived the turmoil at the end of the Pleistocene were the smaller, less specialized, more mobile ones: humans, gray wolves, lions, the smaller ungulates, downsized elephants, rhinos, and horses. Their size left them better suited to the warmer, damper world emerging with the retreat of the ice.

Disruptions caused by the changing climate and vanishing game fueled the trend toward different settlement and dietary patterns. In some regions, groups of people realized that in the midden heaps and latrine areas of their camps food plants they usually harvested from the wild were sprouting and flourishing. Combined with diminishing wild sup-plies, the bounty reinforced their inclination to return to the same campsites repeatedly—humans, like other animals, being creatures of habit and territory—and to prolong their stays.

Coincident with these cultural developments, humans began deliberately breeding their wolfdogs. They culled those that were un-social or overly timid, thereby increasing the likelihood that subse-quent generations would be as easily socialized. In the process, they turned the wolf into a dog. The humans wanted a guaranteed supply of reliable animals, and the wolfdogs wanted security and society.

In many parts of Eurasia, North America, and northern Africa, tamed wolves had proven themselves as hunting partners, but they became more difficult to obtain as people settled into permanent vil-lages, were prone to moving off when they felt the call to mate, and were maimed or killed in combat with large, fierce animals. At a time when hunters had to turn to other species, they needed, more than ever, to be guaranteed the assistance of an animal that excelled at scenting, tracking, and holding game or driving it into ambush. With their speed and agility, the dogs could handle anything from bears to birds, deer, elk, sheep, oxen, buffalo. They also could help guard the village against marauders.

Because no one had many tame wolfdogs—the entire human population of the world at the time was probably around 10 million—efforts to breed them dramatically narrowed the gene pool. For reasons we do not yet understand, that constriction had the effect of releasing the phenotypic variability inherent in the wolf, creating smaller, larger, differently marked animals. Slight genetic mutations—those for lop ears or a particular coat, for example—could rapidly be fixed in a line of dogs and then passed on, allowing bands to develop distinctive ani-mals they could easily differentiate from wolves, a necessity after domestication of sheep and goats.

Although involving a biological process, creation of the dog was fundamentally a cultural act, like making tools, weapons, baskets. Bands in one region turned their captive wolves into dogs and then traded them, the way they bartered other goods, or gave them as gifts during ceremonial exchanges. The knowledge of how to tame wolves was transmitted by people who were traveling. They also mated one of the dogs accompanying them to an animal in another village. Within a few generations, a general type of dog could have become well established and spread fairly widely.

Dogs were valued precisely because they possessed the stellar abilities of the tame wolf but were less inclined to go their own way. The dog was as adaptable as the wolf to different climates, and it was versatile enough to fit a range of needs. In addition to hunting and serving as dinner, dogs sounded a warning when someone approached, helped keep the camp clean of garbage and their people warm. They were playmates for children, totem objects for adults, as were nearly all animals that figured prominently in people's lives. They exhibited a talent for finding their way home no matter what the conditions, which made them in some societies valued guides for the dead to the next world, and for helping people in times of need—pulling them from the water, protecting them from attack by other people or animals. Wounds they licked seemed to heal miraculously, a fact that finds expression to this day in the saying "as clean as a hound's tooth." They also would breed with tame wolves that were still brought into camp— a bonus. It is not surprising that people domesticated the wolf thousands of years before any other animal and that many of them, especially the hunter-gatherers, kept only dogs.

For centuries, Americans and Europeans have underestimated the importance of the emergent dog as a food source, although that was probably one of its earliest functions. Many Native Americans ate puppies, considered the most delectable, on feast days or to honor special visitors, and a number of traditionalists continue the practice. The Aztec and other people in South and Central American and the Caribbean also relied heavily on dog meat for their animal protein, frequently from animals that were castrated and fattened for the purpose. Throughout Asia and Oceania, the dog has remained a highly desirable meat, frequently the primary source of animal protein. During the 1988 Summer Olympics, the South Korean government requested butchers to move their dogs, who can sell for $200 apiece—the price of some hunting dog puppies in the United States—from display in their windows so as not to offend American and European sensibilities. On walks through New York's Chinatown, I have seen dog carcasses hanging in the windows of butcher shops.

Although throughout Europe prehistoric people appear to have eaten dog, at some point their descendants stopped, taking it up again only when no other food was available. Even then, they often did so reluctantly. Traveling along the Columbia River to explore land the young United States had acquired from France as part of the Louisiana Purchase, Meriwether Lewis, William Clark, and their men ate dogs provided by local Indians in the winter of 1806 to supplement their meager rations. Clark wrote that after overcoming their cultural bias, many of them became "extreamly [sic] fond of their flesh." Lewis preferred it to venison or elk. Although not personally "reconciled" to the taste, Clark admitted that he and the men were stronger and healthier for having lived on dogs than they had been for months. Other travelers filed similar reports.

By 15,000 years ago, people around the world were raising dogs, with the centers of activity being northern Europe, including England, northern North America, especially the Arctic region, the Middle East, China, Japan, and Siberia. Presently, the earliest fossil called a dog comes from Obercassel, Germany, and dates to 14,000 years ago, the late Pleistocene or upper Paleolithic. (Pleistocene refers to the geological age; Paleolithic to the human culture.)

Trying to piece together the puzzle of simultaneous domestication around the world, experts assigned certain broad types of dog to specific subspecies of wolf based on perceived morphological similarities and assumed areas of origin. It is a rough evolutionary tree that we hope will be refined as the tools of genetic analysis become more sophisticated.

Canis lupus pallipes, the small Indian wolf, probably gave rise to the dingo and its kin: the Asian pariah dogs, the New Guinea singing dog, and related Pacific Island dogs. It could also have contributed to a few of the Native American dogs. Despite exposure to other dogs, the pariah has bred true to its original dingo type for at least 5,000 years.

Canis lupus arabs, the equally small and closely related Arabian or desert wolf—it and the Indian wolf are now sometimes considered the same subspecies—might have been progenitor of the sight hounds, the basenji and small-game hunters of southern Europe, and a number of dogs indigenous to the Middle East, like the Canaan dog of Israel and pariahs who hang around villages as scavengers and guards. Many of these animals are similar to dingoes in size and appearance, leading some people to suggest that they might, in fact, have a common origin.

Canis lupus chanco, the woolly Chinese wolf, is the possible source of the chow chow and assorted Asian toy breeds, as well as the mastiffs, believed to have originated in the Himalayas, whose bloodlines were ultimately joined by descendants of the European wolf.

Although this association is the most speculative, *Canis lupus hodophilax*, the extinct little Japanese wolf, probably figured in the creation of dogs like the shikoku, kai, the shiba inu, and other indigenous breeds.

Canis lupus lupus, the European gray wolf, lies at the foundation of various herding, guard, and spitz-type dogs indigenous to Europe, as well as some of the terriers, believed to have originated in the British Isles. Along with the North American gray wolf, it is also progenitor to the Eskimo dogs and many Native American dogs, with an assist in some cases from animals crossing the Bering land bridge with migrating people.

The one apparent exception to this rule of wolf origin, which nonetheless proves that domestication was a process occurring around the world, is the Falkland wolf (*Dusicyon australis*). In *The Voyage of the Beagle* (1839), Charles Darwin described Falkland wolves as so fearless and tame that they would invade campsites at night and steal meat from under the heads of sleeping shepherds and sealers. Taking advantage of that behavior, the men would offer each visitor a piece of meat with one hand and knife it with the other. By the turn of the century, the little twenty- to thirty-pound animals, which had fed on birds until the arrival of white men, were all dead. But within the past decade, Robert K. Wayne, an evolutionary biologist at the University of California at Los Angeles who has contributed greatly to understanding canid evolution, conducted mitochondrial DNA analyses of one of the few pelts still in existence, and his results indicated that this extinct animal is most closely related to the coyote. Since coyotes, a North American native, could not have gotten to those remote islands by themselves, the findings lend support to a theory that the little canids were brought to the Falklands by humans some 6,000 years ago.

Degrees of Separation

Though genetically one species, wolves and dogs are quite different socially and culturally. Through at least 15,000 years of human intervention, wolfish traits have been suppressed, enhanced, and even remixed in often subtle ways to create the 400 to 500 breeds we see today, out of 1,000 or so that have existed worldwide. With the possible exception of man, no other animal is so variable.

Morphologically, dogs span a wider range of sizes than wolves, from the 2-pound Chihuahua to the 220-pound mastiff, compared with the 45-pound Arabian wolf to the 175-pound Arctic timber wolf, and show considerably more variety in terms of head shape, from the flat-faced Brussels griffon to the broad-jawed Great Dane and needle-nosed collie. Although both dogs and wolves are highly variable in terms of the color, thickness, and length of their coats, dogs reveal a greater amount of white in mixed pelage, more solid red and tawny yellow. (Like dogs, wolves can be black or white, as well as mixed in their coloration; piebald animals have been reported on rare occasions.) Several breeds are hairless, and others have hair to the ground.

On average, dogs are slighter in build than equivalent-sized wolves, their muzzles shorter and less powerful—1,500 pounds per square inch of crunching power for a mature timber wolf, 1,000 pounds per square inch for a German shepherd—their teeth smaller, their heads more domed, their bones less heavy. (Specialization provides notable exceptions: for example, a forty-pound pit bull reportedly can generate 1,800 pounds per square inch of biting power.) Dogs' tails are curved, and a number of breeds have lop ears. They lack the supracaudal gland on top of the wolf's tail involved in scent marking and identification.

Some scientists have argued that, as with humans, the dog's more domed head reflects a greater development of the prefrontal cortex, which functions to inhibit certain behaviors like killing game, but that is unproven. Young wolves must learn how to hunt, kill, and dissect their prey, as must young dingoes, who since running wild in Australia have proven themselves quite capable hunters. Similarly, the notion that a smaller brain means the dog is less intelligent than the wolf remains speculative, at best, like all arguments relating brain size to intellect. Neanderthal man had a larger brain than modern man, but no one has seriously suggested that Neanderthal man was more "intelligent."

Many biologists suspect that a relatively small number of subtle genetic shifts account for the differences we see between breeds and between the wild and domestic wolf. Some of these changes might be dominant mutations involving just a few genes, which become fixed in a population once they occur: red or tawny yellow coats, the curved tail, and floppy ears are among those believed to fall into this category, as are some forms of dwarfism. Other changes might be recessive, meaning they require close breeding to fix. Still others are multi-factorial, involving a number of genes, which themselves simply code for the proteins that are the building blocks of all biological organisms.

The rate, timing, and sequencing of genes' expression and the extent of their interactions, which are heavily influenced by environmental factors, dictate much of the way the individual develops—within the overall genetic blueprint for a dog or wolf and the more specific ones for breed and line. In fact, changes in the rate and timing of development are believed to account for a number of the significant differences between dogs and wolves. Thus, early sexual maturation and delayed growth (called paedomorphosis) make dogs slighter than equivalent-sized wolves; early sexual maturation and accelerated growth (hypermorphosis) produce dogs larger than any wolf.

Slowing the rate of physical development is believed by evolutionary biologists to produce a phenomenon called neoteny, in which certain juvenile characteristics of the wild progenitor are retained into adulthood by the descendant species. Adult domestic pigs, for example, are said to more closely resemble wild piglets than adult boars. Similarly, a number of experts maintain that the mature dog looks more like a juvenile wolf or even an overgrown puppy than a fully grown wolf. Over the millennia, and especially during the past 150 years, breeders have created small dogs who look like little animated dolls and even enhanced certain features in their larger dogs—shorter muzzles, more domed heads, and more pronounced eye sockets, for example—in an effort to make them look more "civilized" or domestic. Attempting to link behavior directly to appearance, a number of scientists and popular writers have seized on that phenomenon to proclaim that the dog not only looks like a neotenic wolf but acts like one as well, literally playing its life away. But in making that claim, they overlook the fact that humans, not genes, make their dogs perpetual puppies by rewarding their playful behavior.

Although no one knows precisely what in the process of domestication triggered the genetic and developmental changes that led to the physical transformation of the tamed wolf into the dog, inbreeding, which people forced inadvertently by limiting reproductive opportunities and deliberately by selecting mates in order to promote certain characteristics, is a prime suspect. At the same time, the newly domesticated animals, with the stress of living in the wild removed, not only came into heat earlier and more frequently but also produced larger litters of smaller animals. A number of experts have speculated that a change in diet to include more offal, nuts, and grains, along with a reduction in quantity, also permanently stunted the growth of the newly domesticated wolves. Although nutrition clearly is vital to the development and overall size of individuals, it is not clear that the animal's genotype is changed if it suffers from a poor diet. In other words, if its offspring eat well and are healthy, they should reach full size. Whatever their cause, the changes involved in turning the wolf into a dog need only to have affected a few individuals who served as founders of a line to have had far-reaching impact, especially in the case of dominant mutations.

Physical differences aside, dogs communicate in ways that are remarkably similar to wolves. From barks to howls, whines, and yelps, the range of vocalizations are the same, although the frequency and use vary, especially among dogs living alone with people in apartments or closely confined in houses. Dogs, most particularly huskies, apparently howl for much the same reasons as wolves: to call each other together, to end the day, to celebrate dinner if not a successful hunt, to boost morale, to sing of sex. Our Catahoula leopard dogs howl in two-part harmony when we leave the house without them—whether to call us back or bewail their abandonment, I cannot say. After going walk-about on the beach for twenty-four hours, our male announced his return home with howls.

It is commonly theorized that the propensity to bark is an inherited characteristic related to creation of the dog, but that is by no means certain. Some breeds show a disinclination to bark, while individual dogs vary greatly, as does the amount of encouragement people provide. Of our two Catahoulas, the male is a tireless barker when people come near his house, while the female barks only when there is an actual intruder or when she has treed an animal. Neither barks for the sake of barking, leading me to place their behavior in the same class as that of a wolf who barks to warn of a threat. Even the little yappy dog who seems to want nothing more than to hear itself might be telling the world that it feels under attack; it is, after all, highly vulnerable in its eggshell body. Early socialization plays a crucial role in inhibiting barking, as does the reaction of the owner, who can train against the behavior if he or she chooses.

Body language showing fear, submission, dominance, and aggression are similar in dogs and wolves. These include wagging tails, raising hackles, walking on tiptoes, ritual mounting, rolling over on one's back in submission, licking another dog's or a person's muzzle, sticking tails between legs and skulking, pinning ears back or perking them up, cocking heads in query or bemusement, smelling another animal's anus and genitals, and staring. Taken as young puppies from their littermates and raised in relative isolation from other dogs, many puppies fail to learn the cues and thus misunderstand what the dogs they meet in a park or along the street are telling them. Because their handlers are equally clueless, the incomprehension frequently leads to a dispute between dogs and people.

In addition, some dogs have difficulty staring because of heavy lids or hair falling over their eyes, while the overly long coats of some show dogs make it difficult for them to raise their hackles, and excessively long or closely cropped ears are difficult to move. Similarly, docked tails limit communication because they are not easily seen and, in some cases, cannot be raised or lowered sufficiently to convey any message. The problems resulting from these alterations affect the dog's ability to get on not only with other dogs but also with humans. Because the procedures for docking tails and cropping ears are also painful, they are banned in Great Britain and Canada. Many American veterinarians oppose them, as well, but the kennel clubs mandate them for some breeds if they are shown.

Like other canids, dogs and wolves follow their noses through the world, using them to find mates, identify friend and foe, hunt, navigate. Their olfactory ability opens to them a reality largely unknown to us, which is one reason dogs are so valuable to us.

In general, the differences in behavior between wolves and dogs—and breeds of dog—are of degree, or emphasis, not kind. In their classic book *Genetics and the Social Behavior of the Dog* (1965), J. P. Scott and John L. Fuller observed that selective breeding by humans has over millennia taken individual variability in wolves and accentuated it in dog breeds so that each represents "one of many possible individual behavioral variations." For example, some breeds—mostly terriers—are more aggressive than wolves, fighting without provocation from an early age, while hounds can run in packs with minimal fighting, much the way wolves do. Their sociability does not prevent hounds from being tenacious in the chase or from occasionally biting another dog or person. Dogs also respond with different degrees of curiosity, fear, and aggression to olfactory, auditory, or visual stimuli. Although as a general rule specific combinations of these responses are associated with particular breeds, the correlations are not precise. Often there is more variation in talent and ability among dogs of a certain breed than between breeds.

The most significant differences between the wolf and dog are sexual, social, and cultural. The domesticated wolf learned to accept the human as its pack leader, to subordinate its interests and, to a large degree, its instinct to its two-legged companion. Wolves are generalists who adapt to varied natural environments. Wolves work to care for themselves. They are social to wolves. Dogs devote their talents to the service of their human handler—or sheep or other animals to which they have bonded—with more dedication and concentration than a wolf could ever muster.

Scott and Fuller suggested that the period in which socialization could easily occur has been extended in dogs through artificial selection, noting that a wolf pup will bond to humans in doglike fashion only if adopted for hand rearing before it is weaned, at about five weeks. After that time, the wolf puppy's fear response to strangers and bond to its own kind become stronger, and it is well on its way to becoming a wild animal. Extension of the optimum bonding period to fourteen weeks in dogs reflects millennia of selection for sociable animals. Even after fourteen weeks, dogs can be socialized and trained; it is just more difficult. They usually remain kennel dogs.

Acceptance of a human as pack leader had profound consequences, foremost among them destruction of the culture of the wolf pack and alteration of the wolf's psychosexual habits. Dogs mature sexually at six to nine months of age, as opposed to two years for wolves, and, as a rule, come into heat twice a year rather than once for the wolf and other wild canids, including the dingo. (A few dogs, like the basenji, also have yearly estrus cycles, for unknown reasons.) In captivity and when the alpha, or breeding, female dies in the wild, wolf females will come into heat around their first birthday, indicating that the process of sexual maturation might be suppressed through social and environmental, not genetic, factors.

In wolf packs, the alpha, or dominant, male and female generally produce the annual litter, which the rest of the pack—really an extended family—watches, feeds, and educates. Occasionally there might be extra breeding pairs, if food is abundant, but they are usually on their way to establishing their own pack. As a rule, the breeding of subordinate wolf females is suppressed socially: it is not done. In dingo packs, on the other hand, the dominant female kills any other litter that might be born. The favored method of birth control is learned from the parents.

In allying themselves with humans, dogs effectively expanded their pack system and launched a sexual revolution. They renounced much of their canid autonomy but gained the freedom to breed virtually unchecked, except when humans intervened, and rid themselves of the burden of caring for their young—beyond the time they are weaned, for the dam; totally, for the sire.

Unless they have no other choice, wolves do not inbreed in the wild, as if there were some kind of taboo. For example, the wolves on Isle Royale in Lake Superior come from one breeding pair that crossed the ice pack from the mainland in pursuit of game during a particularly cold winter earlier in this century and apparently have not been joined by other animals. They had to inbreed or die. Similarly an alpha male might mate with one of his daughters if the alpha female is killed. On the other hand, dogs, captive wolves, and dingoes are regularly encouraged in incestuous behavior by isolation, confinement, and human preference. Virtually every breed of dog we have today resulted from some degree of inbreeding. When properly done, the results can be healthy and unique in their temperament and habits, but too frequently, they possess genetic defects that would destroy a wild population.

Male wolves participate in the feeding and rearing of the young, as do male dingoes. Male dogs do not. Often they are not on site. Even when present, they do nothing, making them unique among canids. Humans become the primary caregivers after the puppies are weaned, frequently removing them from their mother and placing them in other homes, whereas wolf pups generally stay with their parents until they are two or three years of age, forming the core of the wolf pack.

Because humans provide food, protection, and social context, most dogs never learn how to hunt for themselves, care for their young, or organize a traditional, independent pack. Hounds who hunt in groups and huskies who pull sleds in teams, which some people confuse with a pack, are discouraged from forming hierarchical social structures or acting in dominant fashion toward each other. Hounds struggling for social status at the base of a tree where a bear is perched can maim each other. Curs tearing at each other rather than bunching cattle will allow a herd to scatter to the four corners of the compass, not to be brought in that day. Huskies fighting while hitched to a sled will leave their musher in the middle of a frozen tundra with injured dogs. In each instance, the humans are indisputedly in charge, enforcing their rule and social structure through early socialization and more directly by tying dogs in a yard or kenneling them, so they cannot mingle when not working, as well as by selecting against dogs exhibiting dominance aggression through breeding and culling. (Not all dogs need to be tied; I have seen many leopard dogs and black-mouth curs lying around ranches waiting to work or respond to a threat, and even some huskies are allowed to intermingle. People with multiple pet dogs often leave them loose once they are socialized to each other.)

Dogs often will form close friendships with members of their own and of the opposite sex, and given the chance, females will choose their mate, often of their breed or type, from among a number of suitors, but as a general rule, they lack the organizational skills of wolves. During the mid-1980s, Luigi Boitani, an Italian ethologist, and his colleagues at the University of Rome studied a population of feral dogs in Abruzzi, Italy, and found that although they banded together, they could not establish a well-defined pack. As a result, all the females bred, and the males and other group members did not help with rearing the young, causing most of them to die. Lacking the skills to hunt and kill they would have learned from wild, independent parents, the feral dogs were more scavengers than predators. In fact, the population sustained itself through steady recruitment from among village dogs. Studies of feral dogs in other parts of the world have produced similar findings. None have continued long enough to reveal whether such groups could ultimately become independent, the way the dingo did in Australia, but there is no reason to assume they could not, given sufficient prey and a good climate.

Although instinctively they stalk, pounce, grab, and engage in other hunting behavior, young wolves, dingoes, dogs, and African wild dogs, among other social carnivores (coyotes being a possible exception), must be taught how to isolate, kill, and dissect their prey. They might eventually learn on their own, but they generally die of starvation beforehand. Humans usually train dogs to abort the hunting sequence before or just after they draw blood. For example, a group of curs herding cows are really engaged in an attack, which they stop only because they have been taught by their handler or fellow dogs to back off. Border collies must also learn not to kill and ultimately not to bite the sheep they are being asked to herd and even sheep-guarding dogs must be discouraged on occasion from feasting on their charges. Thus, the celebrated disinclination of many dogs to follow through on their attack is a matter of learning from the pack master and of selective breeding for biddable animals, not of production of animals preprogrammed to stop.

Among dingoes and wolves, what wildlife biologists call submissive behavior, and we might call the art of sublimating one's will to that of the group in order to coexist peacefully, is also learned at an early age. Laurie Corbett, an Australian wildlife biologist, says that a dingo puppy raised in isolation and then placed in a litter will aggressively seek to dominate the other young dingoes. Because it does not know how to be submissive and never learns, it quickly becomes the leader of its peer group, while its elders attempt to ignore its unacceptable behavior. Dominance aggression of this sort in dogs leads to situations in which the pet rules the house, terrorizing one or more of its human inhabitants, which is why early socialization is perhaps the most crucial element of dog raising.

Clearly inheritance and environment—upbringing—are responsible for the dog. Year-round fertility for males and two annual heat cycles for most females have a genetic component, as do sociability toward humans and other personality traits. The inclination toward retrieving, hunting by sight or scent, stalking and pointing, running fast without apparent aim, herding—all have a genetic foundation usually in combination with other basic traits. Beyond that, culture plays a role, transmitting traditions from generation to generation in ways we have probably underestimated. Absent interference from humans or some natural disaster, wolves learn from birth how to survive in their environment and operate in their pack, although some wolves apparently never learn how to hunt proficiently. Dogs learn to operate in the human world, often by performing certain tasks—even if only acting the clown.

At the same time, humans grow accustomed to expecting certain behaviors of specific types or breeds of dogs and treat them accordingly. When the dogs, who are intelligent and adaptable, respond correctly they reinforce the human perception of them. To a degree not yet determined, dogs act according to our expectations, the way children and strangers do. Even when we make adjustments to accommodate individual eccentricities, we do so within our notion of how a Labrador or German shepherd or a cur responds.

The nature of the "pack" in which dogs find themselves is often poorly defined. Many dog owners do not realize that they are in charge; others adopt a model that leads them to want to impose a sort of iron discipline on their pet, believing such behavior to be analogous to that of the alpha wolf. Dominance hierarchies among wolf packs are not as fixed as some researchers and popular writers—following the human tendency to see what we want to believe—have traditionally made them appear. In fact, the rigid hierarchical organization researchers have ascribed to nearly all animal packs and troops over the past fifty years is based less on animal behavior than on an unconscious desire to find in nature a correlative to our hierarchical structures, be they business, the military, or the "traditional" family with Dad on top.

In nature, relationships are more fluid, responding to changing conditions. Male and female wolves maintain separate hierarchies within the pack, which shift over time. More important, in nature the alpha pair are, by definition, the breeding male and female, usually the oldest adults, the parents of younger pack members. But in human society, dogs breed without being allowed to become fully dominant. In effect, we demand of them greater flexibility in behavior and control over their "instincts."

The differences notwithstanding, people with multiple, unrelated

pet dogs, frequently attempt to establish what they call a "pack situation," often in a genuine effort to end the kind of fighting based on
jealousy, missed communication, and improper responses to each
other in which they will engage. Such dogs will eventually establish a
pecking order, but its resemblance to a pack largely exists in the mind
of their owner. Often unconsciously, he or she has imposed a hierarchical structure on the group through training—letting dogs in and
out or feeding them or wiping their feet in a particular sequence,
for example—rewards, and corrections. Or the owner might tolerate
aggressive behavior on the part of a dog he or she feels is the dominant
one while helping to suppress it in others.

Reading the Trail

In Lappland, the Sami people have long employed a variant of
the northern spitz-type dog, which dates back at least 7,000 years,
to herd reindeer. The porokoira is a thick-coated animal, black and
tan or black and white or black, tan, and white, weighing forty to
sixty pounds. Curled in the snow, it resembles a ball of soot. Although
snowmobiles and dirt bikes nearly sent the dogs into extinction, they
have made a comeback of sorts—I saw one in Finnish Lappland who
rode on a snowmobile—even as fences have cut the range of the
herds and made it difficult to think of reindeer as only semidomesti-
cated. For thousands of years before the fences, the Sami followed
reindeer—caribou are their North American cousins—in their
migration, taking from the "wild" herd what they needed for meat,
hides, transportation. There was no imperative to settle into fixed
communities.

Domestication, the next step beyond that of tracking and herding
reindeer, requires a way to gather the wild animals and keep them in
one place—tasks at which the dog excels. While the dates for those
events, as for the creation of the dog, are constantly shifting, some
10,000 years ago, first goats and sheep, then cattle and pigs, were
brought under human domination to ensure a steady supply of meat
and hides. Simultaneously, plants were being actively cultivated. We

take those events as the beginnings of the shift to an agricultural way of life, the dawn of the Neolithic Age.

Ranchers in the southern and southwestern United States continue to use dogs to capture feral cattle and hogs. Often, the dogs themselves are tough, half-wild creatures, capable of grabbing, holding, and, if necessary, killing the animal, especially the hog. They were that way 10,000 years ago as well—quick, tough canids who could bring into line an animal considerably larger and stronger but far less agile. The dogs leaped snarling and slashing with their teeth, bunching the game and holding it in place by circling it until the humans selected the animals they wanted for eating. From there it was a small step to bring the prey into a corral. Once the animals were collected, dogs helped keep them from wandering and protected them from other predators—cats and wolves. In that sense, dogs created animal husbandry, as a number of nineteenth-century French natural historians were fond of proclaiming.

Barring disaster, domesticated animals and plants provided a steady, fixed food supply, a prerequisite for stable communities. As populations increased, social structures became more complex. But whether agriculture itself created a better, as opposed to a different, life remains subject to intense debate. Certainly leisure time decreased as people devoted more hours to cultivation of plants and animals. The security of a steady food supply brought with it the insecurity of dependence on crops that might fail, animals that could run away, be stolen by raiders, or die of epidemic. Even people were exposed to new diseases because they were living in greater proximity to others; in wetlands which they would have abandoned when migratory during the rainy season but now occupied throughout the year because of their crops, thereby exposing themselves to yellow fever and malaria, among other maladies; and in close quarters with animals that bore parasites, including various worms, and diseases transmittable to humans.

Given those drawbacks, agriculture sounds like a bad decision, but those of us peering back from the end of the second millennium A.D., 10,000 or more years after the fact, cannot make such a judgment. We are too far removed from that time and, in many cases, from agriculture itself to understand fully its origins or the series of conscious and unconscious decisions that led to domestication of plants and animals. Yet at the same time, we are products of those decisions and the ones that followed with apparent inevitability. Agriculture provided the opportunity to increase material and cultural wealth, although clearly not everyone was enriched equally. Socioeconomic and gender divisions became more rigid and finally codified through laws that protected inheritance and privilege. Needing water, land for crops and livestock, animals, labor, and raw materials, growing communities waged wars of conquest and destruction against each other.

By all evidence, dogs accompanied people quite well into the new order they had helped create. Agriculturists began to breed dogs for appearance and size to distinguish them from wolves and to enhance their abilities to fill certain roles, the assignment of which represented the same kind of codification and stratification that was going on in society. Thus, there were hunting dogs, war dogs, sheepdogs, companions, dogs fit for eating and sacrifice. The hunters and war dogs, which were often the same, along with the companions, stood above the rest, the way nobility dominated the laborer. Rising class and caste systems placed the dog below privileged men on the chain of being but, depending on their purpose, either above or in line with servants, slaves, women, and children.

Puppies and companion dogs or lapdogs were able to get physically closer to people than any other type. Yet although they rated well above servants, who were required to pamper and even nurse them, because associated with women and children, they were not considered in the same class as the hunting and war dogs, notwithstanding the fact that some of them may have doubled as ratters. These distinctions appear to have found their greatest expression in the Middle East, Europe, and China—wherever empires arose.

Based on hieroglyphics from Egypt and other documentary evidence, most experts surmise that the earliest specialized hunting dog was the sight hound, dating to 5,000 or more years ago, although it is doubtful that it relied on its eyes to the exclusion of other senses. The lean Ibizan and pharaoh hounds, which are probably the same dog, are highly refined versions of this early hunter, developed to run down game in open terrain. A smaller variety is the cirneco dell'Etna, fifteen to thirty pounds; it hunts by sight and scent in Sicily, where its forebears were deposited millennia ago by traders. The related podengo Portugueso, found on the Iberian Peninsula since antiquity, ranges in weight from nine to fifty pounds, in height from eight to twenty-five inches, with the largest variant found on the Canary Islands. Like its counterpart on Sicily, and probably the early Egyptian hounds, the podengo points, trails, and retrieves birds and mammals. It is equally adept at hunting alone or in a pack.

The Egyptians appear to have kept both large and small sight hounds, often with curled tails, and a dwarf harlequin version. Frederick E. Zeuner in his widely respected 1963 study, *A History of Domesticated Animals*, observes that they also had mastiffs, probably from Mesopotamia, and pariahs or mutts. Other evidence clearly places the mastiffs on the end of Assyrian leashes, and it is assumed that those large dogs arrived there at an early date, probably through trade with Asia.

The most famous sight hound in the world today is the greyhound, the often abused racing machine on which people bet millions of dollars annually. Usually said to date from antiquity, the track racers have, in fact, benefited from crosses at the turn of the century with the large bull and bear dog that bulked their muscles. The resultant animal hits and holds speeds of forty miles per hour while chasing a mechanical rabbit around a tight 600-yard track and perhaps slightly more while running down a coyote in open country, where some of them have throttled themselves on a fence strand the prey has slipped under and they, single-minded in pursuit, have not seen.

Greyhounds lack the aerobic capacity of a distance runner like the Alaskan husky or foxhound, but that is largely because they do not need it. Selective breeding has produced an animal with 95 percent or more fast-twitch muscle fibers, which produce fuel anaerobically, compared with 40 percent for a human sprinter, 50 to 65 percent for long-running dogs.

Marvelous though the dogs are, their life at the tracks is dismal. If they do not run to victory and are not lucky enough to be adopted, they are killed. Even those who win are given only enough care to keep them running. "They might as well be plastic," a veterinarian familiar with the tracks told me. Campaigns against the abuse and changing demographics appear to be taking their toll; a number of states have moved to eliminate greyhound racing, and in many areas attendance and gambling are in decline. Ironically, as a result, more dogs are put to death prematurely.

In Europe and England, prototype sheepdogs and hounds had been added to the fundamental division between large and small dogs by 3500 B.C., indicating that people were breeding for purposes. Inveterate breeders not only of dogs but also of birds and livestock, the Greeks decreed that sheepdogs should be white so as not to scare the sheep and be easily distinguishable from wolves; guard dogs black and dark brown to intimidate intruders. Both were to have lop ears; variegated dogs were forbidden because it was difficult to distinguish them from wolves. The Roman writer Columella repeated this injunction in the first century A.D., and it became custom. The Greeks also celebrated the fidelity of their dogs: Argos alone recognized his long-absent master Odysseus on his return from his adventures following the Trojan War, then died. Of course, Argos would have been the oldest dog on record at the time, but no matter. He was devoted.

At the dawn of their empire, the Romans recognized companion, hunting, war, draft, and guard dogs, sight and scent hounds. Extant descriptions and portraits indicate that the companion dogs were small, while the draft, war, and guard dogs resembled variants on the mastiff—the essential large dog they called the molossus—the primary differences probably being in size, training, color, and temperament, meaning that individual dogs from single litters could go to different purposes. Those large dogs fought in gladiatorial games, against each other, humans, and other animals. They marched to war with the legions, drove and guarded livestock. Mixed with sight hounds for speed, they probably formed the basis of the scent hounds.

The Roman historian Tacitus wrote of large wolflike dogs in the Rhine valley of Germany, leading modern historians of the breed to conclude he was speaking of their German shepherd. (The Romans thought the tribes in northern Europe were savage, as well, much the way the northern Europeans later classified non-Europeans and their dogs.)

The Chinese *Book of Rites* (A.D. 800) mentioned three classes of dog: hunting dogs, watch dogs, and food dogs. By A.D. 1,000, another category had been added—that of pampered pet. The emperor Ling gave his dogs royal rank and decreed that the little pug-faced creatures, which people like to trace to the modern Pekingese, be suckled by the imperial wet nurses, provided a stipend, and guarded by court eunuchs. Although the current Pekingese are products of selective breeding, they initially were created by grotesque human manipulation. Puppies were starved to stunt their growth and confined in wire corsets. The cartilage in their noses and between their shoulders was destroyed to reshape them. Changes produced in that fashion are, of course, not inherited.

Several hundred years later, when Marco Polo visited the court of Kublai Khan, he found dogs drawing sledges for freight and passengers in addition to hunting and war hounds, companion and food dogs. While he led the People's Republic of China, Mao Zedong regularly denounced dog ownership as bourgeois recidivism. During the 1950s and 1960s, heavy taxes were imposed on pets, which were periodically slaughtered, the intent being to keep dogs only for police work and research. But in the 1980s and 1990s, the emerging urban professional class in China once again began avidly keeping dogs.

In seventeenth-century Japan, the shogun Tsunayoshi's edict that each street keep a set number of dogs fed and housed roused resentment among the populace and created a public nuisance, as the dogs harassed pedestrians. This story, reported by Engelbert Kaempfer in his *History of Japan* (1690), has come down to us as a case in which the shogun owned 100,000 dogs and imposed an unpopular tax to feed them. That said, dogs apparently never achieved the culinary reputation in Japan that they enjoyed in the rest of Asia in large measure because of Shinto prohibitions against eating land mammals. In Japan, they seem to have served primarily for hunting and hauling. In the nineteenth and early twentieth centuries, the 150-pound tosa was developed as a fighting dog by mixing an indigenous breed, the shikoku, with a large, fierce animal from Nagasaki and mastiffs from Europe. But, as a rule, before the modern era, when Japanese began collecting dogs from around the world, breeds were based largely on geographic and size distinctions. Many of them performed multiple tasks.

I keep returning to that point because it is significant. In essence, the dog, no less than its wild cousin, is a generalist capable of hunting, herding, hauling, and guarding to varying degrees. It became a specialist of rather unstable perfection by human design and training. In the Arctic and other areas where extensive agricultural societies did not develop, different tribes or groups of people had dogs of a particular type: spitz, husky, dingo, or Native American dog. Broad distinctions were sometimes drawn between big and little dogs, but in general the dogs were nonspecialized.

While today we have dogs from Japan and China, as well as the rest of the world, the tradition that has most shaped ours in the United States is European, more specifically British, dating from the Middle Ages, with ancient Greek and Roman prescriptions at its base. Shaping those attitudes was the deep ambivalence of the leaders of the Catholic Church toward dogs. Were they unclean or shining examples of fidelity? Gyrating between poles, Church leaders often found themselves at odds with each other and their flock. After all, who guards a flock but the shepherd and his sheepdog?

The fifth-century Saint Christopher, patron of travelers recently demoted from sainthood, was portrayed with the head of a dog, an appropriate bit of iconography. Francis of Assisi, the thirteenth-century saint who so thoroughly embodied Christian values, was friend to all creatures great and small. The Dominicans wore the cynosure, the "dog's tail," from the Greek *kunosoura*—also the name for Ursa Minor and the Pole Star—identifying themselves as hounds in the service of the Lord, just as Jesus was at times called the "hound of heaven."

A more venerable order than the late-arriving Franciscans and Dominicans, the Benedictines, founded in the sixth century, bred dogs in their various monasteries. The most famous of these was the Belgian

Benedictine monastery of Saint Hubert, which developed a line of superb tracking dogs around the ninth century. Known to us as the Saint Hubert bloodhound, the dog is considered to be descended from the ubiquitous Roman molossus crossed with other mastiffs. Generically, a bloodhound was any large dog with hanging ears and pendulous lips who tracked by scent and caught its prey, especially human meat thieves, in its teeth, although now it does not attack. Into the nineteenth century, several distinctive lines of bloodhounds existed, most particularly the Saint Hubert and Talbot from England.

Throughout Europe, monasteries developed and preserved lines of dogs. Often the Church Fathers complained that the brothers and sisters were spending more time with their animals than their prayers, and although the edicts to desist generally went unheeded, they sometimes led to violence. In rural France, some twenty-five miles from Lyons, a cult of Saint Guinefort, a martyred greyhound, emerged among the peasantry in the eleventh century. According to the legend, a knight returned to his castle with his lady and baby's nursemaid to find Guinefort, who had been left to guard the noble child, standing next to the overturned cradle, his jaws dripping blood. Assuming the worst, the knight slew Guinefort in a vengeful rage. The child was subsequently found alive under the cradle, as were bits of a giant serpent scattered about the room. Guinefort had nobly defended his charge and been ignobly executed. The remorseful knight threw his greyhound's corpse down a well, covered it with stones, and planted an oak grove. Peasants began bringing their sick children there, believing they would be healed by the dog saint.

The Church periodically complained but took no action until the thirteenth century, when the Dominican friar Stephen of Bourbon, more nearly resembling a hound of hell than of heaven, exhumed what he claimed were the saint's bones and scattered them to the wind. He also clear-cut and burned the oak grove. It was a crime, he decreed, for anyone to visit the site, although peasants continued to do so for another 600 years, the dog being more reliable than the Church or state. They quit when antibiotics became a better remedy.

The tale reveals not only the Church's hatred of "paganism," as manifested in turning a dog into a saint, and ambivalence toward dogs but also the attitudes of common people toward animals. Moreover, it subverts the prevailing order by juxtaposing the disloyal, irrational knight with the eminently sane, faithful greyhound. On a more general level, the legend shows the great divergence that often exists between written culture and actual practice: the former is the product of what the elite wants to believe about its world; the latter is how people behave. To the Church, seeking to impose its will on a recalcitrant and superstitious peasantry always in danger of slipping from the true faith, dogs and other animals were instruments of the devil, paganism, and heresy. Throughout the period, real peril resided in the packs of feral and unattended dogs who marauded around the countryside, terrorizing livestock and people, but that alone does not explain the attitude of the Church.

The mixing of dogs increased in the twelfth and thirteenth centuries due to the Crusades and sweep of the Mongols west under the command of Genghis Khan and his heirs. More civilized than many of the people they conquered, those nomadic horsemen from Central Asia opened direct trade routes between Europe and Asia after defeating the Ottoman Empire, which had served as a broker for centuries. The Crusaders, of course, brought dogs, especially quick sight hounds, back to their castles, along with whatever else they could pilfer. They doubtless incorporated those dogs into the bloodlines of their hounds. They probably also used them in the creation of companion dogs, who were presented as symbols of gentle fidelity and domesticity.

The dogs of nobility were deemed superior to all others, although many working animals kept their type—that is, produced puppies looking like their kind—as surely as did those of the aristocracy. Nonetheless, to ensure the division, the serfs, even those who handled the dogs of the nobility, were forbidden from owning hunting hounds for fear they would poach royal lands and neglect their work. They could, however, own curs, and with those many of them hunted through noble forests, their owners complacent in the belief that no peasant's dog could match their hounds and spaniels. Inheritance equaled wealth, privilege, intelligence, and power, after all, and inheritance was determined strictly by how wellborn one was.

The sixteenth and seventeenth centuries accelerated the process of breed formation through hybridization, as colonists, adventurers, traders, sailors, and soldiers carried their dogs to distant shores and brought back others. In 1576, the Cambridge University physician Johannes Caius attempted a classification in his *A Treatise of Englishe Dogges*, prepared at the behest of the Swedish naturalist Conrad Gessner. The result was considerably more complex than the seven categories of the Romans, although, like them, Caius grouped his dogs according to function. Thus, he identified the Bludhunde and Harrier for smelling; the Gasehunde for quick spying; the Grehunde for swiftness and quick spying; the Leuimer, a cross between the Harrier and Grehunde, for its nose and agility; the Tumbler, a sly and crafty dog who bunched game and caught it in its jaws, like the curs we know today; and the Theevishe Dogge, a poacher's cur who hunted silently at night. Caius cast the Tumbler and Theevishe Dogge as noteworthy for subtlety and deceitfulness. The Terrare, or terrier, celebrated for its small size and ability to go to ground—that is, follow prey into a den—or to get in the face of bears and other large game, was grouped with the Leuimer, a dog now lost to history.

Caius named two groups of Gentle or Fowling dogs: the spaniells (so named because they were believed to have originated in Spain), French dogs, and setters who found birds on land; and the water spaniell, or Fynder, a kind of archaic poodle, like the barbet, who fetched from the water. The Spaniell Gentle, or Comforter, reportedly came from Malta and is claimed today by supporters of the Cavalier King Charles spaniel and the Maltese. Probably, it was a generic dog who contributed to many of the modern longhaired toy breeds. Certainly, it was larger and more robust than any of its putative heirs.

"Dogges of the courser sort" were the Shepherdes Dogge, who responded to voice or whistle, and various mastiffs, large dogs used for hunting, fighting, and guarding. The Bandogge, for example, excelled at bull and bear baiting and was distinguished from other mastiffs because it was usually chained. These fearsome mastiffs guarded the Tower of London, preventing jail breaks, and even had their own cemetery on the grounds, a potential treasure trove for people studying canine history that has not yet been exploited. Caius called them frightful to behold, fierce, fell animals—traits reflected in their name, believed at the time to be derived from either *bana* (murderer) or *ban* (cursed).

Another mastiff was the Butchers Dogge, who caught and held a bull or steer by its nose while the butcher bled it to death, the belief being that an animal terrified before slaughter would taste better. With their shortened muzzles, strong jaws, and large powerful builds, the Bandogge and Butchers Dogge were similar in size and temperament. Although they have passed from history, it is postulated that the American bulldog, who can reach 130 pounds, resembles that old type. Similarly, it is said that the pit bulls and bull terriers were derived from a cross of the old bull- and bear-baiting dogs with terriers in the nineteenth century.

Other dogs of the "courser sort" were the messenger or carrier dogge; the Mooner, whose purpose is unknown; the Water Drawer; the Tynckers, or Tinkers, cur; and the defending dog. The Tinkers cur appears to have been another kind of poacher's dog.

The hounds, spaniels, and rustic dogs all kept their type, Caius said, although the range in appearance was far broader than among the refined breeds of today, but among English "dogges" were also the mongrels, the "rascals" who did not breed true. Those included the wappe, the turnespete, and the Dancer, perhaps a beggar's dog. The turnespete, or turnspit, as we know it, literally turned the spit for roasting meat or the wheel for making butter. (If one keeps breeding mongrels to another type of dog, eventually that type will out. Mongrels bred consistently to mongrels will revert to one of the basic dog types.)

In France at the same time were a variety of hounds, lapdogs, spaniels, and sheepdogs, as well as dogs who guided blind people. Giving voice to a view among many churchmen and thinkers, the mathematician René Descartes declared dogs and other animals to be machines incapable of consciousness or feelings. Although in the eighteenth century many naturalists in England and North America began to challenge that view, it remains current, so the debate continues to swing back and forth with shifting intellectual tides. Due in large measure to the influence of the animal-rights movement, the flow in recent years has been toward granting animals volition and emotion.

Near the close of the seventeenth century, Richard Blome published *The Gentleman's Recreation* (1686), another look at the dogs of the British Isles. Caius's types were joined by beagles—downsized Harriers—from the north and south of Britain, and a small lapdog who sometimes joined them in hunting rabbits and hares. Blome named lurchers (crossbred hounds) and a terrier created by crossing a beagle and mongrel mastiff, proving that the term applied not to the dog's breeding but to its habit of pursuing its prey to ground. In fact, until the rise of dog shows in the nineteenth century, what distinguished a type was its way of working *and* its basic appearance.

Proper Distance

Establishment of different classes of dogs complicated but did not resolve the more difficult psychological problem that plagued the Church Fathers, and like so much else having to do with these animals, persists to this day: how to define the boundary between humans and dogs, who themselves straddled the border between the domestic and wild. Humans were dependent on dogs for management of their animals, protection of their homes, companionship. Able to see and smell things beyond humans' senses, they seemed to have access to another reality, which made them an ally to be treated with respect and fear. The wolf, so recently the creator of the dog, became the enemy, an evil force preying on sheep and goats. The dog was valued insofar as it fought the wolf and hunted game for food and collection. But when it failed to defend the livestock or turned killer itself or came up empty on the hunt, whenever it brought misfortune, it was deemed worthless, a traitor, a misbegotten creature.

Many cultures strengthened the boundary between humans and dogs by turning "dog" or "bitch" into an insult, suggesting an excrement or garbage eater, an indiscriminate fornicator, a lout beyond the bounds of society. A human-dog was lowborn, dirty, ascetic, rude—

whatever qualities were deemed unacceptable. The dog itself was something to beat into submission and abuse, the way one abused lesser humans: children, women, slaves, and the lowborn.

What many people feared was the closeness to an animal that was domestic yet wild, trainable but independent, so close to humans that there was—and still is—concern the intimacy would become too intense. Judaic law, for example, frowned on a widow keeping a dog, deeming it unseemly in a sexual sense and, in general, considered dogs to be dirty, a view picked up by Islam and Christianity and shared by Hinduism, even while the first two also celebrated the dog's fidelity and skill in the hunt. Many tribal societies also developed elaborate means of dividing the two species conceptually if not always practically.

In medieval Europe people, especially women, were persecuted as witches for being too intimate with animals and uncultivated plants that could prevent or abort pregnancy. Bestiality was declared a capital offense in Britain in 1534 and remained so until 1861, with a few brief intervals of legal sanity. In 1679, a woman and her dog were hanged in Tyburn Hill, London, for fornicating.

There is an abiding fascination with and fear of bestiality, which undeniably occurs with dogs and other animals. For example, estimates are that 1.2 percent of the U.S. population has had congress with a dog. Alan Beck and Aaron Katcher in their 1983 book, *Between Pets and People*, report on a female psychiatric patient who stunned a class of medical students with the revelation that "she had regular sexual intercourse with the family dog." The Internet has sites devoted to the subject, which, like so much else on the Internet, are largely tedious, and Michael Ryan confessed in his 1995 memoir, *Secret Life*, to having had sex with the family dog in his youth, thereby placing himself in an elite literary company including the former madame Xavier Hollander. Bestiality, however, is not to the taste of most people, and never has been. It is of interest here because of the phobia that stands behind it.

Beyond the fear of dependence on dogs lay the horror, which persists to this day, of feral dogs marauding around the countryside attacking people, livestock, and even other dogs, spreading rabies. Although never very widespread in the human population nor as great a threat as epidemic-causing diseases like cholera, smallpox, or the plague, rabies was a cause for public hysteria because it always brought a painful death. Even today, a century after Louis Pasteur developed his vaccine, fear of rabies remains palpable: Treatment for infected humans is painful and not readily available in poor countries, nor are vaccinations for animals. Over the past decade, Morocco has slaughtered on the order of 2 million dogs to quash an outbreak of rabies. Shanghai, China, put more than 5,000 to death in 1995 for the same reason.

The fear of rabies fueled the image of the dog as a harbinger of death and destruction, an image that stood in stark contrast to the perception of it as a healer and guardian. The news media–fueled panic over pit bull terriers and other "vicious" breeds of dog during the 1980s and early 1990s, which led many communities and countries to ban ownership of them, echoed that age-old fear, as do periodic reports of free-ranging dogs invading a zoo and wantonly slaughtering antelope, gazelle, or other animals. In a sign of their evil, they are said to kill without eating—a trait most associated with human hunters.

Yet for all the taboos and phobias, the dog has remained fixed in our affections, making the leap with us from the cave to villages, farms, towns, cities, and the modern metropolis. Although the keeping of companion animals predates the origin of the dog itself, pet keeping as we know it began in the late eighteenth century with the rise of the urban middle class, the bourgeoisie. As the dog was brought fully into the home, human perceptions of it changed so that it became a paragon of virtue and wisdom. It was groomed, cleaned, clothed, pampered.

With the growth in scientific knowledge and societal interest in natural history, including animal husbandry, in the nineteenth century, the dog became an object of experimentation—in the laboratory where it was dissected, often while still alive, and in breeding kennels where it was altered to fit human conceptions of beauty and utility. Even supposedly ancient dogs were transformed once they fell into the hands of the emergent fancy, the world of the kennel club. Generally, they became more refined and uniform in appearance, and unfortunately the process continues with the search for "primitive" and unspoiled breeds. Not surprisingly, most of our attitudes toward dogs, including the intellectual lens through which we view them, were, like the dogs themselves, formed during this period.

BIG DOGS AND LITTLE DOGS

Basic Division

In Alaska, a surprising number of mushers have house pets, generally little dogs, in addition to their working huskies. My favorites were a toy poodle who rode in the truck and boat and generally had the run of the house, a black-and-white crossbred border collie and heeler, and a little curly-coated white dog named Rebarr who loved to run—whether with dogs or people mattered not at all. When she got hot, she flopped down in the water, then charged out, dripping a trail of mud. "Her parents were real small," Martin Buser told me, "so we got her to ride in the sled. She got too big for that, but she's too small to be a sled dog even though she's fast."

At thirty pounds, Rebarr is a big small dog, just as a thirty-five-pound husky is a little big dog. Whatever the cutoff—for some people, it is thirty pounds; for others, twenty; and for still others, it is simply the structure of the dog—the divide between big dogs and little dogs is the most ancient and fundamental in dogdom. Small dogs are ideal for killing vermin in and around the house, for distracting game so a hunter can draw near, for companionship in close quarters. At their best, they are lively and amusing. Used for protection and work, be it hunting or hauling, big dogs traditionally have been yard or kennel dogs; in fact, only in the past 150 years have they taken up residence in the house in any number. Given their positions in human society, it is hardly surprising that many archaeological sites feature puppies or little dogs, not large animals.

Among some North American tribes, the tradition of large and small dogs existed long before the arrival of Europeans. For example, the Athabascans of the Alaska interior and Canadian Northwest had big village dogs and little dogs, under twenty pounds (called the Tahltan bear dog in modern times), whom they pampered, fed well, and carried in baskets on their hunts until they drew close to their quarry. Released, the Tahltan dog would charge and distract the bear while the men approached with their spears for the kill, just the way any number of terriers and feists have long performed for European and white American hunters.

The generally black-and-tan or black-and-white dogs were fearless, agile, aggressive, able to follow an animal to its den or into a deadfall—places their larger mates could not go. The large dogs, on the other hand, had range and power for hunting caribou or, among the coastal Inuit, pulling sleds. Sadly, the Tahltan bear dog went extinct in the 1970s or 1980s—no one marked the date—having been rendered obsolete by high-powered repeating rifles that made killing bears a relatively easy, long-distance affair and also having failed to find favor in the show ring.

The English reinforced the biological distinction between large and small dogs with laws—also common on the continent. From the time of Henry II early in the twelfth century, "every dweller inhabitant within any forest of any worth may keep a mastiff about his house for the defense of his house and his goods," according to the laws of the forest, but it had to be expeditated, or lawed, to prevent it from harassing the forest owner's deer and other game. A mastiff was defined as any dog descended from the molossus. Included in the definition were "curs of the mastiff kind," also known as "barking curs" because they were kept in the yard to protect the property when not hunting. The standard of measure for a large dog was a small iron stirrup through which its forepaw had to pass.

Every three years, dogs in and around the forest were checked. If they failed the stirrup test, unless the owner had a royal charter allowing him to keep mastiffs and purebred hunting dogs—greyhounds and spaniels—they were taken for expeditation. Their forepaws were placed one at a time on a foot-square block of wood eight inches thick, and the middle three claws were chopped off at the flesh with a single blow from a mallet on a two-inch-wide chisel. A three-shilling fine was levied against any person found with an unexpeditated mastiff. If caught with large dogs, poachers—usually soldiers and lesser nobility, not peasants—could have their testicles and eyes removed as punishment, although apparently that brutal penalty was seldom applied.

Established with the Norman Conquest, forests were preserves granted by royal patent to favored noblemen. "Every dweller" referred only to farmers and wealthy freeholders, not to field hands and laborers. They could keep unexpeditated little dogs, as could the mastiff owners. This arcane bit of law, probably honored as much in the breach as in practice, persisted at least into the seventeenth century, barrister John Manwood having set it forth in *A Treatise and Discourse of the Lawes of the Forest*, printed in 1598. By that time, aristocrats had begun to convert their land to enclosed pastures for raising sheep. The process, known as enclosures, led to the abolition of the commons, areas the community used for grazing and collecting wood. At the same time, throughout England, woodlands were felled at an alarming rate to build and rebuild the fleets of the growing empire.

While the nobility hunted with its hounds, mastiffs, and spaniels, the poor concentrated on other dogs. Because in addition to mastiffs, laborers could not keep hunting dogs and could not afford to maintain packs in any event, they kept multipurpose dogs—curs, weighing thirty to probably around fifty-five or sixty pounds—and smaller terriers who made up in agility and tenacity what they lacked in size and strength. Of course, the curs could go up to one hundred pounds, but the large dogs were not desirable if one had dealings with the forest. They were welcome, however, as guardians and draft animals in some areas.

Whenever they hunted on their own in the royal forests—and there were few other places—soldiers, small freeholders, and, to a lesser degree, peasants were poachers subject to arrest. Their descendants were accorded the right to hunt legally only after they entered the New World—where their survival often depended on it. Then, not surprisingly, their big and little dogs formed the rootstock of those they bred in North America: the big curs and coonhounds; the little treeing feists.

Although the feists and some hunting terriers uphold the honor of small dogs, many of those we know today are mutants maintained to feed human vanity. Like the Pekingese, some are achondroplastic dwarfs with bowed and stunted legs, a punched-in face (brachycephalic head), and exaggerated coat. Others, like the Pomeranian, are midgets or ateliotic dwarfs, well-proportioned miniaturized dogs, like the feists. Nearly all of these animals—pugs, Boston terriers, Yorkies, Scotties, toy poodles, miniaturized spaniels, Maltese, Shih tzus, among them—are at the limit of their biological viability, unable to whelp naturally or exist without human intervention. Some are so distorted in temperament and appearance that it is hard to consider them dogs at all; others resemble fragile, animated dolls. Many are unable to digest their food or relieve themselves properly. For all their problems, they remain popular among people who want canine companions but consider real dogs too much bother.

Similarly, many of the giant breeds so popular today, especially the mastiffs, Saint Bernard, Newfoundland, and even the venerable Great Dane, have become parodies of the large fierce dog on which they were modeled. The majority suffer from congenital cytoskeletal problems, like hip dysplasia; all have a reduced life expectancy because they are physiologically too large for their hearts. A pair of Great Danes of my acquaintance spent the first two years of their lives unable to walk and then became ambulatory only after undergoing extensive surgery costing thousands of dollars. (It goes without saying that the dogs should have been put down, but their owners were fond of the idea of saving them.)

The tradition of big and little working dogs remains strongest in the American South, although its future is threatened by the same economic, social, and environmental upheavals that are transforming the world. The full maturation of industrial capitalism with its concomitant wholesale migration of people into sprawling cities and suburbs and expansion of "factory" farms has nearly obliterated the natural world and now threatens the rural way of life that for centuries has been the mainstay of many societies. According to projections, nearly three-quarters of the world's population will live in metropolitan areas by 2025. Fewer people on diminishing amounts of land will follow the hunting and small farming culture that sustains the tradition of big and little working dogs. The vast acres of cultivated pines—call it the pine monoculture—that have taken the place of virgin forests and farmland are inhospitable to many types of wildlife. In fact, "wild" has already become an adjective more often applied to human fashion and behavior than the world outside ourselves. How is a dog to escape the fate of the Tahltan bear dog or the Scottie prancing around a show ring, its coat dragging the ground?

The Large and Small of It

Driving his old white pickup truck on a warm, overcast Saturday morning in January 1995 past rows of farms turned to piney woods because of government subsidies that pay more for trees than food crops, George Cauley, a large, soft-spoken man who was born and raised in the roadside community of Soperton, right here in rural central Georgia, talks about the little dogs he breeds and uses to hunt squirrels. "When I was growing up," he says, "everybody had a little dog they called a feist or fice and a big yard dog, a cur."

As their names imply—and by the official definition of kennel clubs—both were mongrels. More specifically, they were dogs of a particular type bred, sometimes carefully, to a purpose but not to a rigidly defined standard. They treed everything from squirrels to raccoons, bears, bobcats, and cougars (when they could still be found), tracked hogs, cattle, deer, and any other game their owner asked them to pursue. (The hogs are descended from pigs early colonists brought to the New World. Left to "root hog or die," as Davy Crockett used to say, they rooted with a vengeance, becoming wild, mean, and a terror to ground-nesting birds and snakes. In much of the South, in Australia, Hawaii, and other places were they have naturalized, these feral pigs—sometimes supplemented by Russian wild boars introduced in this century for trophy hunting—are an intrusive, unwelcome, destructive species that must be rooted out.)

Folks in the South argue nonstop over the relative merits of a mountain feist or lowland feist, a Stephens cur, yellow blackmouth cur, leopard cur (including the Catahoula leopard dog), Camus cur, Canadian cur, or any of more than a score of strains representing either a regional variety or a famous breeder's line. They most likely will not even agree that they are the same dog, although they are. They contend over whether their dog scents air or ground, whether it follows a cold trail, whether it hunts predominantly by sight, sound, or smell, how it barks and bays when it hits a track and again when it finds its quarry. Does it open up, or sound off, as soon as it strikes scent or wait until it has actually treed its game? Finally, one or two of them admit that the dogs have the same basic talents but differ in the devotion they bring to the task, the predilection they show for a style of work or particular prey.

Despite the disagreements, the debaters agree on several points: The feist is the little dog, under thirty pounds; and the cur is the big dog, over thirty but usually forty to one hundred for a big Catahoula leopard. The feist is better for small game, especially squirrels, but will work hogs and cattle, the usual domain of the cur, if asked to do so. It will also flush birds, hunt turkey, turtles, and bear. Similarly, the cur will tree squirrels and coons with fervor, but it delights in hogs, cattle, mountain lions and smaller cats, and bear. In the eighteenth and nineteenth centuries, colonists regularly ate black bear meat—fresh, smoked, salted—because the animals were plentiful and large enough to supply a family with meat for many months. A successful bear hunter could be a man of some stature on the frontier: Davy Crockett's fame, for example, arose from his storytelling and bear hunting. Like feists, curs have also been known to hunt quail and other game birds. I heard of one in Kissimmee, Florida, who pointed quail on the weekend and herded cows during the week.

Choosing one type of dog over the other is a matter of personal taste, although certainly the cur has greater range and strength while the feist is more agile and can get into tight spaces better. Hounds hunt with single-minded devotion; they do not herd. The best are fearless and intent on bringing their prey home, meaning they will go for the catch and kill, if needed. Feists and curs work close to their owner, checking in from time to time, unlike hounds who have been known to take to a trail and not be seen for several days. That habit makes the curs and feists ideally suited to hunting in areas where access to land is restricted and straying dogs considered open targets. Feists and curs make excellent pets and watchdogs. Old Yeller, the tragic canine hero of the book and movie, was a yellow blackmouth cur, or cur-dog, said as one word in the South. (It is, of course, grammatically redundant to say "cur-dog" and "feist-dog," since by definition curs and feists are dogs; but practically it is correct, since the cur and feist are types of dog that breed true rather than mismatched mutts.)

Although both will pursue and tree black bears, they do not all take to the task naturally. (The same is true of hounds.) A young dog that a black bear has slapped around may never want to engage one again. Even fewer dogs will voluntarily tangle with a grizzly, which is nearly twice the size of a black bear, faster, stronger, and less inclined to put up with dogs or people. A grizzly does not seek protection in a tree; it runs and then turns and fights. The significant point is that dogs must learn when to pursue certain game and that people will disagree on the best way to teach them. They recognize that it is easier for a dog to learn by running with trained dogs, but beyond that they cannot agree on whether to train them on many types of game or to force them to specialize. Even training a young dog with an older pack has its perils, for it might be slow in learning to think and tree for itself.

A number of houndsmen start their bear dogs on raccoons to get them used to running with other dogs and successfully treeing animals before they take on a black bear. That form of training recognizes that the hunting dog is at heart a generalist, like its wolfish forebear. Problems arise when a dog consistently strikes the trail of deer or some other unwanted "trash" game. A good trainer knows how to redirect that drive to the desired prey through encouragement and positive reinforcement. Sometimes the trainer will yoke the miscreant to a more devoted dog, so it cannot deviate. In recent years, trainers have adopted electric collars designed to deliver everything from a mild shock to a more serious jolt to straying or disobedient dogs. Promoted as humane and effective training tools, those devices remind me of flexible cattle prods. I have not met a man who would voluntarily put one around his own neck.

Curs and feists are not the only hunting dogs, and many people will give you what for if you claim they are the best—and with good reason. The country dogs are all-around animals, whereas some of the hounds are more specialized for particular kinds of scent work. The treeing Walkers, bluetick, redbone, and black-and-tan coonhounds, Plott hounds, and crosses between all have their advocates, especially for raccoons, cougars, bobcats, and bears. Masters of the hunt would not dream of running anything other than foxhounds after their quarry. A few hunters use Airedales and swear that they can track as well as any hound, as long as they are motivated. Some kennels are still breeding beagles to pursue rabbits and trail wounded deer. Hunting terriers are used to tree squirrels and go to den with bears and coyotes; a U.S. Department of Agriculture predator-control specialist used wirehaired fox terriers to tease coyotes from their dens, so he could shoot them. A few of his colleagues are now employing curs for that purpose.

Expounding on the differences between dogs, George Cauley expresses a view common to many feist and cur owners: "A hound hunts for himself; a feist hunts for his owner. A foxhound or coonhound will just run after that game, but a feist always wants to be close to humans. It hunts only for approval of its master, so if you sell a started dog it won't work until the new owner wins its confidence." He admires that loyalty, adding that he has a feist who will not even permit his brother to touch it.

While houndsmen might take exception to part of that statement, it is true that the best hounds follow their noses wherever they lead. They pursue game without looking or coming back. They quit when they lose the trail, play out, or tree or corner their prey. They take vast acres to run, which is why some cur breeders argue that their dog is the best hunter where there is not room to roam. It is biddable, meaning among other things that because it wants to please its owner, it can be taught to leave a track.

In an effort to perpetuate the traits they find most successful, many breeders inbreed—mate closely related dogs—for generations, believing that they can sort out problems through culling, the time-honored way of obliterating one's genetic mistakes. Those who are not too flawed to survive and work are declared super dogs, near clones of the great sire or dam. These breeders sometimes succeed because many desired traits are recessive, meaning that mating two closely related dogs will produce a high number of offspring with those characteristics. The puppies who most closely resemble their breeders' favorites are treated with certain expectations, which, being dogs, they eagerly try to meet. Random success being the greatest reinforcement there is, the excellent products of inbreeding are rewarded and celebrated, the culls forgotten.

Biological reality says that the results of inbreeding are as frequently disastrous as wondrous because the practice not only limits the genetic viability of the dogs but also fixes in the line a number of debilitating and fatal genetic defects, among them neurological disorders, blindness, deafness, and blood, skin, and kidney ailments. Like the desirable traits, those problems commonly are recessive.

That is why inbreeding is not the only culprit. The Catahoula leopard dog is renowned not only for its working ability but also for its distinctive spots and splotches often in a blue, gray, or red merle coat and its glass (pale blue to nearly white) eyes. Yet the dogs can also be brindled, patched, or solid black, red, chocolate, or yellow. In most litters the puppies will represent several of the possible types of coat and eye color. But as the Catahoula has become consolidated and popular, breeders have produced larger numbers of the prized glass-eyed, merle dogs by mating two animals with those recessive characteristics. Whether between related or unrelated dogs, the matings will produce a litter of puppies with the desired eyes and coats; unfortunately, a number of them will probably be deaf, blind, and epileptic. The blue irises are associated with changes in the "merling" gene, which, in turn, is related to various neural and anatomical conditions. Culling would merely destroy dogs with manifest problems while undesirable genes would continue to lurk, unexpressed, in the healthy dogs until they meet their match through a seemingly ideal mating.

This problem is easily solvable by not pairing two dogs with glass eyes and merle coats or even glass eyes alone. Mating a blue-eyed red merle to a brown-eyed blue or gray merle appears to present few difficulties, and usually three or four of the puppies will end up with glass eyes and leopard markings. Solid dogs bred to glass-eyed leopards will also produce a few of the desired dogs without the risk. Although most people familiar with the breed know of the problem, too many of them ignore it, and many hobbyists, attracted to the leopard dogs because of their unique look and reputation, have proceeded out of ignorance of the danger they run. The results, as a number of cowmen and hunters attest, are dogs with temperament and health problems.

Today, as owners of curs, feists, hounds, and even border collies are moving to consolidate their breeds, ostensibly to save them from extinction but also to cash in on the rising interest in basic dogs, sloppy breeding practices are becoming more problematic. In fact, while I was working on this book, the United Kennel Club, the second largest registry of purebred dogs in the United States, after the AKC, announced that it would register as separate breeds blackmouth curs, leopard curs, southern blackmouth curs, treeing curs, and treeing Tennessee brindles, along with treeing feists. Although that new policy will suit people wanting to compete with their dogs, by enforcing narrow divisions, it will prove detrimental to the animals.

Before the pressure to establish breed standards became so intense, curs and feists were largely bred in scattershot fashion. The families who kept their own lines might have engaged in inbreeding, but they always could cross out to other dogs with better abilities. Because they were yard dogs, they probably took care of most breeding matters without much human interference. People would then select the best of the accidental offspring based on their ability to perform, not to meet an idealized standard and prove blood purity.

After all, these dogs represent the finest in mongrelization, crosses between the dogs colonists brought to these shores in the seventeenth and eighteenth centuries and the dogs of the Native Americans. The Fredericksburg, Virginia, Dog Mart, now a country fair built around dog exhibitions, began in 1698 as an annual market where settlers and Indians traded their dogs, furs, whiskey, and other goods. Similar trade marts existed around the colonies, with many surviving in rural areas until the middle decades of this century. In fact, a number of historians of the feist believe that terriers hybridized with the Indian dogs, and one plausibly speculates that the terriers themselves carried bloodlines brought to Europe by Spanish conquistadors and early English explorers.

Feist Dogs

George Cauley—Mr. George, as the young hunters respectfully call him—is a squirrel hunter to the bone, a recognized authority on feists and their training. His brother, Wayne, uses the little dogs on hogs and cattle but not on squirrels and also sponsors hogdog contests in which curs and various mixed breeds are required to bay or catch a boar in a pen.

George and Wayne Cauley grew up hunting. As we pass his house in Soperton, George says, "My daddy fed eight kids by hunting and fishing. He used a single-shot 410-gauge shotgun on everything from squirrels to deer. He never had a regular job. He'd help neighbors round up their cattle or butcher hogs, but that was it." Although he did that in the first half of this century and many folks in Alaska still live that way, because of socioeconomic changes it has become difficult in the lower forty-eight states to follow a way of life similar to that led by the colonists who settled here 250 years ago with their dogs.

Mr. George does not live off hunting. He works for the state roads department and breeds, trains, and hunts his feists, although he says that he's getting out of the breeding business to concentrate on hunting and training dogs. "I sold a man a couple of pups once," he says, "and in a year he called me to say the dogs were no good. They wouldn't learn anything. He had kept them in a cage, feeding them all they wanted, occasionally letting them out but basically giving them no attention or training until they got to be around a year old. Then he decided it was time for them to become squirrel dogs, but they wouldn't respond.

"I took the dogs back, but I couldn't teach them anything either. They were hopeless. I'd show them something, and they'd forget it the next day. I couldn't figure it out, then a little while after I got those dogs back I was watching a program on television explaining how if a human baby was left in a crib, fed but given no affection, its brain would fail to develop. I thought to myself, it must be the same with those dogs.

"Feist pups should start going in the woods as soon as they are able, although you don't start them on squirrels until they're three or four months old. Around that time you might also test to see whether they're gun-shy, as they sometimes are."

Many people will start off with a small-caliber gun, say a .22, that makes relatively little noise. (Plume hunters in Florida at the turn of the century killed hundreds of birds at a time out of rookeries using .22's because their shots could not be heard above the normal sounds of thousands of nesting birds.) Some breeders put down metal garbage can lids that the pups clatter around on while playing, just to acclimate them to loud sounds. Gun-shy dogs will often develop phobias to fire-crackers, thunder, and any strange popping noise. Frightened, they can turn destructive. At many kennels, such dogs are culled in the belief that their fear is hereditary; indeed, some component of it may be. (A dog does not have to be a gun-shy hunting dog to develop those difficult-to-break phobias.)

Whatever you do, Cauley says, you should not abuse a dog you're trying to train. "If you go slamming and framming a dog, you'll ruin it, so it won't do anything for you. It won't hunt. It won't even come when called." "Slam" and "fram" are regional dialect for beating and abusing.

As often as not, when a person mutters, "That hound won't hunt," he's left out the final phrase, "for me." He also has failed to recognize—as he takes it out to shoot or lock in a pen until he finds someone to take it off his hands or beat or shock with more voltage—that nine times out of ten he is the reason the hound chases trash game or fails to follow a trail or tree.

Sagacious as he is when it comes to training, Cauley holds to particular, somewhat superstitious ideas about breeding, the one subject that many excellent dog people refuse to consider rationally. He breeds his females at first heat, usually when they are around six months old, an act that was once commonplace but is now considered improper. Such a young dog is not mature physically or mentally, but Cauley believes that early breeding settles the females down, makes them responsible. He also engages rather extensively in close line breeding, calling it tight breeding. Like most people who follow the practice, he figures the best way to produce the reliability and consistency he wants is to breed within the family. That way, he knows the sire, the dam, and the merit of both. It is possible, of course, to find excellent, unrelated dogs—that's what competition hunts and shows are about—but most breeders prefer to stay with what they think they know until it fails.

For now, Cauley has some nice little dogs that are as feisty as any. They are always eager to hunt and, like many of their kin, nearly wild in some of their habits. He tells the story of one female he had "who would go into the woods, eat all she could, and then come back and regurgitate it for the pups." His dogs are medium by feist standards, around twenty pounds, white and black, white and tan, black and tan. They have a distinctive habit of sticking the tip of their tongues through their slightly parted front teeth.

Cauley is master of the regional hunt of the American Treeing Feist Association, a nonprofit group formed in 1985 to turn into an official breed what it calls the distinctive little treeing dog of the American South. (Several other groups register the little dogs, but this association is the most responsible and the only nonprofit one.) While helping to preserve the feist, consolidation will force a degree of standardization that these dogs have escaped for centuries. The stud book or official registry was closed on July 1, 1994; however, the ATFA board reserved the right to approve registration of additional dogs in order to ensure that no feist goes unrecorded. Participants at a hunt can still enter unregistered dogs, providing an official finds them the proper size and able to tree squirrels.

The standard of the American Treeing Feist Association specifies that males stand ten to eighteen inches, females, ten to seventeen inches, with the maximum weight for both being thirty pounds. They may have stub tails—although most are full length and curve over the back or sideways—and either lop, prick, or (the most desired) semi-prick ears. They must feature long muzzles, powerful hindquarters and chests, thin waists, and short coats in black, white, tan, red, yellow to lemon, or any variation thereof. They are to be silent on track and then bark loudly and incessantly when they tree a raccoon or squirrel, not leaving until the prey is downed or they are called off. They will retrieve, killing wounded squirrels if necessary to bring them home. As the description and rules have stood, rat terriers qualify as feists, as does, more significantly, any small dog that will locate and drive game up a tree. But a feist is not a rat terrier or any old small dog; it is by definition a hunter dependent on its nose, eyes, and ears to locate its prey, its speed and agility to pursue it.

All that is needed to establish a breed of dog is a registry, called a stud book because to this day many people wrongly think, as did the ancient Greeks, that virtue in a dog comes from the sire; and a standard, a written description of the idealized form and function of the breed. As so often happens, however, there are competing groups with different standards for feists and curs. Among feist breeders are those who believe that there are red mountain feists, black-and-white feists, brindled feists, and a number of other regional varieties. If accepted, such distinctions would create even smaller, artificial breeding populations, as has too frequently been done by people interested in showing, as opposed to working, dogs. In 1964, for example, the Kennel Club of England recognized the Norwich terrier as distinct from the Norfolk terrier solely on the basis of its prick ears, and in 1979, the American Kennel Club followed suit. (The Norfolk terrier has semi-prick ears.) The ever popular golden retriever is a red version of the now black flat-coated retriever.

Driving to hunt squirrels, the dogs riding in the back of the pickup truck in their dog boxes, Cauley asks a companion what he thinks the difference is between his mountain feist and one of Cauley's black-and-white dogs. Stumped, the man stammers while looking for an answer, and Cauley laughs. "There is no difference," he says, "except the mountain feist is usually red. People make these things up so they can make money."

But the money a feist breeder might make does not begin to match what is paid for top show dogs or police/guard dogs or even herding dogs, trained hounds, and bird dogs—all of whom can bring $3,000 or more. Still, a proven feist occasionally commands $1,000, and Cauley talks of having sold his top dog to a man who paid "more than you can imagine." Puppies fetch $100 to $150, a fair amount for a small "mutt" with talent. Registered feists command higher prices because they can compete in sponsored hunts and become recognized champions.

While sharing the fear of many observers that consolidation of the feist into a breed will open it to commercial exploitation and the diminution of talent associated with show dogs, I recognize that the little dogs have benefited from the renewed attention. As recently as a decade ago, they were threatened because of socioeconomic changes in the South that caused a decline in rural populations and squirrel hunting, especially with feists and curs, and because of biases in favor of pedigreed hunting dogs. But publicity surrounding the feist, which coincided with a growing interest in animals unspoiled by over-breeding for the show ring, a scarcity in land available for running hounds, and increasing squirrel populations have produced a remark-able resurgence of interest. The American Treeing Feist Association closed its registry with 800 dogs, and other groups have additional animals. That is not a lot compared with the 126,393 Labrador retrievers registered by the American Kennel Club in 1994 and representing no more than half of those born that year, but it will likely be enough to keep these historic animals from meeting the fate of the Tahltan bear dog.

Approximately one hundred people show up at the East Dublin community center the night before the competition for a dinner featuring squirrel soup and Wayne Cauley's barbecue. It is an affair for husbands and wives, a smattering of children, blessed by a local Baptist preacher. There are a few speeches about the American Treeing Feist Association and the upcoming hunt, but most of the conversation is about dogs, competitions, and controversies past. The men are proud of their dogs and curious about those of their fellow competitors.

The next morning twenty-two of the diners turn out at 6:30 for the cast. By lot, two hunters and their dogs—one for each man, there being no women who take to the field—are assigned a guide, who also serves as judge and scorekeeper, and hunting ground. They hunt for two hours, then return to headquarters where the women tally their scores. In a competition hunt, the dog who trees first receives 125 points, providing the squirrel is seen by the judge; the second dog receives 50 points for joining the tree within two minutes. No squirrels are shot, a rule that Cauley says is hard on a well-trained dog because it has nothing to retrieve. The first time out after a competition, the traditional feist man carries his gun so that the dog can retrieve freshly killed squirrels.

A night of rain makes the morning cast a dicey affair; most dogs have difficulty working scent under those conditions, and the squirrels stay in their nests until determining which way the wind blows. As host of this event, Cauley is sensitive to any suggestion of home-field advantage, so he has chosen to take his two men to an area well outside of town where he has hunted squirrels on only a few occasions. Too often, he explains, guides make a beeline for fields they know have been baited or are flush with prey.

Indeed, the winner, Spuds MacKenzie, has the good fortune to hunt a field where hogs and cattle are regularly fed. Despite the dampness that kept them in their nests in more wooded areas, the squirrels had come down to feed and so Spuds was once able to tree two simultaneously. The dogs with Cauley—Poncho, a two-year-old red mountain cur belonging to Ellis Nichols, and Stallion, a four-year-old rat terrier, owned by Dennis Eiland—are stymied. Stallion leaps from the truck onto an opossum as big as he is and begins to "worry" it—rip at its coat—before Eiland can call him off and hang it in the crotch of an oak tree. Some people hunt 'possum, but many others consider them trash game. Most dogs just like to jump them.

Within five minutes, Stallion trees the first squirrel of the day. Poncho refuses to join him, so the score is 125–0. But Stallion, whom, the evening before, Eiland had declared a treeing dog of extreme tenacity and brilliance, finds no other game and after ninety minutes quits hunting. He limps along at Eiland's knee, favoring first his right forefoot, then his left. Meanwhile, bounding over downed wood and crossing streams, Poncho trees two squirrels, but despite several tentative stands, he finds no more.

By the end of the two hours, Eiland, a thin, soft-spoken man, is frustrated, wondering whether the observers present are distracting his Stallion—the observers being two men who recently purchased a feist puppy from Cauley and have come to learn about squirrel hunting, and me—or whether he is simply not suited for competition hunting. Noticing that Stallion cannot decide which foot hurts, Cauley observes that rat terriers have a habit of feigning injury if things do not go their way on a hunt. He also tells me that Poncho could have had three more squirrels to his credit, for a respectable score of 625, had his owner not been shy about calling a "tree." In the hunt, it is up to the owner to tell the judge and other hunter when his dog has treed. From that time, he has two minutes to wait for the other dog to join his. Then he ties his dog and has two minutes, with the help of everyone else around, to locate the squirrel and show it to the judge. So well do squirrels blend into the bark and foliage of a tree that unless they move, an observer often will not see them, no matter how hard he or she looks. On a hunt where every point counts, people will circle the tree, shake vines, even climb partway up to find the game.

That Poncho, for all his good intentions and energy, was thwarted by a reticent owner is not surprising, but it is also not good. False trees are embarrassing and time-consuming for the hunters, which is why many novices, like Poncho's owner, are reluctant to claim that their dog has found a squirrel. But calling a false tree might also encourage the dog to believe that all he has to do to succeed is literally "bark up the wrong tree." That is a bad habit that's hard to break. But calling a dog off a tree when it has located a squirrel can undo years of training and ruin a good dog. In other words, the key to success is to learn when to trust your dog, and only experience can teach that.

Ellis Nichols and Poncho learned their lessons well and began to excel in competitions. Poncho became such an outstanding hunter that he earned the title ATFA Squirrel Dog Champion and the right to compete for the coveted Grand Champion in 1996. In little more than a year, the little red dog became a legend.

Big Dogs

Perhaps the most famous of the cur breeds is the leopard dog, established as the state dog of Louisiana in 1979 and called the Catahoula leopard dog. The designation was based on the claim that the spotted-up cur was indigenous to Catahoula Parrish, named for the savage Indians of that lake country. It makes a good story, but it is, shall we say, exaggerated in the name of Louisiana chauvinism. Leopard curs have long been found throughout the coastal region of the Gulf of Mexico, along the Red River, and into Mexico. They are a common type, reportedly a mix of colonists' curs, the Indians' piebald dogs who by then might have incorporated bits of the remnant Spanish war dogs whom Hernando de Soto had jettisoned on his mad meander to death on the Mississippi, and the red wolf, but their origin is no more certainly in Louisiana than in Florida, Alabama, or Texas. The folks in Louisiana simply decided to make their local curs a breed. You can still find leopard curs working elsewhere and not necessarily registered with the National Association of Louisiana Catahoulas.

In all likelihood the leopard dog is the spotted, sometimes solid, patched, and brindled version of the generic large dog, the cur, whose history and lineage it shares. The red wolf, like the Spanish war dogs, figures minimally, if at all, while there doubtless was mixing with indigenous dogs, just as colonists mixed with the Indians, when not fighting them. Some of these curs, crossed with bloodhounds, foxhounds, and French hounds, figure in the formation of the coonhounds and other treeing hounds found in the rural South.

We have two leopard dogs: Marlow, a Louisiana Catahoula; and Clio, a Florida cur, registered as a Catahoula with a group in Texas called the Animal Research Foundation. We call Clio a cracker dog. Marlow and Clio are different "breeds" only because of human intervention. They behave similarly in their desire to keep things in order and pursue what they consider game. Both love to eat mangoes, oranges, and grapefruit. Both are tenacious, although Clio is sweeter and less leggy. As with all dogs, their differences are greater than their similarities.

So dysplastic that at six months she had no ball-and-socket formation in her hips—well-developed muscles have compensated, and she has been pain free for ten years—Clio accelerates faster but does not have the top-end speed of Marlow (named for Joseph Conrad's narrator in *Lord Jim* and *Heart of Darkness*). He lacks her turning ability and her total disregard for her physical well-being when charging through scrub. The habit once left her hanging from a rock by her forepaws in an abandoned Vermont marble quarry, with nothing between her and the water one hundred feet below; I climbed down and pulled her up by the scruff of her neck.

An active watchdog, who barks vigorously at strangers, Marlow is more fearless and more aggressive in taking what he wants. Although that is commonly considered one of the significant differences between male and female dogs, Marlow's daughter exhibited much the same mentality at seven weeks of age, whereas her brother, who by four months of age already outweighed his sire, is sweet tempered and nonaggressive. Marlow is also more inclined to be a catch dog, using his considerable speed to race ahead of a moving person or animal, spin around, and grab it. (He will desist only when told to run along, and then he becomes bored.) Clio prefers to flush, drive, and bunch.

Marlow craves attention and is quite content to curl up in my lap or that of my nephew or niece, although less so with my wife, Gina; the habit dates to his two-week bout with parvovirus—often fatal to puppies and older dogs—when he was eight weeks old. The veterinarian who saved his life correctly predicted that he would always be an "attention freak," as are many dogs who suffer early trauma. He is friendly toward those he knows, aloof around strangers. On the other hand, Clio is a licker who loves having her belly rubbed but hates lying in anyone's lap, perhaps because she considers that Marlow's right. She also despises the "down" command, proving that her submissiveness has its limits. Friendly toward strangers, she often greets those she knows with a tennis ball, inviting them to play catch with her. They toss the ball in the air; she catches it and tosses it back with a flip of her head. She loves small children but is not fond of puppies or kittens.

Although Marlow barks more frequently, Clio is an alert guardian as well, barking or baying at threats. He is silent in pursuit of game; she sounds off as soon as she picks up a scent. Both have an astounding array of vocalizations, ranging from yaps to gurgles, belly-heaving chirps, bays, and howls, with Clio taking the high notes and Marlow the low. On the whole, he is far more of a "talker" than she.

Both Marlow and Clio are typically shorthaired, his being a little coarser, with large patches of three shades of brown and touches of red over white. She has a white blaze but is predominately black and gray, with rust on her feet—what is called blue merle. He has double glass— nearly translucent pale blue—eyes; she has one brown and one blue with a slice of brown. She has pendant ears; his are "rose," meaning that while they usually hang down and a little away from the head, they frequently fold back, like a greyhound's.

Whatever their origin or registry, curs are tough. A rancher in Utah, John Child, told me about a friend of his who had bought a ranch along the Arizona–New Mexico border with a permit to run 450 head of cattle on U.S. Forest Service land. The new owner wanted to see how many cattle he actually had, so he bought some leopard dogs and over the next few years took 800 head of feral animals from that land. Disregarding what that says about nonmanagement of federal lands, it shows the value of dogs. The man could not have found and rounded up those cattle without dogs who were fierce and half-wild themselves. Child, who had a pack of distinguished bear hounds, one of whom worked with Hal Black from Brigham Young University on his study of black bears, was impressed not only that the dogs hunted cattle but also that they had treed five bears on their own initiative.

Like many of his fellow ranchers, Child had struggled to find a tough cowdog, having rejected border collies as too soft and heelers as incapable. All the heelers wanted to do was bother the horses, he said. So working with what was available, Child finally crossed a border collie and Airedale and found the offspring to be such good catch dogs that he violated his own rule against inbreeding and mated brother and sister. But his crosses were getting old, and in the long run, I could tell, he had his eye on the leopard cur, who would take on and stop a bull or steer weighing twenty times as much and then tree a bear for pleasure. That, to his way of thinking, is a dog.

Florida Curs

Jeff McDaniel, a rancher in Hendry County, Florida, flush in the Big Cypress Swamp, recalls that a man who wanted to hire on to hunt cows sent a videotape of himself working his dogs. "The tape was something," McDaniel says while driving across the graded shell roads of his ranch, his own dogs in a horse trailer behind his truck. "Those dogs would tear at the cows, then he'd take them and throw them over the gooseneck of the trailer. He'd grab a dog by its rear legs and bang its head against the trailer once or twice, bang it again, then look right at the camera and say, 'I guess it needed that.' I wouldn't have a man like that on the ranch."

Freelance Florida cow hunters have been known since the nineteenth century as crackers—a derogatory term that originally referred to people so poor all they could afford to eat was cracked corn (grits) and salt pork. (In some accounts, the name cracker is derived from the cracking sound of the long whips cowmen used.) They were deemed dirty, shiftless, uncouth white trash. Today, they can be "roady," a rough, low-class lot living on amphetamines snorted in the form of "rocket fuel," marijuana, and alcohol. Even by those standards, the cow hunter who sent the video was "trashy."

Yet, as with dogs, generalizations about people are always hazardous. Cowmen can as easily be hardworking, serious, if relatively poor, as roady. Jabbo Smith, a cowman who works blackmouth curs, as well as crosses between blackmouth and leopard curs, takes as much pride in breeding and training as in working his dogs. He also has a passion for horses that is shared by many of the men who make their living on the Florida range. He takes pride in his outfit, while admitting that, on the whole, Florida cowboys do not approach their western counterparts in sartorial splendor. Of course, in the heat and humidity of this country, it is hard to maintain a starched look or keep mildew off leather.

The 23,000-acre McDaniel Ranch starts above the Big Cypress Seminole Indian Reservation, itself nestled above the Miccosukee Indian Reservation, lands set aside after the tribes fled into what was considered the impenetrable vastness of the Everglades to avoid persecuting federal troops and state militia in the interminable Seminole Wars of the first half of the nineteenth century. Those tribes were primarily composed of Creek immigrants from Georgia and Alabama, with a few runaway slaves, who had migrated into Florida after the indigenous peoples finally succumbed in the eighteenth century to 200 years of Spanish and English disease, enslavement, and murder.

A century of drainage, which has created in excess of 1,000 miles of canals and spillways and altered the hydrology of all of South Florida, has opened hundreds of thousands of acres, formerly inundated for much of the year, to agriculture: sugarcane, vegetables, and citrus. But even without that drained land, the region, which includes the Kissimmee River, the Everglades, and Big Cypress Swamp, was always a mosaic of plant communities, from saw grass sloughs, which hold water throughout the year, to marl prairies flooded in the rainy season (May through November) then subjected to drying out in the winter; hardwood hammocks of towering palms, great spreading live oak, and, farther south, mahogany and gumbo-limbo; cypress strands and domes where trees festooned with bromeliads and orchids line deep water (most of the venerable old-growth trees were logged out in the middle years of this century); dry pinelands and palmetto that together form the palmetto prairie. There are alligators, panthers, wood storks, egrets, various herons and other wading birds, otters, raptors, deer, black bear, maybe a jaguarundi or two (the elusive black cats of Florida), turkeys, hogs, cows, caracara, vultures, and snakes. The McDaniel Ranch has them all.

The terrain follows an inverse topography, with areas of standing water in the dry season marking the deepest depressions in the limestone that lies, sometimes barely, beneath the soil. Stretched out under an open sky, the rest is flatter than the Great Plains. At best the temperature is mild; at the height of the rainy season it holds in the double nineties—ninety degrees and rising; 90 percent humidity to rain. The cattle that roamed this scrub in the nineteenth century were scrawny, 500- to 600-pound feral creatures as tough as any wild animal and kept small not by domestication but by the heat; the insects, especially mosquitoes so thick they could suffocate an animal or make a man faint from loss of blood, ticks, and horned flies, called sharpshooters, with a bite so annoying they drive the cows from cover when they hatch in May (call them "herding" flies); parasites; infection; and, for all the lushness, poor fodder. But there was a huge demand for Florida beef in Cuba, and so the ranchers would hire the cracker cowboys, each with a horse, whip, gun, and cur-dog, to hunt those cows out of the palmetto and cypress and drive them to Punta Rassa or Tampa on the Gulf of Mexico, where they were shoved onto boats, breaking legs and necks in the process. The scrawny cowmen were paid in gold doubloons, which became the currency of exchange on the palmetto prairie.

From those days, the spring work—just after the winter dry season—has been called a hunt rather than a roundup, and, indeed, finding cows in that dense vegetation more nearly approximates hunting than herding. But now the animals weigh 1,000 pounds and up, and they go by truck to slaughterhouses in the United States rather than by boat to Cuba.

Frederic Remington visited the palmetto prairie along the Kissimmee River, north of Lake Okeechobee, and filed a less than flattering report and sketches for *Harper's New Monthly Magazine* in June 1895. The cattle were "scrawny creatures not fit for a pointer-dog to mess on." The men were not worthy of being called cowboys, like Remington's beloved western *vaqueros*. "A strange effect is added," he reported, "by their use of large, fierce cur-dogs, one of which accompanies each cattle-hunter, and is taught to pursue cattle, and to even take them by the nose, which is another instance of their brutality."

Those leopard cur-dogs were used until the 1930s, when a screw worm epidemic caused many of them to be phased out. The worms arrived with Herefords brought in from Texas to improve the native stock and laid eggs in lesions caused by catch dogs and the hard life in the scrub. Once hatched, the larvae ate through a calf in twenty-four hours, larger game in a bit longer. Although the dogs were blamed and run from many pastures, folk continued to raise them for hunting hogs and their own cows, after the infestation cleared.

Jeff McDaniel's grandfather bought the ranch in 1936. His father switched from horses to trucks for cattle herding in the late 1960s, but in 1987, Jeff, the youngest of four sons, returned to the old way of working. His three older brothers supervise citrus and sugarcane production, which along with land rented to vegetable farmers, join cattle to make the four musketeers of the Big Cypress ranch—and, by extension, South Florida agriculture.

McDaniel, a solidly built man around six feet tall with a straight-ahead look, even through the sunglasses that are ubiquitous in this country on bright days, talks in a rapid-fire way that would lead a stranger to think he was from the North were it not for his accent, colloquialisms, and narrative skill that set him squarely in a long southern tradition. He says he returned to dogs and horses for hunting cows because trucks, which the rough rangeland tore up, did not provide proper "management," a favorite word that means all aspects of animal husbandry. Most of the cattle raced in front of the onrushing, bouncing, fume-belching trucks, their drivers honking the horns, banging the metal roof of the cabs, bumping laggards. The wilder cows ducked into cypress heads, where they hid until the roundup was over. All were stressed.

"That was cruelty to animals," McDaniel says. So having taken over the cows, because "I always liked a cow" and everyone else in the family considered them more trouble than plants, he told his father he was going to the dogs.

His father and brothers thought he was, well, bull-moose loony.

But he says, "Crazy as it sounds, the idea just lit me up. I'm a Christian, I've got my faith, and I'd say, 'Lord, please tell me if I'm wrong.' But he didn't. And so I sold an old swamp buggy for $4,500 and bought eleven dogs. Then people really thought I was crazy. My dad said I couldn't do it."

At the time there were 3,200 head of crossbred Brahmas to withstand the climate and insects on the ranch, and none of them had seen a dog. All they knew to do was scatter when trucks entered their range. "The first two years, I had some real rank, raily dogs," he says. "It was ugly, I'll tell you."

"Rank" in this country means "tough to the point of viciousness; willing to pursue, catch, and hold anything no matter how big; barely fit company for man or beast." "Raily" means fast and rangy, with not an ounce of fat. Weighing forty to seventy-five pounds, they were Florida curs, shorthaired, a mix of assorted southern curs, especially the yellow blackmouth and Texas and Louisiana leopard curs, as well as whatever else came along that looked good and worked better.

Those rank, raily dogs will take on a 1,000-pound cow or a 1,500-pound bull, following it into a cypress head or standing water and teasing it out or taking it by the ears or nose and bringing it to ground or to heel. They will agitate a cow—or hog—so much that in rage and frustration it chases them; thus, they actually herd from the front. They also will bunch or "wad up" the cows and continue "windmilling" around them, dodging horns, and nipping at their faces, ears, and shoulders, until they tire of fighting. "Those cows are ready to go when they turn their heads into the group and point their tails out," McDaniel says.

But the rank dogs had all they could handle and more than McDaniel sometimes thought he could. "It was a lot of Rolaids days, I'll tell you that. You'd start out and bunch those cows, and then one would take off and the dogs would get on her. While they were doing that, another'd run for the cypress. Pretty soon the other cows would learn to follow, and they'd be scattered. If you start off that way, you're better off going home because you'll never get those cows together till they calm down."

McDaniel, who likes to talk in football analogies, knew it was

fourth and one with the game on the line. Those wild and unmanage-
able cows had to be "broke" to dogs and horses. To do that, he had to
weed out the cows that learned to duck for cover, leading others along.
"You've got to get the troublemaker off the ranch," he says, "send her
to market and make hamburger out of her."

After two years, he had proven the skeptics wrong and successfully
taken the ranch back to a more suitable and humane way of managing
the cows. Even the family had to agree. "I don't care how good a
cowman you are, if you can't work dogs, you can't get it done," he
says. "Working cows without dogs is like stirring up a bucket of
roaches. But you've got to break the cows first. Some of these dogs
aren't worth a flip with cows that aren't broke. They'll scatter, and I've
seen dogs ruined because of that." The failure to hold the cattle
bunched undermines their self-esteem.

"Those first dogs were real gritty," McDaniel says. "They were
mentally different. They were biters, and now I needed to take some of
the bite out of them. After you've got the cows broke, you don't need
so many real tough dogs, just one or two for the hardheads and bulls.
So you go for slightly less fierce cur-dogs because they're the only ones
that will do for hunting cows. Those border collies and heelers won't
do. The border collie's eager enough, but it can't take the heat or the
cockleburs that it picks up in the cypress. And they can't handle these
cows. The first one I saw out here, a cow hooked and broke its back."

Border collie fans, who as a group consider the dog the smartest,
most versatile creature in dogdom, doubtless will take exception, as
will those of the other herding breeds, but many cattlemen make the
same point. The dogs do not work well on open ranges with large, feral
animals. Gina and I once watched three border collies drive a dozen
cows from one pasture to another in England's Lake District. It was a
bucolic scene worthy of John Constable's brush, but the distance was
short, the cows cooperative, and the farmer working in their midst.
Curs, on the other hand, go out and hunt any tough, independent
cow. (Some cow hunters use Australian kelpies in Texas and other
western states, as do a number of ranchers with more settled herds.)

When I met him late in 1995, McDaniel had just lost his top dog,
Willie, a more or less full-blooded leopard dog from Texas lines, to a

heart attack, at age five. "I'll tell you, dogs like Willie and Cowgirl [still living but spayed and slower] will take on anything. They're as rank as they come, and you need a couple of dogs like that. But Willie also knew just what to do, how rough to get, and he kept windmilling the whole time. He'd get the other dogs to do it."

The current cur-dogs were young or just not as rank. Red Prissy, a pet, is friendly in a lupine way: she stands on her hind feet and delicately touches people and animals with her paws, as if feeling them. But she works with single-minded intensity and is a McDaniel favorite because of her ability to follow hand signals to bring in cattle that break from the group in a dash for freedom. She also keeps track of the cowmen following the herd, but she does not like to work alone. Rowdy, a raily black, white, and tan eight-month-old, is keen but a baby; Tough, a beautifully muscled black-and-brown brindle, has, at fifteen months, reached neither his full physical nor his full mental maturity, although because he is Willie's son, McDaniel has high expectations. Cowgirl sets an example, teaching the others how to be cowdogs. Several of the dogs bear the unmistakable markings— abstract patches and splotches—of Catahoula leopard dogs.

In the wings is CH, a three-month-old red-and-white with a bobtail—the tails are docked by some breeders—who might not even windmill his first cows for another half year. Even at six months, young dogs can be too uncoordinated to work without accident. Once injured, a young dog, not surprisingly, often becomes hesitant, a trait that can be fatal, so a smart person does not ask a pup to tangle with a cow, no matter how dog-broke she seems. Told he cannot get in the trailer to go with the other dogs, CH lies in the sand, depressed. When the dogs are loose with him in the yard, he likes to grab their ears or necks, like a good catch dog. They tolerate him without complaint. When he does begin to go, he will learn from the more experienced dogs and McDaniel how to follow and control his instinct. His attitude, drive, and breeding suggest that he could be one of those rare, great dogs, like the departed Willie.

Tough, Rowdy, Cowgirl, and Prissy leap into the trailer with the horse, and we set off for a pasture where McDaniel has to move thirty head, with calves, about a half mile out of a field scheduled for plowing. Cows with calves can get testy, he says, and he usually has an extra man. But the cows start bunching as soon as they see the truck and trailer, and by the time McDaniel sends the dogs forward with a barely audible command, "shoook," they are ready to wad up. They are also intent on protecting their calves, which have moved to the center of the circle.

The dogs race across the prairie and immediately start circling or windmilling around the cows. Occasionally, one lowers her head and charges, trying to hook a dog with her horns, but the dog dodges away, twisting, and then drives her back, snapping and barking the whole time. The dogs are fast and agile. They work without hesitation. It is a beautiful, clear day in the upper seventies, but the sun is intense and they are soon panting.

Seeing that the cows are all facing the center of their bunch, McDaniel calls off the dogs and sits talking while they cool down. Soon he moves off, Rowdy and Cowgirl following his horse, Tough and Prissy acting as outriders for the cows as they trot through a pair of gates toward a cypress dome.

The entire effort takes twenty minutes. After he has closed the gates, McDaniel releases the dogs, who plunge into a canal. "These dogs don't have any quit in them. They only need that 'gator-ade,'" McDaniel says, motioning toward the water. "A dog'll get 'thumped' in the heat if they don't get water. It can ruin a dog if it gets too hot. I don't know what it is, but I call it breaking an animal's wind. If they survive, they just can't take the heat anymore. But gators love to eat dogs, so you got to watch out." Fortunately, the McDaniel Ranch has abundant water, and the full hunts occur in May, the beginning of the rainy season. (Hyperthermia, or heatstroke, can damage internal organs and cause death.)

McDaniel's concern for his dogs is everywhere apparent. Their kennels are clean, although they are often allowed to roam the grounds, along with the pet potbellied pig. His daughters play with them. "I know some cowmen would never put up with this," he says, as Prissy stands to touch me for the sixth or seventh time, then turns to my wife, then the horse, lightly placing her paws against its flank. (She does it with cows, too.) "They'll kick the dog or just ignore it, and if you ask why, they'll say, 'A dog's just a tool.' I don't want them to be pets, but I have to say it's nice coming out in the morning with coffee and tending to the dogs. It's nice and peaceful."

Fearless as they are with cattle, around us the dogs are calm and well mannered. Tough and Rowdy nose a greeting, then proceed with their day. Cowgirl hangs close without soliciting or responding to attention. Like the puppy he is, CH is into everyone's business.

McDaniel's dogs reflect his outgoing personality, his drive and enthusiasm, his belief that if you treat a person or animal well, he or she will respond. Although not obedience trained, they trot around with their tails up and go to work with vigor, attentive to the slightest command, especially any hint that he is loading the gooseneck trailer. They work not out of fear or because he intimidates them but because they want to hunt cows.

"You've got to be patient in this business," McDaniel says. "You don't want to go at it like you're killing a snake. The main thing I'm learning now is the breeding part. I haven't got that figured out yet. You can't just take a good stud and good gyp [bitch] and say if I put them together I'm going to get good dogs. It's not that easy, but I'll tell you, if you find a combination that works, you better keep at it. I didn't breed my Willie enough." For now, he tries to match unrelated dogs of good character and talent, trading breedings and pups with other cowdog men.

"I know the best dogs are the ones you raise yourself. They understand your moods and how you talk. And the merle Catahoulas are not so good. You want a little of the leopard, but if you get too much the dogs are timid. I don't know why it is." It is clear that McDaniel wants dogs of a certain look and attitude, a style, and the merles do not fit it. Beyond that, my guess is he's seen too many dogs from lines where the dams are fearful and the dogs are mated purely for their blue or red leopard spotting and their glass eyes, but short of seeing bloodlines, there is no way to tell.

Observations like McDaniel's, which are common among dog people, put in perspective the claim made by many historians of breeds

that their particular favorite was formed through the principle of survival of the fittest, the constant breeding of "best to best." The argument shows a profound misunderstanding of Darwin's theory of
evolution, which basically holds that those animals that survive are by
definition the fittest. In fact, because they are always the first to get on
the cows or track a recalcitrant bull into thick scrub, the best working
dogs, like Willie, often end up dead from an accident before they can
breed extensively. Even if they do breed, their offspring will not necessarily be their equal in talent and accomplishment, which in dogs, as in
people, is a matter of temperament and will, neither of which is auto-
matically inheritable, and of training, which has nothing to do with
genetics. Frequently, survivors are the more cautious dogs, and the best
sires and dams—in all species—are not the top performers who put
their energy into their work and exceed their natural talents.

Although some of his colleagues will kill dogs who don't take to
cows, McDaniel gives them away to friends, primarily to one hog
hunter who finds them just fine for trailing game. McDaniel himself
says that his leopard cur Jill, now pregnant, came to him when she was
a year old because the man who owned her was going to shoot her. "I
saw something I liked, so I said, 'Let me take her,' " McDaniel relates.
"For a long time she wouldn't do nothing. She'd just lie in the field
and watch the other dogs work, and I'd look over there and wave and
say, 'Hi, Jill, how you doing?' Then one day she just joined in and
started windmilling with the other dogs, and she's been great. The guy
who wanted to shoot her told me, 'If I could have all my mistakes
back, I'd have great dogs.' "

I visit the McDaniel Ranch again in May 1996 for a real cow hunt.
After a cold winter that had taken its toll on the vegetation and cows—
we find two dead and leave them on the isolated pastures for vultures
and other scavengers—the summer rains have finally started, dropping
two inches the night before and threatening more that day. Sculpted
cumulonimbus clouds overlap each other in the sky. All the cowmen
but Jabbo Smith have come with their slickers tied behind their
saddles; he joins this city dweller in chancing a soaking. We win; by
midmorning, the clouds are thin enough to let the sun shine through,

not actually a welcome event when cow hunting, as the temperature and humidity rise with its unveiling.

Rowdy, who liked to run deer as well as cows, has gone to a man in more settled country with less wildlife and been replaced by Becky, a raily yellow blackmouth cur from Kissimmee, barely a year old but already working on her fourth owner because of a habit of singling out one cow for her undivided attention. Still, she loves to hunt cows, and having learned that horses always go with cowmen, she spends her off-hours in the horse stalls, waiting. A seven-week-old blackmouth cur, as popular a cowdog as the leopard cur and gaining more adherents because of a sense that it has not been bred exclusively for eye color and coat markings, waits in the kennels, along with one of Jill's puppies from the winter, a nice little leopard. Although going with us, CH is on probation, with McDaniel thinking he has no interest in cows, and his breeder, Smith, saying that at nine months, he is still young. Indeed, whatever his reason, cows are not yet on his mind; he just runs with the other dogs.

Smith has brought eight dogs—blackmouth curs or crosses with leopard dogs averaging around forty pounds—and one of the other cowmen has a cur, so that together we are nine men and thirteen dogs. Actually there are seven cowmen and two guests—a friend of Smith, who ends up taking the indomitable CH home as a pet, and I are along for the ride. McDaniel puts me on Smut, a slow-moving gray horse who hangs his tongue out of his mouth; he is a fine choice for someone who has not been on a horse in thirty years.

McDaniel and I ride through cypress heads, where we occasionally have to dismount and walk the horses, so impenetrable are the vines and interlocking branches, the thickets of Brazilian pepper, one of the exotic plants that has invaded South Florida over the past century. "You can tell people you hunted cows through some of the roughest country there is," he says, laughing seriously. I realize why once a trail is started, animals and people stick to it; no matter how twisting its course, it is easier to follow the trail than break a new route.

We encounter one group of about ten cows and calves on the wrong side of a fence. Faced with dogs and men on horses, they decide to go through the barbed wire rather than follow it to a gate and literally tear through, snapping the fence posts and leaving us to lead our horses across the tangle to prevent injury. That the cows came through unscathed I take as testimony to their toughness.

When sent to bunch cows, the dogs take off at a dead run and immediately begin churning around them—often in opposite directions—in a tightening circle. Cows that break for cover are quickly cut off by two or three dogs who spin around them, until they return to the herd. Becky, who weighs forty pounds when fully fed and wet, takes on solo escapees herself, herding them as if she were a kelpie or border collie, while, freelancing, Tough charges into any group he can find, apparently for the joy of turning cows. Dogs like Becky and Tough put the lie to frequent reports that curs herd only in groups. Some, like Prissy, are that way, but these two are so intense they could care less whether another dog follows them.

Once the cows are bunched, Smith or McDaniel—depending on whose pack has worked—calls off the dogs, and we wait until they are settled before walking them toward the cowpen, where the next day they will be counted, bled, and sorted for sale. Running cattle in this heat would be disastrous; in fact, the dogs are regularly led away from the herd toward the nearest canal or pond, where they swim and drink. As we walk along, a swallow-tailed kite wheels in the distance; turkey trot along a canal bank. Although alert like the men, the dogs show no interest in the proceedings unless one or more cows try to break away or the men send them out. With 130 cows, including bulls, collected from distant pastures and dense cypress domes, we move at a pace, I think, that is proper for the place, more suited to the flow of animal blood than the high speed of the car that brought me here or the jet that crashed not two weeks earlier in the Everglades, taking 110 people with it.

Hunting

I could dodge this issue by saying that treeing squirrels for points and baying up cows are not, strictly speaking, hunting. Or I could state that to hunt simply means to detect, approach, bring to a stop, kill (or

let someone else do it), and eat, sometimes after retrieving, and therefore a truffle dog is as much a hunter as a wolf or hound. Carrying that
argument a step farther, I could observe that hunting is an innate dog
talent that humans have always valued. But the fact is that hunting is
one of those "hot button" issues that rouses passions on both sides, as
if there were only two.

Even the competitions are not without controversy. Just before
leaving Miami Beach to visit the no-kill squirrel hunt in East Dublin,
Georgia, I read an exposé of hogdog trials, in the Humane Society of
the United States magazine, claiming that often the boar's tusks are
snapped off by the human sponsor before it is released into a pen
where dogs bay and hold it. According to this report, the curs tear at
the cornered, exhausted, and defenseless hog.

Although a number of their sponsors deny ever detusking hogs,
enough of them do that the events have been banned in Florida and
several other states as inhumane. But whether they are inherently evil
or cruel because the dogs and hogs occasionally draw blood strikes me
as problematic. The trials themselves have their roots in bull and bear
baiting, outlawed in the seventeenth century in England as noisy,
bloody entertainments that not coincidentally attracted crowds of
potentially riotous poor people. Of course, there the dog was bad-
gering and harassing the bull or bear, riling it, prior to its slaughter.

It is hard to see how anyone could object to a no-kill hunt, but
there surely are those who do, complaining about noise, the fact that
the hounds travel in boxes in pickup trucks, and the stress that pursuit
by dogs causes the animals. A number of old-time hunters grouse that
the competitions have begun to change the type of hound being bred;
participants in coon hunts, for example, look for fast dogs who work
close to their handler and quickly strike a trail, rather than rangy
hounds. The dogs compete in a brace of two or three hunters but must
work alone rather than in a pack. Because the hunts are held at night,
their handlers often track them with electronic collars, so they can be
reached easily to locate and score the tree. On the other side are many
people who simply find the notion of hunting with dogs offensive.

Through public referendums, voters in Colorado, Massachusetts,
Oregon, and Washington have imposed bans on hunting black bears

using bait and hounds, and opponents to those and other hunting practices regularly launch ballot initiatives in other states. Houndsmen throughout the United States and Canada are appalled. They want to blame animal-rights activists—"anti's" is the polite name they use— rather than recognize that their wide-open spaces are being hemmed in by housing developments. Not always without cause, these newcomers are afraid that hunters and their hounds will injure them and decimate the wildlife, including cougars and bears they both admire and fear.

The irresponsible methods of hunting employed by many houndsmen often contribute to their public image as lower-class louts who tear after their dogs in pickup trucks and jeeps—sometimes running over them in the process—then blast away at some poor animal without killing it. I remember seeing one videotape of a cougar hunt in Idaho, in which the guide drove the hunter to within one-hundred feet of where the hounds had treed a big cat. The hunter, his belly hanging over his pants, climbed from the Jeep, crossed a U.S. Forest Service road, and emptied a .357 magnum revolver—six bullets—into the animal. It fell to the ground and began fighting with the hounds, who tried to tear it apart even while it attempted to kill them. The hunter reloaded and finally killed the big cat. The dogs hunted; the human engaged in brutality. In some parts of the country, houndsmen regularly blockade forest-service and sometimes residential roads so their hounds can pursue deer or bears. It might be safe for the dogs, but it is bad citizenship.

Where it is not prohibited, hunters with and without dogs often bait fields to attract their prey. The hunter might believe he is improving the odds that he will succeed in getting meat he needs for the table, but to most of us the act is unfair. Drawn to the food, the cougar, deer, or bear becomes easy prey.

Nor are houndsmen the only culprits. I was riding my bike in Vermont one Saturday morning during deer season when I saw a group of hunters in a field putting their guns and coolers into empty pickup trucks. Hunters are common there, so I thought nothing of the scene until a few moments later one of the trucks pulled beside me and the passenger discharged a 12-gauge shotgun by my ear, presumably to see whether I would fall off my bike from fright. I had within the year been hit head-on by a car while riding, so I was not about to be frightened by a shotgun. But I was enraged enough to give chase and lucky enough not to catch the miscreants. Unfortunately, brave hunters of that sort also occasionally kill their fellow hunters or innocent people "by accident."

I will say here that I am not a hunter—never have been—nor do I run my dogs in hogdog trials or various no-kill hunts for squirrels or coons. I have fished, collected snakes and turtles, taken in an owl for healing, killed and skinned a few animals that others have wounded then left in pain because they could not end the suffering they had brought on, and fired guns at targets, with some success and satisfaction, but I have not hunted. Nonetheless, I do not oppose it, as long as the hunter is taking the game for food, for himself or someone else.

Hunting for food and clothing is what humans have done for much of their existence, and I believe those who desire to take their meat in that fashion should be able to do so, there being something more honest about shooting and dressing your own food than purchasing shrink-wrapped feedlot beef, factory-produced poultry, force-fed pork or veal. I do not want animals hunted to extinction, but I also have no desire to deny that humans are hunters—excellent ones with dogs. In South Florida, there are a number of hog hunters, who care more about their dogs than about their families. That is not virtuous, but it is fact. They will weep when a hog mauls a dog, a not uncommon occurrence, or when one gets shot or run over. As a veterinarian friend says, "Their dogs are their link to *hog*." And the hog is everything wild and free.

That said, I have no tolerance for the type of "sport" hunting that predominated in the nineteenth and early twentieth centuries, when gunners slaughtered whatever they could put in their sights by the tens of thousands, leaving fields of blood and gore wherever they roamed. No one can kill animals in that quantity now, but trophy hunting persists in all its horrible splendor. It should end, as should the killing of predators.

Canned hunts, in which previously caught coyotes, bears, or more exotic animals are turned loose in a pen for the "great hunter" to lay waste with his pistol, shotgun, or rifle, are cowardly at best. They serve only to satisfy bloodlust. A variation on the canned hunt is the guaranteed kill. For example, a hog-hunting guide will turn a captured boar out in front of his dogs, who cannot help but bay it up for the client to shoot in the head, if he does not panic and miss. Shooting released birds over a baited field is equally unsavory to me, but that is strictly personal; I would rather shoot wild birds, were I to hunt them.

My rules for hunting are simple:

1. Eat what you kill, or make sure it is eaten by someone.
2. Anyone who leaves a wounded animal in the field loses the right to hunt. Anyone who kills another person through negligence or folly, well . . .
3. Do not abuse your dogs by kicking, whipping, and beating them, shocking them excessively using remote-control electronic collars, shooting them if they fail to meet expectations.
4. Follow your hounds on horseback or by foot, but not in motorized vehicles, and use tracking devices to help locate them, so they do not go roaming through people's fields. Too often the good ol' boys in trucks run over their dogs or tear up land just so they can avoid walking or sitting on top of a mule or horse. Sometimes, they are so lazy they rig their dog boxes so they can open them without getting out of the truck. The hounds charge out on the trail of bear or coyotes. There is neither sport nor fairness in that behavior.
5. Respect other people's rights and do not go tearing across their property or blocking roads. This rule applies equally to the good ol' boys in their pickups and the wealthy hunt club members riding to hounds on their Thoroughbred horses, in their proper attire.

For their part, nonhunters must stop thinking of everyone who lives on a farm or ranch as a cracker or bumpkin or redneck or any other form of old fool. It has become commonplace for suburbanites to complain about the smells or sounds of the ranch or farm down the street and demand an ordinance be put in place to get rid of them.

The prohibitions are an abuse of democracy. Farmers, ranchers, and houndsmen—often the same people—live within a culture that has as much right to exist, as long as they are behaving responsibly, as the suburban culture—maybe more. Many of them care as deeply for the land as environmentalists and new homeowners, although just as many of them do not.

My rules do not account for the ethical conflict surrounding hunting because I believe there is an overriding principle, which involves accommodation of different lifestyles and cultures. Hunting is not inherently evil; too many hunters are. Their goal is to shoot as many animals as possible, to run their dogs into the ground in the pursuit of game or brutalize them for failing, in the process drinking themselves stupid so that they are dangerous to man and beast. On the other hand, I have met men and women (although hunting remains largely a pursuit of men) who have never taken a shot at a target they could not clearly identify or left a wounded animal to suffer. There are also men and women who treat their dogs with respect.

Without exhaustively debating this issue, we should remember that at the end of the Pleistocene growing numbers of human hunters with dogs did contribute to the extinction of a number of species of large mammals. But the human efforts were just a part of major shifts in climate and ecosystems that put those populations at risk, and the entire process took thousands of years. During the past 150 years, humans with increasingly powerful guns have hunted numerous large and small species of birds and mammals to extinction, engaging in wholesale slaughter for profit and pleasure. Humans have also destroyed millions of acres of habitat on land and sea with petroleum-powered machines, explosives, and toxins. In short, in less than two centuries humans have accomplished that which had previously taken thousands of years.

Observing that deer have proliferated so much in the northeastern United States that they have become pests and that the populations of a number of predators have begun to increase does not alter our sordid history. Deer have rebounded because of a cessation of nearly all predation in suburban areas. There are many reasons to hunt deer or elk or moose where they abound. There are scant reasons to hunt mountain lions, wolves, grizzly bears, or any other predator, although the lions and bears occasionally kill humans, and the wolves will take out livestock and pet dogs. But just as opponents of hunting must recognize that there are times and places where it is useful, hunters must realize that relative abundance does not mean they can hunt whatever strikes their fancy or that populations are equally plentiful in every region. With too many people chasing too few resources, moratoriums are necessary for populations to replenish without interference.

Hounds need not vanish. In fact, hunting dogs have found new targets that do not involve killing. Scientists use hounds to locate bears, Florida panthers, seals in Alaska, and other animals in order to study and preserve them. Presently, New Zealand huntaways, black and tan, barking herders created in this century to gather sheep, are being considered for rounding up feral hogs in Hawaii, which are destroying native flora and fauna, for "humane disposal." Curs would work better, but the U.S. Department of Agriculture does not want to use such rough dogs for fear of offending its partner in this venture, the animal-rights group PETA (People for the Ethical Treatment of Animals).

Hunting dogs and terriers are employed around the world in detecting contraband and dangerous organisms. Even the various no-kill hunts and field trials give the dogs an opportunity to do what they have always done. The point is that the reward given the dog at the end of a successful hunt does not have to be a chunk of freshly killed meat. The hounds can apply their talents to other purposes quite well.

Chapter Three

COMMON SCENTS

Following Scent

Hounds are justly famous for their ability to detect and follow scents of particular animals, including human, up hill and down dale, across ice sheets and flowing rivers. But their reputation derives from their excellence at discriminating among different odors to find and follow a trail, more than from their ability to smell—a trait shared by many dogs and increasingly employed with spectacular results in fields far from the hunt.

For the past several decades, dogs have been bringing their noses to urban problems, the way they once turned them to help their weak two-legged companions find food for the fire. Now the prey is considerably different. Skillful trainers are teaching dogs to sniff out narcotics—marijuana, cocaine, heroin, methamphetamines, LSD—termites, gypsy moths, mold in lumberyards, chemicals like gasoline used to start fires, guns, explosives, contraband food, snakes, money being smuggled out of the United States in quantities exceeding the $10,000 limit, cows going into estrus, and leaks in underground gas pipelines. As one trainer suggested, if an object has an odor, a dog can be trained to identify it. The most venerable, culinary, and lucrative of these offtrack uses is truffle hunting. The Italians employ farm-bred dogs resembling pointers to locate that subterranean fungus with the value of gold and swear by their genius for the work with a fervency matching that of the French extolling their truffle pigs.

No one keeps a census of the number of dogs involved in scent-detection work, but it reaches into the thousands in this country alone, when one includes dogs employed by the police and military—often cross-trained to detect narcotics or explosives as well as to perform traditional protection tasks—and search-and-rescue squads. Specialized in finding the victims of disasters and lost individuals, those dogs received national acclaim in the wake of Hurricane Andrew's assault on South Florida in 1992, the 1994 Northridge earthquake in Los Angeles, and the 1995 bombing of the Oklahoma City federal building. In the company of their handlers, they pick their way through the rubble detecting the scent of victims and then alerting rescuers to their location. The best among them distinguish between the quick and the dead.

Often the scents they detect are tantalizingly faint odors taking an impossibly convoluted course through an impenetrable jumble inaccessible to the most refined mechanical device. In other words, if dogs are not brought to a disaster site early, survivors are almost guaranteed to die. When the teams are attempting to find a person who has jumped from a plane or been thrown from a wreck, there is no track at all, so the dogs, like bird dogs or hounds, must make casts until they detect something. Then they weave in and out of the scent in a narrowing cone until they reach the source. That is the style of air scenters.

With the exception of Dade County, Florida, home of Miami, and a few other locales, search-and-rescue squads are composed of volunteers with their own dogs. In South Florida, the dogs and handlers are professionals with the Fire Department's search-and-rescue squad, one of only two in the nation designated for international duty. The unit was professionalized so that it would be on call at all times, ready to be in the air within six hours of receiving a call for assistance from anywhere in the world. As good as they are—and some are superb—volunteer groups can suffer from political infighting, plus insurance and scheduling problems, meaning they cannot always guarantee such a response. There are sixteen dogs and handlers among the fifty-eight-person Dade county team, including a bloodhound, added because, according to director Skip Fernandez, bloodhounds are "natural trackers," moving at a speed comfortable for people on foot.

Fernandez works with a female golden retriever named Aspen,

who has achieved renown in search-and-rescue circles for her performances in the wake of Hurricane Andrew and the Oklahoma City
bombing. In the twisted ruins of the federal building, she found the
remains of three victims. Aspen is an active, thin-coated golden with
high prey drive, meaning she would not even be allowed in the show
ring. She hails from a kennel that produces a litter every three to five
years to give the owners and their dogs time to recover and mature.

"I'm not going to tell anyone that golden retrievers are the best
dogs for search-and-rescue work," Fernandez says during an interview
at Dade County's Fire Department headquarters. "They're not. In
fact, until a few years ago only German shepherd dogs were used. I
have goldens because I like them. I've had them, and I'm partial
to them. That's why I have females, too." In the more macho world
of police work, females are seldom used, in part because they are generally less aggressive than males. In fact, only since the mid-1990s
have police departments begun to recognize the value of dedicated
detection dogs, whose presence frees their police canines for their preferred tasks.

Given proper training and handling, any dog with a good nose and
strong desire or drive can do scent work—with the possible exception
of some of the toy breeds, which are physically not up to the effort of
work. Retrievers, Brittanies, field-stock springer spaniels, pointers,
border collies, Australian shepherds, Catahoula leopard dogs, Jack
Russell terriers, and beagles are among those currently employed.
According to trainers, the key is to select a dog with the physical size
and agility to perform the necessary tasks, the instincts to hunt and
retrieve. Those instincts are often referred to as "prey drive" or
"retrieve drive," both somewhat imprecise, nonsynonymous terms that
refer to the dog's desire to seek and find objects—to hunt, as it were.
Fernandez says the successful dog is trainable, agile, and has a greater
tendency for "fight rather than flight," meaning it is bold and assertive,
unafraid of strange or new situations. Some people call that aggression,
but others shy away from the term because of the implications of violence toward other dogs or people, which is not tolerated, the Jack
Russell terriers chasing and killing brown tree snakes on Guam
excepted. Often those little predators were given up by owners who

found them too aggressive. (Although out of vogue among animal behaviorists, who consider them vague, "prey drive" and "retrieve drive" are common shorthand among trainers, breeders, and handlers for a complex of agonistic behaviors, and for that reason I use them throughout.)

Many detection dogs are rescued from animal shelters, given up by owners who lack the ability or desire to train them, or donated by breed rescue clubs, although those groups most commonly place their dogs in private homes. The U.S. Customs Service also receives dogs from schools for the blind who are too energetic and aggressive to make good guides. These secondhand animals demonstrate what consistent training and solid handling can accomplish. As long as their noses are healthy and they can focus on what they are doing, they should succeed.

Studies by Lawrence J. Myers, professor and founder of the Institute for Biological Detection Systems at Auburn University's School of Veterinary Medicine, have revealed a greater difference in scenting ability among individual dogs within breeds than between breeds themselves. In an apparent paradox, a small study Myers conducted indicated a slight but significant difference between a line of hunting beagles and "pet grade" beagles in his clinic. He could not determine how much, if any, of that difference was due to selective breeding for scenting ability, in part because the houndsman was culling dogs based on their performance whereas "pet grade" dogs are by definition culls, rejects a breeder sold or gave away because they were deemed unfit for the hunt or show ring. That question aside, a working Labrador probably can match noses with a bloodhound—although the Labrador might not track as well—and the hounds and curs are generally equal in scenting ability while differing in their style.

Myers is one of the foremost researchers in this country in canine olfaction, a little-understood talent given the faith we place in it and the price of failure. Paradox rules the field, as evidenced by the following examples of inconsistency in trained, successful scent dogs. On one occasion, a retriever able to detect minute quantities of cocaine entered a warehouse filled with the narcotic and did nothing. On another, a beagle skilled at finding oranges, apples, mangoes, pork, and beef tucked in travelers' luggage ignored a bag literally oozing ripe mangoes.

Sandy Seward, a handler and trainer for the U.S. Department of Agriculture's Beagle Brigade, asked the beagle, Jessie, to reconsider. She declined, and so Sandy followed her own nose and opened the bag. "There must have been 500 mangoes in there," she says. "Jessie was embarrassed. But I decided there was too much odor. She didn't know what to do."

Apocryphal though they sound, these tales are true, and they raise tantalizing questions about what precisely detection dogs, whose numbers are skyrocketing, are smelling and how accurate they are. The short answers: no one knows for sure; and above 90 percent of the time for the best dogs *and* handlers. Inattentive, poorly motivated humans can bring that rate down to 75 percent or less.

Although scientists have deciphered the steps in the biochemical processes governing canine olfaction, they do not know precisely what a dog smells—whether whole bouquets of scent or particular components. The average dog has 220 million scent receptors, for example, compared with our 5 million. Unfolded and flattened, the smell receptors from an average dog's nose could cover it like a second coat with hair dragging on the ground. Basically, odor molecules become trapped and concentrated in the nasal mucous membranes, which contain smell receptors. The concentrated odor undergoes a chemical reaction with the cilia, the fine strands radiating from the smell receptors, that fires an electrical impulse along the olfactory nerve to the olfactory bulb, an area between the main brain and nose, before heading off to other parts of the brain. Those include the cerebral cortex and, most significantly, the limbic system, which controls the emotions and such behaviors as eating, drinking, and sexual arousal. Used-up scent is washed out with mucus and probably passed through nasal blood vessels. In addition, dogs possess a vomeronasal organ (located above the roof of the mouth, behind the incisors) that appears to play a role in reading pheromones, the chemical compounds released by animals to communicate their sexual receptivity or other states to their fellow dogs, cats, roaches, or whatever.

The frequently observed habit among dogs of smelling the anus of each dog they meet, which finicky owners find disgusting, represents one of their primary means of identifying each other. Strong evidence suggests that the anal sacs secrete chemicals that bear each dog's signature odor. Whether they tell more about its condition and intentions is unknown. It is clear, however, that by snuffling urine and feces, a dog can determine the sex of the responsible animal, as well as its sexual receptivity. It is also possible that dogs of a particular type are able to recognize their kin through methods that at least partly involve scent.

Through their olfactory system, dogs experience a rich, complex world, which is why they seem so oblivious to our commands at times when they are smelling something. To a dog, scent is what an engrossing sight is to us. But having a good sense of smell is not guaranteed. Myers has estimated that as many as 35 percent of all dogs suffer temporary or permanent diminution or loss of their natural scenting ability, the major causes being thyroid problems, injury, or diseases like distemper, diabetes, and kennel cough.

Debates rage over what a dog smells when it tracks a person, with the most accepted current hypothesis being "skin rafts," tiny particles of bacteria-laden dead skin that are constantly shed. Some researchers have argued that dogs are, in fact, zeroing in on odor from one part of the body—an elbow, for example—when they track an animal or person. Those odors are believed to be unique, so that when presented with another part of that person's anatomy to smell, the tracking dog cannot make a proper identification. But scant evidence exists to support such assertions.

Similar arguments arise over whether an animal brought into a trail on the perpendicular can turn the proper direction to the source. Most evidence suggests that dogs have difficulty with this problem, but a few experts swear that they can be trained to go the correct way. The question then becomes, as it so often does in scent work, is the animal receiving cues from its handler? Or is it really discerning very subtle differences in scent intensity? Without answers to these and other questions—money is not available for the research—all we can say with certainty is that dogs perform feats that amaze and perplex us.

"We have dogs that will alert to drugs three decks up on a ship or five to six stories up in a building," says Carl Newcombe, director of the Canine Enforcement Training Center for the U.S. Customs Service. They generally pluck those scents from ventilation systems.

Larry Myers says that dogs appear to follow a scent along a gradient to its source. The odor itself emanates from, say, a mango, in a plume that dissipates as it drifts away, usually downwind. A dog picks up the scent when its nose enters that plume. It tracks by following slight changes in intensity to the source, a task complicated by the fact that scent spreads in clumps and clusters—a chaotic flow— rather than uniformly, and in collapsed buildings it follows air currents twisting through piles of rubble. Exactly how slight the variations can be before the dog loses the scent is unclear—and doubtless varies from dog to dog, although it certainly reaches parts per billion, even per quadrillion. According to Myers, this hypothesis can account for the failure of some dogs to respond when confronted with a large amount of drugs or mangoes or whatever. It also shows why dogs pursuing a particularly faint or powerful scent weave in and out as if lost.

"The concentration of an odor should be proportional to the surface area of the source," he says, "so if you have a very large source instead of a point source, the concentration would be high over a large area and the difference in intensity would be very low. In close proximity, the dog would then have no gradient to follow."

But the dog need not always head toward the source. A crossbred bear hound of John Child tracks backward along the trail when working for Brigham Young University zoologist Hal Black. "We want to see where the bear has been and what it's done, not what it's doing in response to our running it with a dog," he explains. Still the hound is working in a seemingly counterintuitive fashion, tracing the scent from strong to faint.

The Customs Service retriever and USDA beagle that missed their scents were excellent dogs with skilled trainer-handlers, who identified and corrected the reasons for their errors. As Sandy Seward had surmised, the dogs were so inundated with scent that they saw no need to point to the source—they were in it. While it is true that a dog cannot track what it is literally standing on, it should be able to tell its handler when it is drowning in the odor it is trained to detect.

The way around the apparent dilemma is to vary the amount of scent a dog is exposed to in training. For example, the beagles are usually schooled on single apples, mangoes, pieces of meat, while the narcotics dogs are tuned to pick up trace amounts. The key is to find the source of that faint odor. Skillful trainers like Seward and Newcombe figure that you must therefore train the dogs to alert to huge amounts of scent as well, so they vary the quantities, locations, containers, and times of day that they work the dogs. They also take care not to contaminate the samples with other scents, putting their bare hands all over a sample of plastic explosives, for example.

These practices have the added advantage of keeping the dogs from learning shortcuts—something they are notorious for doing, no matter what their task. A police narcotics dog in Alabama, for example, developed the habit of alerting to Ziploc baggies because his handler stored all the training samples in them. Although it is true that they are a traditional conveyance for drugs, a dog alerting to plastic baggies is not technically finding narcotics and, therefore, should not be used. Unfortunately, they often are because defense attorneys have not consistently challenged the dogs' reasons for the detection or its reliability.

Nontraditional scent work gathered momentum during the war in Vietnam and then the "wars" on drugs and terrorism. Trainers began to tune the canine nose to more exotic targets: narcotics and new generations of incendiary devices and plastic explosives. Carl Newcombe says, "People realized that we could do more with dogs than we had been, and so they began experimenting with different odors." They also began to train dogs purely to perform detection work, rather than attempting to force guard dogs to do double and triple duty, and they looked to breeds other than those traditionally used in police work. The key was to use positive reinforcement to shape behavior, rather than compulsory methods, including physical punishment. Success bred more experimentation, with many people now believing it is possible to train a dog to detect anything that emits an odor.

In 1984, the USDA's Animal and Plant Health Inspection Service organized the Beagle Brigade to patrol airports and international postal depots for contraband fruit and meat. Wearing green Beagle Brigade vests and trained to sit when they detect any banned food, the dogs were so efficient—an accuracy rate of more than 90 percent after two years in the field—that 44 teams worked in the nation's busiest international airports and postal facilities in 1995, and other nations were starting their own programs. By contrast, that year the U.S. Customs Service had 433 canine teams in the field, which seized narcotics with an estimated $2-billion street value. Around the nation, local police departments receive millions of dollars annually as a result of drug seizures and property forfeiture under controversial racketeering laws.

Although the most lucrative, drug detection is probably the least important task the dogs perform. Less costly, more maneuverable, and often more accurate than machines—if machines for what they do exist at all—dogs often serve as the first line of defense against agents that can cripple entire industries and as keys to unlocking mysteries. Contraband food can carry insects like the Mediterranean fruit fly, citrus canker, or other pathogens that could threaten the nation's multibillion-dollar fruit, beef, and pork industries, not to mention public health. Brown tree snakes from Australia, New Guinea, and the Philippines have extirpated nine of Guam's twelve native bird species, and officials fear that they would do the same in Hawaii were they to arrive there on airplanes or cargo ships from Guam. Yet until Jack Russell terriers were employed a few years ago, no sure method of searching cargo and killing the snakes, which can reach ten feet in length, existed; by 1995, eight dogs regularly patrolled Guam's airport and harbor. According to those involved in the decision, the USDA selected Jack Russells because the little terrier had a reputation for tenacity and aggression and it wanted a dog who would seek out and destroy its quarry.

Other USDA researchers experimented in the early 1980s with Catahoula leopard dogs and German shepherds as a solution to a vexing dilemma: how to determine when a dairy cow is in estrus. They found that the dogs could detect estrus cows with accuracy rates of 86 to 97 percent. The dogs also anticipated, 64 percent of the time, by one to two days when a cow would go into estrus. Since there is a relatively small window of opportunity for impregnating the cow (around twelve hours), knowing precisely when she enters estrus is important to farmers, but short of using dogs and human guesswork, which usually involves looking for homosexual behavior, the only way to determine that is with expensive radioimmunoassays. The research was dropped because the scientists did not like having to reward the dogs for each correct detection; they felt this practice was too labor-intensive. They also worried that the dogs were picking up cues from their handlers, thereby increasing the probability of false positives.

Curiously, the researchers were concerned about the very thing that makes detection work successful. Normally in training dogs, variable reinforcement is most effective, but for detection dogs, who must discriminate between odors, rewards for each correct identification are necessary. The same is true of other tests or puzzles the dog is asked to solve. No one seems to understand fully the reasons for that, although they seem to have to do with keeping the animal informed of the question it is being asked to answer: for example, are you smelling a mango or a papaya? The need for handlers to reward their detection dogs for each correct identification does increase the possibility that the dogs will learn to read cues and cut corners. A good example of this false identification is the police dog, mentioned earlier, who alerted to baggies rather than drugs. The dogs might also begin to watch for a hitch in the stride of a handler who suspects that he or she is going to find some contraband.

The bombing of the federal office building in Oklahoma City graphically exposed the importance of programs that screen for bombs in public spaces. In the aftermath of that attack, a worker at the Internal Revenue Service office in Miami called the police and asked for a dog to come scan the mail for explosives. Told it was already x-rayed, he said, yes, he knew that, but he trusted the dog more than the machine. Some organizations, like the U.S. Secret Service, the military, the Federal Aviation Administration, and a number of police departments, have long employed dogs to locate explosives. Following the tragedy in Oklahoma City, more law enforcement agencies began training bomb-detection dogs.

Bombings are usually acts of political terror; arson is commonly a crime of avarice or rage. Although less newsworthy, it is more costly and more deadly. (Of course, fires are also started by people who are negligent or, in the case of many of those involving black churches, filled with prejudice and lacking even marginal intelligence.) In 1993, the last year for which figures were available, arson cost insurance companies and consumers $2.4 billion; 560 civilians lost their lives in those fires. Because learning why a fire started often leads to determining who caused it—frequently the property owner seeking to escape defaulting on a mortgage and having to declare bankruptcy or wanting to collect insurance—two insurance companies, Aetna and State Farm, sponsor programs to put into fire departments around the nation dogs trained to detect traces of weathered gasoline or other flammable chemicals (accelerants) in burned-out buildings. Between 1992, when the first program started, and 1995, nearly forty of the dogs, most of them Labrador types, went on duty.

The arson dog I met in Seminole, Florida, a small community just west of Tampa, in the spring of 1995 was a black female Labrador retriever rescued from the animal shelter when she was nine months old and named Villain after she was caught stealing a pizza by her handler-trainer Bill Whitstine, a wiry, intense, pleasant man in his early thirties, who, like most people involved in detection work, loves training as much as working his dog. Whitstine says that when he was accepted by State Farm into the training program it sponsors at the Maine Criminal Justice Academy, he selected a dog from Florida, rather than taking one provided by the school, because he believed a dog born and raised in the state would have a thinner coat and greater physiological tolerance for its hot, humid climate than one from the Northeast.

"We started using dogs," he says, "because in a burned-out building where you have a collapsed roof, caved-in walls, and four miles of melted wire, the visible physical evidence of arson is usually destroyed, so you're looking for a needle in a haystack. The dog sniffs and then points to an object with a trace of accelerant on it, say something in parts per billion. With a mechanical sniffer, even if it were equal to a dog, and it is not, I'd still have to point it at just the right spot to make it register. The dog does the pointing, and I just have to take the sample."

In one case, Villain indicated that a woman had gasoline on her clothing, and she was questioned as a suspect in the burning of a building. The woman said she had, in fact, bought gas at a nearby gas station and then went on to describe a fellow customer, who proved to have started the fire.

In another instance, a police dog tracked suspects from a fire at a car dealership to an apartment. Summoned to the scene, Whitstine asked if he and Villain could speak with the occupants about the blaze, which was the talk of the neighborhood. The two men agreed. While Whitstine questioned them, Villain sat and raised her paw, indicating that she smelled gas residue on their clothing, although as far as they were concerned, she was just being a dog, offering to shake hands. The men were arrested and later convicted.

On yet a third of the sixty-three occasions when her work has led to arrests, Villain sat next to a man being questioned after a suspicious fire and pointed to his pants. The man defended himself by saying he had just purchased gas, and further investigation confirmed that he had—to fill a can that was found at the site of a fire.

Raised with dogs—his collie learned to climb the forest-fire lookout tower where his mother stood watch—Whitstine considers arson dogs the best investigative tool to come along in the past twenty years. Furthermore, he firmly believes that detection work should be left to dogs like Villain trained to a passive or at most a nonaggressive active alert, not to police dogs. In a passive alert, the dog sits and possibly points at the source of the odor. (Secret Service dogs lie down.) In an active alert, the dog will seek to uncover the object, the way a truffle dog digs for its prize, a drug dog scratches at the cache, or a search-and-rescue dog attempts to uncover a living person trapped in rubble. Search-and-rescue dogs are also trained to bark, like a baying hound, when they find a lost person to indicate their location. The significant goal should be to separate detection from other police-dog work, such as crowd control and apprehension of suspects, to relieve stress on the dogs, ensure higher-quality performances, and decrease the number of accidental bites.

Virtually everyone involved in detection work agrees that the handlers cannot smell for their dogs, but they can enhance or detract significantly from their performance. The best handlers allow their dogs time to parse scents while also watching for signs they are confused, because the object causing their befuddlement usually requires additional investigation. Dade County rescue leader Skip Fernandez says that handlers learn to read the dog's body language, to see when it becomes focused on an object. When they work well together, human and dog are a formidable team capable of feats of hunting not only for food but for the minute particles that indicate the presence of a lost soul or provide evidence of a crime or merely an act of omission that could have grave consequences.

Basic Training

These are dogs no one wanted: Stanley, chained to a pole in a yard in Texas for the first year and a half of his life and given neither attention nor training; Cricket, a refugee from the Broward County, Florida, animal shelter; Crusty, a wheezing veteran of a veterinary school dog food test who barely knows what to do outside a cage; Charlie, a donated dog who tries hard to learn without much effect; and Bagels, who proved himself a hound rather than a lapdog by barking and wandering and, thus, was expelled from his first home. Annie, Quincy, and Barney are repeaters, dogs who this time will make the grade or be sent to new homes. They comprise the class for the Beagle Brigade that commences on May 1, 1995, under the supervision of chief trainer Sandy Seward, about as patient and thoughtful a dog person as can be found. Tall, blond, plainspoken, she has put a top obedience title on a bloodhound, a breed considered virtually untrainable in that fashion. The accomplishment not only proves her mettle as a trainer but also reveals how often assessments of a particular breed's "intelligence" are based on human bias, not canine ability.

Regional supervisor for this Beagle Brigade, headquartered in Miami, is Lourdes Edlin, who learned from training dolphins at the Miami Seaquarium how to shape behavior with rewards. "You can't put a leash on a dolphin and give it correction," she says with a smile. Edlin has a whippet—another breed deemed difficult to train by experts in canine intelligence—who not only has an obedience title but also retrieves. Edlin's border collie, Cisco, is a beautiful animal trained in the German protection-dog sport of Schutzhund and in herding. But he excels at Frisbee competitions.

Given enough time, Edlin and Seward can probably train any dog they encounter, although, like most dog people, they prefer working with those who possess a high food or prey drive, meaning they are motivated to go after what they want. Carl Newcombe at the U.S. Customs Service, which trains its dogs to an active alert, seeks animals with "a natural desire to retrieve" and so favors the sporting breeds. The dogs must also be friendly, comfortable in strange environments, and capable of staying focused on their task for a full day. German shepherds and Malinois used in security work often do not adjust to full-time detection, he says. They are too energetic and are motivated only for short periods of time. Although they are capable of detecting anything when trained, asking them to do scent work all day is like asking a sprinter to run a marathon.

Overly fearful or clinging dogs are washed out of virtually all programs because they are difficult for any trainer, to say the least. They can freak out at odd situations or moments and turn into biters of strangers, hardly behavior wanted in a crowded airport. That aside, good trainers know that they have to lay aside their preconceived notions and work with what the dog has in terms of talent and interests.

This class of beagles will challenge Seward and Edlin's ingenuity and patience, causing them to ask serious questions about where to find dogs. But, for now, like trainers with virtually every other agency in the detection business, they have no choice but to take rescued or donated animals. They cannot afford to have dogs bred and then farmed out for a year or year and a half, until they are mature enough to train—an optimum situation but not one for which the government or public, for all the value of these animals, is willing to pay. Even if they were, finding responsible breeders in the United States would prove difficult. They exist, to be sure, but they are widely scattered and their dogs are in such great demand that they have waiting lists for their puppies. Across the board, the reputation of American breeders and their dogs is so bad as to be embarrassing. In light of that, taking unwanted animals actually saves their lives and taxpayer money. But it means that trainers must deal with what is available. (Most search-and-rescue dogs are raised from puppies by their handlers; police dogs come from kennels specializing in their breeding, which does not prevent them from having a high failure rate.)

With their high food drive and nonthreatening demeanor, beagles—the term here includes crossbred animals like Cricket who resemble the little hounds—make the perfect tool for snorting through people's personal belongings without invading their privacy. Wearing their distinctive green vests, they sit down by the offending bag and wait for their handler to find the contraband and reward them with a kibble. Generally, culprits are carrying food for their journey, which they hand over with a smile because it is difficult to get angry at the little dog with the long ears and gentle demeanor. Moreover, children love the beagles, which becomes a problem when they run up to pet them or grab their tails, thereby distracting them from their work. Worse, such behavior can lead the dog to bite out of fright or surprise. It is a rare and unwelcome occurrence, but, to paraphrase a Buddhist koan, dogs bite. Savvy trainers know to ask well-wishers and children to let the dog finish before allowing them to say hello.

Travelers who deny the beagle's suggestion that they are carrying a banned food are given a signed slip indicating that they must pass through a USDA inspection station, where their bags are searched or x-rayed. If the hounds are found correct, as they usually are, the offenders face a fine. It is much easier to hand over the food to the dog's handler.

The largest complaint, according to handlers I have talked with, seems to be that a few people become indignant when they learn that the little hounds are kept in a kennel when not working, either a portable crate at the airport or a large boarding kennel with indoor-outdoor runs and doghouses at a USDA field station. Some animal shelters will not even release dogs to the Beagle Brigade for that reason. Occasionally, the objections are based on ignorance, but increasingly they appear to arise from animal-rights supporters who identify kennels with crowded prison cells for their own ideological and psychological reasons. Many of us, for example, do not like to board our dogs when we are going on vacation to have "fun," and we project our separation anxiety onto all dogs.

I spent considerable time with the Beagle Brigade and can attest that the dogs receive better care than many house pets. They are fed daily, groomed and cleaned regularly, given prompt medical attention, and exercised. They work in close proximity to people where they are rewarded for using their canine talents. For all of them, life in the Beagle Brigade represents liberation from an awful fate: abusive owners, close confinement with no attention, or death. I have often seen dogs "living" as pets who are confined to narrow spaces in the owner's yard or a corner of the basement and given no attention, the way Stanley was before Sandy Seward took him for training.

Not all detection dogs are kenneled. Arson dogs are traditionally kept with their handler, so that the two can form a tight bond and the dog can train daily: if it has not worked a fire site, it detects samples of weathered gasoline dabbed around the house or yard so it can receive its daily quota of food, since all of its calories are consumed as a reward for detection. Search-and-rescue dogs live at the home of their trainer-handlers, just as police dogs are inseparable from their handlers, the need for a strong bond being paramount. On the other hand, U.S. Customs Service narcotics dogs are also kenneled. Tradition plays a role, as does recognition of the personality and drive of the dogs. Seward explains that beagles are notorious escape artists, which means they must be kept confined or they will go out hunting, and because they detect food, they must keep their noses clear of the smells they are being asked to identify. The Customs Service wants its dogs to use all of their energy in their work.

After rescuing her from the animal shelter literally on the day she was to be euthanized, Lourdes Edlin took Cricket to her house, where the little street dog delivered eight puppies, two of whom resembled beagles closely enough to become working dogs when they grow up. Once homes were found for the other puppies, she was brought to the kennel in Miami.

When the man who owned and ignored Stanley brought him to a Texas airport for Seward to evaluate his temperament and apparent intelligence, he pinched the dog on the ear for a perceived misdeed. Stanley cried in pain. Not a person prone to mincing words, Seward recalls reassuring Stanley while dressing down the owner and demanding to know where he learned such a "mean trick."

"From a dog trainer," the man replied. Indeed, it was once common for trainers of bird dogs to press a bottle cap into the ear of dog who was not obeying quickly enough or holding its point long enough, and some people still employ an ear pinch, with or without the cap. Ear pinching represents one aspect of what can be called the compulsory style of obedience training, which was refined by the military and justified on scientific grounds during and following World War I. Compulsory training is based on the premise that the best-behaved dog is the one most afraid to disobey. Whether the punishment consists of grabbing an ear, slapping the dog with a cattle prod, whip, or switch, pulling it up short with a choke collar, or zapping it with a shock collar is a matter of personal preference. Animals trained by such methods are known to "shut down" or quit working after a few years, but for the people inclined to abuse them, that has traditionally been no problem. They get a new dog before the corpse of the old one is cold.

Watching these beagles—generally one to two years of age, prime time for serious training to begin—struggle against the baggage of their past, which the trainers often are hard-pressed to discern but must somehow overcome in order to turn the dogs into proud animals, is an education in training itself and in the myriad ways that people can screw up their dogs. It is fashionable in the circles of animal behaviorists to suggest that people must not feel responsible for bad dogs, and in some cases that is true, but in the majority of instances it must be said that left to their own devices dogs do pretty well. It is people with their strange notions of training and discipline, their unwillingness to deal with the individual, their abuse, who cause the problems. Unfortunately, many of those attitudes represent received wisdom or knowledge gleaned from countless books on dog behavior, intelligence, and training, the bulk of them misleading at best. Fortunately, that state of affairs is changing in many parts of dogdom.

The trainer of a working dog must deal with the personality of each animal. The handler must learn to trust his or her dog and to command it when necessary, for the worst thing a handler can do is pull a dog off a scent, that is, not give it time to decipher what it is smelling or where it is coming from. The second worst thing is to reward the dog for error, thereby reinforcing bad behavior. The third worst thing is to treat it inconsistently. Dogs are creatures of habit with keen associative minds and long memories. It does not take much to undo weeks of careful training. Not surprisingly, those rules are identical to the ones set forth for training and handling a treeing feist or any other dog, even a pet.

Like the best trainers today, Seward and Edlin employ positive reinforcement to shape the dog's own drives and desires. When given for egregious or repeated offenses, corrections generally consist of a firm "No" punctuated when necessary with a quick jerk of the leash to tighten the choke collar. (A number of trainers use a collar with blunted prongs that applies equal pressure to the dog's neck, thereby lessening the chance of injury from an improperly used choke collar.) But the general rule is to reward correct behavior. The beagles receive individualized attention—tutoring, if you will—geared to their needs and abilities. They also are given minimal obedience instruction, just enough to learn their name and to come when called (even though they always work on a leash), sit, and stay.

The Customs Service's Carl Newcombe says that undergoing obedience training makes narcotics dogs too fearful and too attentive to their handlers to hunt through large buildings effectively. "We use no compulsory techniques," he says, "and make corrections only in the case of aggression toward people or other dogs. We want a natural response and so try to enhance their behavior by making work fun." A number of corporations and school systems would benefit from that attitude.

Food, of course, is not the only reward that can be used. Edlin trained Cisco from puppyhood with a Frisbee. Schutzhund trainers commonly use a tennis ball and padded sleeve, while U.S. Customs narcotics dogs are rewarded with a rag that frequently has a sample of the drug attached. Dogs do not consume narcotics the way people do: the sample reinforces the message that they are to find that substance if they want to play with their towel. There are also attention freaks among dogs, who, like our Catahoula, Marlow, consider praise enough. But food is a powerful and easy-to-transport reward. A handler or trainer need only reach into a belt pouch or pocket to find a morsel for good work.

On the first day of training, Stanley is raising a ruckus in his crate, barking, scratching, agitating dogs and people. He refuses to respond to verbal correction, and so Seward fires a stream of water at him from a large syringe. It takes several repeats to catch his attention, but once he gets the message he settles down. Agitated dogs do not work well, so Seward waits until all are settled down before beginning the drill. As she takes the dogs through their paces, she keeps notes on their performance so that by the end of the training period, she will have a complete record of what was done when not only with the dogs but also with the handlers, who will enter the class after about eight weeks. In fact, this training period will cover four months, due to delays caused by hurricane threats and other unforeseen interruptions.

For the first session, each of six boxes turned upside down on the linoleum floor of the double-wide training trailer holds an apple, so the beagles cannot miss. The goal is to introduce them to the scent and to the process of sitting when they detect it. For smelling and sitting, they receive praise and the reward of a small treat of dog food. The exercise should be easy, but the dogs are what Seward calls "spastic," mentally ranging all over the trailer (they cannot do so physically because they are on leashes) as they are taken one at a time through the drill. As the exercise is repeated, apples are randomly removed from boxes so that the beagles do not associate the box itself with sitting for a reward.

Stanley goes first through the drill, and although his nose is fine, he is more interested in looking out the windows than locating the scent emanating from a box. He also has a difficult time making the connection between snorting the apple and sitting. He will be a project.

A tightly wound bundle of energy, Cricket vaults onto boxes, tries to bounce off the walls. She also will not pay attention to another handler if Edlin is in the room, viewing Lourdes, rightly, as her savior. Despite her energy and speed, she manages an approximation of a sit at each box.

Crusty takes a full header into the first box, wheezing as he strains against the light choke collar that will be exchanged for a broad nylon number to ease the pressure on his trachea, which apparently was injured when he was a test dog. Crusty knows about food but not much else—the horrible result of keeping a dog in a small cage and depriving it of any experience other than what the experiment demands.

Charlie is a nice dog, who tries hard but is too conscious of what Seward might want to be much good at anything. She craves approval but has not a clue about what to do with it.

Bagels starts late because of an infection and never catches up. He is the first one dropped from the training.

Of the three dogs who are repeating the training: Annie walks right through the drill, sitting and receiving her reward, while Barney and Quincy are allowed to miss the opening sessions.

The description is easy, the work, backbreaking for Seward who bends and taps the box at least one-hundred times, repeating in a calm voice, "Seek, sit, good dog," as she hands out the reward. Consistency in commands and delivery of the reward are crucial. But by the end of the day, some of the green dogs are beginning to focus with varying degrees of comprehension on the task at hand.

As training proceeds, suitcases of different shapes and sizes replace the boxes, and new smells waft through the air after the dogs have learned to identify apples consistently. Keeping their spirits, attention, and drive high by promptly rewarding proper performance and reforming bad behavior is the key to successful training. Cricket, for example, must learn that vaulting onto luggage is not acceptable, but at the same time Seward and eventually her handler must be careful not to kill her great exuberance. She is the only one of the five new dogs who passes the class and is assigned to a handler. Joining her in meeting all protocols—meaning they can alert to apples, oranges, mangoes, pork, and beef in varying amounts—are the three repeaters,

Barney, Annie, and Quincy, whom Seward will keep as her working dog. Thus, four of eight dogs from the class are placed with handlers.

Beagles who wash out of the program are given to people eager to have Beagle Brigade dogs because they know that even if they cannot do serious scent work, they are of sound mind and body. If they were not, they would not have been selected for training. Cricket's classmates failed for a variety of reasons. Halfway through the training class, Stanley, who had been progressing smoothly, walked into the trailer and behaved as if he had never been taught to alert to an odor. Seward decided that the probable cause of his regression was an allergic reaction to pesticides sprayed outside the kennel by the Department of Agriculture's grounds crew and sucked inside by an industrial fan used to keep it cool. Because he missed a week of training, she determined to hold him back for the next class, but in the following months he failed to recover his drive for the work and so was placed in a home. The other three nongraduating beagles also went to private homes: Charlie because she was uninterested in using her nose to work; Bagels because he was too erratic and unpredictable in his performance, not his temperament; and Crusty because he just never learned to get beyond diving into the box for food.

A failure rate of 30 to 50 percent is not unusual in the world of working dogs and, odd though it sounds, is pretty good, considering that more than half of the German shepherds evaluated for guard work are rejected on the basis of bad hips alone. But to the trainers, every failure hurts, and they have begun to seek more refined evaluation criteria. Carl Newcombe instituted new tests in 1995, which focus on retrieve drive and what he calls possessiveness, and saw the graduation rate for Customs Service dogs increase 10 to 20 percent—to 70 percent. He expects that figure to go as high as 75 to 80 percent once only dogs selected according to the new criteria are in training.

To make any system work, evaluators must have a full understanding of canine behavior and an ability to see the dog's talents. Although dogs bred to work in a certain way—to follow their noses, for example—have a predisposition to do so, the extent of their desire and ability to perform can vary greatly, often in inverse proportion to their physical talents. Piled on top of that natural predisposition, no matter its strength, are layers of environmental influences: the health of the mother, her treatment of the puppies, their early stimulation and socialization, their experiences with people and life in general, whether and how they were trained or abused. Research has revealed that nutrition also plays a major role in the development, physical health, and mental acuity of the dog.

No one has yet sorted out the relative contributions of these various, often competing influences; in fact, even experts can misread them or become impatient with a dog who is a slow learner. Nonetheless, it is certain that too many negative influences can severely limit the ability of a dog with abundant natural talent to fulfill its potential, just as positive handling and training can help an average one become superior. Annie, for example, went through three classes but was never placed because she was never the best dog. Her nose is fine; she was just a little slow. This time, she is the best dog, obedient, cheerful, always ready to do her job. She might not have quite the drive of Cricket, but the full package is impressive enough to gain her assignment to a handler from the busy Los Angeles International Airport. Cricket, Barney, and Quincy work in Miami, which after JFK Airport in New York is the busiest international airport in the country.

The star of the class is Cricket because of her exceptional nose, her exuberance, and all she has overcome. Observing her with her handler, a young woman with a firm but fair attitude, Seward says, "She's really excited that she's got a nice person, and I love that because someone was really rotten to this dog. Somebody's idea of training her was to call her and beat the crap out of her for whatever she did wrong—if she chewed something, for example—and they didn't realize that in her mind they beat her for coming. And then when she got pregnant, they got rid of her. Dogs are all very trusting initially, but when they have that trust betrayed it's difficult to win it back."

The ability of the beagles and other rescued detection dogs to overcome their environment and move on to productive lives speaks volumes not only about the resiliency of dogs but also about the capabilities of the trainers who reshape their behavior, helping them to triumph over what other people have put them through.

I asked Sandy Seward once what kind of dog she would recommend to a person who wanted a pet that never demanded attention or exercise, never messed up the house or misbehaved, that sat around all day being nice and looking pretty. "I'd tell them to get a stuffed animal," she said.

At the end of the class comes a series of trials. The dogs walk through their drills at the airport with their new handlers. The teams are learning to wander through a crowded international-arrivals baggage area, attentive to each other, to the passengers, to baggage carts. Working the dogs, the handlers must keep moving without pulling them off scent—a delicate balancing act because sometimes the dogs are uncertain. Different scents, sights, and sounds are competing for the attention of both the dog and handler. They become distracted. The handler walks too quickly past a bag, misreading the beagle's hesitation as a failure to detect rather than an attempt to sort through stimuli, to concentrate on the task.

Handlers in most programs are a highly motivated group of people who see the canine patrols as a chance to vary their routines and to work with an animal they respect. They get an opportunity to move through the airport or harbor rather than stand behind a counter. Those who see it solely as a promotion usually seek a transfer after they find themselves with a balkish dog and sore feet.

Although the dogs are new to their work, already they have their own styles. Cricket no longer vaults, but she still is constantly on the move, assertive, in need of slowing down a little to be certain of what she smells. Annie is deliberative and professional; however, her handler is tentative, not a good sign. Barney is laid back, almost gentle. Quincy just goes about his business. As they age and gain experience—largely in the form of successful seizures—they will clarify their style, the way any animal devoted to a task does.

As part of a test, I stand in the path of the four beagles, like any other arriving passenger, with an apple hidden in the backpack that lies on the floor between my feet. Only two of them—Cricket of the outstanding nose and Quincy, handled by Sandy Seward—detect it. The other two dogs walk past, probably because their handlers know who I am and never think that my bag might have something interesting in it. Of course, that is no excuse, and in the remarks that follow the session, Seward observes that the apple was missed. One should never assume that a bag has nothing in it. Similarly, one should never mistrust the dog: people sometimes save an apple for later eating, stuff it in their bag, and forget about it in the rush of arrival, remembering only after gentle questioning from a handler with an alert little beagle.

Watching veteran handlers and dogs reveals the extent to which detection work is equivalent to hunting in an urban world. Abbott, the old pro handled by Willie Harris at Miami International Airport, rests his chin on the circular baggage carousel and smells the luggage from a Boeing 747 that has just arrived from Germany as it passes him. Children gather around, trying to pull his tail, but he is not deterred. When Abbott smells something interesting, he promptly sits with an expectant look on his face, and Harris, if the baggage carousel is moving, quickly marks the suspicious luggage with his eyes, then moves to pull it from the rotating mass. Abbott waits patiently for the inspection and his inevitable reward—he is seldom wrong—the way a good treeing hound waits for its piece of squirrel or raccoon at the end of the hunt. It is a complex but effective dance, as Abbott and Harris snare a half-dozen apples in fifteen minutes. "The Germans bring in a lot of apples," Harris says, commenting on national preferences for food.

He then works a flight from South America—meat and mangoes are popular imports—with Molly, the dog Lourdes Edlin usually handles. Molly likes to stand on her hind legs to investigate handbags and then checks luggage on the ground, weaving quickly through the crowd. Before starting, she routinely stretches and scratches herself on the floor.

Talking to a group of Beagle Brigade handlers, I suggested that to better understand their dogs, they might consider getting down on all fours—more to scale, lying on their stomachs—and looking at the international-arrivals area in Miami, New York, or Los Angeles from the vantage point of the beagle. Sandy Seward and one other trainer promptly said that they had done so—to the amazement of their colleagues. Of course, we do not see, hear, or smell like a dog, so the exercise is one in approximation, but it does allow an empathetic person to gain some feel for the way a dog views a crowded world full of exhausted people wanting nothing more than to grab their bags, clear passport control and customs, and figure out where they are going in a strange city—or a hometown, which exposure to other cultures has rendered alien. From ground level, you see feet flying in every direction on pendulumlike legs attached to weaving bodies and heads talking, yelling, nodding side to side as they fight sleep. People and carts move randomly, move everywhere, and you must hustle along, connected to one of those tall beings by a string. Thousands of bags abound with scents no dog would believe and sometimes among them something that brings you a morsel. And as you hunt for them among the rubble, children appear chattering, delaying the boss, keeping you from your prize, and the kids grab at your tail and pet you as you hunt.

A number of the handlers asserted that from working with dogs daily, their own sense of smell and awareness of who was carrying food had improved markedly. Some, like Sandy Seward, have detected food their hounds have missed, for reasons not completely mysterious. Bonds of that sort, based on empathy and mutual trust, make detection dogs better than machines. The question is why we do not use them more.

A Question of Odor

Generally, scent dogs are trained on the substances they are seeking, but because human cadavers are difficult to obtain, narcotics are tempting to keep around, and explosives are dangerous, some trainers will try to use substitutes or pseudo scents, either concocted at home or purchased from Sigma Chemical Company, the only manufacturer in this country of those artificial odors. In training puppies, hunters have long used the pelt or wing, if not the whole carcass, of the game they want their dogs to find. The Italians substitute moldy fontina cheese for truffles in training their hounds, an act appearing to be an olfactory oxymoron. But the use of chemicals created to resemble a real narcotic or person is somewhat more controversial, because of concerns that dogs trained on pseudo scent will not, in fact, detect the real thing, paving the way for serious court challenges or even loss of life.

Pat Carr, director of corporate compliance and forensics marketing at Sigma, told me when I interviewed her by phone for an item on scent detection dogs in *Scientific American* (September 1995) that the company became involved in the business in 1990 when it was asked to produce "pseudo cocaine" and "pseudo heroin" for use in training narcotics dogs. The Customs Service made the request because having developed those scents for its own training purposes in 1977, it was forbidden by law from manufacturing them.

Sigma's 1995 inventory included substances known as "pseudo distressed body" for training animals to find victims of trauma or natural disasters; "pseudo corpse" for finding buried bodies; "pseudo drowned victim" for release on water; "pseudo explosive"; "pseudo narcotics"—cocaine, heroin, and marijuana, with LSD and methamphetamines on the way. "Pseudo corpse" and "pseudo drowned victim" are especially useful in search-and-rescue work because of the unavailability of human corpses and body parts.

In the January 29, 1996, issue of the *New Yorker*, author John McPhee wrote about a team of "cadaver dogs" from Tuscaloosa, Alabama, trained to find human corpses. They were, McPhee reported, rewarded with pieces of each corpse they uncovered. He also repeated a common fiction that the dogs could not find cadavers after they had eaten because they no longer had hunger to motivate them. No one I have interviewed in the detection field has ever heard of such a team. All observed that a dog feeding on a corpse would disturb the crime scene and therefore invalidate what was found as evidence; that training a dog on cadavers is not possible because cadavers cannot easily be obtained and using them, if they could be found, would violate state and local laws; and that a dog that is well fed is better able to work than a hungry one. Beyond those technical issues, allowing a dog to feast on a corpse would doubtless draw cries of outrage and a lawsuit from the family of the deceased. In past centuries, dogs were trained not only to find cadavers but also to hunt people and rewarded with meals of their flesh, and the practice might have continued until fairly recently in some areas, but such reports today of flesh-eating government dogs are legends.

Many police-dog trainers believe that "pseudo distressed body" actually resembles what they call "fear scent," an odor they claim is secreted by people who are fleeing the scene of a crime. They refuse to accept Sigma's statement that no scientific evidence confirms the street lore, itself based on the simple observation that dogs have the ability to detect and respond to emotional and physical states. A few dogs have been trained, for example, to anticipate when their owners are about to have epileptic seizures, an astounding feat, but they are reading a host of cues of which scent might be one.

The simple fact is that dogs naturally chase moving targets, be they cats, cows, deer, elk, moose, raccoons, squirrels, or people. If the animal or person stays in one place, there is scarce likelihood that a dog will chase it, especially a police dog, who is trained to pursue someone running away from it. Even if dogs can smell fear—and many dog owners aver that their animals seem to understand when someone is afraid of them—it does not follow logically that a person fleeing them or a crime scene is guilty because afraid. Clearly someone who sees a dog charging in his or her direction is going to be fearful, so even if people secrete a particular odor when terrified, there is no guarantee the fear has any cause other than the dog.

The use of "pseudo distressed body" for teaching dogs to attack humans has raised serious ethical and legal questions. But citing proprietary concerns, Sigma has refused to make its products available to independent researchers for evaluation. Although responsible trainers recognize that dogs trained on the artificial scents must ultimately be certified on the real thing, especially in the case of narcotics, there is a sense among some experts that the animals might be engaged in the sort of association that led the Alabama sheriff's dog to start alerting to baggies. Presented in court with blind sample of pseudo cocaine and real cocaine, for example, a dog might consistently prefer the pseudo, allowing a good attorney to challenge whether the animal can detect cocaine at all and casting doubt on the integrity of the prosecution's case.

It is not necessarily a difficult challenge, because neither Sigma's chemists nor anyone else can say with certainty what dogs actually do smell. The pseudo scents represent chemical brews resembling those from the substance in question, which are then field tested—the fake being declared good if dogs trained on it will alert to the real thing. The pseudo scents are clearly useful in training dogs for search-and-rescue work, where corpses are not readily available, but their abuse by trainers threatens not only the industry but the legitimate uses of scent dogs as well. There are regular reports of unscrupulous kennel owners attempting to cash in on the interest in detection dogs by cutting corners in training and relying heavily on pseudo scents they have concocted on their stoves. A trained detection dog can bring $10,000 or more, a hefty incentive.

The concerns have caused trainers and handlers, primarily associated with government agencies, to seek ways to develop certification programs for the dogs. A number of states, including Florida, New York, Massachusetts, Michigan, California, and Utah, have already established criteria for police dogs used to detect narcotics and explosives, and it is possible to expand those to include other detection dogs as well as to apply carefully developed national standards. Detection dogs are tools that must be used with respect and caution for their abilities and their power to injure the life of someone falsely accused of a crime; to allow a lost person to go unfound and die; to fail to block a fatal bomb attack by mistaking plastique for plastic.

They must be trained with care. More important, their handlers must be trained. "Dogs are easy," Whitstine says. "It takes fifteen minutes a day to train the dog and forty-five minutes for the handler."

Unwinding

Like other top trainers today, Skip Fernandez, director of the Dade County Search and Rescue Squad, practices a form of training that relies on positive reinforcement. The rules are simple: provide individual attention, reward the good, ignore or correct the bad, with a word if that will suffice. What you want to avoid is the sort of escalation of violence that makes a hardheaded dog more stubborn and ultimately nonproductive. But recognizing that search-and-rescue work is as psychologically and emotionally wearing on the dogs as on the people involved—only the dogs cannot decompress the way people can, with conversation, counseling, and exercise—he implemented a program for mandatory "de-stressing" after work. In Oklahoma City, the team found a park and for an hour after each shift took the dogs to play ball, to run, to do whatever dogs do when left to their own devices. It is a form of payback for a job well done, the ultimate reward. Most good handlers, whether they engage in such extensive activities with their dogs or not, recognize the importance of ending each shift or each training session on a positive note, to keep the dog and themselves enthusiastic.

Chapter Four

GNASHING TEETH

Fighting

One afternoon in December 1995, while I was writing this chapter on canine aggression, I heard Clio, our female leopard dog, bay twice in the backyard, her signal that something unacceptable was happening. Then I heard Marlow race from the house to investigate. Knowing Gina was outside trying to bring order to the yard, which had grown into a jungle after a particularly wet rainy season, and figuring the three of them could handle the situation, I continued working.

A moment later Gina screamed, "Get out of here! Get out!" Clio bawled, a vocalization she reserves for major prey. Nothing from Marlow, which meant he was in action. But why? Fearing someone had come into the yard, which is surrounded by a six-foot-tall wood fence, I bounded downstairs and out the door. Across the pool, I saw Marlow lunge for a squat white animal that was forcing its way through the fence, springing six-inch-wide boards from their cross-pieces. Gina was beating on it with a stick, to no avail. I grabbed the garden hose, turned it on full, ran around the pool, and opened up the nozzle on both dogs.

Marlow backed off, the way almost any dog will. The squat white dog launched itself at his throat. I turned the jet of water full into its face, but it kept going for Marlow, its beady black eyes focused on nothing. Frustrated, I lashed the dog across its back with the hose, as hard as I could—and I am six-foot-one and fit from more than twenty years of daily exercise. Oblivious to the blows, the dog bored forward as Marlow retreated.

Angling around them as they neared the pool, I sought a way to grab Marlow and the white dog by the scruff of the neck simultaneously, a technique I have used to separate fairly sizable dogs in the past. But because of the aberrant behavior of the beast attacking Marlow, I did not want to miss, assuming it would come at me instead. I thought of pushing them in the pool. Bent next to Marlow, I could see his clear blue eyes bulging with effort, as if they would burst from his head. The white dog snapped for his cheek. Marlow avoided its teeth and using his superior height and strength—their weight was nearly equal— savaged the dog, even as it continued to grab at his face and throat.

It was a horrific fight of the sort I had just watched on a videotape of a battle between pit bulls. I had been thinking of making contacts in the violent subculture of the pits, although I find it abhorrent and did not want to seem to be celebrating it. Now I had a dogfight in my backyard, as violent if far less organized than any I would find in an abandoned warehouse in the far reaches of Dade County—fighting being popular in portions of Miami's Anglo, Hispanic, and African-American communities.

Marlow, behaving like a rank and raily Catahoula, slashed with his canines and dodged with his head, looking for leverage to take down an animal already low to the ground. Despite the beating it was taking, the white dog continued to attack. After breaking loose, Marlow reared, leaving his chest open to a raking slash, then he closed on the dog's skull.

While I was angling to shove them into the pool, the neighbor came through the hole in the fence and grabbed his dog by its hind legs. As soon as he dragged it free, the fight stopped. It had lasted nearly five minutes. I held Marlow, saliva and blood hanging in a long unbroken string from his mouth, his chest covered with dirt and more saliva and blood. My heart raced. I was wired for battle, as was Gina. Marlow was on alert, ready to engage again if needed. He had about him what can only be described as a deadly calm.

The neighbor said, "They were just defending their territory."

I said, "Breaking through a fence is not territorial defense. Your dog has been racing up and down, barking insanely, battering its head against that fence for a month, and you have done nothing."

"He'll never do it again, I assure you," he said. "The good thing is that if it had been a fight to the death, your dog would have won."

"There is nothing good about a dogfight," I said. At that point I held little rancor against the man, whom I had met only once, but if I had owned a pistol, I would without hesitation have put it to his dog's head when he was attacking Marlow and pulled the trigger. I have seen many dogfights in my life. I recall a neighbor's boxer who, when I was a kid, came through a screen door to attack our Dalmatian. I broke up fights between two one-hundred-pound dogs. I saw my fifty-five-pound German shorthaired pointer pin a Doberman twice his size, who had attacked him while its owner stood by approvingly, and watched in horror as two eighty-pound females tore at each other through Gina's legs in a friend's kitchen. Her legs were slashed; the dogs were uninjured. I have always believed myself unwilling to condemn any dog to death for being mean, but the animal that came through our fence was different. It did not behave in normal fashion.

Our neighbor hauled his dog away, and I washed off Marlow, then cleaned and treated four puncture wounds on his neck and right ear, as well as a couple of shallow, ragged gashes on his chest. He had, it turned out, nearly killed the neighbor's dog, a bull terrier, an animal bred for the fighting pits of the nineteenth century and then, according to the official propaganda of the breed club, the American Kennel Club, and the Kennel Club of England, tempered down through "careful" breeding so that today it really is the doll-like animal known as Spuds MacKenzie on the Budweiser beer commercials, pawed at by scantily clad female models, not the old fighting dog that General George Patton hauled on his charge across Europe in World War II. Patton knew better than the breed clubs.

As Gina and I reconstructed the event, we realized that the dog had been coming through the fence to get her. She was working right where he sprung the boards. He could have detected only motion and scent because the boards are spaced in such a way that one cannot clearly see between them. Clio was in another part of the yard, and Marlow was in the house. Clio had responded to the first breech in the fence with her warning call, and Marlow had answered, as he had for more than eight years.

I do not tolerate fighting in my dogs, and Marlow is not a fighter, although he is a fit and muscular sixty-five-pound male. I do, however, have a rule that if the dogs are attacked, they have the right to defend themselves. Nothing else would be fair, and in his life Marlow has done that four times. Clio leaves the fighting to him.

The first time Marlow fought a dog, he was less than a year old and put in its place a nasty hundred-pound malamute my father owned. The dog jumped Clio, and Marlow, weighing at the time maybe fifty pounds, came to her defense before I came to his. Malamutes have a reputation for aggression toward other dogs, so we might assume that my father amplified what already existed in this dog through his sometimes rough treatment of him. Not only did that dog hate other dogs, it also was churlish around children. As Konrad Lorenz observed in *Man Meets Dog* (1964), canines often take on the demeanor and habit of their owners.

The second time, Marlow was six and turned away a ninety-pound golden retriever who attacked him and Clio while they walked with me on the beach. The dog had ridden up to us on an all-terrain vehicle belonging to its owner, who had let it leap down and then driven off, as if wanting to watch what would happen. The dog attacked, but Marlow, treating it as if it were a bull, spun it around and sent it back to its indignant owner without bloodshed. I told the man never to let that dog near us again, and he has obliged. Still, whenever Marlow hears an ATV approaching, he turns to confront it so that he will not be surprised as he was that morning.

The third time this type of incident occurred, Gina and I were walking Clio and Marlow on leashes through the neighborhood when someone let a large Labrador out of his house and allowed him to charge up behind us. Gina was ahead of me with Clio. The Lab tried to race past us to get to them, but Marlow slipped his collar—our dogs do not wear choke collars except when going to the veterinarian—and again turned the dog completely around with his chest, deep growl, and a warning snap. He was seven. There was no blood drawn.

The fourth time was the bloodiest, and we hope the last. But what it showed was the way in which Marlow will defend his territory and his family—his pack, if you will—with fearlessness and tenacity. Actually, like most mature dogs, Marlow is forced to occupy a border zone between being the dominant or alpha male and the subdominant one. He follows my commands, Gina's, and generally those of my parents, nephew and occasional house sitters. But he has mated, fought to defend his property and pack, and when not directed, operates on his own—all behaviors usually reserved for the alpha male. In dog matters, he is usually right. Not all animals are, and even he must be watched closely to make sure he does not decide incorrectly. From the time he was a puppy, he has hated the sound of skateboards and rollerblades. He growls and prepares to charge them as if they were bulls or bears to be brought under control—clearly not an acceptable action. He also has on occasion manifested a strong inclination to sneak off after feral females in heat. As I have learned from bitter experience, letting a dog wander from home is a sure way to get it killed.

Having been jumped on several occasions while a puppy by larger dogs, Clio goes out of her way to avoid potentially violent encounters. When this bull terrier started through her fence, however, she reacted with a cry of warning and for help. Similarly, Marlow has never attacked another dog, preferring to check the dog out and then go about his business. But if he or his pack is threatened, he becomes fury; he will back down from no animal and no one. Without regard for his safety, Marlow saved Gina from what could have been a serious mauling, as just two years earlier he and Clio had prevented a man from breaking into the house.

I talked to the bull terrier's owner two days after the attack, and before I could even voice my opinion he said that he was giving the dog away as soon as it healed and that the new owners would know its history. "But first, he has to heal," he said. Half the dog's face was swollen to twice its normal size. On its head were several deep lacerations. Its neck bore numerous bites. "This dog was nearly unconscious when I brought him back here, but, you know, if your dog had killed him, that would have been all right. I won't have a vicious dog. I spent all that night thinking, 'What would have happened if he had gotten into the adjoining yard, where those children play?' "

"What would have happened," I said, "if the dogs hadn't been in our yard?" I decided that for all his seeming insight, he did not understand his dog, and so I was at least intellectually prepared for what followed.

After we talked, he invited me to see the house he was restoring, and I agreed. As I walked into the living room, he said, "See, Willie's just as gentle as can be."

Willie allowed me one step before he quietly circled from behind me, smelled the toes on my left foot—one of the benefits of life on Miami Beach is that you can wear sandals year-round—moved to the right foot and then up my leg. I froze as soon as he started sniffing and then said, "Actually, given that he's smelling the dog that just mauled him, I don't feel very comfortable about this."

My neighbor locked Willie in a room. "He's not been the same since he fought with a man who broke into the house. The guy kicked him in the ear, and it's still not healed."

Willie was around two years old, an age when many males begin to try to assert dominance in their pack. A young wolf ultimately moves off—often around that age—to find a mate and start his own pack. The dog has scant option and so tries, if so inclined, to claim top ranking for himself. It is a time for the owner to maintain the upper hand, not through force but through firm handling and training aimed at turning that drive into something positive. Ignored or dealt with ineffectually—either with too little or too much force—the assertiveness can turn into a major problem that gets someone, most commonly the owner or a family member, bitten or maimed.

In Willie's case, the battle with the intruder, during which he was behaving in quite a respectable manner, could well have traumatized him, making him more defensive of his territory, more aggressive with strangers—dog and human. His incessant barking and battering at the fence indicated heightened fear and aggression, which his owner failed to address. When he sprung the boards, he responded in the nature of his breed, attacking and fighting like a pit dog. He might have been a nice dog before the trauma combined with a poorly handled, age-related rise in aggressiveness to make him something else.

On the other hand, he could be suffering from what animal behaviorist Nicholas Dodman of the Tufts University School of Veterinary Medicine has dubbed "seizure-induced compulsive behavior," a genetic disorder common to bull terriers. Dodman describes the condition in his 1996 book, *The Dog Who Loved Too Much*, as involving obsessive-compulsive tail chasing and other behaviors, apparently brought on by epileptic-type seizures associated with an inability to process zinc and perhaps copper. Hydrocephalus (fluid on the brain), kidney failure, and heart disease are also common in the breed and associated with the disorder. Certainly, Willie's pounding into the fence was obsessive behavior. An expensive, detailed medical examination, including CT scans and EEGs, might reveal the nature of Willie's problem.

The dog's problems might also be human rather than behavioral or biochemical. Many owners deliberately make their dogs mean or fail to teach them civility through ignorance and indifference. They also refuse to rid themselves of vicious dogs because they are emotionally attached to the animal and psychologically deny that it is really that bad. My neighbor seems to possess elements of each of these states. He has manifested interest in Willie's physical prowess, failed to give Willie away despite evidence that he is violently unstable, and taken to chastising him erratically when they are outside together and the dog starts barking—either pleading with him to stop or physically punishing him. On another occasion since the attack, Willie attempted to come through the fence, leading me to tell his owner that a repeat would leave me no choice but to report both to the authorities. (On the opposite end of the spectrum are those owners who dispose of a dog for the slightest infraction or threat, especially if they perceive that it is directed against them.)

The incident raises numerous questions about Willie, the demonic bull terrier, the breed and type to which he belongs, and vicious, dangerous dogs in general. Beyond that, it points to the difficulty faced in trying to decipher what in dog behavior is instinctual, what upbringing, what the result of trauma or training for the fight, and finally what is the result of genetic defects. What makes the question so pertinent is that more and more people are buying big dogs for protection and so demanding fierce, assertive animals.

USA Today reported in 1993 and again in 1995 that 38 percent of American households with dogs owned them because of their fear of crime, with the number steadily rising. That concern has translated into an explosion in sales of rottweilers, German shepherds, Malinois, pit bulls, Dobermans, mastiffs of various sorts, chow chows, and exotic breeds like the fila brasileiro and Argentine dogo, not to mention crosses like the wolfdog.

Coincident with the increase has come a proliferation of the sort of stories that led to condemnation of the pit bull in the 1980s: accounts of savage dogs or wolfdogs maiming innocent people. The human mind being given to prejudicial thought, the breeds of the miscreants have been blamed, with condemnation of all large dogs being the next step. One half expects the return of expeditation, along with mandatory defanging and neutering.

There is a problem, to be sure. Experts estimate that more than 3 million dog bites occur each year in the United States; of these, 585,000 require medical attention. Fatalities average twenty a year, an insignificant number compared with those deaths arising from gunshots—making dogs far better *and* safer protection—or automobile accidents, but bites are very frightening to people because the dog in these cases appears to betray our trust and reveal itself as a sneaky wild animal that will turn on the very people who care for it. Disproportionate to their numbers, pit bulls, German shepherds, Siberian huskies and malamutes, rottweilers, Dobermans, wolfdogs, and chow chows (including mixed breeds) account for bites requiring treatment, maimings, and fatalities. Often left out of those statistics is the hard truth that in 80 percent of those cases the dog launching the attack belongs to the victim or a neighbor: it is known to the person it mauls. Also, most of those killed are young children and elderly people who are going about their business and relatively unable physically to defend themselves.

Those are the facts. The truth lies somewhere else. Almost all large dogs, and many medium ones, serve by their mere presence as a deterrent to crime. Fearing attack, many people treat them with caution. There is good reason: in their house, yard, or car, they will probably stand on alert, bark, growl, or act with some degree of territorial aggression toward a perceived threat. Many of them will not, however, know how to separate friend from foe.

Exceptionally intelligent and mature dogs can make those distinctions, but they are not foolproof. Suppose, for example, that the dog has learned to run off anyone attempting to enter through the window and then one day a friend of yours decides to climb through an open ground-floor window to surprise you and runs right into the slashing teeth of your pet doing its job. Suppose that the dog is chained and a child runs too close. Suppose the dog is standing next to its owner and a person dashes by. Suppose someone jogs up from behind and the dog turns in surprise and fear.

Those hypothetical cases become more problematic when people own dogs bred for heightened aggression. They assume that if they purchase a dog who looks fierce and has a reputation for meanness, then train it to be fierce and mean, they will have a greater likelihood of being secure. Unfortunately, they usually end up not with a Schutzhund champion, trained daily, but with a randomly vicious, uncontrollable dog for which they paid a great deal of money.

Many poorly trained protection dogs add their owners' terror to their innate "fear aggression," as experts call it, so that they become unreliable biters who attempt to attack and run away simultaneously. Next door to Willie, for example, is a Doberman—the breed is notorious for its fear biters—whose chief occupation is barking in the backyard. Kept out of the house, undisciplined, and basically uncared for, the dog would be useless against intruders.

A trainer for a local police department told me one day about a family who wanted an attack-trained Doberman to protect their children, so a kennel owner sold one to them for $18,000. A year later, the dog had forgotten everything it had learned because the people had never practiced with it—and probably because it was poorly trained to begin with. The $18,000 dog was merely fearful and territorially aggressive and dangerous to the children it was supposed to protect. Miami is not unique in having a large number of broker–kennel owners who will sell "trained" guard dogs for exorbitant prices, but the buyer must approach them with caution. A few are honest and expert;

more than a few are in business for a quick profit. They can exert control over a dog without properly training it.

That said, it is also true that dog owners must educate themselves, their own family members, and guests about how to behave around a dog. Some rules are simple: never put your hand in the window of a car to pet a dog, no matter how cute or small; never stick your face in the face of strange dog or an upset dog or a shy dog, unless you want a new face; never bend over a strange dog to pet it because in doing so you are dominating it in an unfriendly fashion; never leave dogs and children who are not fast friends unattended, but by the same token do not through your actions set up a situation where the pampered pet feels it is vying with the child or another person for your affection. A child launching itself on the head of a sleeping dog is a child who might get maimed.

I heard a story about one of the world's highest-paid models, who, after completing a shoot with a poodle, took the dog's muzzle in her hand and blew into its nose. Taken by surprise, the dog's handler—all animals in films and modeling sessions have handlers—thought, "Oh, my God, what is she doing!" Telling the story, the handler said, "I could just see that dog tearing her face off." Nothing of the sort happened, but it can, even with nice dogs.

Around our house, there is another rule: never feed the dogs scraps at the table. I had not realized how firmly we had drilled that home until one night during a dinner party when a new guest reached down to give a morsel to one of the dogs and four other guests in unison said, "Don't feed the dogs at the table." Doing so creates beggars. It also sets up a potential for a dogfight as the animals compete for food at close quarters. (Our dogs are trained to allow Gina or me to take food from their mouths.)

A good animal behaviorist and trainer can help break dogs and people of bad habits that lead to biting. Unfortunately, their numbers are small. The field has only recently begun to receive attention at most veterinary schools, and many of the "experts" who pass out their cards at dog shows are trainers with too little knowledge or skill to help. The problem dogs end up abandoned or killed.

By the same token, it is essential for dog owners to work at educating people. We took our eight-year-old niece, Nichole, to a Frisbee-dog competition in Orlando in the spring of 1995. Like many children, she is fascinated by dogs, and she wanted to watch the array of high fliers competing in that event. I walked with her, explaining that she had first to ask the owner whether it was all right to pet his or her dog and, receiving permission, had to approach the dog slowly— no sudden movements for its head. "Hold out your hand," I said, "and let it come to you."

Nichole followed instructions and talked immediately to Lourdes Edlin's border collie, Cisco, and her Australian shepherd puppy, Skylar, who at eight weeks thought he was the foremost dog in the world. She met Sandy Seward's little terrier, Chancey, and then two Great Danes big enough to lick her face while they were lying down. Then we approached a couple in their thirties with a malamute. Nichole had bad dealings with her grandfather's dog and was curious to see whether every representative of the breed was that way.

"Is this a malamute?" she asked, trying to be polite.

"Of course," the owner snorted. "He's a champion; in fact, we're thinking of starting a line from him to compete in the Iditarod."

"Can I pet him?"

"We don't touch strange dogs," the gentlewoman replied.

Nichole was crestfallen. Too angry to speak to them, I took her to see another dog, explaining that she had done everything right but the owners, rather than admit they had an unpredictable or mean dog, wanted to put the problem off on her. I also told her that neither the dog nor its owners would be able to tell a sled from a go-cart.

After Marlow's fight with Willie, I checked the Dade County ordinance outlawing pit bulls and any dog resembling them, which was passed in 1989 in response to public outcry over attacks on people, especially children. Challenged in federal court, the ordinance was ruled constitutional, and in subsequent years more communities and Great Britain joined suit in banning dangerous breeds.

A number of experts argued at the time that such ordinances failed to address the true problem of vicious dogs, observing, among other things, that the top biter in absolute terms was the German shepherd.

Although the first ordinances were passed against pit bulls, they soon included German shepherds—except those owned by the police—rottweilers, Doberman pinschers, Akitas, chow chows, the Japanese tosa, and a number of other breeds deemed vicious, as well as wolfdogs and mixed breeds. Insurers began requiring extra premiums from people owning the American Staffordshire terrier and its kin, boxer, bull terrier, chow chow, Doberman pinscher, German shepherd, Great Dane, rottweiler, and Siberian husky.

Despite the concerns of insurance companies, in Dade County and elsewhere, bull terriers escaped banning largely because they were dogs of the rich and famous while the pit bull belonged to the poor and minorities. The American Kennel Club describes the bull terrier as having been "bred by gentlemen for gentlemen" who enjoyed the sport of dogfighting in a rougher time. Elaborating on the theme, the attorney for the county proclaimed in Federal District Court that the bull terrier, the "Spuds MacKenzie dog," was a "lapdog, as gentle as can be."

In fact, it is nearly impossible to get the Animal Control Department to cite the owner of a vicious dog who is not a pit bull. When I finally called about Willie's attack, I was told that the owner could be cited only if a witness other than a member of my family could corroborate the event. As it turned out, another neighbor's maid had seen the ruckus from a window, but she reported that I was attacked by the dog. Until Willie attacks and maims, virtually nothing can be done to force his owner to give him up or restrain him.

Fighting pit bulls are bred for a compact size, extreme aggression, direct attack without warning, powerful jaws, a high tolerance for pain, and nonresponsiveness to the usual signals of surrender—a yelp or whimper, a loosening of engagement. Manifesting a quality called "gameness," they press forward for the kill unless pried away, often by a handler with a "parting stick." They often are trained to sudden violence and killing with either cats or dogs, many of them stolen. They are also run on treadmills to increase their stamina.

The recognized breeds of pit bulls are the American Staffordshire terrier, the Staffordshire bull terrier, and the bull terrier, all registered by the American Kennel Club; and the American pit bull terrier of the

United Kennel Club, a private registry. All were bred and used as fighting dogs in the nineteenth century—in fact, the American Staffordshire terrier and American pit bull terrier are the same dog— and continue to do battle today, although the "sport" was declared illegal in England in 1835 and the early part of this century throughout most of the United States. But as recently as 1940, the United Kennel Club was printing its "pit rules" of engagement, and it is still possible to find them included in pamphlets like *Combat Rules*, the edition I have a copy of dating to June 1975 and published by Sharon and Raymond Holt. Arizona made dogfighting a felony only in 1977. Lax enforcement and weak laws in other states help the activity flourish.

The dogs derive their name from the pit in which they fight. By the rules of the United Kennel Club, which no longer sanctions fights, it was to "14 feet or 16 feet square with sides of $2 \frac{1}{2}$ feet or 3 feet high, with a tight wood floor." A "scratch line," behind which the dogs were held, was drawn seven feet out from opposing corners.

The rules of engagement concern themselves with washing the dogs, guarding against cheating, and the etiquette of the "turn" and "scratch." Arcane and stilted in their presentation, these rules exist to put a sheen of respectability and fair play on a brutal combat. Before each fight the dogs are washed to ensure that poisons have not been placed on their coats. They are handled according to prescribed ritual, then released into battle. After one dog turns its head and shoulders away from its opponent, they are separated and taken to their corners. Many dogs "turn" to protect their faces when fighting but in doing so expose their necks, and so this movement is considered not only bad form but also a sign of "softness." In the fight I witnessed between Marlow and Willie, neither dog turned.

Following the break, the dog who "turned" must "scratch," meaning that after being turned loose by its handler, it must cross its scratch line and move directly across the other scratch line to engage its opponent. Should it fail to start, stop along the way, or refuse to engage the other dog, it has lost. After the first "turn," the dogs alternate subsequent scratches—the way basketball teams alternate jump balls. If they fight until one can no longer continue because of injury or death, without either turning, no more scratches are required. For the dogs, only victory matters. Dogs who refuse to engage or quit before death or physical separation are killed. Those who lose the fight die, at the hands of either the other dog or their "owner."

Because it is illegal and generally held reprehensible in contemporary American society, the world of organized dogfighting represents a violent, secretive, outlaw subculture, frequently tied to the manufacture of methamphetamines, the trade in drugs and guns. In Cuba and other nations, however, it continues to enjoy a wide and active following. For centuries in this country and Europe, battles between dogs were as acceptable as those between humans; dogs and humans; humans, dogs, and other animals. Where they persist, boxing, bull-fighting, dog and cock fighting are reminders of a more violent time.

While the various Staffordshire terriers and pit bulls have been singled out for banning, a few honest dog books admit that the bull terrier cannot be kept with other dogs because of a strong tendency toward aggression. And some localities have banned it along with its cousins. In truth, without early and steady socialization, the bull terrier can be as dangerous as its cousins. That is hardly the description of a lapdog. The AKC's own publications observe that the bull terrier, American Staffordshire terrier, and Staffordshire bull terrier derive from the same early-nineteenth-century "bull and terrier," created by crossing the bull-baiting dog (bulldog) with a white English terrier. Later breeders crossed in Dalmations to create a white form.

That bull-baiting dog was a mastiff who worked without preliminaries and did not turn from its task. Terriers have long been celebrated for high pain tolerance and aggressiveness toward other animals: dogs, people, cats, vermin, whatever. Many of the smaller terriers were used through the nineteenth century as ratters. In rat pits, where competitions were held, it was not unusual for a single terrier— or whippet—to kill 2,500 or more rats during the course of a day. Virtually all of the terriers were initially bred and trained to engage immediately and directly, which makes them often inappropriate as pets despite their now dandified appearance. Thus, the bull and terrier, by whatever name, was created to combine strength and fearlessness with brutal aggressiveness, tenacity, and agility.

Before the bull terrier invaded our yard, I argued that the vicious dog ordinances were misbegotten because they did not address problem dogs. They merely engaged in the sort of breedism—racism applied to dogs—that obscured the larger problem of dogs who attack people. I still believe that, but now I also think that some types of dogs may be more inclined to attack a person or another animal without provocation or warning. They suffer from some form of extreme aggression, be it dominance or territorial or fear or predatory—all categories applied by behaviorists in an attempt to describe certain classes of behavior.

Not a fan of government regulation, I nonetheless think that vicious-dog ordinances must be strengthened and firmly applied, so that problem animals are retrained or removed from society. Those ordinances must be directed at the behavior of individual dogs, not at specific breeds. It is possible, for example, to require that anyone with a dog who bites in other than a clearly accidental way be required to attend sessions with a certified animal behaviorist and trainer, then demonstrate competence in controlling the animal. Dogs adjudged a threat to human safety should be destroyed. By the same token, people who train their dogs to be mean should be prosecuted. To avoid such measures, people owning aggressive dogs must take the responsibility to train their animals properly and thoroughly, so that they can control them.

Whether some breeds are inherently vicious and untrustworthy is unknown. Kennel club officials and dog owners who deny that pit bulls are natural fighters, for example, are caught in a web of their own devise because they actively promote the notion that through breeding the character of a dog can be known. Thus, their dog shows are organized around the notion that a judge looking at a dog for several minutes can determine its temperament and how well it is capable of performing the function for which it was created in the first place. By that rule, the judge is required to determine how good a fighter the bull terrier standing before him or her would have been, while joining its owner in asserting that over the past century—roughly fifty canine generations—it has been turned into a gentle house pet, not even in need of constant socialization, the exception to that claim being dogs who are "unregistered."

Media hysteria over pit bull attacks in the 1980s—the assaults were real, but the focus on one type of dog was misdirected—spawned a fair amount of research into the genetic basis of canine behavior and repeated attempts to identify the "vicious gene" that set them apart from other breeds. No gene was found; in fact, researchers observed more genetic variation between individual dogs than between breeds of dogs or even between dogs and wolves. But the few studies of the inheritability of behavior that exist suggest that it is complex and rather conservative, meaning that it can be altered in degree but not kind through deliberate or sloppy breeding. The question then becomes how strong and unique those predilections were in the first place.

The bull terrier who came into our yard, for example, behaved in typical fighting-dog fashion. Once it set its mind to attack, it stopped at nothing. It recognized no pain. It would literally have fought until it or Marlow died. Stories of attacks by pit bulls carry the same message. Diane Dehay, the trainer for the Miami Police Department, told me that when her police dog was still green, they were attacked by a pit bull. Initially the dog fled, but when he saw his handler coming under attack, he reversed course and came to her defense. She had been bitten on the thigh. The pit bull was shot and killed. The dog guaranteed that he would continue working with a fine officer rather than be farmed out to a rent-a-guard dog operation, the customary fate of dogs who fail to make it into a canine corps.

Pit bulls are the epitome of "gameness," and, despite attempts to gentle their instinct through breeding, they retain the capacity to attack. Moreover, some lines of dogs are still bred to fight and probably have enhanced "gameness," as opposed to the reduced "gameness" of the show and pet lines, meaning simply that people have not selected for overaggressiveness, not that they have successfully changed the nature of the beast. Those are points on a continuum, not qualitative differences. Thus, a pet pit bull can be turned into a fighter through the efforts of its owner or poor handling or trauma, while a fighting pit bull can be a calm pet—if you start young and are good at handling dogs. All are best kept out of contact with other dogs, however, the way some recovering addicts must be isolated from the product to which they were addicted.

Although some biologists have suggested that the absence or shortage of certain neurotransmitters, like dopamine, in the brains of pit bulls or similarly aggressive dogs might account for their imperviousness to pain, which is a major factor in their ability to continue attacks, that is speculative. Not enough is known about canine behavior, genetics, or development to make such statements more than tantalizing hypotheses.

All we know now is that no "vicious" gene has been found for the pit bull and probably none will be, behavior being much more complex than that. But it is equally true that people will continue to look for a genetic cause for the behavior, building on a recent claim that a line of research mice created through rigorous inbreeding were hyperaggressive. This claim strikes a chord in people who wish everything to be predetermined by inheritance alone. It is a type of faith.

Explaining the behavior of other apparently hyperaggressive dogs is much more difficult and provisional than addressing that of pit bulls, an indication that it is literally a complex dance between the individual animal's breeding and upbringing, including its early socialization, training, and daily handling. The sole exception to that observation appears to be the chow chow, who rates off every chart in terms of its desire to dominate its owner, protectiveness toward property, aggression toward children, and untrainability. It doubtless has endured for so long because it was regularly eaten in its native China and, therefore, not expected to be a pet.

There are plenty of hyperaggressive dogs, of all sizes, and so when the breed-specific ordinances began to take effect, many people abandoned or killed their pit bulls—abandonment usually meant that animal shelters did the killing since the dogs were deemed unfit for human or animal society—and turned to rottweilers, who had a reputation for fierceness and a devilish demeanor. An enduring image from the aftermath of the bombing of the federal office building in Oklahoma City in the spring of 1995 is of a rottweiler named Brutus wearing a collar of gun cartridges at a militia meeting.

Rottweilers who attack apparently behave in much the same fashion as pit bulls, and due to overbreeding, they are equally unreliable. I once pulled a rottweiler from the canal near our house, which is lined with sea walls that prevented the dog from climbing out itself, but when I went to lift it from a narrow ledge to dry ground, it snarled at me, prepared for attack. I called the Fire Department—Dade County's Animal Control Office was not open, and in any event it does not respond in timely fashion to emergencies. Firefighters arrived within minutes from a firehouse across the street and muzzled the dog before lifting it, shitting and growling out of fear, to safety. The dog apparently had taken a dive off its owner's dock while pursuing a balloon with intent to maim. It was two years old and already obese.

But the allure of the rottweiler among the cognoscenti has already faded despite its large numbers of registrations. Reports of fatal maulings of young children and subsequent legal bans have made it too high profile for people seeking a guard. Randall Lockwood, an animal behaviorist with the Humane Society of the United States who tracks dog attacks on humans, observes that during the past twenty years the fierce dog of choice has gone from the German shepherd to the Doberman pinscher to the pit bull in all its incarnations to the rottweiler and now the wolfdog.

I occasionally have visions of the more vicious among the macho crowd racing out to replace their wolfdogs and rottweilers with leopard dogs, thinking they have found the ultimate in studly guards—these animals are almost exclusively male. That would be a grave mistake. Leopard dogs, like other curs, are basic dogs, often lupine in their demeanor and outlook. They can do Schutzhund and obedience work, but they do not do it happily. Harsh handling and compulsory training ruin them, perhaps because, although fearless and aggressive in pursuit of prey, they are sensitive to abusive treatment. It will send them into hiding or cause them to quit, even though, treated fairly, they are intelligent, diligent workers. Upon meeting Marlow for the first time, our two-year-old nephew, Daniel, walked up to him, took his face in his hands, stuck his mouth up against his, and growled. It was a frightening moment, but Marlow, who was not raised with children, did nothing but growl back in the low gurgling roar he uses when working and lick Daniel's nose.

Due to bad breeding, a number of spaniels and even some golden retrievers, who are traditionally bred to live peaceably with people and other dogs, have shown up with sudden rage syndrome. Without provocation, they attack their owners or any other person within reach, biting them multiple times before returning to their "normal" state. This condition appears to be inherited and basically incurable— some experts speculate that the dogs suffer mild epileptic seizures— leaving people little choice but to put the afflicted dog down unless they wish to risk their own life and limb. A number of these and other breeds also suffer from dominance aggression, apparently arising from poor early socialization.

In the case of springer spaniels, the appearance of sudden rage syndrome was traced to a winner at the Westminster Kennel Club Show who became a top stud by virtue of his victory. That is probably the case with other breeds as well. Selective breeding should free the line of the problem. In fact, field lines of the springers do not manifest the behavior. Socialization and training, of course, are the responsibility of owners.

Rottweilers, Dobermans, German shepherds, and other working protection dogs have been bred for generations to be aggressive, strong, active animals, able to perform demanding tasks including attacking people. But defining the underlying basis of that behavior is difficult. Folk wisdom says that these are dominant, alpha dogs, equivalent to the alpha wolf in a pack. That is off the mark. Certainly the males— and males are more likely to display dominance aggression against people and other animals than females—are strong, active dogs who often need a firm hand to guide them. But the person behind that hand must learn whether his or her dog is also fearful of new experiences, places, or sounds; sociable; possessed of strong hunting instinct; biddable.

Too often, owners seek to assert their total dominance over their dogs, forcing them to submit to their will, to follow their commands immediately. They have been taught to do that by their parents and any number of training manuals, including those by Barbara Woodhouse, the British expert who enjoyed enormous popularity in the 1970s and 1980s in print and on television. Woodhouse believed in total domination of the dog, without realizing herself that such an approach created dogs who believed the way to get on with people and other animals was to dominate them. Adding abuse to that creates a recipe for disaster. Dogs treated harshly may well become aggressive either out of fear or anger or an admixture of both. Dogs taught to fight by owners eager for a rough-and-tumble wrestling companion often do not know when to stop.

At an obedience class, I watched a middle-aged man with an attitude problem become increasingly shrill with a Doberman nearly as big and far more handsome than he because the dog was responding slowly or not at all to his commands. Clearly, the behavior was not new, nor was its cause a mystery. The more angry and violent the man became, the more recalcitrant the dog grew until finally the instructor wisely told him that if he did not tone down his correction and voice, he would end up with a vicious dog. A week later, he was back, worse than before, and the instructor invited him to leave. There are some cases when the man deserves to be bitten by the dog.

Malcolm Willis, an animal behaviorist at the University of Newcastle-upon-Tyne, suggests in an essay in *The Domestic Dog* (1995) that the media frenzy over the rottweiler as the heir of the pit bull among the vicious dog crowd has at its base a belief that the breed is dominated by alpha males. His own research, on the other hand, shows "few alpha-type dogs, but a great many owners who [do] not understand their animals and, in some cases, could not even play with them." He further theorizes that problems could arise within specific lines descended from a dog or dogs with behavioral problems, as in the case of sudden rage syndrome.

Like Willie, many male dogs have a tendency to attempt to assert dominance over other dogs and their owners when they are between one and three years of age. If training alone fails to correct the behavior—and this is the time when full training should begin—neutering will often bring it under control. Not coincidentally, this behavior manifests itself at a time when the dog is beginning to reach its full physical and mental maturity. People remembering how difficult their teens and even early twenties were should expect no more of their dogs.

Other aggressive behavior includes protection of territory or possessions and fighting with other dogs, especially of the same sex. Dogs bred for guarding or protection work usually show a high level of territorial protection, especially when chained, leashed, or kept in a confined space, although their sense of territory often extends to their people as well. As I have noted, many of them are aggressive out of fear. Overaggression in defense of territory or owner must also be treated firmly so it does not get out of hand, although many people encourage the behavior, a recipe for disaster that is then blamed on breeding.

The evidence on aggression is confusing, as it so often is with dogs and people, in part because few people will even agree on how to define the behavior. Invariably they are describing symptoms rather than identifying causes. All one can say, given the current state of knowledge, is that the pit bulls in all their variety are perhaps unique among dogs in their overall level of aggression, their reduced sensitivity to pain, and their inability to recognize the normal signs of surrender, whereas many other dogs accused of viciousness are victims of sloppy breeding and either poor or deliberately cruel training. As is so often the case, the link between genetics and behavior is complicated. Certainly, there is a predisposition toward certain responses, which socialization and training can temper and shape, even among the fighting dogs. Some dogs are vicious by birthright, but the majority are made that way by human action and inaction.

The Dance

His admirers claim that Phil Hoelcher can train anything that walks on four legs, but he is especially expert at the most rigorous of all obedience and protection competitions, Schutzhund ("protection dog"), a stylized version of police-dog work. After the novice or beginners class, which tests the dog's attentiveness to its handler and ability to ignore distractions, there are three levels of achievement, the first being Schutzhund I and the highest, III, which is roughly equivalent to a black belt in karate. Schutzhund requires of a dog and trainer absolute discipline through a prescribed, increasingly rigorous routine involving tracking, obedience, and protection, or attack work. The dog must follow the path of a human who is nowhere to be seen and find lost objects; heel, come immediately and at a run when called, retrieve a dumbbell over a high hurdle, and climb up and down (no jumping) a steep inverted V with slightly raised bars for footholds; literally get in the face of an intruder and bark incessantly to warn him that he best not move; and finally catch him by the arm, which is encased in a padded sleeve, when he flees. The catch must come on command, be made with full force, and be unbreakable except on command. While waiting to perform, the dog must lie down. Movement or any show of aggression toward other dogs or people brings immediate dismissal. Schutzhund dogs are trained the way all police dogs should be but frequently are not, with the result that civilians too often get bitten.

In 1995, Hoelcher won the North American Schutzhund Championship with a ninety-seven-pound German shepherd, Doggie, returning him officially to the top of a sport he has excelled in for several decades. In addition to national titles in 1983 and 1984, he is one of the three or four people who consistently rank among the top finishers in any competition. A man who at a glance can evaluate a dog's potential and nature, be it a puppy, adolescent, or adult, he helped establish the police canine programs in Dade County, Florida, which enjoy a national reputation. When not training horses and dogs for films and television with his wife, Nancy, with whom he operates Trademark Animal Talent out of Miami, or giving seminars, he serves as chief guru for practitioners of Schutzhund.

Compactly built, his hair thinning, he intently studies the interaction of dogs and people to decipher what each is doing and what both are doing together. Like many top trainers, he is convinced of the rectitude of the methods that have served him so well, yet he is also willing to spend hours discussing dogs, their talents, and ways to utilize them. When he works a dog, he wants it to obey. It is not surprising that people speak of Hoelcher with more than a little awe even if they whisper on the side that, yes, his methods are sometimes compulsory, but he's working with the most aggressive, powerful dogs around.

One of those German shepherds, Eros, weighs in at around 130 pounds and packs so much power that he has nearly knocked over a backpedaling 200-pound man when hitting the Kevlar sleeve. Through his black mask, he stares at people with such intensity that few are willing to take Hoelcher's word that they can go up and pull his tail and ears if they desire. Trained by Hoelcher, but handled by his owner or her son, Eros has won the national Schutzhund II title and finished second in the Schutzhund III competition behind Doggie.

A Miamian who trained his first dog in 1953, at age eight, Hoelcher prefers German shepherds from German breeders. This is because it has become axiomatic that good working dogs are not to be found in the United States unless they come from imported lines, and then the cost is high, the wait from one of the few breeders producing quality dogs long. Like many modern breeds, the German shepherd has deep roots in rustic farm dogs, in this case those found in the Rhine River valley for millennia. Consolidated at the turn of the century into a breed, with standard and stud book, it became the darling of armed services and police departments around the world, as well as services training guide dogs for the blind. British veterinarian Bruce Fogle believes that the enormous popularity of the movie dog Rin Tin Tin, beginning in 1918 and continuing well beyond his death in 1932, fueled demand in the United States and abroad for the German shepherd, much the way Lassie elevated the collie in public eyes and the 1990 movie *Turner and Hooch* set off a short-lived boom for the surly French mastiff, the dogue de Bordeaux.

By the 1920s, there were already grumblings that the German

shepherd's popularity among the fancy was leading to dilution of its working abilities. But it was not until after World War II that the problem became acute, as the fancy and commercial breeders turned the majestic shepherd dog into a genetic nightmare with exaggerated down-sloping hindquarters. In the minds of judges and people in the show world, that conformation presumably makes it look as if the dog is always ready to spring into action; in practice, it guarantees that the animal cannot. American German shepherds are notorious for their high incidence of crippling hip dysplasia and temperament problems. Many are overly fearful and nervous, which can make them aggressive toward strangers and other dogs.

In much of Europe, breed clubs control breeding and attempt to guarantee that only champions at work and conformation will produce puppies. In Germany, for example, a German shepherd must have at least a Schutzhund I title before the parent club authorizes its breeding. That does not prevent unhealthy dogs from being born; in fact, Europeans are overbreeding to meet skyrocketing demand, and in many ways they are more obsessed with notions of purity and the absolute inheritability of behavior than their American counterparts. But as a rule, the dogs from Germany are more likely to have the size, strength, physical soundness, intelligence, and ability to take intensive training—the look and feel—that people have long valued in the breed but that the vast majority of American animals lack.

Despite his preference for German shepherds, Hoelcher says that any large dog—and even some medium-sized animals like pit bulls and border collies—with the proper prey drive and temperament can excel at Schutzhund. Serious training does not start until the dog is around eighteen months old, nearly mature physically and mentally able to take the pressure of obedience work. Even with those allowances, however, Hoelcher estimates that only 10 percent of males and .2 percent of females of any breed can make it to the top. A Labrador retriever finished second in the international championship in the early 1990s, setting off a ministampede toward the breed, which previously had been considered too friendly, or nonaggressive, for the work. A bouvier des Flandres took top honors in 1996, with Hoelcher fourth. On the whole, however, participants prefer the German shepherd, Doberman pinscher, rottweiler, giant schnauzer, and the Belgian Malinois, a dog who has gained a large following in recent years because of a shortage of the more traditional breeds. (Smaller in stature than the German shepherd and prone to an erratic temperament, the Malinois is actually the brown, shorthaired form of the Belgian shepherd, which includes the black groenendael, curly-coated laekenois, and longhaired Tervuren. It is wrongly considered a separate breed in this country.)

Whatever their drawbacks, these breeds are perceived as being more inherently aggressive and devoted to their owner than a hound or gundog. But the Labrador's success suggests that the perception is of limited accuracy, that its breed is less a measure for the dog's ability to do Schutzhund than, say, its desire to catch, retrieve, and hold on to its prey—its "prey drive," or predatory aggression, which the best gundogs and hounds, like the top shepherds, have in abundance.

The bias toward the big European stockdogs is also culturally determined. Although official records on dogs used specifically to keep public order date to fourteenth-century France, the modern practice began in Hildesheim, Germany, in 1887, where Great Danes were first deployed, followed soon by German shepherds. In 1899, Ghent, Belgium, established the first canine training center for police dogs. Given those origins and their lupine appearance—leading people to assume they are more aggressive and frightening than their kin—it is hardly surprising that the German and Belgium shepherds are the dogs of choice for police work. But in addition to these and other traditional breeds, police trainers use Airedales, bouvier des Flandres, beauceron, Newfoundlands, malamutes, and Dutch shepherds, as well as pit bulls, Rhodesian Ridgebacks, Akitas, crossbred shepherds, golden retrievers, mastiffs, bloodhounds (still a favorite tracker), standard poodles, Chesapeake Bay retrievers, and Caucasian sheepdogs.

Sporting competitions for protection dogs began shortly after they joined the ranks of police forces. Founded in 1903, DVG, Deutsche Verbard der Gebauchshundsportvereine, is the oldest and largest Schutzhund organization in the world, with 30,000 members in Germany and the United States. Similar competitions were established in Belgium and France about the same time. Although they are less precisely choreographed and less popular in the United States than

Schutzhund, they also measure the protection and obedience skills of their canine competitors. However, they limit the dogs they allow to compete to the traditional police canines, with a few exceptions in the United States.

Currently, along with an assistant, Karen Greer, Hoelcher is working with a ninety-pound, four-year-old Doberman from Germany who moves like fury. "When that dog started, he was all over the field," Hoelcher says. "I got him because the previous owner couldn't control him. But for this work, we want a highly aggressive animal, then we try to channel and direct that aggression and energy." In January 1996, he took his first step toward a Schutzhund title.

Actually, the former owner had nearly sent the dog into a psychotic breakdown by demanding that he show increasing aggression during his routine and consistently raising the level of punishment meted out with a shock collar during training. There are trainers who do not use these devices, a few who do so sparingly to correct only the most egregious behavior, and a larger number who use them the way a channel surfer wields a remote control—punching buttons at the slightest offense. By analogy, imagine that you begin screaming at and beating your puppy—or child—to make him behave in a way he does not understand. As he grows, he may become totally cowed and submissive, with a sneaky mean streak, or so enraged at the abuse and inured to the punishment that he will strike back at you or someone else. A bully is created, not born.

Properly trained for protection, Schutzhund dogs are not vicious, nor are they animals that will attack without warning. "You can have a high-scoring Schutzhund dog without an aggressive bone in his body," Hoelcher says. "Such a dog will not bite anybody if he's not wearing a sleeve. It's trained to prey on equipment." The key with less aggressive dogs is to build their prey drive, encouraging them to chase and grab tennis balls, something most dogs enjoy, then moving to a rag and on to a sleeve. The dogs who tend to excel, however, are those with an edge, high dominance and predatory aggression, that is directed in such a way that they attack or bite when ordered, no matter the context. Untrained, they would tend to attack according to their desire to prove themselves top dog. As noted earlier, dogs can also be aggressive because of fear, like many Dobermans and German shepherds, and although they can be trained to Schutzhund and other tasks, they are projects. The fear makes them unpredictable in strange situations and around new people.

Thus, the key to success in Schutzhund, no less than in any other activity, is to combine training with natural talent. Although the great champions benefit from both, those with lesser talent can rise to significant heights with training, while those with great innate ability and either too little or too much training can falter. The latter are frequently no better off than the dog with neither. Schutzhund is about control: the trainer's control over himself, or herself, and the dog; the dog's control over itself.

During a practice, Doggie marches through his drills with precision, heeling with his eyes fixed on Hoelcher for the slightest indication that he should do something else. On command he races across a yard to confront an "intruder," dressed for protection in a Kevlar-lined, padded suit, who is hiding behind a portable partition. Doggie positions himself directly in front of the unwelcome man and barks incessantly. When Hoelcher gives the command, he stops. Then the man runs, and Doggie is ordered to apprehend him. Launching himself from a full sprint, Doggie grabs the padded sleeve and holds it while the 200-pound man swings him up and off the ground. Then, on command he releases his grip and walks the subdued suspect back to a bench, sitting him down, and staring. It is clear watching Doggie, with his rough tan-and-black coat, why people often confuse a full-grown German shepherd with a wolf. In size and power, he resembles nothing so much as our mental image of a mature gray wolf, but it is finally only a mirage.

Hoelcher says, "I love wolves, but they are wild. They can't do this work. Sure, if you back a wolf into a corner, it will attack you and tear you apart, but I guarantee that it will be pooping and peeing at the same time from fear. The wolf is everything we've been breeding away from for 10,000 years."

Like other wild animals, wolves will not respond to compulsory training. Wolves will usually not even consent to walk on a leash without recoiling. A number of breeds of dogs, including hounds and curs, also have a tendency to look askance at a leash: it offends their sense of independence. Not surprisingly, these are the types of dogs that many human trainers consider unintelligent and primitive. Whatever their disinclinations, they are social to people, like all dogs, even when afraid.

Wolves are generally unsociable, fearful of humans, and averse to confinement or restraint, as well as compulsion. Despite that, it has become popular in recent years among people wanting fierce protectors or exotic pets to cross dogs and wolves. They boast of the results, but experts who evaluate these animals invariably say that the majority of them possess a wariness and distrust of humans that increases with age, making them difficult for all but the most expert handler to manage. In the 1970s and 1980s, two breeds of hybrids were recognized in Europe by the Federation Cynologique Internationale (FCI), the Czech wolfdog and the Saarloos wolfhound, a creation of Dutch geneticist Leendert Saarloos. Both involved crosses between wolves and German shepherds and are said to have a pronounced tendency to be timid, even fearful, around strangers and aggressive toward other animals.

In the United States, attempts are under way to establish a wolfdog breed and a so-called Amerindian breed, which can include wolf-to-dog and coyote-to-dog crosses. People involved justify the breedings on the grounds that ancient people and Native Americans mated their dogs to wolves and coyotes with some regularity and, therefore, they are simply reviving a traditional type of dog. While hybridization occurred, its frequency probably was not as extensive as these modern breeders claim once the wolf had become dog. Dogs, wolves, and coyotes tend to keep to themselves, even when living in proximity, unless their social structures are unbalanced by disease or human predation.

Traditionally, people making crosses usually bred right back into their dog lines because they found the hybrids less reliable—that is, more timid and less social—than dogs. The crosses were made to rejuvenate the dogs in a particular line or village, not to create a new kind of animal—a significant difference. Also, selection of tame wolves and hybrids was rigorous, with unsocial individuals being driven from human society or killed. Today, the captive wolves may or may not be properly evaluated and tamed. Even when selection for sociability and fearlessness occurs, it lacks rigor and derives from a smaller pool than that used in the past or in tribal societies, where the boundaries between wild and tame were less rigid and the animals used did not come from the cages of researchers. The puppies of these contemporary matings, whose future temperament cannot be accurately determined, are sold as pets.

Beyond the shaky historical justifications, the hybrids spring from the insatiable appetite among some humans for vicious animals to serve as extensions of their personalities. Often, they get more than they bargained for or can control. Rationalizing their desire, wolfdog owners argue that bulk breeding of dogs for the show ring and to match the demand of people wanting guard dogs has produced animals of poor physical and mental characteristics, making Doggie the exception rather than the rule. Hoelcher emphatically agrees with the assertions that high demand has caused the ruin of many breeds used in protection work. He says that during the past few years rottweilers have been turned into "grumps," while Malinois, which police departments across the United States buy through importers from European breeders for as much $5,500 apiece—individuals pay as much as $25,000 for "trained" rottweilers and other guard dogs—are "being bred stupid."

Difficulty in finding a solid guard dog does not translate into proof that wolfdogs are inherently more physically and mentally sound; in fact, many are not. Hybrids are not routinely tested for hip dysplasia or other inherited disorders, on the faulty assumption that they cannot have them by definition. Nor does everyone involved in the breedings test the sire and dam for sociability and temperament, with special emphasis on the wolf. Even if all the wolfdogs produced are genetically excellent, the fact remains that too often they are being reared in the close quarters of a kennel or yard without proper training or care, conditions that are trying enough for dogs.

Hounds of Hell

Guard dogs, police dogs, military dogs—these are the most numerous working dogs in the world, patrolling military bases, airports, businesses, city streets. As aggressive as Doggie, many lack the training that keeps him under control, and consequently they are barely fit for human society. Indeed, with their handlers, the dogs have compiled an unenviable record of attacking people for extralegal reasons.

In Alabama and other southern states, dogs were one of several weapons—including cattle prods, water hoses, and billy clubs—turned against civil-rights protesters. More than a few people, white and black, who protested against the war in Vietnam or drug busts on their college campuses also felt the hot breath of dog, followed by the searing pain of teeth puncturing and rending flesh. Fans attending rock 'n' roll concerts in the 1950s and early 1960s were frequently greeted by snarling, vicious dogs, agents of society's disapproval of the music of its children, which it deemed subversive. Labor union pickets and demonstrators for other causes have also encountered dogs.

Sadly, more than a few police around the country continue to turn their dogs loose on "suspects" or people being arrested for minor offenses or acting in an "insolent" fashion. Because the primary reward for police dogs is the chance to attack the "sleeve," the renegade officer often sees his action as one of positive reinforcement. The extent of this problem is unknown, but a lawsuit was filed in King County, Washington, home of Seattle, to end the practice in 1996 and anecdotal evidence suggests that it is not uncommon nationally, although most often not reported. The behavior casts doubt on all dogs and makes the job of responsible canine officers that much more difficult. It also instills in many citizens a fear of dogs that affects their entire lives.

In the Netherlands, Scotland, and several other European countries, police dogs are called to identify criminals in court, a practice dating back at least a millennium. Indeed, into the nineteenth century throughout Europe and Great Britain, dogs, cocks, and cats could testify in court to identify suspects, absent human witnesses. Today, cats and cocks are considered unreliable, but the testimony of dogs is still deemed valid and justified on scientific grounds. Although dogs have superior olfactory abilities and can make scent associations that save lives and money, there is scant evidence that they can positively identify a person who has committed a crime; indeed, it is likely that more innocent than guilty people have been punished based on such testimony.

Scandals involving the terrorization of innocent civilians have dogged police canine programs for decades, leading some communities periodically to disband them. That is unfortunate because, properly employed, they are tremendous assets. Well-trained dogs patrolling on foot are known to deter crime much more effectively than punitive jail sentences, and, as we have seen, they are excellent at detecting explosives and tracking suspects and lost souls. In prisons, anecdotal evidence suggests that the dogs are effective in preventing violence because, as Samuel Chapman points out in *Police Dogs in North America* (1990), the definitive text on the subject, it is easier for a prisoner to back down from a dog than a guard. Not only does the inmate not have to fight the dog to prove his toughness but he also knows that he would probably lose.

Despite their documented value on foot patrol, most canine units operate out of cars, which makes them good only for crisis situations and investigations, not crime prevention—their strength. In fact, it is for drug detection that many police departments are rushing to acquire and train canines. Thus, the programs, like the dogging of innocent people, are manifestations of a society at war with itself. If peace is ever declared in the "war on drugs," we might expect many of the dogs to be cashiered, as has happened in the past.

Usually the programs are abolished because they are considered to create too many administrative and morale problems. Dog handlers must be given compensatory time off for training and tending to their dogs, which causes jealousy among other officers who do not consider such activities work, and the handlers frequently form cliques within the department that create command problems. Even within the generally supportive world of detection dogs, police canine officers are often perceived as having a "macho" attitude, meaning they believe themselves and their dogs tougher and rougher than anyone else. They then use their dogs as instruments of their aggression. Even with the income from drug seizures, those negatives sometimes become too great for many departments to bear. Without the money, there is no contest.

The situation is unfortunate, to be sure. Many canine officers are dedicated men and women, like Diane Dehay, the first woman trainer for the Miami Police Department, who has brought new, less compulsory training methods to the program and worked to break down the fear—born of bitter history—that many minority men, women, and children have of police dogs. Only through those efforts will dogs retain their positive role in law enforcement.

American police departments are not the only organizations with a history of turning dogs on innocent people. Former prisoners reported from Chechnya in 1995 that their Russian captors had let dogs maul them. During the Cold War, East German security forces employed thousands of dogs to keep people from crossing the Berlin Wall; in fact, when it tumbled in 1989, a 7,000-dog canine corps, composed of massive 130-pound Caucasian sheepdogs, among others, was demobilized. Homes were found for many of them, but usually sentinel dogs cannot make the transition to civilian life and are killed when their working days end. Military kennels in the Third Reich kicked out 50,000 trained dogs, which worked on the front and behind the lines, including in the death camps. Ian McEwan's haunting *Black Dogs* (1992) documents fictionally some of the abuses perpetrated by German forces with dogs during World War II and the terror they unloosed on civilians.

And the Germans were not alone. During World War II, countries at war employed more than 200,000 dogs as messengers, as shipboard early warning systems for dive-bombers, as sentinels, rescue dogs, and bomb carriers who would die on delivery. As early as the 1930s, the Alaska Territorial Guard patrolled on dogsleds against Japanese incursions. The Soviet Union trained dogs to carry mines into tanks, where an electromagnetic trigger would detonate them, while the Japanese strapped bombs to dog-drawn carts. The Russian dogs were starved and then taught that food was to be found inside tanks. All they had to do was crawl through open hatches to scavenge. It was a clever, if cruel, system of training.

Use of dogs in modern warfare has its roots in World War I, when "scientific training methods," involving compulsory obedience exercises and rigorous discipline, were developed; thus, dog training more closely approximated boot camp than school, with the graduates commonly resembling soldiers suffering from low morale. In the Great War, dogs hauled munitions across mountains by cart and by sled, helped seek out the wounded, and served as messengers and sentinels. By the Vietnam War, dogs were trained to detect mines, human infiltrators, tunnels, and drugs, as well as for their traditional guarding roles. But they were no longer needed to draw carts or carry messages.

Fighting intruders is wolfish behavior, and so it is tempting to say that dogs fought for their human companions from the start. Certainly, they served as camp sentinels and defenders, perhaps even joined their humans on forays against another village. But because tribal conflicts are generally a pale version of what we call war, involving raids more than pitched battles, it is more likely that war dogs began to establish themselves with the formation of standing armies. As societies consolidated themselves and began keeping livestock and cultivating land, it became important to protect territory beyond their own village or homes. As land was farmed out or livestock depleted through illness or mismanagement, those people would look to neighboring villages and farmsites for replenishment. Dogs, who had already proved themselves successful in rounding up animals and defending the camp, became essential forces for battle in Europe, the Middle East, Japan, China, Mongolia, and parts of India.

To the dogs, humans were simply another form of prey. Soldiers and civilians who had never encountered vicious dogs could be routed by one. Indeed, the purpose of the dogs, who often led the charge, was to wreak havoc and strike terror into enemy ranks. Probably the Egyptians used dogs in battle 5,000 or more years ago. The ancient Greeks had guard and assault dogs. The Romans employed the molossus in their conquest of Europe and the Middle East, as a drover, livestock protector, and war dog—the selection for task being based as much on temperament and performance as on parentage. Various Celtic, Gaelic, Anglo-Saxon, and Germanic tribes fought with dogs, some of them large enough, it is said, to pull a man from his horse. Breed histories say the Irish wolfhound is a reconstruction of the ancient Celtic warrior, but more likely it is a figuring forth in flesh and bone of an imagined animal.

The Greeks, Romans, and Celts fitted their dogs with spiked collars for cutting horses' legs. At other times, they were given padded vests to protect them against arrows and spears. The Greeks tied pots of burning oil to the heads of some of their dogs so they could burn the bellies of enemy horses. In addition to weapons, the Celts trained their dogs to catch the noses of horses, a clever and effective use of the dog's natural inclination to grab and hold large game.

Dogs were so common in war and as members of traveling armies that it is probably impossible to find a group in Europe or Asia that did not use them. More significant from a canine standpoint was the mixing that occurred as those forces swept out of their homelands into other parts of the world.

The sixteenth-century Italian naturalist Ulisse Aldrovandi observed that the sheepdogs of antiquity were the same as the dogs of war except that the latter were taught to attack humans; the sheepdogs were white and war dogs black, brown, or some other combination of dark colors. Clearly, they could be littermates. Aldrovandi's description reads remarkably like the program still in use today to train police and Schutzhund dogs: a man wearing a protective suit runs away from the dog, is caught, and attacked. Citing an authority named Blondus, he writes, "The war-dog . . . should be a terrifying aspect and look as though he was just going to fight, and be an enemy to everybody except his master." The dogs were most common in Spain.

Spaniards in the fifteenth, sixteenth, and seventeenth centuries—the period of their greatest empire—so masterfully converted the dogs of war into hounds of hell in the New World that their own priests regularly filed protests. John Grier Varner and Jeannette Johnson

Varner lay out the history of the Spanish war dogs in gruesome detail in their 1983 book, *Dogs of the Conquest*. As they observe, the conquistadors employed lessons from earlier conflicts. In 1480, for example, Pedro de Vera Mendoza subdued the Canary Islanders with his monteria infernal, his abominable chase hounds. In the 1480s and 1490s, war dogs devoured children abandoned on the steps of churches and mosques during the expulsion of the Moors from Spain.

The savagery was a rehearsal for the slaughter that was to sweep across the New World, fueled by the Spanish concept of blood purity, *limpieza*, which applied to people and dogs; fanatical Catholicism; rigid morality that viewed any non-Spanish behavior as depraved, unless the nobility was engaged in it; and an obsessive quest for wealth and territory. Although no dogs sailed on Columbus's first voyage, they were on the second, and soon the whole array of Spanish war and hunting dogs—the lebrel, a chase hound; mastin, a mastiff; alano, a wolfhound; perro de ayudas, an aid dog; and perro de presa, a catch dog—were in the New World. The noblemen who maintained these dogs sought to keep their bloodlines pure in much the way they sought to preserve those of their families: by ensuring proper mating.

Sailors landing for food and water at Puerto Bueno, Jamaica, on May 5, 1494, panicked at the sight of natives they took as hostile, opened fire with crossbows, and unloosed a dog. The natives scattered, and the Spaniards quickly spread the word: terrified of the dogs, the "savages" were easy prey. The indigenous dogs, after all, were small creatures kept as scavengers and pets, fattened for the banquet table. The people had never encountered a dog who tore them apart.

Christopher Columbus used wolfhounds and mastiffs to hunt down and kill rebellious slaves on Hispaniola, but it was after his imprisonment and return to Spain—a result of disgruntlement with his incapacity to govern—that abuses worsened. Spanish dogs roamed the countryside, killing game, livestock, and Indians, who were considered worth less than the dogs. On at least one occasion a nursing infant was torn from his mother's breast and fed to hounds who ripped him apart and consumed him. Mastiffs frequently disemboweled by accident and design caciques, or chiefs, the Spaniards were ostensibly trying to cultivate. When their followers rebelled, they were tracked, killed, and eaten by dogs, who, according to tradition, were trained with cuts from their prey.

By the 1520s, dogs had become so numerous on Hispaniola that they were preying on the game and livestock, presenting a problem that more dogs, to guard the flocks, were needed to correct. Dogs were sweeping across South and Central America, helping a small number of invaders conquer and destroy the empires of the Aztec and Inca, as well as numerous smaller tribes and cultures. These societies were obliterated without mercy or remorse. Their fear of the hell hounds of Spain doubtless contributed to their defeat at the hands of an enemy with fewer troops but more powerful weapons and unparalleled disregard for life and suffering.

Juan Ponce de León, famous as the discoverer of Florida, was notorious in Puerto Rico for his use of dogs to suppress slave rebellions and terrorize the populace. His favorite war dog was Becerrillo, a medium-sized mastiff, reddish brown with black nose and eyes, who wore a padded cotton *escaupil* (body cover) in battle. His worth was deemed so great that his share of spoils amounted to one and one-half times that awarded a crossbowman. It was, in fact, common for the war dogs to receive a share of the bounty exceeding that of foot soldiers and often equal to junior officers. Of course, that booty helped fill the coffers of the owner. Becerrillo eventually ran into a flight of arrows while swimming clear of an attack, dying like his master before him.

A son of Becerrillo, named Leoncico, accompanied Balboa across the Isthmus of Panama to the Pacific, feasting along the way on Indians the conquistador wanted to punish for homosexuality and other sexual perversions, paganism, flight from slavery, rebellion, and insubordination. The Indians, of course, did not see those behaviors as mortal sins, but their mores were of no concern to the Christian soldiers.

Cortés used dogs to defeat the Aztec. Hernando de Soto took dogs on his ill-fated trip through Florida to the Mississippi, where he perished, and his command passed to Luis de Moscoso, who finally arrived in Mexico City in 1543, six years after setting out, with the remnant force and no dogs. (The stragglers are the ones believed to have influenced the leopard curs.) Pizarro and his dogs tore apart the Inca empire.

Trails of brutality, of ripped-out guts, torn and eaten flesh, criss-cross the map of conquest and settlement. Occasionally priests protested to the Crown, which issued reprimands and orders to the conquistadors, who ignored them. Abandoned dogs proliferated and marauded through the countryside. They also gradually fell into the hands of Indians, who learned to fight rather than fear them. The dogs themselves changed in the New World, the Spanish nobles unable to breed consistently according to their notion of *limpieza*, just as they themselves sometimes interbred with the natives, although often keeping the Indian women as concubines rather than wives. Hybrid vigor, of course, has long been recognized as the most positive result of this mixed breeding, but, unfortunately, the power elites through much of South America—and, to be fair, the rest of the world—have never wanted to apply that lesson to themselves and so they regularly denounce miscegenation as the way to bring degeneracy to the "people," whoever they may be.

The Spaniards were not the only conquerors willing to use dogs against the people they met and enslaved. Benjamin Franklin was among the North American colonists who agitated for hounds to run down Indians. In the mid–nineteenth century, Florida plantation owners hatched a plan to use Cuban bloodhounds, known as "nigger dogs," to pursue Seminole Indians, but it met with such public opposition in the Northeast that it was canceled. However, with much less public protest, the dogs—believed to have been a mix between mastiffs, sight hounds, and Saint Hubert bloodhounds—were unloosed on runaway slaves, a common practice throughout the South in the eighteenth and nineteenth centuries. In addition to the Cuban bloodhounds, wolfhounds, foxhounds, and mastiffs were employed in hunting down runaways and punishing disobedient slaves. One particularly gruesome torture involved placing a naked slave in a circle of leashed dogs and then allowing them enough line to tear at his flesh before they were reeled in.

Overseers of the notorious southern work camps of the late nineteenth and early twentieth centuries, where prisoners, convicted often of nothing more than vagrancy or being poor and black, served their time in virtual slavery, boasted of the foxhounds and bloodhounds they used to hunt fugitives. The camps in Florida and Alabama, where prisoners tapped the sap of pine trees for processing into turpentine and rosin, were especially notorious for the sadism with which prisoners were treated. The situation in Florida was so grotesque that in the 1920s it was called the American Siberia.

Today, bloodhounds are still brought on manhunts for escaped convicts, the most notorious case in recent years being that of James Earl Ray, the assassin of Martin Luther King, Jr., who broke out of the state penitentiary in Petros, Tennessee, in 1977. While it is ironic that dogs more commonly used to hunt down slaves and black convicts should haul in the avatar of white supremicism, it also underscores that it is people who turn dogs to particular ends of good and evil. The dogs themselves simply perform according to their nature.

Chapter Five

THE CULTURE
OF INSTINCT

Hard-working Dogs

The French explorer Alcide Dessalines d'Orbigny reported in his *Voyage dans l'Amerique Meridionale* (1826) on a sheepdog from Uruguay he called *perro ovejero* (literally a sheep-guarding dog) and compared to the Roman molossus. Suckled on ewe's milk from the time it was born, *perro ovejero* guarded and herded the flock, without any human intervention. It left its charges only to run to the farmhouse for what d'Orbigny called a meager morsel of food. *Perro ovejero* nudged the sheep into a corral at night and then slept among them. It did not allow strange men or dogs to come near. The devoted sheepdog also hunted jaguar and partridge with its human master, who, for all of that, d'Orbigny said, abused it greatly, beating it with sticks, slashing it with a knife when it did something wrong. Yet the dog remained singularly loyal, a quality d'Orbigny found preferable to the habit of well-bred European hunting dogs to follow any old fool who called them.

Familiar with d'Orbigny's work, Charles Darwin sought out the sheepdogs of Argentina while voyaging on the *Beagle* and found them remarkably similar in training and behavior to *perro ovejero*. In *The Voyage of the Beagle*, Darwin praised their intelligence and devotion to duty. "It is a common thing," Darwin wrote, "to meet a large flock of sheep guarded by one or two dogs, at the distance of some miles from any house." They drove off foraging feral dogs, often by their presence alone, and at night brought the flock home.

The sheepdogs d'Orbigny and Darwin observed had their roots in the dogs Spanish conquistadores unloosed on the Americas and their counterparts as far north as New Mexico, where they were adjudged superior to English herding dogs by virtue of their size and gentleness with the stock. They were most likely a mix of the Spanish mastiffs, hounds, livestock guardians, and, where they existed, Native American "half-wild curs," as the English-speaking invaders called them. They tracked fugitive slaves and game, but more important from the naturalists' perspective, they tended flocks by themselves or with only a few others, guarding them, walking them to and from their corrals, taking them by the ear to lead them back to the fold.

It was amazing and illuminating for privileged individuals like d'Orbigny and Darwin to watch a crossbred cur perform more astonishing feats than the purebreds then gaining popularity among the moneyed classes of their native lands. D'Orbigny thought that the behavior of *perro ovejero* had to represent ratiocination as well as instinct, while Darwin found in the Argentine sheepdog confirmation of his notions that dogs possessed intelligence, emotion, reason, imagination, morality, a sense of beauty, language, and even belief in the supernatural or spiritual world.

"Only a few persons now dispute that animals possess some power of reason," Darwin wrote in *The Descent of Man, and Selection in Relation to Sex* (1871). "Animals may constantly be seen to pause, deliberate, and resolve." Like d'Orbigny, he did not know how to distinguish between the "power of reason and that of instinct" in dogs, but he was certain both were at play. Unfortunately, having elevated genetic determinism to the status of divine predestination, a number of scientists today would like to remember the Darwin who talked about inheritance and instinct while ignoring the naturalist who argued for volition and intelligence, the ability to learn and cogitate, in animals. The process is called selective reading.

Darwin and d'Orbigny believed that the sheepdogs of the New World represented a type more "primitive" than the sporting dogs of their native lands—a notion that, as we have seen, lingers. These basic dogs also combined talents long believed cleaved by selective breeding: guarding and herding. In their versatility, the sheepdogs of the New World resemble the curs, with the important distinction that the latter are presently deemed too rough for use on sheep. Ranchers do not want their sheep's wool torn by dogs nipping and biting at them, nor do they want them wadded into a bunch and held until a shepherd moves them. Rather, they like a herding dog who will gather, then walk or drive the flock into its pen.

Both guarding—territorial defense—and herding fall under the general category of agonistic (popularly called aggressive) behavior, which J.P. Scott and John L. Fuller defined as patterns associated with conflict and with hunting. Dogs showing a greater inclination to confront directly anything perceived as threatening them or their territory were made guardians or warriors, while those who stalked and attacked their game in more slashing manner were herders. Other factors combined to divide dogdom—dictates on color and size, for example—but those outward characteristics notwithstanding, for millennia selection was based on performance and human preferences. Breeding in many areas was not restricted solely to dogs of a particular body type. Rather, drive, energy, and availability of the dogs, the size and inclinations of the livestock, the contours of the land—all figured in the type of dog employed.

Before the consolidation of working breeds began in the nineteenth century, there was considerable overlap between types of sheepdogs of the sort d'Orbigny and Darwin observed. The major difference in behavioral terms was that herding dogs viewed livestock as prey whereas guarding dogs treated it as their pack. Beyond that, the herders were generally smaller, more active, and more agile, although the largest of them were the same size as small guarding dogs and, in fact, served both functions. For example, many curs will move quite happily along with a herd of cows they have just bunched, looking the part of placid livestock guards; a number of the European shepherd dogs serve double duty as well. Local types displayed individual idiosyncrasies of style: heeling, bunching and driving, "baying up." But the narrowing of behavior and appearance that proceeds apace because of human desire has generally harmed the rustic farm dog, whose chief value lay in its independence, intelligence, and versatility.

•   •   •

Piecing together the origin of the several score or more of sheepdogs we see today is a fascinating undertaking, which ultimately leaves many questions unanswered. Sometime deep in antiquity, people in the trade belt from the Fertile Crescent to Tibet and Mongolia began using large, wide-muzzled dogs to guard their homes and flocks, sheep being considerably more defenseless against predators than cattle. The mastiffs moved with shepherds and sheep from pasture to pasture. Their reputation for ferocity and their size helped them spread into Greece, Rome, central Asia, the Balkans, western Europe, and England. Tracking the precise routes of dispersal is currently an impossible task, but similarities in body types do indicate where the dogs traveled, especially after the ancient Greeks established and the Romans spread the tradition of the white dog as the sheep guard. Not only was it easily distinguished from wolves, but it also was deemed more acceptable to sheep because it "looked" like them.

Many cultures lacked the Greek and Roman concern with coat color, and so it is possible to find sheep-guarding dogs who are black, white, and all shades between. Their coats range in texture from short and rough to the long corded hair of the komondorak (corded coats occur when the dog's undercoat grows as long as its guard hairs), their weight from 60 to 200 pounds. Because of their wide use, they are often referred to as Eurasian guard dogs. Although a number of them are still bred in the traditional way—to purpose more than appearance—many have been standardized by breed clubs, often from a small number of animals, or founders. For example, the Great Pyrenees (Pyrenean mountain dog) and Tibetan mastiff, who is popularly considered the forerunner of all the giant dogs, were reconstructed by British breeders at the turn of the century to match their notions of the lost originals. The Maremma of Italy, on the other hand, represents a consolidation of two types—short-coated Maremmano and rough-coated Abruzzese mountain dogs—while others have been split into separate breeds. Thus, the large Turkish guard was cleaved into the Anatolian, or karabash, dog, with a tawny coat and black-and-white muzzle, and the akbash dog, with a white coat. Although promoters of these breeds vigorously argue the case for their uniqueness, the distinctions have more to do with human desires than with dogs.

As they dispersed, the Eurasian mastiffs met indigenous sheepdogs in the Middle East and Europe, who ranged in size from small to large. The northern European dogs probably derived initially from the gray wolf. Whatever their origin, the behavior and styles of work of these early farm dogs spanned the spectrum. Especially in mountainous and other regions where pastures were small and sheep were kept bunched for fear of thieves and predators, shepherds preferred large dogs prone to fierce defense of their flock (pack) and territory. In more open terrain with abundant forage, where flocks would scatter, smaller, more agile dogs worked best for gathering, driving, even guarding sheep or other livestock. The sheep, of course, adapted to the type of pasture and dog they were dealing with, so that over the course of generations a complex culture emerged, involving animals and humans.

In addition to guarding livestock, some of the large farm dogs pulled carts. In the cities, they served as the primary beasts of burden for people too poor or cramped for space to keep horses or oxen. During war, they proved invaluable for hauling supplies and munitions in mountainous terrain. Saint Bernards, who are from the same stock as the Pyrenean and Swiss mountain dogs, were crossed with Inuit dogs in the Canadian Arctic in the nineteenth century to produce the large Mackenzie River huskies used by the Royal Canadian Mounted Police and greatly diminished in number since the advent of snowmobiles and planes.

Mixing of dogs occurred in markets and villages, so in more isolated areas, little outbreeding might occur, leading to formation of unique, autochthonous breeds. In the main, shepherds wanted dogs who behaved and looked like the ones who worked best for them; also acceptable were different-looking animals who performed their duties superbly. Dogs who failed were killed, abandoned, or given to someone else. It is a simple, effective form of selection.

We can reasonably assume that the highly variable type of "rough shepherd's dogge," as they were known in sixteenth century England, sprang at some date from the mixing of indigenous spitz-type herders with the larger mastiff. That shepherd's dogge was trained to respond to whistles and hand signals in order to gather and move sheep grazing in small clusters or to drive cattle to markets. Purer northern dogs were the heelers, including the dwarf corgis, intent on nipping at the feet of their prey. Demand for herding dogs increased dramatically during the eighteenth and nineteenth centuries as the English gentry expanded their flocks.

In seventeenth-century France, there were at least seventeen types of guarding and herding dogs adapted to terrain, grazing conditions, and cultural differences between regions. Most of those dogs, of whom the briard and beauceron are best known in the United States, served as both guardians and herders. In Germany, there were what the Romans called "wolf" dogs, as well as precursors to today's schnauzers, rottweilers, and Great Danes. Similar types of shepherd dogs existed in the Low Countries. In Hungary were dogs with corded coats, like the small, active puli and the large komondorak.

During the seventeenth century, fishermen in Newfoundland crossed the Pryenean mountain dog with a black water dog (probably a cur) from England and created the dog who gave rise to the Newfoundland and also influenced the Labrador (more cur than mountain dog), Chesapeake Bay, flat-coated, and curly-coated retrievers.

With its vast ranches or stations, Australia has proved a fertile ground for developing new herders, foremost among them the kelpie and cattle dog, formerly known as various blue and red heelers. New Zealand has produced several remarkable lines of border collie and the huntaway. Well regarded though it is in Australia, where it is notorious for walking across the backs of tightly bunched sheep, and among a small group of fans in the United States, the kelpie is generally rated below the border collie by most American sheepdog fans. It looks more basic, works farther afield, and is more independent, although it too has the "eye," the intense, direct stare that is said to mesmerize sheep. A few border collie aficionados claim the kelpie barks too much while their dogs are always silent. People make many exaggerated claims about dogs; border collies can bark with the best.

Some dogs are innately too active to become flock guardians. Whether whole breeds are is difficult to answer, although by virtue of their energy, the border collie, heelers, and kelpie might be. More certain is the fact that the rigid distinction between large guard and smaller herding dogs that we take for granted is probably an artifact of nineteenth-century England. In consolidating breeds, the fancy assigned them specialities that did not reflect the full range of their behavior, and divided them on the basis of physical characteristics.

For all the efforts to divide them, many of the dogs seem to embody a description set forth by Douglas English in his 1924 book, *Friends of Mankind*: "Sheep-dogs are of many breeds, but are characterized as a class by exceptional courage, fidelity, vigilance, memory, and touchiness. In no dogs do we see the nervous irritability of the race in stronger evidence." In addition, he found them humorless and easily "offended by rebuke." Remarkably, those observations continue to hold among dogs bred for herding, who find even verbal chastisement unacceptable. On the other hand, breeders of sheepdogs, like the German shepherd and Malinois, for protection and police work, as we have seen, select against that sensitivity to create animals with a high tolerance for correction. Those dogs are not more intelligent or talented; they are simply better able temperamentally to withstand the rigors of compulsory training.

In an effort to find a sheepdog unspoiled by selective breeding, at home in an established sheep-keeping culture, I visited the Navajo Reservation in August 1995 with Hal Black, a zoologist at Brigham Young University. In the early 1980s, Black and a team of students investigated the Navajo's use of small mutts to protect their mixed flocks of goats and sheep from predators. Similar small dogs are used by poor ranchers in Sonora, Mexico, and in Namibia with success equal to that of the Navajo. The dogs work because they are bonded from birth with the sheep, as were the animals d'Orbigny and Darwin described more than a century ago, as livestock guard dogs have been for millennia. I chose the Navajo dogs not only for their link to that tradition but also because they are small to medium-sized mutts, not the large purebred Eurasian dogs widely publicized in the American media and some academic circles as the best livestock guard dogs to be found. The Navajo sheepdogs are raised, not bred, to their work. They do not fit the standard definition of a guard dog, yet they seem to perform the task quite well.

That trip followed by several months a visit I had paid to an American Kennel Club–sanctioned herding trial, which in keeping with British tradition involved sheep, not cattle. Also on the program was an instinct test designed to measure whether a dog had innate herding ability. The test proved an amusing commentary not just on the dogs and their owners but also on the relative merits of the first dog to win an AKC herding title, a Belgian Tervuren, and an old farm dog, a border collie who had killed sheep in his youth, spent most of the next two years tied to a tree untrained, and then been adopted and put to work as a herder. Somewhere in that story lies instinct.

Guarding

Told I have come from Miami Beach by way of Alaska to observe Navajo sheepdogs, a shepherd who calls himself Chee looks at me and says, "You travel too much. I've been here all my life." Thin, softspoken, in his midfifties, he waves past his corral of logs and chicken wire and his small, cinder block house to the phantasmagoric red sandstone buttes and mesas of Monument Valley where lightning splinters to earth. Chee's sheep and dogs walk placidly across his bare red yard, dotted with puddles from rain the night before, to the shadow of a cliff, while we stand in the sun broiling our big brains, making me wonder about the relative intelligence of animals.

"Yes," I say, "I travel too much."

I generally find reservations depressing, stark reminders that the genocide launched against the indigenous people of the Americas 500 years ago, and pursued with singular cruelty for the better part of 400 of those years, continues to this day in less bloody form. Occasional outbursts of militancy and tribal revivals have not stemmed the tide, and although the spread of casino gambling and bingo parlors have proved to be lucrative sources of revenue on some reservations, there is no guarantee they will succeed in buying a better life any more than has the uranium found in Navajo country or the oil in Alaska.

Nonetheless, the 25,000-square-mile reservation of the largest tribe of Native Americans in the United States contains some of the most starkly beautiful country in the world. It is a region I have always identified with spirits, although I am not inclined toward religion, a landscape wind and water have carved like a pair of deranged and sublime artists working in tandem at cross-purposes. It is a place one could never want to leave. Yet, as Hal Black and I talk to Chee and reflect on my flight from Anchorage, I remind myself that the Navajo and Apache were once travelers, Athabascan speakers who made their way from their ancestral homes in Alaska and western Canada down the front range of the Rockies into this land of high deserts and pueblos that seem born of the rock itself.

"How high are we?" Chee asks after we have talked about Miami Beach and the ocean.

"About 4,500 feet," Black says.

Chee shrugs.

The Navajo, the newcomers here, adapted their herding culture from the even more recent Spanish colonists early in the eighteenth century and have sustained it through war, exile, and confinement after 1868 to a reservation that excluded most of their best range and today appears to be largely barren. Looking at the poor forage, Black wonders how the livestock or people can survive. Yet approximately 170,000 Navajo occupy 110 chapters, or communities, living not only in densely clustered housing but also in scattered sheep camps, often with traditional hogans and corrals near small cinder block houses or trailers.

A friendly man in his fifties, with a gracious, open demeanor and full head of blond hair, Black is by training a mammalogist. He has studied bats and more recently black bears in the mountains of southern Utah, with his students making several important discoveries concerning their diets, territories, and travel patterns. He first came to the Navajo reservation to observe the sheepdogs in the early 1980s, after ranchers had begun adopting the Eurasian guard dogs—among them, the Great Pyrenees, Anatolian shepherd, akbash, Maremma, komondorak, and kuvasz—as deterrents to coyotes, marauding dogs, and other predators, like wildcats and bears. Unpoetically referred to as LGDs, livestock guarding dogs, the Eurasian dogs were introduced as an effort to find an alternative to the poison 1080, banned in 1972, that would emphasize protection from, not destruction of, wildlife. Liberally spread throughout the West, the toxic compound had become the major weapon in the official war of extermination launched against the coyote in 1916. It is estimated that at least 4 million coyotes and countless other animals, including pet dogs, died during that campaign, which put not a dent in the coyote population. Like many animals under stress, they bred more to replace those that were slaughtered, and they learned to avoid the poison, the knowledge entering their culture, not their genes.

The Animal Damage Control Division of the U.S. Department of Agriculture's Animal and Plant Health Inspection Service and the Livestock Guard Dog Project of Hampshire College, under the direction of evolutionary biologists Raymond and Lorna Coppinger, heavily promoted the use of the Eurasian dogs, widely perceived here as the only livestock guarding dogs in the world. The bias was born of ignorance—there being no tradition of guard dog use in Anglo North America—and grounded in the histories of breed clubs, which made extravagant claims for the animals they celebrated. In a case of self-fulfilling legend, those fictional histories became reality.

Experience soon revealed that while generally effective in slowing or stopping predation in fenced pastures, the Eurasian dogs, usually employed alone or in pairs because of their relative unsociability to other dogs, have problems protecting large flocks on open ranges, in broken country, and where coyotes are numerous. Some stray from the sheep; others are aggressive toward their charges. At $300 to $400 a puppy, they are also expensive, given that 38 percent wash out in the first two years, and half are gone after three, according to statistics compiled by the USDA's livestock guarding dog program.

According to the National Agricultural Statistics Survey, in 1994, predators killed goats worth $5.48 million and 368,050 sheep, roughly 40 percent of those lost to all causes, valued at $17.7 million. The continuing losses and a growing understanding of the limitations of

Eurasian dogs have caused some people to turn to llamas and burros, which will deter predation. But Black's often overlooked research shows that those ranchers who want dogs can be flexible in the type they choose, as long as they raise puppies four to five weeks old with sheep, minimize their contact with humans, and deploy them in sufficient numbers to guard hundreds of animals. Already, some ranchers are beginning to use more dogs and to crossbreed in an effort to produce a more tenacious animal.

I had come across Black's work while researching eastern coyotes and was intrigued because the Navajo appeared to place great trust in dogs with whom they had little interaction and because the animals themselves were not purebred. If you ask Navajos what kind of dogs they use, they say, "They're just dogs"—who *look* and *act* like Navajo dogs. Although the Navajo do not purposefully breed, buy, or sell sheepdog puppies, they engage in a form of selection, choosing whenever possible small to medium-sized rough-coated dogs, with erect or semierect ears, culling those who do not perform properly. In 1981, Black studied 230 dogs on seventy-two ranches scattered throughout the reservation to test for regional variations, which did not appear. He found the range of weights to be fifteen to sixty pounds, considerably smaller than the one-hundred-pound Eurasian livestock guards.

"Those big white dogs are no good," Chee said when asked about the Great Pyrenees and its kin. "They scare the sheep." The Navajo, who never fell under the Spanish mission system, established their herds with sheep and goats stolen from Mexican colonists and other Native Americans. It appears that from the start they turned their own dogs into flock guards, incorporating other types as they came along. Nowhere do you hear the cultural shibboleth of contemporary Anglo-Americans, following the ancient Greeks and Romans, that the white dogs are successful because they look like sheep and because they are big, perpetual puppies in mind if not in body who disrupt predation by offering to play with the hunter—a view put forth by the Coppingers in articles in *Natural History* and *Smithsonian* magazines that has given many people a distorted impression of the big dogs' behavior and abilities.

The Navajo dogs are mixtures of every type found on the reservation, including German shepherds and other hogan or house pets. Chee has a longhaired sheepdog whose sire was the house dog and mother a sheepdog. Expecting a mélange, I was amazed that half of the sixteen dogs we saw at three widely scattered sites resembled the mummified remains of the Basketmaker dog, the small black-and-white animal with a rough coat, shortened muzzle, and prick ears that perished near here some 2,000 years ago.

Chee had four of the Basketmaker type among his seven dogs, guarding approximately ninety sheep and goats—four to five dogs per flock is more common—although like other Navajo, not excepting his question about altitude, he had little interest in our attempts at quantification. When asked how many dogs he had, he said, "Enough." Similarly, he described their size as "not too big and not too small" and the amount of food he gave them as "not too much," in order to keep them from becoming "too active." (In light of studies showing a direct relationship between quality of diet and the levels of activity and aggressiveness in dogs, the Navajo attitude toward nutrition reflects a shrewd insight.) To supplement their diet, the dogs scavenge trash, graze on the sparse grass, kill small game and lizards. Like working dogs in many parts of the world, they appear underweight but not emaciated.

Chee, in fact, was more forthcoming than many Navajo, who tend to view Anglos asking questions about their dogs with a combination of bemusement and suspicion. To overcome that, Black, who visited the reservation by invitation, used one of his Navajo students as an interpreter and kept his interviews as informal as possible. For example, he and his coworkers recorded responses from memory after returning to their van. As a result, they were able to elicit fairly detailed answers to a series of questions regarding the upbringing, care, and behavior of the sheepdogs.

Recognizing that Navajo sheepdogs are products of a rich and unique tradition and that their flocks are smaller, with 17 to 300 mixed-breed sheep and goats, than the typical Anglo operation, with 500 to several thousand pedigreed sheep, Black sought to distill the basic principles that made their dogs successful. He concluded that the Navajo "recipe" for creating a sheepdog requires only that the puppy be raised in the corral preferably from birth but absolutely from four to five weeks of age and given minimal human attention. The mothers of pups whelped in the corral usually shuttle between nursing them and guarding the flock. When the pups are ten to twelve weeks old, they are encouraged to go with the sheep, if they are not already following their mother or other older dogs. The method is as ancient as the use of guard dogs, be they for livestock or people. As Darwin observed in *The Voyage of the Beagle*, the dog raised with sheep thinks of them "as its fellow brethren." The flock is its pack, the range and corral its territory.

The phenomenon is no mystery, as behavioral studies since those of Scott and Fuller at Jackson Laboratory in Bar Harbor, Maine, have repeatedly shown: dogs have a genetic predisposition to form lasting social bonds with their own and other species. The imprinting begins at around three weeks of age and continues until the twelfth week. Thus, a puppy raised with sheep and given only minimal human contact during that period will usually stay with sheep and avoid humans, to whom it might become somewhat acclimated during a second bonding period, around four to six months of age. The same is true if they are raised with kittens or any other species. (They will bond, to a lesser degree, to particular sites, such as corrals, or objects.)

No one has studied whether starting the puppies at four to five weeks with sheep is essential or waiting until they are seven or eight weeks old is sufficient, although evidence supports the view that the earlier time creates a more lasting bond. From four to six weeks, puppies bond with other dogs in the form of their littermates. Taken from home at that age and raised with another species, they forge a close union and identification. The Navajo dogs regard the flock and other dogs as their littermates. (Puppies removed from their litters at four to six weeks and raised solely by humans tend to become overly dependent on them and poorly socialized toward other dogs.)

Within the context of the flock, the puppy develops its personality and style, just as it would if living with humans or in a kennel or among a group of feral dogs. None of those who reach adulthood seeks to dominate the sheep; in fact, many are openly submissive to them.

But some appear indifferent, as if simply traveling along, and still others seem to shepherd them in a nonconfrontational fashion. Black observed one small female who rode and slept, spread-eagled, on the back of a large ram and a group of dogs that divided itself to cover each segment of a flock that fragmented while grazing.

At one homestead, we watched four dogs walk their flock home and straight into the corral, after which a buff Basketmaker-type male remained on the outside. Lying down, he faded into the landscape. Moving, he skulked, eyeing us warily. We could not approach him. Lying among the sheep, the other three dogs also kept a close watch on us.

Some of the dogs always stay among the sheep and goats, even in the corral, while others hang around the periphery, ready to pursue any intruder. Black was once driven into his car by one of the dogs, and he has observed them routing horses, burros, cattle, stray dogs, and coyotes, which they will kill. Chee told us that the night before, his dogs had fought with and driven off a coyote that approached the corral. At another ranch, Black and I watched two longhaired dogs chase a German shepherd 200 yards to its house while three other dogs moved slowly with their sheep, as if nothing were happening.

The dogs clearly exercise their own judgment. At the ranch with the buff dog, we encountered a six-month-old pet German shepherd who had regularly played with the sheepdogs, to the dismay of the grandmother who owned the flock, until one day "it did something" and they ran it off, never to engage it again. When we went to the corral to take photographs, the puppy followed, but he did not interact with the sheep or other dogs. We speculated that he must have attacked one of the sheep and been shunned by his former playmates forever.

The Navajo want their dogs to be vigorous in defense of their sheep and goats but calm, even placid, in their presence. A few days before our arrival, Chee had shot one of his dogs because it was "bothering the sheep," a deadly sin. Playing, biting, killing, even too much motion—all fall into that category. Navajo shepherds will scold dogs or tie them to the corral if they stray, deny them food or attach a heavy object to their necks to break them of wandering. Some will tie a pup to a sheep. Occasionally a shepherd will cut off the tips of ears of a miscreant or dock its tail before giving up on it. How effective such tactics are is unclear, but Black observed 44 of 230 working dogs with docked tails and one without ear tips. A few dogs were born tailless; others had had their tails docked by people not only for chasing sheep but also out of a desire to make them look like Navajo dogs and not like coyotes. A few people simply disliked long, wagging tails on their dogs. Incorrigibles or those who kill are put to death or banished— given away or driven from the ranch to join the groups of feral dogs scavenging garbage dumps. In turn, those groups occasionally provide recruits for the ranks of sheepdogs and household pets.

The survivors perform along a sliding scale of competency, with some of the laggards spending part of their time at the hogan and the best becoming the sheep's guardians and guides. The only commands many of them recognize are a whistle, for food, and *dibe* (Navajo for "sheep"), meaning "get with the sheep," issued—rarely for mature dogs—with a wave of the arm or thrown object. Most are wary of people, although a few have names and seem to have formed secondary bonds to their herders.

Black found that two-thirds of the Navajo herd their flocks for part of each day—the older women are believed to keep the tradition alive, but many family members participate. The remaining third turn their sheep, goats, and dogs out unattended with varying degrees of frequency, trusting the animals to fend for themselves. Animals are lost each way, but the dogs hold predation to an acceptable level, a remarkable achievement considering that the reservation is open and rugged country.

While recognizing the critical role of early socialization to sheep, many Anglo ranchers continue to rely exclusively on the giant Eurasian animals. Jeff Green, director the USDA's livestock guarding dog program and coauthor of one of Black's papers on the Navajo dogs, said he and his colleagues did not promote mixed breeds vigorously as an alternative to the purebreds because they feared the failure rate for those dogs would exceed that of the breeds to which they were already committed. They had no empirical basis for that, but given the initial difficulty faced in persuading ranchers to adopt a new approach to predator control, they did not want to deal with additional uncertainty.

A number of the failures of the Eurasian dogs had to do with inadequate bonding to sheep. The Coppingers, among others, initially argued that early bonding was not essential because the dogs were genetically programmed to stay with and guard sheep, as if they were machines. Accepting that argument for genetic predetermination, many ranchers purchased one of the dogs, put it with sheep at eight weeks of age or later while teaching it to walk on a leash and come when called—bonding it to humans, in other words—and then expected it to guard the flock day and night. The fact that roughly half of the dogs succeeded in the face of such human inconsistency is as much testament to their intelligence, adaptability, and capacity for secondary bonding (meaning they will adopt a species other than the primary one) as to their breeding. That they faltered along the way was a reflection of the difficulty involved in adopting only a piece of a culture—in this case a pastoral one involving sheep-guarding dogs.

Far from being machines, they manifest the full range of dog behavior, like their Navajo counterparts. Ranchers who have employed dogs like the Great Pyrenees report that in addition to feeding on dead lambs, some of the dogs will kill and eat small game, fawns, and occasionally their charges. Many have a tendency to wander, and more than a few are too timid in the face of predators—a result of years of nonselection for the sort of territorial defense and aggression that made them famous. The best are those bonded to sheep at an early age and left to do their work, but even they have trouble in open country and where coyotes abound. They simply are overwhelmed by the speed and numbers of their adversaries.

To test his recipe for a sheepdog, Black purchased a greyhound puppy from a rancher in Idaho who bred them to hunt and kill coyotes, and raised her with sheep from four weeks to eight months of age when he gave her to a Navajo family. Black thought the big, sleek dog worked well, but the Navajo subsequently "got rid of her" because she was "too big and too active." She was not a Navajo dog. Using the same method, Raymond Coppinger successfully turned several Chesapeake Bay retrievers into livestock protectors. Black observed a Chesapeake working on the Navajo reservation and in Oregon where the rancher told him the retriever was the best livestock guard he had ever had. The big male had apparently just taken to the sheep from an early age and opted to live with them.

The success of nonstandard guard dogs suggests that people can be flexible in their selection, but the USDA and the Coppingers continue to promote the Eurasian animals to the exclusion of others. When I asked him about that, Coppinger said, without citing numbers, that the Chesapeakes have a higher failure rate than the Eurasian breeds and that the greyhound was too active because of its genes (he did not perceive that the Navajo's rejection of it reflected their cultural bias against big, active dogs). He also argued that when the Navajo cull animals, they are engaged in selection.

They do reject dogs who continually bother the sheep. But they make no attempt to mate those who work out, and it is not clear how many new sheepdogs are recruited from the working population, which is 77 percent male. Of those, nearly 30 percent are castrated to make them stay with sheep. Black found that sheepdogs came from many sources, including the roadside. In fact, the Navajo actually tolerate a wide range of behavior and working styles. There are "sometimes" sheepdogs, for example, just as there are house dogs who sire sheepdogs, leading me to suspect that there are some dogs who are just temperamentally not suited to the task of living with sheep full-time, the same way there are dogs not able to live with humans. They become strays or feral animals because of fear or trauma or a desire to be free. Doubtless those inclinations have a genetic basis, but there is scant evidence to suggest that they are breed specific.

More likely guarding and protecting are behaviors common to all dogs. Sandy Seward, trainer for the USDA's Beagle Brigade, told me the story of a pregnant cairn terrier she found abandoned on the road and took home. After the dog delivered and weened her mixed-breed puppies, Seward placed her with an elderly couple in central Florida. The man had been diagnosed with inoperable cancer and given six months to live, and he and his wife wanted a dog to brighten his waning days and provide her with companionship after his death. Five years later, the man's cancer was in remission, and the dog had earned a place in their hearts and home. For years the couple had fed squirrels, and as they had aged, the squirrels had become bolder, tearing through window screens to enter the house and demand food. The little terrier had driven the squirrels out and back into their trees, allowing the couple to repair their screens and attain a modicum of peace for the first time in years. The little Navajo dogs engage in the same type of behavior, only their home is the range, their couple a flock of sheep and goats.

Continual early socialization to sheep is the most crucial ingredient for creating livestock-guarding dogs. Closely following that is a human culture that winnows out dogs who do not live up to expectations—killing them is not necessary—and allows those with promise to develop. Along with the sheep, they will help train puppies to the way of their flock.

Herding

There is speculation among fans of the black-and-tan English shepherd, a breed consolidated in recent years in the United States, that it descends more or less directly from the large farm shepherd that colonists brought to these shores some 300 years ago, whereas the border collie represents the small variety that stayed home. Although it is hard to fathom why the large dog would make the crossing while the small one remained, the farm shepherd might well represent an early form of herding dog, from which eventually sprang the collie, the Shetland sheepdog (a small collie), and the border collie, deemed in at least one book on "canine intelligence" the smartest dog in the world.

Of course, in the 1940s and early 1950s, when Lassie was in his/her glory—the gender confusion a result of a male being used to play a female in the fashion of Elizabethan England when boys played girls on the stage—the collie was considered among the most brilliant of dogs. Now it is recognized as dull, having been bred for a long narrow snout and beautiful coat but not brains and good health. Among obedience judges, the German shepherd still rates high, as do the poodle, Shetland sheepdog, Labrador and golden retrievers, and Doberman pinscher. Of course, now it has become fashionable in some circles to rate the Australian shepherd as the world's most trainable and intelligent dog.

The Australian shepherd, or Aussie, is also promoted as the best house pet because it is less hyperactive and destructive than the border collie. Unfortunately, the claim is not always true: a number of Australian shepherd breeders report that the dogs are, on average, more destructive when bored than border collies. In fact, the energy levels of individual dogs, their drives, and the way people raise them count for far more than any generalization and can even alter genetic predispositions.

In a perpetual feedback loop, reputation leads to expectations, which when even vaguely met, reinforce the reputation as long as the animal or person is in vogue. Thus, the border collie or Aussie is the smartest dog in no small measure because people expect it to be that way and find what they seek. The expectations are themselves based on human measures, primarily the willingness of the dog to submit to the rigors of obedience training: sit, stay, lie down, come, and fetch on command. Books and television programs have been devoted to the subject, but on the face of it, we can say that if obedience is the measure of intelligence then a docile, submissive, hardworking slave is a genius.

The origins of what we call obedience training lie in the nineteenth century when dog enthusiasts in Europe, England, and the United States argued that teaching the dog to behave according to human standards was a way to break it to human will, to overcome its animal nature. The process gained momentum in the first decades of the twentieth century and has rolled along ever since.

Obedience requires a dog to be totally conscious of its handler, which ruins it for actual work as a hunter, herder, or racer, when it must also exercise its own judgment. Schutzhund and field-trial dogs are the same way—trained to respond to their handlers' every command. They are amazing to watch, but their performance must not be equated with intelligence. Many independent, inquisitive dogs are, in fact, extremely intelligent; they just prefer to operate either on their own or at a remove from their owner.

Leida Jones, a breeder of border collies and Australian shepherds, who uses her dogs to herd sheep, to compete in sheepdog trials, and to prance around the show ring, says, "I do a little obedience training, but I think obedience is a sickness, an obsession. Some people are just into that control. They want to control everything their dog does."

The collies, of which the English or farm shepherd is surely one, are a type of herding dog once distinguished according to size and region of origin that gathered and drove sheep and cattle. They were the British equivalent of the shepherd dogs of Germany, the Low Countries, and France. Thus, we now have the sheltie, the rough and smooth collie, the border collie, the English shepherd, the Australian shepherd (really from the United States), and, from Australia, the kelpie and the cattle dog. The bearded collie is related to the old English sheepdog (formerly the English bobtail sheepdog), which itself is kin to a score of shaggy European drovers. The Aussie and Australian dogs are of recent vintage, and various regional heelers, which somewhere in the past are linked to the corgis, continue to be bred throughout the sheep-rearing English-speaking world.

The border collie has achieved near mythic status in the United States among those who believe it a canine genius of the first rank. Leida Jones says that border collie aficionados have a habit of viewing the world "in black and white," the predominant colors of their breed. I have met some amazing border collies and some that are physical disasters, crippled by bad hips, blinded by progressive retinal atrophy, an inherited eye disorder, and so high-strung they bounced off walls or vibrated uncontrollably while waiting for a command.

Whatever its intellect, the border collie is prized here and abroad for its skill in managing sheep in pastures. In this country, many of the dogs work exclusively, if at all, at sheepdog trials, designed to measure the dog's performance under the strict supervision of its master, who gives directions by whistle. In Great Britain and New Zealand, on the other hand, where sheep herding is still a way of life, the dogs work on the farm and then attend the trials as a way for their masters to show them off and arrange for sale and breeding. The trials are televised affairs where the border collie's responsiveness to command, its drive, its fast style, and its eye have brought it innumerable championships and contributed to its reputation for genius.

Leida Jones believes that because trial dogs are handler conscious rather than independent, it is necessary for people using their dogs only for trials to outcross with other good working dogs in order to instill self-possession. "Trial dogs have less initiative than farm dogs," she said, "so if you keep breeding title to title you end up with nothing."

Aware of that, many fans of border collies in this country look abroad for their bloodlines. A number of them have learned from bitter experience that although they might receive top working animals from England or Scotland, they are as likely to receive a dog with bad joints or eyes. Jones spent months looking for a border collie bitch to use for working the sheep on her seventy-acre farm in the rolling hills of central Florida, only to be thwarted each time she demanded hip X rays of the dog. She was told that working dogs are not x-rayed as a rule, the philosophy being that if they work, they are sound. Combined with rising demand, that practice has produced the sort of proliferation of health and temperament problems that plague other purebred dogs.

The United States Border Collie Association and individual breeders are fighting to keep the dog in proper physical and mental form, but as long as its popularity remains high, they are likely to have difficulty. Now that the dog is in the show ring—accepted by the AKC as one of its officially recognized breeds over the strong protest of the USBCA—their odds of success have fallen close to zero. The AKC made clear nearly a decade ago that once the border collie became an official breed, the dogs would have to conform to a narrowly defined standard. In their unrecognized state, they were too variable in terms of coat length, size, and coloration to please show judges.

I met Leida Jones because she was the breeder of Cisco, the Frisbee-playing border collie belonging to Lourdes Edlin. Jones rescued Cisco's sire, Scotchie, from a tree where he had been tied for the better part of two years because when freed he baited and then killed sheep, an offense that would have gotten him shot in many parts of the world.

"Some herding dogs will show kill maneuver traits," she says, meaning they will stalk, pounce, and bite. "You want to stop that right away. Usually, if a border collie kills a sheep, he's chased it to death, whereas German shepherds used as herders might kill two or three sheep a year."

Jones redirected Scotchie's energy to herding by teaching him to abort his attacks and move the animals in a prescribed direction, not to kill them. "He's a good farm dog," she says, "not a good trial dog. In training a working dog, you want to encourage him to think on his own, so you guide his instinct. A farm dog has to be a good thinker."

She also rescued Cisco's brother, whom she had sold to a man who wanted him desperately as a pet for his son. "He called me six or seven months later and said, 'We have not been good. We didn't spend time with the dog. When we let him loose, he'll chew up something in the yard or in the house. He's undisciplined.' I took the dog back. He was easy to train. You just had to show him something, and he did it." Too many people purchase the putative super dog and assume it can figure out everything because of its breeding. It winds up a mess. Jones missed rescuing one female that her owners had left in a kennel on their property for eight months, until she began to mature physically and they felt she was ready for training. "Then they took her from her pen and put a leash on her, and she flipped out, and they shot her." It is easy to begin training dogs at seven weeks of age to come and perform other simple tasks, because they are eager to learn and please. But without stimulation and socialization, they are emotionally abused, intellectually deprived creatures.

The "breed rescue" in which Jones engages represents one of the finest movements in dogdom, especially among clubs devoted to particular breeds. Around the country, members work to take dogs people no longer want and then to place them in good homes. The effort keeps those animals out of shelters, where they might meet an early death.

Jones attempts to ensure that her dogs go to good homes. She breeds only one to two litters a year of both border collies and Australian shepherds, depending on requests she has for dogs and her own needs. Like other responsible breeders, she never advertises, and she interviews all potential buyers. "I had a person call and request a blue merle Aussie with blue eyes. I sent them someplace else." Like the blue-eyed merle leopard dog, the double blue (or blue-eyed and red merle) Aussie is prone to hereditary eye, hearing, and neurological problems, especially if it is the product of two dogs with those features. Because that look is highly popular among buyers, unscrupulous and ignorant people are breeding for it, with dire results. Unlike many breeders, Jones not only guarantees the health of her animals but also will replace one with a congenital disease without demanding the ill animal back.

I visited Jones's farm in mid-May 1995 and again on a Saturday morning in early June to watch a herding trial sponsored by the local chapter of the Australian Shepherd Club of America and open to American Kennel Club–registered herding dogs. The AKC began involving itself in herding trials in 1990 in an attempt to refute criticism that its dogs were so overbred for the show ring that they had lost their working ability, a charge that virtually every responsible breeder of working dogs and independent observer of canines agrees is true. Until it was annexed by the AKC, the border collie was not allowed to compete in AKC-sanctioned herding trials.

Jones and other Australian shepherd breeders say that their dogs have already split into heavy-boned, long-coated, relatively talentless, and often brain-dead show dogs and smaller, more energetic working dogs. In addition, several famous show lines are dysplastic and plagued with eye and temperament problems, meaning they are biters.

A prominent United States Border Collie Association official had warned me that the AKC herding trials were a sham. Too easy to count as real competition, she said, they were designed to make people feel good about their dogs. She was right: the event I attended compared to serious sheepdog trials the way a Harlem Globetrotters contest resembles a National Basketball Association game, which is to say that they both employed balls, baskets, and five-man teams. The competitors were sincere and hardworking, their dogs well cared for and, in some cases, talented, but the event itself was noteworthy for its lack of rigor.

For the first event, each dog was required to move three sheep—driven into the middle of a small, fenced pasture and fed to keep them in place until the competitors arrived—through a series of obstacles representing pens and gates, receiving points for each one successfully navigated. A smooth-coated border collie kept order among the sheep used in the competition, which were so accustomed to dogs and the drill that the best among them followed the route on their own.

Although no border collies were entered, the first run involved one solid working dog, Leida Jones's Bob, an Australian shepherd bred by a man who maintains the line his grandfather had started by inbreeding and culling those failing to perform according to his standards. Jones says that the practice has in some cases produced Aussies prone to epilepsy and other disorders, although this line seems free of them because of the breeder's rigorous culling. Bob simply vibrates when in his kennel and stares intently at sheep, cattle, horses—anything on four legs that moves. He has high drive, almost overdrive, and because he is young, it is difficult to tell whether he will turn into a brilliant herding dog. For now, he is proof either that the breeder has loose standards of excellence or that he better think about some intelligent outcrosses. Bob's genealogy resembles a telephone pole; his personality and temperament are those of a person walking a tightrope over the deep canyon of insanity. If he settles into a good working dog, Jones will probably breed him with one of her dogs.

On an overcast morning that brought welcome release from two weeks of blistering hot weather that would have forced cancellation of the two-day event, had it persisted, Bob won the first test in the advanced class without much difficulty. The category is for accomplished herders, but the corgi who took second and the puli receiving third-place honors were no match. They worked competently and unspectacularly. The fourth and fifth dogs were misplaced. A German shepherd could not move the first three sheep she drew, which headed directly for the exit gate, and then failed to keep the next trio together.

In all, twenty-nine dogs were entered in three classes: advanced, intermediate, and started, for novices with some experience but not much skill. About seventy-five people attended, a respectable number given the weather. Most of them wanted to put their dogs in a small corral with sheep in the afternoon's "instinct" test, an AKC-designed event to show dog owners and the world that "herding" breeds have a natural affinity for livestock no matter what the fancy has done to them.

Except for Bob, a corgi, and a young Aussie in the started class, the dogs were undistinguished. A Pembroke Welsh corgi in the intermediate class, meaning it had scored enough points in various competitions to be promoted from the started class, failed to pick up the sheep or move them. He obeyed his owner but had no sense of how to deal with three thoroughly docile sheep. Bearded collies, one of whom actually finished second in the started class, simply walked behind the sheep, which walked behind the handler, who walked backward through the course. I assumed the calm dogs reassured the placid sheep, which were resigned to covering the circuit so they could return to the shade, but the official AKC guide would say the bearded collies were acting as drovers, according to their nature.

The winner of the started class, an Australian shepherd named Chelsea, had seven homes before she was ten months old and was completely untrained. Now a little over a year old, she was working on an advanced obedience title, herding with credibility, and doing occasional television commercials from her home in Louisiana. She was a hyperactive dog, always investigating something, if only a bug, which is probably why she ran through so many homes. But she was also confirmation to what kind people can do with a dog. The corgi finishing second to Chelsea moved with quickness that belied his stubby legs, nipping at the feet of the sheep, relentlessly driving them forward. Together, they demonstrated different styles of work. They were fairly judged, as Leida Jones observed, according to their method, not a single standard laid down in "black and white."

In England and New Zealand, the handlers at sheepdog trials are almost exclusively men, the farmers who daily work their dogs. Here, the opposite is the case. The majority of the handlers are women, and for many of them dogs are sport. They engage not just in trials but also in obedience work, search and rescue, even the show ring. Many of the men who participate appear primarily interested in adding herding titles to the list of their dog's accomplishments so they can drive up the price of their offspring. If the majority of those dogs see sheep on a regular basis, it is to practice the routine followed in the trials, not to move them around a farm. That certainly is preferable to doing nothing with the dog, but it would be nicer to see how the dogs performed in more demanding circumstances.

When it came time, following a break, to collect six sheep for the afternoon "instinct" test, only one herding dog was to be seen, a Belgian Tervuren, the first AKC national herding trial champion. A big, well-groomed dog, with a flowing reddish black mane, he accompanied three officials into the pasture and with them futilely chased a small band of sheep for twenty minutes. Each time the sheep saw the dog and people, they shied away. The Tervuren was unable to gather them.

Seeing the impasse, Leida Jones unloosed Scotchie and, with him cantering beside, eyes fixed on the sheep, drove her little all-terrain vehicle to the rescue. Within ten minutes the sheep were in a holding pen tended by the Tervuren, who barely succeeded in preventing their escape through the narrow passage he blocked. He was snappish, like his owner, the chief judge for the event, who commanded him with the roar of a drill sergeant. She was intent on control over events that neither she nor the dog could muster.

For the test, three sheep were brought into the corral with the human impresario, a kindly man who competes with a Samoyed, the white spitz. Armed with a shepherd's crook to beat back any dog who tried to bite the quarry, he called dogs and handlers into the ring, their order of appearance determined by lot. Once inside, the dog, on a lead with its handler in tow, was supposed to chase the sheep, moving them in a circle around the circular corral. The official and handler often appeared to herd the dog, coaxing and cajoling it to take an interest and run. Any half-decent dog should do that, and indeed the sheltie, Aussie, crossbred kelpie, beauceron who washed out from ring work in France—the equivalent of Schutzhund—and cost its new American owners $3,000, and collie with hips so bad it could hardly walk straight waltzed into certificates of instinct.

What precise quality they possessed is unclear. The weak-hipped collie moved only after heavy coaxing by both humans and after the official set the sheep in motion directly under its nose. Then it lunged forward before retreating. The sheltie pranced around in the neighborhood of the sheep without any notion of what it was doing or what they were. The kelpie mix chased the sheep, although it seemed to have no awareness of what it was doing or why. It was merely caught up in the excitement of the ring, with sheep and people scurrying about. The beauceron was a big, strong, but not agile dog probably better suited for driving cattle or moving along with a large flock, like a guard dog. An Australian shepherd, a beautifully trained, veteran search-and-rescue dog, was so handler conscious that he did not take his eyes off his owner. Unfamiliar with sheep or her gestures toward them, he simply stayed glued to her knee while she ran around the ring, herding sheep with the judge. Like the others, the dog passed. Unlike most of them, he clearly had talent; it was just obscured by his other training.

As the border collie has gained popularity in the United States in the past two decades, several strong bloodlines from New Zealand and Scotland have achieved international renown, leading to numerous reports about their outstanding qualities, their innate drive to herd sheep with their fixed "eye." In the most extreme cases, they are said to manage the woolly creatures by their stare alone, as if all they have to do is point to a spot and the hypnotized sheep will go there. Forgotten because of their popularity is the simple truth that dogs, no matter their breeding, are only as good as their trainers and handlers. John Child, the bear-hunting rancher in Utah, tells the story of the border collies his father imported from a famous New Zealand line. After their arrival, he put them in the pasture and told them to "get sheep." They did nothing. Thinking they were having trouble getting acclimated, he waited a few days before trying again. Nothing. Frustrated, he whistled at them, and the dogs immediately set to work. He called the breeder, who said: "Oh, we forgot to tell you, they're trained to work to a whistle. They ignore voice commands."

THE UGLINESS
OF BEAUTY

The Show

On my return from the 1995 Westminster Kennel Club Show, the 119th meeting of what bills itself as the second-longest-running sporting event in the United States, behind the Kentucky Derby, I found a fax in my machine: "I hate Scotties." From a prominent veterinarian, it reflected my feelings while watching the upset victory of Ch. (Champion) Gaelforce Post Script, a.k.a. Peggy Sue, the Scottish terrier declared Best in Show (out of some 2,700 entrants). Churning around the center of Madison Square Garden on her dwarfed legs, her long black coat flapping, she had looked like a mop that had swabbed too many kennels without a rinse. Whatever her charms, she represented the appalling human practice of breeding mutant animals for ego satisfaction. But to the judges, including Jacklyn Hungerland, a Carmel, California, psychologist who made the final decision, the bitch with the long black coat and exaggerated nose had more nearly resembled "a little cart horse" with a desire to win. To hear her fans, she had sensed her moment and seized it, the way a great athlete rises to glory in a crucial series, while the favorites—the German shepherd, boxer, poodle, Akita, and Afghan—faltered.

For her effort, Peggy Sue won a silver cup in which she sat, a celebratory dinner at Sardi's Restaurant, dutifully recorded in the *New York Times*, and her choice of suitors—champion, American Kennel Club–registered Scottish terriers only. She was queen of the premier event of the fancy, so venerable it predates formation of the American Kennel Club, whose policies its sponsor profoundly influences.

The German shepherd, Ch. Altana's Mystique, owned by Jane A. Firestone and the most decorated member of its breed in AKC history, was reportedly the odds-on favorite before the show, but she mysteriously failed even to take the herding group. That is one of the seven general divisions into which all breeds formally recognized by the American Kennel Club are sorted, the others being sporting, non-sporting, working, toy, terrier, and hound. In fact, in the gossipy world of the fancy, word was spreading in the fall of 1994 that the German shepherd was going to win. Betting was reportedly heavy. But there were more invidious rumors that the bitch was barren and therefore should not even be allowed in the ring, which is designed to honor "breeding stock." We will never know what combination of rumors and judicial opinion spelled her demise, but it was a stunning blow. Rumors are a fact of life in the fancy, the breadth of their distribution increasing in direct proportion to their viciousness and the success of the dog in question.

Biff, the most decorated boxer in breed history, who competes as Ch. Hi-Tech's Arbitrage, also failed to take his working group, despite a send-off in the February 20 and 27, 1995, *New Yorker*. "If I were a bitch," wrote Susan Orlean, "I'd be in love with Biff Truesdale. Biff is perfect." A Japanese businessman had once offered a blank check for the dog, only to be rejected. Orlean predicted Biff would take the working group but not Westminster, observing that the judge for Best in Show was known as "a poodle person." (Clearly, her line of gossip differed from the one I heard and was equally wrong, which is what keeps the fancy lively.) The judge for the group thought differently, and Biff retired to become a stud, taking with him the breed's peculiar talent, according to the official description, of standing on its hind legs and boxing with its forepaws when fighting.

In my notebook I had predicted that the big Akita, Ch. Tobe's Return of the Jedai, also known as Ben, the winningest representative of his breed in history, who had come out of semiretirement for another run at Westminster, would trot off with top prize. He had raced to Best of Breed and then Best of Working Group—beating the boxer—to loud cheers from the crowd. The *New York Times* had run a glowing profile of the eight-year-old, ancient by standards of show dogs, on Monday, February 13 (1995), the day Westminster opened its two-day run.

To my untrained eye, Ben was not the best Akita in the ring that morning, but he was the sentimental favorite of the large crowd that gathered to see him and I expected that to carry him to victory. He played to them, raising his head, licking hands while waiting his turn to trot around the ring on the end of his leash. All the while, a handler in a diaphanous evening gown that fully exposed her back—the other woman handlers wore conservative suits and dresses—and long, dark hair piled high on her head, courted the judge. Hand resting ever so lightly in the small of her back, he kept her dog in for a final flounce around the ring with the other finalists.

My companion and I laughed. Well, he commented, she entered into the transaction, so you can't accuse the judge of sexism. Indeed, the same attire did not carry her past the initial cut in the Afghan ring later in the day where a woman was judge. (When a lot of dogs are entered, judges usually review the field, then choose a handful of favorites for further consideration.)

Of course, one should never challenge the objectivity of the judge, a person skilled in the measure of dog flesh, capable of discerning which is best after ten to fifteen minutes of watching thirty or more males and females circle the ring on their thin leashes—thus the phrase "dogs on a string"—and stand for quick inspection to ensure the coat is the dog's and its testicles number two. (On at least one occasion at a different show, a monorchid dog surgically implanted with a second testicle had its own undescended ball drop in the middle of such an examination—mirabile dictu.) In the course of those observations, the judge, we are told, can also discern the dog's temperament and talent, all virtue being derived from how well it conforms not to the standard, per se, but to the judge's interpretation of that standard. Terrier handlers help the process by throwing a squeaky toy mouse in front of the dog, who is supposed to perk up, thereby showing its ratting spirit.

The majority of handlers in the top rank of the fancy are professionals, men and women who love dogs and for a fee will "finish," or "put" a championship on, a dog. Whether they have computer programs, written records, or outstanding memories, they know which judges favor which types of dogs, which shows are least populous and most heavily weighted—points being awarded not just on performance but also on the size of the field. Usually, it costs at least $10,000 to finish a dog, which can occur within a couple of months, and several times as much to campaign it for a serious shot at Westminster. For that, the dog must garner prizes from top shows around the country and walk into New York on the crest of an advertising campaign in magazines devoted to the fancy.

Most fanciers are content with the championship, which means money in the bank in the form of stud fees or puppy sales—$500 and up, depending on the breed and bloodlines, the area of the country in which they live, and their willingness to advertise. If sold, celebrated champions who have won a number of major shows like Westminster or simply dominated their breeds can command as much as $50,000. To be called "champion," a dog must earn fifteen points in AKC-sanctioned shows according to an arcane, weighted formula that changes from year to year in an attempt to provide more points for dogs in areas where competition is fierce. To complicate matters, the points must come from a minimum of three different judges, two of whom represent "majors"—shows at which winners receive anywhere from three to five points for their effort.

At most shows, dogs of a given breed compete in various classes—puppy, novice, bred-by-exhibitor, American-bred, and open—against others of their gender. The victors in all classes then vie for the titles of Winner's Dog and Winner's Bitch in their breed. Those two battle existing champions for Best of Breed. Best-of-Breed winners contend for Best of Group, and those victors prance it out for Best in Show. Only the Winner's Dog and Winner's Bitch for each breed earn points toward their championship, a process that guarantees maximum distribution of the title—to keep people happy.

At a large event, upward of 4,000 dogs will be judged in one day leading to Best in Show. At Westminster, where all entrants are champions, judging starts with Best of Breed and runner-up, Best of Opposite Sex, before moving to group and show judging, where only winners are rewarded, regardless of gender. The dogs compete for trophies, ribbons, prestige, and dollars for breeding and offspring—in short, to gratify their owners' egos and contribute to their coffers.

Although the American Kennel Club, under whose auspices nearly all of the major canine beauty contests in the United States occur, sponsors a number of performance trials, more than 90 percent of its competitors enter dog shows. Annually, approximately 1.3 million dogs strut through on the order of 11,177 shows (an average of just over 110 a show), some of them devoted to single breeds. The remaining 10 percent (150,000 dogs) compete in 4,703 AKC performance events (averaging 32 dogs): obedience trials, field trials, terrier trials, herding trials, and coursing events that test the speed and mettle of sight hounds. In addition to sanctioning the events, which are officially hosted by one or more of the 3,200 groups affiliated with it in some way, the AKC sets rules and regulations, certifies judges, and publishes results.

Although professional handlers are disproportionately represented at shows like Westminster, they are not essential to victory. Owners with the time and inclination successfully show their own dogs, some of whom they even breed themselves. Among the 1995 Best of Breed winners at Westminster was an Irish wolfhound, Ch. Fitzarran Carnasserie Marcus, owned and handled by Jacqueline Carswell, bred by William and Betty Deemer, two of the most respected breeders in the business. Carswell also shows and competes in coursing events—with Afghans and whippets, but it was her wolfhound, a beautiful giant of a dog, who made it to New York.

Carswell explained that Irish wolfhounds are usually shown by their owners because they have a tendency to become overexcited around strangers, which in turn can cause heart palpitations and "bloat," in extreme cases ending in death. Dog books advise that the breed needs plenty of exercise, so it is left to breeders to warn buyers about these problems. They also must caution them that their friendly giant has a life expectancy of about six years, not the eleven reported in many books, and is prone to monorchidism and testicular cancer. The wolfhound itself is a modern "reconstruction" of the ancient Celtic war and hunting dog, said to be capable of grabbing a war horse by the nose and holding it. Crossbreeding a relict dog to Scottish deerhounds and Great Danes is said to have reinvigorated exhausted bloodlines at the turn of the century. Something of the sort should happen again.

Stephen Webb, owner-handler of Ch. Pond Hollow Wild Goose Chase, the winning Chesapeake Bay retriever, had been involved with the fancy for only a year and a half. A self-professed amateur, he had come to Westminster for the experience, having heard not only that newcomers never won but also that professionals had the advantage with judges. Victories such as Webb's keep hope alive in the band of people who cannot afford or choose not to hire a professional. They defy predictions and the odds, just like Peggy Sue. They also drive more than a few longtime participants, who have never achieved such success, to jealous frenzy.

Westminster bills itself as a benched show, one of the few left in the fancy. Through World War II, it was commonplace for dogs to be kept in a benching area when not in the ring so judges, other partici-pants, and visitors could view them at their leisure for the entire two or three days the show lasted. They were breeding stock, after all. At Westminster, only dogs being exhibited that day must be in the benching area—a section of the Garden called the rotunda. The majority of them are locked in their travel crates, often without food or water until after they have competed, handlers not wanting any "acci-dents" in front of the judge. More than a few handlers do not feed their charges for days before a show to make them perky for the ring, where they then receive rewards of jerky, cookies, or even marshmal-lows for trotting or posing. A few lucky dogs are out on a leash, standing for photos with children or sitting next to their crates.

During the 1995 show, the rotunda was uncomfortably hot despite a temperature outside of ten degrees. People jammed the aisles as they meandered through an area containing not only dogs but also every conceivable piece of canine memorabilia: porcelain figurines, bronze statuettes, posters, breed books, videos, photographic and por-trait-painting services, dog food and snacks, individualized collars, leashes, and beds. Handlers groomed their charges. Among the exhibitors was Take the Lead, a group devoted to helping former or current dog people with AIDS or other terminal conditions pay for their medical treatment through grants. The only requirement is that the person have been active for at least five years in the dog business as represented by the AKC. (Assuming they could not attract support from corporations and wealthy individuals for what was widely perceived as a homosexual disease, organizers expanded their mission and played down the AIDS connection publicly while pursuing their good work.) Associations representing owner-handlers and professional handlers also had their tables at the backstage carnival.

On the Garden floor, the dogs pranced and postured in seven rings. The most numerous breed was the Chinese shar-pei, with fifty-four entrants; the smallest the Sussex spaniel, with two. Crowd favorites were the rottweiler; German shorthaired pointer; toys like the Pomeranian; Akitas; and dogs with long flowing coats, which were also darlings of the television cameras. Properly groomed, with highlights and an occasional touch-up, the long coats billowed like formal gowns as the dogs trotted around the ring. The dog on the string can be beautiful, to be sure, but it might as well be a mechanical doll.

Roger Caras, ringside announcer for the event, president of the ASPCA, and author of several popular books on AKC-recognized dogs, solemnly intoned about the "intelligence," "nobility," "antiquity," and "working ability" of each breed, except the companion dogs, their "beauty" and purpose being self-evident. For the terriers, he added a line about their innate aggressiveness being tempered through careful breeding. Dave Frei and Joe Garagiola, announcers for the live evening television broadcasts by the Madison Square Garden Network, largely echoed the party line, except when Garagiola could not help but notice that a dog could not see because of hair in its eyes. At that moment, Frei leaped in to assure viewers that it could, of course, see quite well, presumably the way one looks through a blindfold.

What struck me as I walked from ring to ring was the uniformity within breeds. It was especially noticeable among those with a single-colored coat: the red Irish setter, silver-gray weimaraner, reddish brown vizsla or Pomeranian. Several popular breeds were divided into separate varieties based solely on coat color and texture: black, parti-colored, and ASCOB (any solid color other than black) cocker spaniels; white and colored English bull terriers; German shorthaired and German wirehaired pointers; shorthaired, wirehaired, and long-haired dachshunds; smooth- and rough-coated collies; smooth and wirehaired fox terriers. In some cases, the variability was scrubbed out because only dogs of a certain color—chocolate mousse among Chesa-peake Bay retrievers, for example—were winning. There was dis-turbing uniformity in size; in fact, beagles and poodles are divided purely on the basis of their height.

With one exception, the Labrador retrievers were short legged and overweight, despite a 1994 change in the standard mandating that they be taller and leaner. (A group of disgruntled Lab owners challenged the change in court, where at this writing the controversy sits.) All of the Labs were yellow or black, not brown, an accepted color, or any of the shades of red-yellow that one sees in working Labs. The most out-standing dog—lean and almost white, a color seldom seen among working retrievers—did not make the cut for final judging.

As a matter of institutional policy, the AKC promotes a narrowing range of possible looks. A campaign begun in the 1980s calls for breed clubs—called "parent" clubs and representing about one-third of the 450 organizations in the AKC—to revise the standards, ostensibly to cull out ambiguity (re: differences) so judges can better understand what to reward. The old standards, some of which date to the nine-teenth century, allow for considerable latitude in the appearance and judging of animals, although even they are narrow versions of what appears naturally. Critics within the clubs charge, however, that the real purpose of the "standardization of standards" is to aid the drive to create a circuit of dog shows throughout the world, which would require a breed to conform to international standards. If that is the case, the dogs of the fancy are facing worldwide as well as domestic ruin.

• • •

The 119th Westminster Kennel Club Show came two months after *Time* magazine ran a cover story, "A Terrible Beauty" (December 12, 1994), exploring the decline of American purebred dogs. The article followed a negative report about puppy mills on ABC's newsmagazine *20/20*. In many ways the *Time* story was a reaffirmation of, and elaboration on, issues raised in my March 1990 article for the *Atlantic Monthly*, "The Politics of Dogs." I explored charges, which had been floating around the fancy and dog world for years, that over-breeding dogs for the AKC show ring was producing dogs unable to perform their traditional functions or even enjoy healthy lives. If anything, the stories, out of respect for the decent men and women who work daily with dogs, understate the full depth of the problems facing AKC-recognized breeds.

With Westminster as one of its flagship clubs, the AKC bills itself as the "principal registry agency for purebred dogs in the United States," the largest and richest body of its type in the world. Of the 50 to 57 million dogs in 35 million American households, some 12 to 15 million possess AKC papers, certifying that they are purebred. That represents about 50 percent of those eligible for AKC registration. Approximately 6 million more are registered with other organizations, the largest of which is the United Kennel Club of Kalamazoo, Michigan. Each year, Americans purchase some 500,000 puppies from retailers, representing 25 to 40 percent of the dogs the AKC registers, depending on how many of their owners pay for papers.

Clearly, the AKC and the roughly 140 (an expansion drive makes the number subject to change) breeds it recognizes—out of the 400 to 500 believed to exist—dominate dogdom. In addition to its *The Complete Dog Book* containing information and photos on each breed, its official magazine, the *Gazette*, videos, and shows create a market for AKC dogs. *The Complete Dog Book*, for example, is the best-selling canine reference book in the United States, although far from the best. Even the shows sponsored by other organizations tend to follow the AKC model while publicly criticizing it.

In essence, breeders, veterinarians, animal-rights activists, trainers, and dog owners have argued first that the American Kennel Club defines quality in a dog primarily on the basis of appearance, paying scant heed to health, temperament, and work habits. Destructive forms of inbreeding have produced millions of dogs capable only of conforming to human standards of beauty. A great many of them cannot even do that.

Second, because it benefits financially from the registration of dogs produced and sold commercially, the AKC has failed to take a stand against the puppy mills, pet stores, brokers, and commercial breeders that exploit purebred dogs. It encourages registration of those animals—although, produced and sold under inhumane conditions, many are of questionable pedigree and genetic fitness—while refusing to cooperate with authorities seeking to regulate the kennels breeding them and the brokers selling them.

Finally, critics charge, the AKC and its clubs define purity in a breed according to a nineteenth-century notion of inheritance that is destructive for the health of the dogs and genetically unsound. The result is that the AKC has repeatedly ignored the horror of inherited diseases afflicting purebred dogs at an astounding rate. Fully one out of four dogs, or 25 percent, from AKC-recognized breeds suffer at least one of the more than 300 genetic disorders identified to date, with the rates among specific breeds running as high as 90 percent for some ailments. Those genetic problems cost dog owners at least $1 billion annually in veterinary care alone.

Attempting to address the problem, more than a dozen states, including California, Florida, New York, and Massachusetts, have passed lemon laws in recent years, requiring in one way or another that breeders take responsibility for their defective puppies. Generally, they mandate that the breeder or pet store replace the dog, refund the purchase price, or, in some cases, pay for treatment. The AKC opposes those bills as onerous, without offering any alternatives or realizing that states *must* act to protect consumers if the producers—in this case the AKC and breeders of its dogs—will not police themselves.

The articles and news reports continue to appear because there are serious problems with AKC-registerable dogs. Consumers are beginning to pay heed, and AKC registrations as a percentage of eligible dogs are falling. The AKC responds with attacks on the writers and producers, demands for retraction, complaints that it is misrepresented. Immediately after my article appeared, AKC officials met with the magazine's editor and demanded a retraction. He refused. They organized letter-writing campaigns and sent Alan Stern, the vice president of communications, to attack me on radio and television talk shows.

The AKC also retaliates against handlers, breeders, judges, and officials who fail to hew to the party line. Their dogs suddenly fail to win in the ring, they no longer receive assignments, or they find themselves without a job. AKC president Kenneth Marden, now a member of the board of directors, was fired shortly after the *Atlantic* piece appeared, ostensibly because he did not place enough emphasis on dog shows. Marden had told me for the article, "We have gotten away from what dogs were originally bred for. In some cases we have paid so much attention to form that we have lost the use of the dog."

In its attack, the AKC overlooked several important facts. The *Atlantic Monthly* has a checking department that verifies every fact in every article in the magazine. Second, people, including many in the fancy, are outraged over what has been happening to purebred dogs and the AKC's failure to act. The horror stories one hears are often worse and always more numerous than those that are printed; thus, on call-in talk shows in the spring of 1990, virtually every participant confirmed what was in the article and added accounts of their own travails with purebred dogs. Had the organization listened to its conscientious members and to veterinarians, it might have known that.

Breed clubs around the country requested permission to reprint the *Atlantic* article, which I granted without charge, believing it more important to make the information widely available than to collect reprint fees from groups with little money. I continue to receive letters from people seeking help with their problems, the most moving from a woman with a Dalmatian who was not allowed to compete in AKC-sponsored obedience trials because it suffered hereditary deafness. The dog was trained to respond to sign language. Some 8 percent of Dalmatians are born deaf, a condition for which the Dalmatian Club of America, the AKC-affiliated breed club, recommends euthanasia. On the other hand, it allows the 22 percent who are carriers of the genetic defect and often deaf in one ear to reproduce and compete.

I also received an appeal for help from the Cavalier King Charles Spaniel Club, USA, which in 1994–95 was locked in a desperate fight to avoid annexation by the American Kennel Club. More than 90 percent of the club's members had repeatedly voted to stay free of the AKC. The club has a strict code of ethics forbidding the sale of puppies through pet stores, a restriction the AKC does not permit its breed clubs. Members feared that their delicate, difficult-to-breed little spaniel would become a darling of commercial kennels if recognized by the AKC. At the same time, the AKC moved to register the border collie, who like the Cavalier King Charles spaniel had been in its miscellaneous class for a quarter of a century—a limbo status where the dog can compete in obedience trials but not conformation or performance events.

The AKC justified its actions much the way it had the annexation of the Australian shepherd in 1990. More than 90 percent of the Australian Shepherd Club of America had vigorously opposed recognition by the AKC. But after a minority of its members petitioned the AKC to register the Aussie, the club reluctantly agreed to go along rather than compete against a separate AKC-sponsored group as guardian of the breed. Theoretically, the dogs care nothing for these machinations. Practically, they are profoundly affected. As a condition for recognition, the AKC demands that variability in size and conformation be eradicated, which can only be accomplished by limiting the gene pool through inbreeding.

Like the Australian shepherd, the border collie and Cavalier King Charles spaniel achieved considerable popularity as non-AKC dogs. Bringing them into the fold means increased revenue for the not-for-profit AKC, which earns about $30 million a year, some 75 percent of which comes from registration fees for puppies, of which only about 2 percent is devoted to education and research. For those reasons, the border collie and Cavalier King Charles spaniel clubs fought back with vigor. By 1996, defenders of the little spaniel were holding their own, aided by the fact that the number of dogs involved is relatively small and they have friends among people influential with AKC officials. On the other hand, border collie lovers failed. The Best of Breed winner at the 120th Westminster Kennel Club Show appeared to lack "eye," the distinctive fixed stare that is a signature of the breed, and possessed the small, refined head favored by the fancy.

For writing of the problems with purebred dogs, Ann Blackman, the reporter for the *Time* article, was subjected to much the same treatment as I. From AKC board chairman James W. Smith, a packet went to members of the AKC's 450 clubs providing copies of letters he and senior officials had written to *Time*, along with a request that they voice similar opinions. In his letter to *Time*'s editor in chief, Smith talked vaguely about the AKC's good works without offering any substantive criticism of the article. The letter from Wayne R. Cavanaugh, vice president for communications at the AKC, attacked Blackman's "journalistic ethics," accusing her of using "shareholder's [*sic*] money to concoct and advance a story for her personal use." Again, he offered no specifics for that absurd charge. Sadly, the letters confirm that the AKC's response to criticism amounts to little more than bombastic assaults, based on nothing, against the integrity of its critics.

AKC governance reflects its attitude toward the public and the dogs it purports to honor. The clubs—the AKC expelled its last individual members in 1923 on the grounds that they were gadflies—send representatives to a meeting of delegates, who elect a board of directors, which selects a president. The deliberations of all bodies are closed to the media; their decisions appear in the *Gazette*. These undemocratic habits have led critics like Herm David, columnist for *Dog World* magazine, to call the AKC "elitist, grossly undemocratic, and operationally secretive," as well as arrogant.

On the night of the judging for Best in Show at the 119th Westminster, I sat next to staff of the *Gazette*. Like the show's public relations officers, they complained bitterly about the accuracy of the *Time* article and ABC program. Then, as the judging proceeded, they began to comment on how certain breeds, like the Irish setter, cocker spaniel, and German shepherd, had indeed been ruined through overbreeding and how the breed clubs refused to take action to improve their lot. They also agreed, as do numerous AKC officials, that the sale of dogs in pet stores and through commercial kennels must stop. They even said the AKC should play a role. Beyond that, as the group winners strutted before the judge, their images beamed into homes and projected on Madison Square Garden's massive video screens, there was talk about how most of the people in the fancy were so concerned with creating designer dogs that they regularly mated dogs without regard to their genetic health or temperament. Those were the charges contained in the articles under attack.

It was Peggy Sue's night to sweep away the competition and another successful run for the Westminster Kennel Club, which numbered not a single woman among its top officers and board members, despite their large representation among the fancy. But Westminster is about designer dogs and champagne parties, to which commoners are not invited. It is a fancy.

Ruined Dogs

Sitting in the living room of her home in Willow, Alaska, in August 1995, Natalie Norris, who has raised, raced, and judged Siberian huskies since 1946, recalled the last time she took her top sled dog to an AKC-sanctioned conformation show. Straight from Howling Dog Kennel, which she and her husband, Earl, own and operate, her Siberian finished seventh out of seven competitors. The only other working dog present placed sixth. Attending another show, she graded the entrants on her perception of their working ability and produced a ranking exactly the opposite of the judges.

In a sense Earl and Natalie Norris are caught in a bind not of their making. Their huskies cannot win in the show ring, where refined, inbred nonworking huskies flourish, or on the snow, where mongrel Alaskan huskies beat them every time. Explaining why Alaskan husky breeders steadfastly oppose any attempt to establish an official standard and stud book for their dogs, even though they keep detailed genealogies, Martin Buser says: "People make a standard and then want the dog to fit that mold. That doomed the Siberian husky. Breeding to a standard ruined it, just as it does all working dogs." Certainly many cur owners agree.

Having heard for years that the Chesapeake Bay retriever had been ruined by a newfound popularity among the fancy, I sought out the breed competition at Westminster in 1995. Of the thirty-seven dogs entered, sixteen came directly from three different breeders with four or more dogs each in the show. Many of the rest were related to dogs from those kennels. All of the representatives of this rustic water dog, whose permissible colors range from dark brown to light deadgrass (straw), were the color of chocolate mousse. Although working Chesapeakes range in weight from fifty-five to one hundred pounds, the AKC breed standard adopted in 1976 decrees that those in the show ring can reach only eighty pounds (seventy for females). Overweight or underweight dogs are *severely* penalized (emphasis added).

The standard for the Chesapeake also states that willingness to work, love of water, and olfactory ability should be given the highest priority in selecting and breeding a dog, yet no dog show has a retrieving, swimming, or smelling test. Instead, the standard instructs judges to give primary consideration to the texture, color, and oiliness of the competitor's coat, as morphological indicators of its working ability. Of course those characteristics do nothing of the sort, but the fancy believes they do.

Our Chesapeake, Max, born four years before the new standard was written and registered with the AKC, weighed ninety pounds when he was fit, well above the standard. With his broad head, thick chest, and dark brown coat, Max was a traditional Chesapeake Bay retriever from Maryland's Eastern Shore, a dog who would break through ice to retrieve and plunge merrily through rapids or heavy surf. If he saw water, he went in it. But because of his size and a residual "third" ear protruding about a quarter of inch from the right side of his face, he would have washed out of the show ring without a point toward a championship.

The rough-and-tumble, obstinate old-style Chesapeake (known as the Chessie to those who like nicknames), which had gained fame in the days late in the last century when ducks were slaughtered by the thousand for sport and was one of the first breeds recognized by the young AKC, was adopted by the fancy in the late 1970s and early 1980s because it was "unruined" by the show world. By 1995, roughly seven dog generations later, the rustic dog had become a rotating circle of chocolate mousse. Max, who loved chocolate above all foods, would have appreciated the irony, but what I saw made me conclude that the reports of the demise of the Chesapeake were not premature. A well-bred Chesapeake can be found—with difficulty.

I asked an avid bird hunter and renowned veterinarian if he had ever hunted over an Irish setter. "Only once in forty years," he said, "and it was *black*. The show people bred for that small head and got rid of half their brains. They're crazy dogs, but the Russians have hunting Irish setters with the big, square heads." In my *Atlantic* article, I quoted Michael W. Fox, a veterinarian and respected animal behaviorist with the Humane Society of the United States, as saying of Irish setters, "They're so dumb they get lost on the end of their leash." The Irish Setter Club of America screamed foul, but it is hard to find anyone who has recently met an Irish setter that was not a thin-skulled bundle of neuroses and genetic ailments with a flowing red coat. The black Irish setter the hunter had encountered would never have been registered, the AKC standard permitting no trace of black.

At the 120th Westminster Kennel Club Show, the Rhodesian Ridgeback judged Best of Breed was thin and gracile like a vizsla, not barrel-chested and broad of head like the traditional hound from Africa. The winning Saint Bernard could not open its eyes, its lids were so heavy and distorted; it walked as if it were dysplastic; and it wheezed after trotting ten feet. The champion mastiff had an uncontrollable tremor in its left rear leg.

I once met a collie, the putative heir of the great Scotch collie, deemed in many circles the smartest dog in the nineteenth century, who would lie down in the middle of the busiest street in Baltimore when he got tired. A collie along one of my sculling routes barks incessantly then obsessively attacks a dock piling whenever I row past. The collie I encountered at the herding trial in central Florida was weak hipped and mentally slow. Of course, not all canine neuroses are the result of bad breeding, but collies have more than their share of problems. An inherited eye disorder, collie eye anomaly, which can cause blindness, afflicts 90 percent, and many also suffer from skin conditions and epilepsy, which plague highly inbred lines of Australian shepherds and other breeds as well. As if their exaggerated, narrow noses and heads, weak hips and eyes were not bad enough, most collies do not have a clue as to what to do with livestock. The collie's problems are not totally new. As early as 1945, when the military was desperate for dogs for the war effort, it specified *farm* collies in its pleas, meaning it wanted working dogs.

Progressive retinal atrophy (PRA), also a hereditary disease that causes blindness, is afflicting a growing number of breeds, from Irish setters to Portuguese water dogs and border collies. PRA, like collie eye anomaly, is recessive and avoidable through proper breeding. Although the genes responsible for PRA appear to differ in location from breed to breed, diagnostic tests for carriers already exist for Irish setters, with those for other breeds on the way. They promise to improve breeding, if people will use them. Although the Portuguese Water Dog Club of America has attempted to do that, with some success, the record for the fancy at large is not good—for this and other genetic conditions.

Most dog owners are familiar with hip dysplasia, an often debilitating laxity in the hip joint caused when the ball does not fit properly with the socket. Although hip dysplasia also occurs in humans and many other domestic animals, it is epidemic among purebred dogs. Few Saint Bernards are born with sound hips, and other breeds, like the German shepherd, are not much better, although the severity of the condition ranges in intensity from occasional discomfort to such severe pain that either corrective surgery, total hip replacement, or destruction of the animal is necessary. Construction of a pseudo–hip joint through surgery or total hip replacement usually buys a few years of comfort for a high price. Even mildly afflicted dogs can develop arthritis as they age, which complicates their problem. For dogs, the pain is physical; for owners, emotional and financial.

Regular exercise can allow some dysplastic dogs to live pain free for years, as their muscles compensate for poor bone formation, but that is hardly universal. At six months of age, our female Catahoula, Clio, had almost no ball or socket formation in her hips, yet she tumbled, ran, cut, and did back flips all day long. Now nearly ten, she has had few problems, primarily because she is fit, she runs and walks on sand or grass, and we live in a warm climate. Under different circumstances, she might have suffered tremendously.

One of the most beautiful dogs I have seen was a silver Chesapeake Bay retriever named, coincidentally I hope, Mark. Just eight months old, he was in a run at a veterinary clinic in Baltimore, awaiting death by lethal injection. His hips were so bad he cried in pain whenever anyone touched his hindquarters. That was twenty-five years ago, before artificial hips were available for dogs, but given the cost of those, Mark's fate probably would not have been much different.

Virtually no breed in the AKC registry is unaffected by inherited defects. On an individual basis, experts estimate that at least 25 percent of purebred dogs are afflicted with some genetic ailment, from metabolic to bone, joint, and eye disorders. Even the healthy ones often lack the brains, talent, and temperament necessary for productive lives. Dalmatians are prone not only to hereditary deafness but also to skin problems, urinary stones, and epilepsy. How closely these ailments, which can cause death or large medical bills, are associated is not completely known, but in 1980, Robert Schaible, then a geneticist at the Indiana University School of Medicine in Indianapolis, reported on an experiment he had conducted to free the Dalmatian of those defects. He crossed a Dalmatian with a pointer—the two are closely related—and then bred back to Dalmatians. After five generations—ten years—the defect-free backcrossed dogs were indistinguishable from purebred Dalmatians. (Dalmatians were used as pointers early in their history and probably influenced development of the gundogs we see today.)

In 1981, the AKC board of directors approved registration of Schaible's dogs, boldly arguing that the AKC had a responsibility to do what it could to correct genetic defects. The Dalmatian Club of America, the parent club, objected that the purity of its breed was being compromised and forced cancellation of the registration. The AKC board said it had to accede to the wishes of the breed club, but critics observe that it simply bowed to an ignorant minority. Since then, the AKC has failed to educate its members about modern breeding practices or encourage other crosses that might reinvigorate faltering bloodlines. Institutional culture has decided to ignore the simple truth that breeds are the products of human actions to create a limited gene pool from a broader, more diverse one. Their "purity" is a human artifact, which means next to nothing for working ability and less than nothing for health.

The metabolic and genetic problems inherent in the bull terrier apparently were present from the beginning of the breed, yet to this day the breed club will not take steps to insist on their eradication through selective breeding. The club has a committee devoted to genetics and supports research on a small scale, but the majority of its members refuse to take further action. They believe, as do their colleagues in other clubs, that all breeds have trouble and, therefore, nothing needs to be done to change the situation. Bad dogs are simply disposed of or tolerated; too many of them are bred, especially those who are champions in the show ring, where their lousy temperament and health do not weigh against them.

The bulldog and Boston terrier have difficulty whelping naturally, because of their brachycephalic heads, which become wedged in the birth canal. Bitches are regularly subjected to cesarean sections. Along with similar breeds, like the boxer and mastiff, they can have problems breathing, especially in the heat or after exercise. For unknown reasons, whippets also have difficulty giving birth without assistance. Many of the toy breeds are so small and fragile they cannot live outside artificial environments, and a number of them, including the Yorkshire terrier, Maltese, and bichon frise, are difficult to housebreak, inbreeding for size and other bizarre characteristics having affected their ability to defecate properly.

Cocker spaniels, Labrador retrievers, terriers, collies, poodles, and dachshunds appear to have a predisposition toward obesity, which afflicts an estimated 40 percent of the dogs in Europe and North America, leading to skin, joint, and cardiovascular problems, as well as diabetes. (Spayed and neutered dogs have a problem with fatness, as well, but that is controllable through diet and exercise.) Subject to sudden rage syndrome and hydrocephaly, the popular cocker long ago lost its ability to hunt. Certain lines of Labradors have also become prone to dwarfism, which defines basset hounds, Pekingese, the bulldog, Scottie, and similar short-legged breeds. Bedlington terriers (who more closely resemble sheep than dogs) suffer from copper toxicosis, a fatal ailment. Fully fifty pure breeds are prone to autoimmune diseases that affect internal organs and the central nervous system.

By the end of 1994, markers had been found for only 23 of more than 300 genetic ailments, recorded on a computerized data base developed by Donald Patterson and his colleagues at the University of Pennsylvania School of Veterinary Medicine. An average of ten new diseases are added to the data base each year. Despite the AKC's financial contribution to that project, it and other organizations "devoted" to dogs, including the pet industry, have largely failed to support basic genetic research at levels needed to produce results.

At Westminster, I met a sheltie breeder who told me that canine hip dysplasia was not necessarily inherited and was sometimes self-correcting, comments I have heard too often from show-dog breeders. The assertion appears related to the observation that environmental factors, like too much food or exercise when young, can influence the onset and severity of the problem, which by all accounts is polygenic, meaning due to the interaction of an unspecified number of genes. The confusion, of course, lets irresponsible breeders claim that their lines do not, in fact, have a genetic problem. They further justify their posture by arguing that no one has found the genes or genetic markers for hip dysplasia.

A breeder of Australian shepherds told me about a friend of hers, a "collie person," whose dog had finished his championship in four shows—a remarkable feat—when he was a year old. The dog was severely dysplastic, yet the owner had people clamoring to breed to him, and she was granting their desire. This same Australian shepherd breeder discovered that her foundation stud, who had already sired a Best of Breed at Westminster, had produced a litter in which seven of the puppies developed bad hips. Perplexed because she tests all her dogs and knows them to be free of the condition, she investigated and discovered that the bitch she had bred him to, although free of the disorder herself, was the daughter of a dysplastic dog, who nonetheless had been the top-ranked conformation bitch in the country. Although this capacity of dysplasia to jump generations is well documented and not uncommon for polygenic disorders, breeders interpret it as proof of nonheritability.

Breeders of AKC-registerable dogs are not the only culprits in the spread of dysplasia and other genetic disorders. Many breeders of curs, border collies, kelpies, and other working dogs also refuse to x-ray, arguing that as long as they work well, they are fine. While it is true that dogs with severe problems generally become lame, some, like Clio, compensate for their weakness. Bred, those seemingly healthy dogs pass on the genes for their problem. That said, I suspect that extensive testing would prove that hip dysplasia and other maladies among working dogs do not approach the levels found among show dogs.

Optimally, no puppy from a litter with a dysplastic dog should be bred, but because that is infeasible, the Orthopedic Foundation for Animals (OFA), which certifies the hips of dogs through X rays taken after the animal is two years old, has developed a set of recommendations that substantially reduces the number of afflicted dogs, when followed. (The Canine Eye Registry Foundation serves much the same function for eye problems.)

The OFA advises that only normal dogs should be bred; they should come from normal grandparents and parents; 75 percent of their siblings should be normal; and they should have a proven record of producing healthy dogs. The OFA actually rates hips as excellent, good, fair, borderline, mild, moderate, and severe. It certifies for breeding only those with excellent, good, or fair hips.

Because most dogs are finished—earn their championship—and bred before two years of age and because their owners fear what they would learn about their soundness, many are never certified by the OFA. Seeking an earlier detection system, Gail Smith, chief of surgery at the University of Pennsylvania School of Veterinary Medicine, developed during the late 1980s and early 1990s a method of evaluating hip laxity in dogs as young as four months, before clinical symptoms of dysplasia usually appear and before dogs reach their sexual maturity. X rays are used to rate the puppies on a "distraction index"

(DI), assigning the tightest ball-and-socket fit a score of zero and the worst 1.0.

Called PennHIP and marketed by International Canine Genetics of Malvern, Pennsylvania, the method has shown promise as a predictor of which dogs might develop dysplasia. It has also been embraced by many in the fancy as a way to choose sound dogs for breeding before they even reach first heat. A dog bred before two years, especially among larger breeds, is not physically mature and too young in any event to be producing puppies, but many in the fancy are uninterested in such niceties. They refuse to believe what they know.

The story is the same for every breed and condition. A woman who had shown Doberman pinschers around the busy Florida circuit for years told me that she and her mother had quit when they could no longer tolerate what was happening to their breed. Von Willebrand's disease, an inherited disorder that causes excessive bleeding, had become epidemic, and spinal problems had grown commonplace as people bred to a fashion demanding "boxy" dogs, only as long as they were tall, with downward-sloping hindquarters resembling those of the German shepherd. Many dogs showed foul tempers—incorrectly attributed to rage syndrome—or congenital fearfulness.

Too often, breeders choose to hide behind scientific uncertainty to justify practices they know to be damaging to the dogs they claim to love. Intent on winning prizes, they breed to the champion bitch or stud in an effort to secure its good qualities without a thought to the bad they are bringing along for the ride. This widespread practice creates a "founder effect," by which both good and bad characteristics are rapidly and thoroughly disseminated. Seeking to perpetuate those championship traits in their kennels, meaning they select for a narrow band of observable traits—head shape, size, coat color, and length— show breeders engage in various forms of inbreeding. (When mating grandsire to granddaughter, granddam to grandson, or first cousins, they like to call it line breeding. Genetically, it is inbreeding.)

Defenders of the practice observe that all thoroughbred horses in this country descend from six animals and that many new species are believed to arise from isolated groups. Most geneticists agree that while inbreeding is not absolutely evil, it is always risky. Genetic variability is essential to maintaining an organism's vitality and ability to respond to environmental stress. Genetic variability is what is lost through inbreeding. When done poorly and for the wrong reasons, which is to say when flawed animals are not culled, the practice produces genetic disasters. Culling is not foolproof; many asymptomatic dogs can carry one or more recessive genes, which they will pass on to at least some of their offspring. Eventually, those undesirable genes will be expressed. In the fancy, the emphasis on appearance to the exclusion of all else has led to the maintenance and breeding of dogs with severe defects.

Nearly all genetic ailments in dogs are recessive and are fixed along with desired physical characteristics through the founder effect and inbreeding. Some breeders develop in their line an undesirable or unhealthy trait—dysplasia or epilepsy, for example. Others encounter genetic fatigue, a loss of vigor, even sterility. They can no longer produce the type of dog winning in the ring. Those who do not breed for working ability find it vanishes, a clear sign that it must constantly be reinforced. So many dogs have problems that even outcrossing has become hazardous in some breeds, because you might inadvertently bring a disorder into your kennel, the way the Australian shepherd breeder introduced hip dysplasia to hers.

Most geneticists maintain that to breed good dogs, one must start with as broad a gene pool of unrelated or distantly related animals with the desired traits, including health, as possible and then seek to produce puppies who are more healthy, temperamentally sound, and intelligent than their parents. If line breeding is necessary, as it sometimes might be, the key is to cross back out as soon as possible, certainly as soon as a defect or problem appears. Call the whole process one of seeking hybrid vigor, which theoretically is more possible to attain today by travel and the availability of frozen sperm than it has ever been in the past.

It is essential for people not to breed dogs who manifest or carry unwanted characteristics. Yet within the fancy, that simple measure is ignored, partly for fear it would spell the demise of whole lines, if not breeds, some defects being so abundant that no dogs can be found free of them. Even when defects are not universal, mating dogs with traits that arise from recessive genes can lead to problems because so many defects are also recessive. I have already pointed out the problems that arise when Australian shepherds and Catahoulas with glass eyes and blue or red merle coats are mated; similar genetic disasters arise in other breeds where recessive traits are bred among related or unrelated dogs, such as white bull terriers. Believing the look is all that matters for winning prizes and sales, breeders ignore the odds.

I wish I could say the problem does not extend to non-AKC dogs, but I would be lying and self-contradictory, having already referred several times to the problems facing Catahoulas. In fact, several alternative kennel clubs, including the large United Kennel Club, are also in the show business, and the exhibitors participating in those events are engaging in the same harmful practices that have brought so many AKC breeds to ruin. I'll give one example.

A woman called me one evening to discuss mating her Catahoula bitch to our male. We get these calls because many of the Catahoulas in South Florida come from one breeder and her top sire, making it difficult to find an unrelated dog. Our male is from Louisiana. He also has the desirable eyes and coloration, along with a rank and gritty demeanor.

"I want a red merle male with a bulldog head and blue eyes," she said, "because I show my dogs and I know what's winning in the show ring."

"Wait," I said, "I have no interest in dog shows. I don't like them, and I'm not at all sure I want to breed my dog for that purpose. I've written against the show world. I'm telling you this now so you will understand I'm not sympathetic to your plight."

I might as well have been talking to the wall.

"I believe in instinct," she said. "At the last show of the National Association of Louisiana Catahoulas, I entered my dog in that test to see whether they would herd, what do you call it?"

"An instinct test."

"Right. She looked at the cows rather than me, so I guess she has instinct. The people there say the dogs with big heads are hogdogs and the ones with smaller heads are cowdogs. That's the difference between them."

"That's a lot of crap," I said. "Cowdogs will get on cows, bunching them, sometimes catching. A lot of hogdogs are just better trackers or dogs who really aren't interested in cows. Others could work cows as well as hogs, but their owners are hog hunters. It has nothing to do with what their head looks like."

"Right," she said, her voice sounding unconvinced. "OK. Well, I'll call to come look at your dog. Does he have a big head or a small head?"

I told her not to bother.

Thus, the ruination of dogs comes from bad breeding for superficial traits; nonselection for working habits and temperament; and sloppy overbreeding, which allows bad traits to proliferate. As long as the fancy continues its current approach to judging quality in breeds based on appearance alone, the situation will continue to worsen. As it now stands, most dogs sold to consumers by people in the fancy are culls, puppies judged inappropriate for showing. Many breeders divide their litters into three categories: show, breeding, and pet quality. The first has the potential to be a champion, the second to produce "sound" dogs but not to win ribbons, and the third to be too bad for showing or breeding but good enough for living as a healthy pet, as long as it is neutered.

The categories are meaningful only to people attempting to put a price on dogs. When unspayed and unneutered, dogs of lesser quality breed in people's homes, and the offspring are sold as the heirs to champions. No regard is given to their appearance or their talent. Other animals are bred in the deplorable conditions of puppy mills. That any of those dogs turn out well—and some do—is testament to their resilience and the handling of their owners.

The effects of bad breeding are compounded by mass production to meet the public's demand for a "hot" dog, be it a little-known AKC breed or one not recognized by that organization and, therefore, considered "rare." It is a world where faddism meets vanity. The shar-pei was marketed as an ancient Chinese fighting and guard dog rescued from near extinction during the 1950s and 1960s when Mao Zedong campaigned against dog ownership. That the shar-pei was most likely a construct of the period, rather than a victim, receives no notice. In 1968, there were a dozen of these dogs in the United States. By 1990, there were 50,000, with most of that growth occurring in the 1980s, when the demand for non-AKC rare breeds combined with a fascination for the wrinkled appearance of the shar-pei to make it a yuppie dog. Puppies sold for as much as $10,000. The 1983 Neiman-Marcus Christmas catalog carried a pair as its special offering, to the dismay of dog lovers. During the height of the craze, one puppy mill produced 150 puppies a year and sold them for an average of $1,000 each. There were shar-pei, mini-pei, and pug-pei.

Sloppily bred from a limited gene pool—it is depressing how often that statement can be made about a pure breed—the dogs have developed autoimmune deficiencies leading to severe skin disorders and faulty bites that sometimes make it difficult for them to eat. Their hips are bad; their eyelids need to be surgically cut from over the eye. Many display the foul temper of a punch-drunk fighter. They are what veterinarians call a genetic disaster.

In 1989, the breed's proponents sought shelter in the AKC, calculating that as soon as the shar-pei became an official breed it would lose cachet. Probably the health problems had a greater impact, but whatever the cause, the market for the disasters collapsed in 1989. Since then, breeders have worked without notable success to rid the shar-pei of genetic flaws. Without outcrossing or rigorous breeding of the healthiest specimens, if any can be found, their task is hopeless.

Mastiffs, like the dogue de Bordeaux, the Neapolitan, and Tibetan, experienced a surge of interest as the shar-pei failed and people sought large guard dogs to protect them from crime. Hip dysplasia and bad temperament, as well as eye and skin problems, began to proliferate. Many are considered expensive, lethargic dunces.

Watching some of these mastiffs, I have difficulty imagining how they ever could be descended from the ferocious fighting, guard, and war dogs of antiquity. A Neapolitan of my acquaintance, a beautiful black giant, has as his sole distinguishing characteristic a fondness for drinking dirty scrub water. A mastiff down the street from us spends its life in a doghouse, sleeping, except for a few minutes at dusk when it cries. It is not clear the dog can see; its owners never give it attention. It is only three years old.

Despite the rising interest in "rare" dogs, the bulk of the abuses remain among breeds the AKC recognizes, simply because they are most abundant. Many of those selected for pressure are dogs deemed "unruined" by popularity, like the Chesapeake in the 1970s and 1980s. During the decade from 1984 to 1994, the rottweiler underwent a population explosion, as part of the same search for home guardians that brought the run on mastiffs. In 1984, the American Kennel Club registered 21,207 rottweilers. In 1994, the total stood at 102,596—by the AKC's own measure less than half of those eligible. That is nearly a fivefold increase in a decade, roughly five canine generations. Hip quality and temperament have fallen in direct proportion to the rise in population. A great many of the rottweilers are squat and obese, like Labradors. During that same decade, the ever popular, already ruined German shepherd went from 59,490 to 78,999.

There are fine, concerned breeders, but finding them involves a search through breed clubs, veterinarians, kennels, and individuals involved in various aspects of the dog world. For example, the Monks of New Skete, an Orthodox Catholic Church religious order near Cambridge, New York, have produced German shepherds without dysplasia and other problems since 1966, from German lines because American-bred dogs were too unreliable. They will not mate inferior animals; they cull those with defects. Other private breeders are also producing a limited number of solid dogs, especially of the working, hunting, and herding breeds, but like the Monks of New Skete, they do not advertise and frequently have waiting lists of more than a year. They are also selective about their clients, wanting to place their dogs only with responsible owners.

Dedicated though they are, these breeders face a difficult, daily battle as long they remain in the AKC, and many do in the hope that they will have an effect on its policies. They must walk a thin line between producing dogs they know are healthy, good-tempered, and capable and those who are winning in the ring—a different sort of animal.

The problem is so severe in some breeds that people have developed different lines, created new crosses, or registered their working dogs with other groups, if at all. Among Australian shepherds, show dogs are larger and slower than their working cousins. Border collies appear to be undergoing a similar split between show and working lines. Labrador retrievers have been fractured into as many as five distinct varieties: show dogs; dogs competing in AKC field trials; hunting retrievers; dogs used as guide dogs for the blind, who are bred for temperament, trainability, and health; and pointing retrievers, a controversial category, to be sure.

Breeders and owners of working pointers, setters, Brittanies, spaniels, and retrievers often register them with American Field, an organization in Chicago devoted to gundogs. They emphasize working ability and what they call biddability or trainability. Feist, cur, and hound breeders also register with one or more groups depending on their desire to compete in trials and tap into a broader record of bloodlines. The Masters of Foxhounds Association has maintained its registry since 1907 for working foxhounds at hunt clubs in the United States and Canada. As a rule, the master of a hunt will put down a whole litter of foxhounds if one appears with genetic problems, a draconian solution that has nonetheless been effective in keeping the breed relatively free of genetic problems for nearly 300 years. On the other hand, the mushers who breed Alaskan huskies eschew registries, preferring to keep their own records. In their tight-knit world, the people producing good dogs are well-known.

Upbringing also has a profound effect on a dog's working ability. I have seen numerous kennels of people active in the fancy where the dogs leave their runs, with concrete floors, only to enter a traveling crate to go to a show. The animals are socialized, barely, to the breeder and perhaps a kennel hand or handler. Otherwise, they do nothing. They are afraid of grass, which may, in fact, hurt their feet. I have also seen a number of well-run kennels, but they represent, I fear, a minority of the total devoted to producing pedigreed dogs.

I heard the story once of a young female who was raised for six months in a crate. Released for "training," she tripped when she walked on grass, not knowing how to lift her feet. It took weeks to teach her to climb a flight of stairs, and even after mastering that, she was unable to make the associative leap necessary to climb different stairs. She required retraining. Yet the dog's breeder was known for her champions. Stairs are not easy for dogs, but a seven-week-old Catahoula we had with us for a few days taught herself how to go up and down by following Marlow and Clio.

By some accounts, 33 percent of the dogs born in the United States are abandoned or given up for adoption before they reach their second birthday. Half of those dogs are euthanized. Added to those casualities are puppies who die from a disease like parvovirus, which also disproportionately affects older dogs, or "fading puppy syndrome," which appears due to inbreeding and kills 15 to 30 percent before they are weaned. A propensity for parvovirus appears to be innate in some breeds, like the rottweiler and Doberman, probably because of immune system problems, but it has also been shown that puppies in pet stores or large kennels are particularly susceptible owing to high levels of the virus in those areas. Although a vaccine exists for parvo, puppies go through a period of weakened immunity after they are weaned and before their immune systems are fully developed. Inoculations help bridge the gap, but they are not foolproof.

Applying these statistics and those on inherited defects to a hypothetical litter of eight purebred dogs—taken by many experts as a large number—produces an interesting group portrait. Two will die within the first month from fading puppy syndrome; two will become rescued animals and either find new homes or be destroyed; two will end up with one or more genetic ailments other than the fading puppy syndrome that killed their littermates—hip dysplasia or an eye problem being most common; and two to four, depending on the fate of the rescue cases, will make healthy pets, workers, or show dogs, albeit with various abilities. Clearly there is overlap in the figures—many abandoned dogs are quite sound, for example, and some breeds are healthier than others, as are some lines within breeds. For toy and small breeds, which might produce one to four dogs per litter, the situation is worse. There is nothing robust or superior about the dogs of the fancy, except in the imaginations of people.

The Fancy

The charge that breeding dogs for the fancy renders them unfit to perform any function dates to the first officially recognized dog show in England in 1859. Of more recent origin is the depth and breadth of the problem. Dog shows in the nineteenth century involved a smattering of representatives of a relatively small number of breeds. They were creations primarily of the new urban and professional classes, the bourgeoisie, who were caught up in the general cultural drive to perfect nature.

In many cases the results were genetic mutants—"sports"—dwarfs, midgets, giants, often with distinctive coats. Perpetuation and refinement of those dogs became proof not only of the ability of humans to control the forces of reproduction but also of the dog's mutability and devotion. What other animal, after all, would so willingly distort itself for our pleasure?

People had collected the genetic accidents for millennia or, like the Chinese with the "little lion dog," tried to shape puppies to their own design. But the scale of the fancy's effort and its success were unprecedented. Although these breeders did not understand genetics, they could see that within the space of a few generations they could dramatically alter the shape of the dog—much faster than they could with other livestock, which in any event was not as attractive, affectionate, or as intelligent as the dog. Turning the top representative of this or that breed into something I created became the driving force for the fancy.

The definition of "breed," as something with a registry and a "standard," dates from the second half of the nineteenth century. To be officially purebred, then, was to possess a certificate of pedigree—papers—certifying the dog's genealogy, and, of course, to look like its fellow breed members. Today, officials for the AKC and other kennel clubs have gone so far as to argue that without looking at a dog's papers they cannot tell whether it is a collie, a bull terrier, Labrador, or Dalmatian. As absurd as that sounds, it reflects the reality that modern breeds are human constructs often based on the most subtle differences.

The nineteenth-century notion of breed as elucidated in England both supported and was grounded in the racial and social theories of the period, setting out the superiority of the white race over all others and within that assigning worth to individuals based on their class and family. In the ostensibly democratic United States, class divisions also took on ominous ethnic and racial dimensions. Indeed, throughout western Europe, there were justifications for all manner of distinctions based on income, ethnicity, and family blood. The clash of these with democratic ideals, their transmogrification in the horrible eugenics of Nazism, their perpetuation in racism that remains potent—all are stories for other books. Their significance here lies in the way they are reflected in the definition of "breed," the worship of purity of bloodlines, and the assignment of qualities to dogs based less on what they did than on who owned them and where they originated—northern dogs being superior to southern dogs, for example, hunting hounds and sporting dogs to peasants' curs and lurchers, greyhounds racing for gentlemen to whippets running and ratting for workers.

As historian Harriet Ritvo observes in her seminal 1987 study, *The Animal Estate*, the fancy was the sport of the English urban and professional classes, who wanted desperately to be upper class. No matter how hard they tried to achieve that goal, however, they were locked out by virtue not of their merit or wealth, which were often greater than that of the nobility they sought to join, but their birth. They funneled their frustrated desire in a number of social and cultural directions, including establishment of kennels for breeding pedigreed dogs.

The kennels allowed them to play God, directing the evolution of the species toward a desired perfection of form and purity of blood. Ritvo writes of breed standards that repeatedly split the dog world according to appearance: "Although the system appeared secure and stable, grounded in biological imperatives and validating centuries of English dog breeding, in fact it resulted from an impressive collective act of will and imagination."

Dogs could become champions, the most noble of the noble, based on the closeness with which they matched the standards their owners had invented. A few breeds were even dubbed "aristocratic" because of their historic association with royalty: pugs, said to have been favorites of William and Mary; bloodhounds, the quintessential scent hounds with traceable roots to the Middle Ages; borzois, the wolf-hunting sight hounds of Russian nobility; deerhounds, the sight hounds of Scottish nobility; and collies, because Queen Victoria fancied them. Sheep being the cash darlings of the gentry, collies were forgiven their rustic roots.

Yet, as Ritvo points out, no matter how hard they tried, the members of the fancy, precisely because they were not to the manor born, could never capture the essence of breeding or class; they could only record pedigrees and collect brightly colored ribbons or silver trophies. The dogs winning those prizes symbolized, Ritvo says, the "power to manipulate and the power to purchase," which were, indeed, the essence of bourgeois society.

As befit a valued commodity, prices ran high for the popular breeds. In 1891, in England, collies and Saint Bernards commanded £1,000 each, a considerable amount; fox terriers went for £375; and the King Charles spaniel fetched £259. Dog thieves received considerably less, but they still carried on a flourishing business fueling rendering plants, medical schools, or ransoming the household pet for clear profit—£2 to £20, Ritvo reports, in 1844.

The Americans closely followed the British model in most regards, but because wealth and class were more closely aligned on these shores, they could more easily claim the mantle of superiority for themselves and their dogs. Today, AKC officials make veiled references to the entry into the fancy after World War II of the "wrong type" of people—middle- and working-class breeders who manage their own kennels and show their own dogs. The analysis goes: Before and even today at its highest levels, the fancy is the sport of the wealthy few who can hire professionals and are unmotivated by crass "commercial" interests. The people bringing ruin to this gentle sport are the middle and lower classes, who have no regard for proper breeding.

Making the argument, AKC officials reveal the class bias inherent in their organization and also one of the ways in which they seek to avoid responsibility for the sorry state of American dogdom. In producing dogs who win ribbons and have no other redeeming purpose, those "wrong" people are simply being good members of the fancy. Their attitude toward dogs is no different from that of the wealthy collectors who hire professionals to manage their kennels and dogs—they just have less money.

Although never approaching the English in their emphasis on breeding for subtle social distinctions, the nineteenth-century French bourgeoisie engaged in a similar glorification and commodification of the dog, according to Kathleen Kete in *The Beast in the Boudoir* (1995). The primary differences lay in the French emphasis on the concept of breed and view of breeding as a conquest of nature. They placed less emphasis on phenotype than on the entire definition of "dog." Thus, breed histories became moral allegories revolving around the idea that the best dogs were those who had become most incorporated into human society. The French continue to allow dogs in restaurants, to the delight of dog lovers and disgust of those who consider them filthy. During a wonderful lunch at the Manoir du Tertre outside Rennes in Brittany with a team of primate researchers, we encountered a large-boned black Great Dane who stood at table height and politely sampled our meals with his nose. He never tried to taste them.

In England, France, the United States, and other European countries, a significant manifestation of the transformation of the dog into a pet lay in creation of the small companion dogs. Many of them were bred for shortened muzzles that gave them a more human demeanor, and they were miniaturized to make them doll-like. Often they were clothed, groomed, expected to behave like little people. Their feet never touched the ground. The social-climbing, overweight dowager with her pampered sleeve dog or obese, sexually repressed toy spaniel became a standing joke that often understated reality. Canine weddings with the principals dressed in formal attire were common in Paris and are still conducted not only in France but also in the United States, England, Australia, and other nations where certain dog lovers feel their pet is better off masquerading as a person.

The first chihuahua I met, while in elementary school, belonged to an obese woman who kept it in her kitchen. Never letting the dog go outside, she had covered the floor with newspaper to ease the task of cleaning up its excrement and urine. The dog spent its time yapping at strangers and biting her arms. Thirty years later, I learned from reading Kathleen Kete that, despite the current notoriety of Paris for excrement-carpeted streets and sidewalks, nineteenth-century Parisian pets were frequently kept indoors for their health, making our neighbor in Winter Park, Florida, the keeper of a bizarre and twisted tradition about which she was ignorant. She knew only that, outside, her dog, said to have dated from the days of the Aztec empire, became a quivering mass of nerves, frightened of its shadow.

Feeding the fancy was a widespread perception, championed by naturalists, including Charles Darwin, that the dog stood just below humans in the animal kingdom, matched, if at all, only by the horse. It embodied the perfect relationship between master and devoted, obedient, industrious servant—not generally to be found among human servants, to be sure. The dog was deemed not intelligent, although Darwin himself considered it capable of rational thought and all other human qualities of mind, so much as, Ritvo says, "sagacious," wise, and forgiving. It was said that a good dog would do anything for its master: starve itself to death on his grave out of devotion and sorrow, give up its life for him, travel thousands of miles from a place of bondage to return home, fight to the death to protect home and hearth, work until it dropped, swim until it drowned, commit suicide from despair. The dog gave even when abused, thereby showing its superiority as a slave.

Many naturalists in the late eighteenth and early nineteenth centuries considered domestic animals of all sorts superior to their wild cousins precisely because they had submitted their will to that of humans. Wild animals were fit only for slaughter, the more and faster the better, an attitude that found bloody fulfillment in the entire ethos of hunting as adventure, sport, and public service. Nature existed to be conquered, and the more unnatural the dog became the better, as long as it retained some speciality, like any good worker.

Although dog marts, informal comparisons, and competitions existed probably for centuries and by the 1830s workers in England were holding regular ratting events for their whippets and terriers in pubs, the first "recorded" dog show took place at Newcastle-upon-Tyne, England, in 1859, among merchants and professionals. Fanciers organized the Kennel Club in 1873 to impose order on their "sport" and maintain the stud book for their dogs. The first dog show in the United States was held a year later in Mineola, New York, with the inaugural Westminster Kennel Club Show taking place three years later.

In 1884, the American Kennel Club was founded, according to its charter, to promote specific breeds, sponsor shows, and "to do everything to advance the study, breeding, exhibiting, running and maintenance of purity of thoroughbred dogs." Through World War II, AKC shows were multiday affairs involving benched displays and ring judging of what was deemed breeding stock. After the war, shows became shorter, benches were removed from all except the most prestigious, and judging became a race against the clock—all to cater to growing numbers of participants. The increased speed meant that only the most superficial characteristics of the dog were on display. Appearance mattered, nothing else.

During the past fifty years, members of the fancy in the United States have added to the archaic notions of breeding that govern their world a program for the mass production of dogs to meet the demands of a growing human population. At many kennels, the goal now is to produce puppies by the gross, select from among them the most desirable for the show ring, attribute the result to scientific breeding, and sell the rest.

The AKC went along, in no small measure for the money. Like many nonprofit organizations, it is required to spend what it makes—thus, no profit—but if it chooses to spend that money promoting purebred AKC dogs and events, paying handsome salaries, maintaining offices in New York City, and producing slick promotional material, no one is to stop it. It does not spend money encouraging responsible breeding, cleaning fraud from its stud book, and sponsoring research into the problems of purebred dogs, the scant 2 percent of its income devoted to research and education notwithstanding.

In Europe, kennel clubs frequently require that dogs be free of dysplasia and other genetic ailments before they can compete for championships or be certified to breed. Some organizations require that champions distinguish themselves in the field and ring. The AKC has no such provisions. Its only concession to matters of health is to prohibit cosmetic surgery to correct defects, notwithstanding that many alterations go undetected. It is difficult to find a handler who does not speak about illegal surgery as a major problem. The AKC itself proceeds in typically ambivalent fashion, outlawing surgery to correct eye problems that cause pain and blindness while mandating ear cropping and/or tail docking in Doberman pinschers, boxers, Great Danes, and other dogs, which cause pain and adversely affect their ability to communicate.

There are a number of ways to effect reform that would be good for dogs without ruining the notion of the show. First, dogs should not qualify for championships until they prove their working ability through field or obedience trials and are certified free of defects and of sound temperament. That will require rewriting the strict standards now in place to permit judges to consider each dog on its own merit, not according to an abstract definition. In keeping with those changes, ear cropping and tail docking should be banned, as they are in England and Canada. Second, breeds unable to whelp naturally and those unable to live normal lives outside an artificial environment should be modified through selective breeding or eliminated from competition and registration. Third, dogs with congenital defects should be denied registration, their owners discouraged from breeding them. That can be done by selling dogs with "restricted" transfers, stipulating that they will not be bred until they have reached two years of age and are certified free of defects by a veterinarian. If they fail, they are neutered. Owners violating the agreement will not be able to register their litters. Dogs failing the test will be replaced by the breeder.

Some breed clubs have taken that step, without support from the AKC. Choosing not to oppose such a sound policy outright, it has decreed that dogs with restrictions cannot compete for their championships because they are not technically breeding stock. Since most dogs earn their AKC championship before they are a year old, the policy makes the restricted transfer anathema to people wanting to compete. It is a typical instance of the way in which the American Kennel Club pays lip service to quality while enforcing other rules.

In much the same fashion, AKC officials publicly admit that the papers they issue warranting the purity of bloodlines for three generations of an AKC dog are no guarantee of quality, that they would, as then president William F. Stifel told Michael Satchell, a reporter for *Parade* in 1987, register a blind, deaf, three-legged purebred pup with hip dysplasia and green fur, as long as its papers were in order. Yet at the same time, AKC publications and announcers sing the praises of the purebred animal. The problem has become so egregious in recent years that people regularly talk about AKC papers as worthless, fit only for housebreaking the dog or starting a fire.

Sadly, the world of pedigreed dogs has become a manifestation not of the possibility of breeding to perfection or even of bourgeois dreams of social ascendancy—those having been achieved. Rather, it resembles nothing so much as the dysfunctional American family rife with incest, neglect, gender-based favoritism, physical and emotional abuse, slavish devotion to appearances, imposition of the hopes and aspirations of the parents for wealth and success on the offspring. Money and success in the ring—that is, society—are the sole determinants of an individual's worth. Failure brings rejection.

The Dark Underbelly

Not coincidentally, the boom in dogs coincided in the United States with the explosion in population, suburbs, cars, and disposable income following the end of World War II. To the buying public, "AKC" became a name brand signifying that the dog was purebred and of high quality. Producing and selling those dogs to families with kids—the major consumers—became a way for hobbyists to make extra money and kennel owners, including farmers, to earn a living. The "doggie in the window" was, in fact, a mass-produced commodity, shipped by way of a broker from the puppy mill where it was manufactured to a pet store where it was displayed and sold. The AKC earned money each step of the way: with registration of the litter by the breeder, from transfer slips filled out whenever the puppies passed through middlemen, and when the proud new owner registered his or her pup. The AKC grew in power and wealth as the number of dogs increased, regardless of their quality. Expansion of dog shows fed the demand for the perfect dog to match the perfect life of peace and prosperity. In 1956, the AKC had 5 million dogs in its stud book. Since then, it has registered more than 33 million, averaging over 1 million a year since 1977.

The problem was that the dogs often failed to meet expectations. They were foul tempered, in ill health, poorly socialized. They proliferated so greatly in suburban neighborhoods that ordinances were passed requiring them to be fenced, vaccinated, licensed, leashed, and more recently cleaned up after. In the 1960s, under pressure from animal-welfare groups, department stores were required to stop selling pets—not only dogs and cats but turtles, hamsters, mice, guinea pigs. Pet stores, especially chains that were popping up in strip shopping centers, became the chief retail outlet. But backyard breeders and direct-sale commercial kennels were also abundant for the most popular dogs.

Born in squalid, filthy cages that often keep their mother from urinating properly, much less walking, given little human contact, taken at age six weeks or so—legally now eight weeks in some states—and sent for sale at a pet store in the dark back of a hot—or cold—truck, puppies for the retail trade usually spend the most sensitive socialization period in isolation. As a result, they are fearful, prone to aggression and separation anxiety, and largely untrainable. Many end up dead, disposed of like any unwanted commodity. The few who rise above their circumstances are, indeed, exceptional.

In 1970, after extensive lobbying by the Humane Society of the United States and other animal-welfare groups, puppy mills and brokers (the middlemen who shipped the dogs) were brought under the jurisdiction of the federal Animal Welfare Act, which, first passed in 1966, authorized the U.S. Department of Agriculture to license and inspect brokers, exhibitors, transporters, and researchers dealing with animals "not raised for food or fiber." Little changed, as the department fell short of inspectors and will, partly, it is speculated, because the majority of puppy mills were located in midwestern states whose legislators had no interest in stopping them and considerable influence in Washington, D.C.

Despite repeated reports from its own inspector general and in the newspapers, including one in the February 5, 1996, edition of the *New York Times*, the USDA has done little to enforce regulations applying to some 4,600 brokers and breeders, who not only supply nearly 90 percent of the puppies sold in pet stores but also provide, at an average cost of around $250 each, animals to biomedical research institutions. Animals bought from breeders are not the only ones used for research: some 2 million cats and dogs are stolen each year, most of them brokered through dealers to those organizations.

Nor has the AKC evinced any interest in shutting down the businesses that supply, by some estimates, as many as 40 percent of their registrations. My own calculations for the *Atlantic* placed the figure at around 20 percent, based on the fact that some 500,000 dogs are bought each year through pet stores, and the AKC registers around 1.2 million dogs—just under half of those eligible. Thus, I assumed that half of the store-bought dogs were registered. The AKC does not know or will not disclose precise figures.

In the winter of 1980–81, Robert Baker, an investigator for the Humane Society of the United States undertook what remains the most exhaustive undercover investigation of commercial breeders in the Midwest, examining 294 out of 3,886 licensed breeders and brokers. He documented unsanitary, inhumane practices by nearly all of them. Many of the breeders were elderly farmers trying to supplement their income, who regarded their dogs much as they would chickens or any other cash-producing livestock, but others were white supremacist, neo-Nazis, mixing semen with vitriol. In the 1990s, Amish farmers in Lancaster County, Pennsylvania, gained notoriety as operators of puppy mills. Brokers figured that they were above reproach.

Baker also concluded that many of the puppy mills, which produce anywhere from four to one hundred litters a year, were fraudulently registering their dogs with the AKC. (In Florida, a commercial breeder is defined as anyone producing three or more litters annually.) To prove how easy it was to do, he registered a nonexistent litter of Labrador retrievers. After he publicized his deed, the AKC, following the venerable practice of killing the messenger, suspended him indefinitely from any of its activities, a punishment he does not rue.

By now, the horrors of puppy mills have been thoroughly documented on television, in newspaper and magazine articles. At this writing lawsuits are under way in several states claiming that the AKC is engaged in mail fraud and other crimes for misregistering puppies from those factories. Former inspectors for the AKC, who are charged with investigating fraudulent registrations, have come forward denouncing the organization and its practices. States have passed lemon laws. Yet the federal government has not funded increased enforcement of laws already on the books, and the AKC has taken no action to reform or lobby for a halt to the retail trade in animals. Nor have animal-rights groups mounted a serious national campaign demanding abolition, as if they too profit too greatly by trotting out puppy mills as a present evil. Their inaction merely contributes to what is an easily correctable national shame. The sale of puppies and all other animals through pet stores must end. Consumers can do their part by never buying an animal from a store.

Ugly though they are, puppy mills represent only one segment of the dirty underbelly of purebred dogs—commercial breeding. Although precise figures are difficult to find, I estimate that as many as 40 percent of dog owners obtain their pets through a commercial kennel or pet store, with the remainder coming from a friend, relative, neighbor, private breeder, or shelter. I define as a private breeder anyone who produces dogs primarily for his or her own use, selling puppies, if at all, only to individuals. Those puppies are bred for a purpose.

Commercial breeders are people who regularly produce dogs for sale. This definition includes backyard breeders and owners of small kennels who raise one to three litters a year primarily for sale, even though they fall under the federal minimum for licensing. These breeders market their puppies through advertisements in newspapers and dog magazines rather than pet stores. They fuel the dramatic increase in the numbers of popular breeds. If they get from their mass production one or two champions a year, they are satisfied because they will then breed them with an eye toward increased profit. Their kennels are probably cleaner on average than a puppy mill, but often their puppies are scarcely better socialized or more selectively bred. They are, however, the bread and butter of the purebred dog industry in the United States.

Occasional breeders also contribute to the problem when they produce litters for the fun of it or to "teach" their children about birth without regard to the qualities of the dog they have mated, the puppies they have produced. Still, their dogs are often well socialized, a significant advantage.

Commercial breeders and pet stores complain that limiting their business amounts to restraint of trade. It does in a way, but outweighing their "right" to profit from crimes against dogs is the responsibility of society to give those same animals an opportunity to live a healthy life. Animals are irreparably injured through commercialization. Permitting it to continue is cruelty.

Like commercial interests, the fancy rails against critics who seek reform of its outrageous practices, protesting that they know what is best for "their breeds." By their lights, the look they impose on animals is all that is necessary to define their quality. Were that so, dogdom would be a healthier place. Dogs who won championships would be vigorous, fertile, temperamentally and physically sound, varied. The show ring would be a place to study outstanding, accomplished specimens revealing the range of possibilities of size and color of various breeds. In short, the fancy would celebrate dogs, not people.

Absent the sudden advent of that canine utopia, progress might be possible. With assistance from concerned individuals, foundations, and breed clubs, as well as less beneficent support from the AKC, researchers have begun to identify genes responsible for some of the debilitating conditions afflicting purebred dogs. That support should be increased and supplemented with contributions from the pet industry and animal-rights groups—every organization claiming an interest in the well-being of dogs.

The Dog Genome Project at the University of California at Berkeley, as well as the Fred Hutchinson Cancer Research Center at the University of Washington, is designed to map the entire canine genome, with its seventy-eight chromosomes and estimated 100,000 genes. Specifically, researchers hope to locate some of the genes that might code for certain behaviors, a difficult task. Other canine geneticists are working to identify the genes responsible for the genetic ailments that afflict dogs. Those scientists currently number no more than 100 worldwide and, for all the importance of dogs, for the $8 billion that Americans alone spend on the care and feeding of their dogs (the purchase price adds several billion more), they are desperately underfunded. Whatever they find should not be used to justify continued bad breeding practices, but it should help clean up the mess that exists and allow breeders to make informed choices that produce sound, healthy dogs. The tools exist to accomplish the task. The minds are in place. Funds are needed, and they should come from all those who benefit from dogs.

Surveying the damaged bloodlines of pure breeds, Joe W. Templeton, a professor of veterinary pathology and genetics at Texas A & M, says, "I'm disappointed that we haven't been able to educate people better on genetic problems. We can't convince them that they're not good caretakers of dogs. They claim to love them, but they don't."

Chapter Seven

MUTTS OF
THE NORTH

The Long Haul

Billed as "the world's last great race," the Iditarod Trail International Sled Dog Race is a grueling endurance test for dogs and humans, covering 1,100 miles from Anchorage to Nome. The course traverses some of the most spectacular country in the world, crossing the Alaska Range, running along a stretch of the historic Yukon River, tracking the Bering Sea. Snow, ice, and frozen tundra compose the trail. Under optimum conditions, fast teams complete the crossing in just over nine days—an average of more than 100 miles a day. Along the way, each competitor must take a mandatory twenty-four-hour break, one eight-hour stop on the Yukon, and another at White Mountain, 77 miles from the finish line. Savvy mushers run four to five hours, then stop for an equal period of time to rest and feed their dogs, keeping them fresh. Thus, they are actually racing for twelve out of every twenty-four hours.

But optimum conditions are seldom the rule. Crazed moose and careless snowmobile drivers who bash into sleds and through dog teams, fallen trees, soft ice, innumerable camp accidents, spoiled food, broken equipment, injuries, and even unexpected dog deaths can waylay the best race plan. When the weather sours, as it often will in early March, brutally cold temperatures (minus fifty degrees Fahrenheit is not uncommon), drifting snow, blizzards, hurricane-force winds that turn snow and ice into projectiles and drop the wind chill to minus one hundred degrees turn the race into a survival test. In 1996, conditions were nearly the opposite and just as challenging, with daytime temperatures in the thirties and forties, open water, scarce snow, and a trail rendered horrid by U.S. Army snowmobiles, which had traversed it shortly before the race on maneuvers.

The always challenging conditions combined with several years of international television coverage, suspended after 1993 because of controversy over accidental dog deaths, to raise the visibility of the race and the sport of mushing around the world. Iditarod champions, like five-time winner Rick Swenson, four-time victor Susan Butcher, and double record-setter Martin Buser, became celebrities. Their dogs—hard-charging Alaskan huskies—became the best-known animals not found in any popular encyclopedia of dogs. Spectators call the dogs by name—Andy, Granite, D2, Elmer—the way they do any great athlete.

Although most races in the Arctic and sub-Arctic are sprints of less than 30 miles, with middle-distance events of 90 to 400 miles also drawing a relatively large number of participants, the ultramarathons currently attract top professionals, sponsors, and attention. Foremost among them are the Alpirod and Iditarod. The Alpirod is the premier distance event in Europe, where mushing enjoys great popularity as sport and recreation.

Around the world, mushers aspire to run the Iditarod, mushing's equivalent of bicycling's Tour de France. It is a physical and financial challenge just to get to the starting line in Anchorage. The cost of equipping, feeding, and training a team runs to tens of thousands of dollars a year, an amount that requires independent income or sponsorship, even if only from one's own family. In most years, at least one entrant is a wealthy visitor from the lower forty-eight states who leases or buys a team and has an adventure, purchasing with dollars what many Alaskans with dogs cannot afford for themselves.

Yet the real difficulty and allure of the race have to do with the fact that one person—women perform as well as men—with anywhere from five to sixteen dogs (down from a maximum of twenty before 1995) is making the winter run across the big, scenic empty that is Alaska. The Iditarod and mushing in general have come to symbolize the best and worst in the relationship between dogs and humans. That is appropriate in a land where until the snowmobile came into widespread use in the late 1960s dogs were the most common form of transportation for nine months of the year.

Established in 1973 to commemorate a relay to bring diphtheria serum from Nenana (south of Fairbanks) to an epidemic-beset Nome in 1925, the Iditarod has always been about dogs. The lead dog on the last leg of the successful diphtheria mission, Balto, is memorialized with a statue in New York's Central Park and in 1995 was fictionalized into the hero of the cartoon film by the same name. The plaque on the Central Park statue reads: "Dedicated to the indomitable spirit of the sled dogs that relayed anti-toxin six hundred miles over rough ice, across treacherous waters, through Arctic blizzards from Nenana to the relief of a stricken Nome in the winter of 1925. Endurance—fidelity—intelligence."

A visit to Alaska in August 1995 to research the origins and nature of Alaskan huskies—the top Iditarod dogs—for *Natural History* magazine the year after a trip to Finnish Lapland brought forcibly home to me how in so many ways the Arctic remains a frontier, off the major trade routes, sparsely peopled, abounding in fish and game, forbidding in its long, cold, dark winters, tantalizing in its brief, bright, warm summers. It is a region where the earliest settlers became nearly fully carnivorous, living off the migrating herds of caribou, reindeer, moose, bears, seals, walrus, whales, and fish. For all our considerable technological might, it remains a difficult region to develop due to its climate and, I think, the feeling that many visitors and residents have of its remoteness.

Alaska is the American chunk of the Arctic, a landmass one-quarter the size of the lower forty-eight states, as large as western Europe, yet occupied by fewer than 600,000 people, more than a third of them in Anchorage. Alaska contains the tallest peak in North America, Denali (Mount McKinley), and vast stretches of tundra broken by mountains, lakes, alluvial rivers. To fly into Anchorage even in the middle of summer after crossing the glacier-capped Canadian Rockies is to feel that you have entered another country. Despite the recognizable language, cultural and commercial artifacts, the ubiquitous cars and trucks, you cannot avoid a sense of having stepped through a time-space warp. The temperature in Fairbanks, the largest city in the interior with some 45,000 residents, ranges from the eighties in July and August, when day lasts for eighteen hours or more, to minus fifty, without wind, in the late fall and winter, when daylight is a faint memory.

The glaciated mountains captivated me, a flatlander from Florida. Flying back from Denali, our light charter plane dipped into the Great Gorge, a mile deep, with a mile-thick glacier, a river of ice at its bottom. Rock walls loomed so close it seemed the wings would caress them. I stared down at openings of translucent blue ice, as clear as the water in any sparkling swimming pool, but ancient beyond my counting, and at the miles of frozen rapids, whitewater roaring without apparent motion through the gorge. At the glacier's base an artesian spring erupted into a river cluttered with the usual summer deadfalls and salmon, cutting through the briefly green and flowering tundra. We flew over two moose standing up to their chests in a marsh that within a month would be ice.

Spectacular as it is, Alaska is no more paradise than any other piece of this planet, and for all of its excitement, mushing is not the embodiment of Jack London's romantic imagination, where man meets nature with noble and tragic consequences, where the half-wild wolfdog reigns supreme. Yet the reality is sufficient to keep mushing alive in the machine age. There are true stories of sled dogs saving their owners from certain death and of mushers saving their dogs, of moose running amuck through dog teams and of wolves dancing through dog yards at night.

Martin Buser and other mushers talk of the pure pleasure of riding for miles behind a team of smooth-running dogs, the silence broken only by the dogs breathing, the crackle of their footsteps, the glide of the sled's runners across snow. At night, the aurora borealis brings the sky to life in a fluid dance of energy. Dawn and dusk bracket the day with their opposing but equally calming fires. When the full moon and morning sun balance across the sky, earth and heaven unite. Wildlife abounds.

Because those images of solitude and grace, of dogs and humans working in harmony are so potent, advertisers flocked to the Iditarod. But they fled from it after animal-rights groups, including the powerful Humane Society of the United States, made charges that the huskies were being callously run to death in the name of entertainment. There were in fact men possessed of the old miner and trapper attitude that held a dog was good as long as it pulled and did not require too much food, who shot their wolfdogs when they reached an age where they began to show their wolf nature, or who toughened their dogs' feet by laying cinders from a nearby power plant on their yard—enough of these men to lend credence to the charges—even though the growth in prize money and popularity was bringing in a new group of mushers who recognized that their dogs were their livelihoods. Understanding that the happy, well-treated dog ran best, these men and women set out to keep their animals in top physical and psychological condition. Despite the criticism their sport has received, they daily reveal the enduring strength of our bond with dogs.

Whiteout

Martin Buser ran his first Iditarod in 1980 behind a team of Siberian huskies, finishing well off the lead. He was twenty-two, determined to excel in a sport that had captured his imagination as a boy in his native Switzerland. He placed nineteenth the following year with another team of Siberians, the pick of the Norris's Howling Dog Kennel, and swore he would not run the Iditarod again without competitive dogs. He started a kennel and by 1988 was attracting attention with his fast, houndy huskies, descendants of sprint racers. In 1991, he shocked his competitors by driving through a whiteout, a ferocious blizzard that blasted off the Bering Sea just as leader Susan Butcher, trying for a record-setting fifth victory, pulled out of White Mountain for the final seventy-seven-mile push into Nome.

Butcher turned from the storm's fury back to White Mountain. Seeing Buser on his way out of the checkpoint, she told him the trail was impassable, an assessment she repeated for the television cameras. Two other mushers followed her retreat, leaving only Rick Swenson, the new race leader, and Martin Buser to challenge the storm. Ice masks formed over the faces of the dogs; bitter wind freeze-dried, then scoured human skin. Visibility vanished. Buser picked his way inch by inch along the trail, following the tracks left by snowmobiles until he could no longer find them. After losing the trail, he huddled with his dogs for two hours. He woke to intensified wind that rocked his sled as if it were an off-balance cradle.

Realizing that staying put was as physically draining as moving and detecting a slight improvement in visibility—to twenty feet—he set out, feeling his way with his lead dog, Eleanor, next to him. The sled dragged on its side behind the team. As they crept through the blasting wind, Eleanor learned to read the faint signs of the trail, to weave together the bits and pieces of data that she and Buser were picking up. Powerfully built, standing about five-foot eleven, Buser experienced for the first time what it was like to lead rather than drive a team of dogs, how each crossing of the gangline by a dog in the team, each tug and jerk, placed additional strain on the leader. He also felt the dogs staring at him, placing their trust in him "to get them through a situation that they couldn't quite figure out." Trained in Alpine climbing, rescue, and orienteering while serving his tour in the Swiss Army and a veteran of a successful ascent on Denali, he was pressed to the limit of his skill. Finally, they crested a ridge and broke free of the storm.

"My heart started to beat faster," Buser recalls. He sensed Eleanor's impatience for him to right the sled and climb on the runners so she and the other dogs could gain speed. Following a brief rest at a cabin, he pushed on to the last checkpoint at Safety and then raced into Nome ninety minutes behind Rick Swenson, who had tied himself to his lead dogs and sloughed through the storm. Greeting Buser was his wife, Kathy Chapoton, who, knowing only that he was missing, had feared the worst. Buser and his dogs had prevailed.

Despite finishing second to Swenson, who became the first and only five-time winner of the Iditarod, Buser says his dogs came of age during the whiteout and accepted him as a member of *their* team. He was no longer "the guy with the sled" slowing them down. They believed themselves capable of anything, and he shared that belief. More important, he showed the mushing world that the houndy huskies bred for speed, possessed of shorter, thinner coats than the more traditional-looking animals, could stand up to the harshest conditions imaginable. Skeptics called them fair-weather dogs, but they came through the worst the Bering coast could throw at them.

The whiteout became a historic landmark in the annals of Buser's Happy Trails Kennel, a defining moment that shaped his attitude toward his dogs and theirs toward him. The dogs gained enthusiasm and self-confidence, which they pass on to new dogs coming into the kennel, be they puppies or young adults from outside. They transmit the culture of Happy Trails through their tail-wagging enthusiasm, their responsiveness to commands—two of the basic ones being "gee" for right and "haw" for left, the same as for horses—and to the challenge of the trail, their intelligence about their work.

Buser nurtures that attitude. He stops when the team is running well to stroke and congratulate each dog. He huddles and howls with his team, to build their morale. He sings to them along the trail. He issues commands in a normal tone of voice, without shouting or histrionics, saying that the more you shout, the louder you have to shout until it has no effect. He closely observes his dogs' behavior and habits. Studying the sleeping holes made by his dogs on the trail, he observed that one, Wolfie, who had failed to complete three Iditarods, was losing more heat than the others and so prepared foam pads for the dogs to sleep on, thereby allowing them to conserve energy.

In 1992, Buser won the Iditarod in record time with Eleanor and a young dog, D2, as the primary leaders. (Just under three years old, D2 was actually a prodigy among lead dogs, who often do not begin to reach their full maturity until they are three or four.) His brothers, Dave, Hector, Madrid, IBM, and Handy Man, and a half brother, Tyrone, were also in the starting twenty-dog team that had among its other members the large, piebald Milkcow and Clifford, the big red dog. Buser bought Clifford for a dollar from a musher who was leaving the sport and had offered to give him away. "You can't give dogs away," Buser told him. "It's bad form." So Clifford the dollar dog joined the team and became one of its most recognizable and popular members, as well as a bosom buddy to Dave. Dropped from the 1991 race well before the whiteout, Tyrone howled for four days.

In 1993, botulism from food spoiled by unseasonably warm temperatures weakened the team, and an unexpected mating of D2 and Eleanor, while in harness, led to a forty-minute delay. Buser and his dogs struggled to a sixth-place finish. But in 1994, they roared back to finish first in a new record, after running the fastest 300 miles ever—thirty-seven hours and four minutes in the Kusko 300. D2's brother Dave set the pace for much of that race.

In 1995, with many of his top dogs out of action due to illness or injury and Clifford substituting in lead for D2, who was dropped because of a pulled muscle, Buser was second in the Iditarod, behind record-setter Doug Swingley of Simms, Montana, the first non-Alaska resident to win. Finishing in nine days, two hours, and forty-three minutes, Swingley came surprisingly close to cracking the nine-day barrier, the Iditarod's equivalent of a two-hour, six-minute marathon. Buser nonetheless achieved another first: for the third time, he won the Leonhard Seppala Humanitarian Award, named for the legendary musher who led the 1925 relay to bring diphtheria serum to Nome and presented by a vote of race veterinarians to the driver who takes the best and most humane care of his dogs. No other musher has been honored that many times.

In 1996, with D2 home in Big Lake with an injury, Buser started a team including veterans Dave and Clifford in the lead, IBM, Spandex, Tyrone, Polly, Milkcow, and his daughter, Lafite; newcomers Bill, Blondie, Primus, Hillary, Melkior, Ingot, Whaler, and Baraka. First at the halfway point and locked in a tight duel with Swingley, Buser began to run into difficulty as the atrocious trail conditions took their toll on his dogs, fatiguing them and causing nagging injuries. A poorly marked trail change also cost him time. He finished with seven dogs, of whom only Milkcow was a veteran. Blondie, a young reddish-blond houndy husky with a black muzzle, pulled lead for most of the race and won the Golden Harness Award voted by mushers to the best new leader. She is a dog with drive and self-assurance.

The 1993 winner, Jeff King of Denali, cruised to victory in Nome in the second-fastest time ever, nine days, five hours, and forty-three minutes. Swingley was second and Buser third; the next five competitors also broke the ten-day barrier. Although King suggested that Swingley and Buser tired themselves and their teams by concentrating on each other so early in the race, he clearly had conserved his team's energy and marked his time for a strategic push on the Yukon that allowed him to break into the lead. Luck also played a role as he encountered fewer difficulties on the trail than the other top finishers. The warm weather spoiled some of Swingley's dog food, while Buser battled his various mishaps. Clearly, these three competitive men, who exemplify the best in mushing, will be marking each other for years to come.

Buser says that his philosophy is to place his dogs' well-being above all other considerations, including his desire to win the race. He wants to finish with a strong, happy team. For that reason, he drops a dog as soon as he notices it is not quite right—meaning that there is a shift in gait or behavior that would escape the notice of many other drivers and veterinarians. (Dropped dogs are flown to Anchorage or Nome for pickup.) Recognizing that the team was tiring in its chase of Swingley late in the 1995 race, he took an unscheduled rest, losing two hours in the process. Before leaving White Mountain, he turned all his dogs loose to run on Iron Creek, giving them a break from the pressure of the chase.

As soon as Buser stops for a rest, he, like his fellow competitors, tends to the dogs, preparing their food, thawing snow or ice for drinking water for them, putting down straw or foam for their beds, checking the condition of each animal, often along with one of the race veterinarians, tending to minor cuts and scraps. That takes three hours, leaving him an hour or two to eat and sleep. Then he returns to hitch up the team, check their booties if they are wearing them, and set off for another run of four or five hours. Establishing a good, consistent rhythm is essential, he believes, to success, allowing the dogs and himself to focus their energy on racing.

The Dogs

Like virtually all of the other top sled dogs, Buser's are Alaskan huskies, which have emerged from the genetic melting pot of twentieth-century Alaska to put all officially recognized northern breeds—for example, the malamute, Samoyed, and Siberian husky—to shame. In much of northern Europe, a rule that for decades allowed only purebred dogs to compete has in recent years fallen under the weight of its own hypocrisy, as racers were importing Alaskan huskies they misregistered as Siberian huskies or laika, a Russian breed. Although an obsession with breed purity persists in some European and South American nations, the fact remains that even the best Siberians—the most successful of the purebreds—are slow, unwilling to give their full effort, and weak in the feet compared with their Alaskan kin. They will not, as Buser says, "give 150 percent."

Alaskan huskies run to records in sprints, middle-distance events, and ultramarathons. That success has increased demand and price for them: a team dog starts at $1,000, a leader at $3,500, and the best ones cannot be bought. By comparison, top show dogs have been known to fetch as much as $50,000, trained guard dogs close to $20,000, and trained hunting dogs and herding-trial champion border collies $10,000 or more.

Arleigh Reynolds, assistant professor of clinical sciences at the Cornell University College of Veterinary Medicine and a musher himself, has shown that Alaskan huskies possess three times the oxygen-uptake capacity per unit of body weight (VO_{2max}) of the best human athletes. (Typically, comparisons with humans are used because, not surprisingly, more is known about the physiology of human athletes.) While other dogs, including Labrador retrievers, can match that result when properly conditioned, none have yet shown the combination of physical and mental toughness possessed by the Alaskan. Were another type to do so, more than one musher would cross it into their lines and study the result. Indeed, Labradors were employed as sled dogs in Canada during the 1920s, but they were desired for their steadiness and endurance, not their speed.

The Alaskan husky is a generalist runner, able to lope (with one foot always touching the ground) or gallop (with all four off in what mushers call a "floating gallop") at around twenty-two miles an hour in a sprint of twenty to thirty miles and trot or canter (a half trot, half lope) at ten to fifteen miles for four or five hours at a stretch. Dogs competing in an ultramarathon like the Iditarod consume 10,000 to 11,000 calories a day, 65 percent of them in animal fat, which they metabolize quickly into energy. Sprint dogs require considerably fewer calories, but a high-fat diet is best for them as well.

While it should not be surprising that dogs do best on a high-fat diet, since they are carnivores by nature, the results of studies in 1994–95 at Harvard and Cornell Universities, as well as the Medical College at Bern, Switzerland, show that fat has a significant impact on the dog's physiology. Researchers at Harvard University found that VO_{2max} increases 30 to 50 percent in Labrador retrievers subjected to a high-fat diet and physical training over equally well conditioned dogs fed a low-fat diet. Further, the Harvard tests and additional studies on Alaskan huskies at Cornell indicate a significant increase in the amount of mitochondria—which use oxygen to produce adenosine triphosphate (ATP), which, in turn, fuels cells—in the muscles of the trained dogs on a high-fat diet but not in those on a low-fat diet. In humans, aerobic exercise has been shown to increase mitochondria in slow-twitch muscles, but this research is the first to show that in dogs training will accomplish that task only when linked to a diet rich in fat. Thus, the research underscores the signal importance of proper nutrition in canine performance. "If someone had told me this a year ago, I wouldn't have believed it," Reynolds, who participated in the studies, said shortly after the results were known.

By modern definition, the Alaskan husky is not an official breed because there is neither a stud book nor a written standard. Even mushers and veterinarians call the Alaskans mutts. While correctly identifying their mixed heritage, that moniker overlooks their common lineage and the significant fact that everyone involved with sled-dog racing knows Alaskan huskies when they see them. Like the curs of the American South, they are a type easily identified by function and overall form. Arleigh Reynolds defines them as "purpose-bred dogs."

"An Alaskan husky," Martin Buser says, "is any dog that runs fast and pulls hard." It is also distinguished by its good feet, which withstand the cold, although booties are used for added protection in extreme conditions; its competitive desire or will; and its sociability, especially toward other dogs, a necessity for team work. The distance racers must have a good appetite, a strong cardiovascular system, and stamina.

In appearance, Alaskan huskies are balanced dogs, deep-chested, with powerful hindquarters and solid shoulders. Most have the double coat distinctive to northern breeds, with rough guard hairs over a woolly undercoat. They are solid or parti-colored in red, white, black, tan, gray, and shades between, with blue, brown, or pied eyes. Some are the classic husky type, with medium to long guard hairs, curled bushy tails, and prick ears. Others are "houndy," like Buser's, meaning they have longer legs, fuller, more rounded muscles, a sloping croup (rump), an angulated front, and sometimes thinner, shorter coats and flop ears. But those are points on a continuum, not hard distinctions. In weight, the Alaskan huskies range from forty to seventy pounds, averaging forty-five for females and fifty-five for males.

The Alaskan husky is a distinctly modern dog with deep roots in Arctic prehistory. Stanley J. Olsen, an anthropologist at the University of Arizona and author of *Origins of the Domestic Dog* (1985), posits that short-faced wolves, whose fossil remains were found in Fairbanks during the early 1930s and more recently in the Ukraine and Siberia, were the progenitors of the Eskimo dogs, or huskies, some 10,000 to 15,000 years ago. Although we do not know when Arctic people began using dogs as draft animals, Olsen and many other archaeologists speculate that the forebears of the Eskimo, who appeared along the Alaska coast 1,000 or more years ago, had sled dogs. But the Athabascan Indians of the inland rivers, who had hunting dogs, seem to have adopted mushing only in the nineteenth century, from Russian and Canadian fur traders.

The Russians in particular appear to have brought to Alaska from the Chukchi Peninsula in Siberia some of their favorite sled dogs, whom they considered superior for transport. The trappers of

Hudson's Bay Company used teams of four to five large freighting dogs from Canada to haul heavy loads of furs and supplies twenty-five to fifty miles a day. Generally, natives and whites selected the largest, most placid dogs from litters; those ready to sprint off would have been unacceptable for working traplines. Unwanted dogs were killed or left to fend for themselves.

In native villages, headmen would frequently dictate which dog would serve as stud, with the result that each village or region became known for its type of dogs—for example, Huslia or Nenana dogs from the inland; Katzebue on the Bering coast; Saint Lawrence Island, where the huskies, like their Siberian kin, often had blue eyes. But there was sufficient exchange between villages that they did not become distinctive breeds. (The malamute of the fancy is a refined version of one of those village types.)

The gold rushes across Alaska and Canada's Yukon Territory, beginning in 1880 with a strike in Juneau and lasting through 1908 when the precious metal was found at Iditarod (with major finds at Fortymile, Circle, Dawson, Nome, Fairbanks), changed the country and its dogs. Northwest Canada's 1896 Klondike Gold Rush drew 100,000 pilgrims to Dawson, the tiny Yukon River town, their sleds and carts hitched to anything that moved—other men, horses, goats, oxen, dogs, wolves, even turkeys—most of them landing dead in mountain ravines or rivers. Carnivores being more easily maintained than herbivores in that environment, dogs quickly became the draft animal of choice and began to command prices of $1,000. Boatloads came from the states—setters, curs, collies, Saint Bernards, Newfoundlands, Airedales, bull terriers and pit bulls, retrievers, spaniels, pointers, hounds, German shepherds—many of them stolen. Although some people took fine care of their animals, most followed a basic dictum: dogs who worked were well fed and bred; those who faltered were killed or abandoned. The survivors interbred with native dogs, invigorating them without substantially altering their appearance.

This mixed canine corps hauled everything from mail to gold and people on sleds, toboggans, carts, and railroad cars. Traffic jams in towns like Fairbanks quickly became mass dogfights involving thirty or forty animals and continuing until the drivers, or "dog punchers," broke them up with whips and boots. Sometimes the dogs attacked children. Their howls and barks filled the air, their excrement the streets, their corpses the Chena River. For all the mayhem they created, their value was such that people on the street usually avoided them rather than kick them out of the way, a courtesy seldom shown other humans or animals.

When the newcomers and native Alaskans played at the turn of the century, they raced dogs. The first organized contest, the All Alaska Sweepstakes, made the 408-mile round-trip from Nome to Candle in 1908. More races followed in Nome and other cities, with many of them covering twenty to sixty miles. Most of the teams reflected the mixture of dogs used in the territory, but in the 1909 race, Louis Thrustrup drove Russian fur trader William Goosak's team of Chukchi Peninsula huskies to victory. Their success encouraged more competitors to import the small, fast dogs. Natalie and Earl Norris trace their Howling Dog line of purebred Siberians to those Chukchi huskies, many of whom were absorbed over the years into the indigenous stock.

After a hiatus for the First World War, during which some 400 Alaskan sled dogs served the French army as freighters in the Vosges Mountains, racing resumed in 1927, with Fairbanks as its locus. With due respect to the superb mushers who raced during this period and are celebrated in popular histories, including Leonhard Seppala, whose dogs performed so well in the diphtheria serum relay and later races, the most significant person to the development of the Alaskan husky was Johnny Allen, an Athabascan from the lower Yukon who in 1938 became the first musher to average more than fifteen miles an hour for thirty miles. Seppala, a Norwegian, is renowned throughout the world of mushing, while Allen remains a relative unknown, obscurity Gareth Wright attributes to the fact that "white men make the rules." An Alaska native who is the only musher to have won major championships in five decades and is the primary creator of the dog known as the Alaskan husky, Wright has often not received proper credit for his own contributions to modern mushing.

In Johnny Allen's time, Wright says during a long conversation at his home on the Chena River, a white toy poodle dancing near his feet, many of the villages along the Yukon would send teams to the races in Fairbanks and other cities. The mushers would drive their dogs to the race, compete, then drive them home, covering several hundred miles. "Johnny Allen was my hero," Wright says. "We boys memorized all his records. He could make his dogs do a figure eight in the snow." During the 1920s and 1930s, Allen's dogs were his own concoction, a mix of Irish setters, who were distinguishing themselves in Idaho sled-dog sprints, wolves, and native huskies. Gareth Wright admired the dogs as much as the man.

Allen's huskies nearly disappeared during World War II, when the U.S. Army bought almost every available dog in the territory and racing was again suspended. In 1946, Earl Norris joined two other mushers in organizing the Fur Rendezvous Sled Dog Race in Anchorage, which in 1961 was renamed the World Championship Sled Dog Race; it comprised three twenty-five mile sprints on consecutive days, with the best cumulative time winning. In Fairbanks, the North American Championship Sled Dog Derby—now two races of twenty miles and one of thirty on consecutive days—became the premier event.

Mushers ran various mixed-breed teams and Siberian huskies, which were required on the European circuit. Natalie Norris says, "In the 1940s in Fairbanks, the dog community was anti–pure breed." Young Gareth Wright set out in those first postwar years to recreate the dogs of his hero, Johnny Allen. He had found one dog representative of that line and had obtained from a bankrupt Californian the daughter of a field-trial champion Irish setter. Wright crossed these two, then added a cross to a blue-eyed Saint Lawrence Island husky to reduce the size and toughen the feet of that first cross, which others have described as "flighty." From those breedings came his foundation dogs, Queenie and Satan, whose offspring he dubbed Aurora huskies.

Periodically, Wright would cross in village dogs belonging to racers along the Yukon and its tributaries or hounds from elsewhere, but he mainly engaged in close line breeding to fix the traits he wanted: speed, a will to run at full throttle until the race was won, and good feet.

According to legend, targhee hounds from Idaho, a cross between staghounds and Irish setters, figure in the Aurora husky, but Wright says that is not the case. "I tried the targhee hound, but I discontinued them because they had no endurance and they were cripplers." Similarly, his experiments with wolves and coyotes were failures. "Wolves aren't good to cross with dogs. They like to run at night. They quit and won't start." Wright lost his foundation stud, Satan, when a wolf to whom he tried to breed the dog killed him after they mated. The wolf produced no puppies. Similarly, Wright abandoned attempts to cross his dogs with coyotes, which he deemed "too sneaky."

Although the crosses go on periodically in a quixotic quest for tough feet or stamina born of the belief that a wolf must have both in more abundance than a dog, other mushers echo Wright's view. The call of the wild is a siren's song. Dogs are valued for their ability to work with humans, a trait wolf hybrids generally lack: they are considered "spooky" and difficult to handle. Beyond that, they will not run like an Alaskan husky.

"I kept the breed to myself for years," Wright told me, "but I finally had to let it out." He had too many dogs, for one thing. For another, their success had put them in demand, and by the mid-1950s it was becoming difficult to find racers who were not breeding into the Aurora line. George Attla, a young Athabascan who became the most successful sprint musher in history, crossed huskies from his native Huslia, who were "good dogs," with Wright's. "The Huslia dogs were big and strong," he says. "But Gareth had a faster dog than anyone else, so I bred to the Aurora line. Half of my breeding has Gareth Wright bloodlines. You can't escape Gareth's breeding." He added that the Huslia dogs and other native dogs chosen for racing were more leggy and ready to run than the large, slow dogs generally chosen for transport, so that people actually began to keep the animals they once culled.

Wright and Attla both say that the Aurora bloodlines spread throughout Alaska. In the immediate postwar years, a majority of the racers were Indians, a fact that no longer holds because the snowmobile's arrival in the 1960s rendered dogsleds obsolete as a means of winter transportation and the cost of maintaining dogs for sport or recreation is too great for most people. The larger freighters faded into the show ring or from view. Only a few, like the Mackenzie River husky, used since early in the century by the Royal Canadian Mounted Police, remain active.

The wide dispersal means that probably no competitive musher using Alaskan huskies has dogs without Gareth Wright's Aurora husky bloodlines. Even so-called village dogs may be related at some remove to his animals.

Doug Swingley says: "If you go back four or five generations in any musher's kennel, you'll find dogs that came from a one hundred-mile stretch along the Yukon from Tanana to Galena, with spurs off to places like Huslia and Nenana. Gareth Wright's and George Attla's dogs were mixed with those village dogs." As in the past, in some villages a good stud would be allowed to impregnate all of the bitches in heat. On occasion, salukis and other sight hounds were crossed into particular lines for speed. The result is the Alaskan husky.

Both Wright and Attla sold their older dogs and less than exemplary sprinters to "Iditaroders" in the early years of that race, first run in 1973. "Those Iditaroders wanted slow, good eaters with good fur," Wright says. "There wasn't much money in that race, so you had to enjoy being cold." But within a decade those Iditaroders had seized the popular imagination with their runs across the wilderness. Now their dogs are the same as the sprint dogs; their clothes the latest in high-tech, layered winter wear; their sleds built for speed and durability; their dog food the best that can be found.

The rising popularity of mushing around the world has intensified the pressure to produce superior dogs. Sprint mushers strive to have "a whole team of super animals," Attla says. Not fully mature until they are two years old, the sprint dogs are at their peak for around five years, then, according to various descriptions, they burn out or wise up, meaning they begin to pace themselves, to hold something in reserve. (In part to forestall that development, the dogs are never trained at the full distance they will run.) Wright prefers females for sprints, believing they mature faster than males. Distance racers are slightly older—between two and three—when they begin to reach their potential, so it takes time and patience to establish a successful kennel.

"It used to be that geographical divisions accounted for differences between dogs," Buser says. "But now there is so much traveling and interbreeding that good breeders are following natural selection at its finest. People are breeding to their likes and dislikes." Buser shifted the focus in long-distance racing to speed and the mental attitude of the dogs when he began breeding his "houndy" huskies.

Having calculated that each foot of each dog completing the journey from Anchorage to Nome will touch the ground 1.3 million times, Buser wants happy, outgoing, eager dogs with good locomotion, capable of trotting or cantering for hours, then accelerating to a sprint when necessary. Also, because he believes that big dogs commonly end up dropped, he likes males and females of equal size, around fifty-four pounds—an idiosyncrasy not shared by other mushers.

Susan Butcher, for example, prefers dogs with the old-time husky look and coat because she feels they are more adaptable to the bitter cold and require less special care. Her famous leader, Granite, who tipped the scales at sixty-seven pounds, had wolfhound blood. A few other dogs are part border collie; others have the wolfish look of the dog Frederic Remington painted in *Evening on a Canadian Lake*.

Doug Swingley says that his dogs probably occupy a place on the spectrum between Buser's and Butcher's. He favors a slightly longer coat and more muscle mass than Buser but also breeds for the houndy legs and speed, which is what Butcher came to lack in her kennel. A student of genealogy, Swingley had carefully examined the lines of Buser's dogs when establishing his own kennel. Like Buser, he wants dogs with superior attitudes, a willingness to run, and a fierce drive to win.

"Dogs use only 50 to 60 percent of their speed in distance races," he says. "I have an idea of what I want a dog to look like. Beyond that, mental intensity is central. I pick solely on mental abilities. I look for those dogs with the best attitude. Those are the ones I want to breed, but the mind is not easy to transmit. People want a dog like D2, but they don't look at his genealogy. Dagger, his sire, and Angel, his dam, were completely unrelated."

Instead, there is a tradition in mushing, as in most other realms of dogdom, to engage in close line breeding in an effort to perpetuate the best qualities of top dogs and eliminate what is seen as the uncertainty of outside bloodlines. Like people with other breeds, mushers engaging in the practice believe they can spot and weed out those canine genetic ailments that are recessive and often fixed along with positive traits through inbreeding because dogs possessing them will not run well. There is an element of truth in that, and many of these breeders succeed in producing healthy animals.

But the best among them recognize that inbreeding does not guarantee success and is always potentially dangerous. Consequently, they look to maintain hybrid vigor—having dogs from distantly related lines; crossing in another breed; obtaining from a remote village on the Bering Sea, an old-style native husky, who might not have much Aurora blood. "It's a small gene pool that has great diversity, because of the outcrossing," Swingley says. But mushers have to seek that diversity.

In 1994, German shorthaired pointer–husky crosses enjoyed remarkable success in the Alpirod and caused a ripple of excitement through the tight-knit world of mushing. (The occasional success of sprint racers with pointers, border collies, and hounds of various sorts has not had the same effect.) But there are questions as to whether the dogs' feet are tough enough to withstand the rigors of the Alaskan winter, especially on a long haul like the Iditarod. In the early years of Happy Trails Kennel, Buser had a German shorthaired pointer cross named Bruiser who one day along the Bering coast tried to point a ptarmigan while loping down the trail. His instincts literally tripped over themselves.

Similarly, Buser says that mushers who have experimented with border collies as lead dogs have often come away disappointed. The dogs learn instructions with remarkable ease, but the repetitiveness of distance racing bores them. They begin to look for new ways to move the sled—pushing it, stringing it over a tree limb, running circles around the other dogs. On the other hand, border collie-husky crosses seem to perform well.

The cost of not outcrossing is high. Around 1994, George Attla undertook an extensive overhaul of his bloodlines, having run into a genetic cul de sac because of too many years of following folk wisdom that said, "Breed best to best." Too often, people interpret the phrase to mean they should inbreed. "I pushed it too far," he says. Other mushers came up with faster dogs, and his kennel lacked the genetic variability needed for him to respond. The fact is that each successful musher will seek to breed dogs who match his or her notion of which types of animals work best, so that those lines will take on the personality of the musher. The key is to do that while maintaining genetic vigor.

Happy Trails

Martin Buser, Kathy Chapoton, their two boys, Rohn and Nikolai, and kennel hands live in Big Lake, Alaska, a town about an hour's drive north of Anchorage and so small it appears only on the most detailed state road maps. A seemingly endless parade of visitors arrives at the door of the house Martin and Kathy built on land she homesteaded, many of them directed there by local residents. Some stay the night, others linger long enough to see the dogs, buy a Buser booster sweatshirt, and maybe talk about mushing—an endless topic of conversation. From the look of the home, it is apparent that Buser, who makes his own sleds from hickory and sewed the curtains, is meticulous in all he does. He is as fine a craftsman as he is a sled-dog racer.

Lying between Wasilla, home of the Iditarod Trail Committee, and Willow, a weigh station on the road to Denali National Park and Fairbanks, Big Lake is nestled in Alaska's "banana belt," the area around Anchorage that stays relatively warmer than the true north country. It is a region of lakes pierced by the Little Susitna River, rich in salmon during the summer run, and scattered homesteads. Mountains loom on every horizon. When Buser takes Peter Fromm, a three-time European sled-dog sprint champion, and me salmon fishing on the Little Susitna River one Sunday afternoon, he is hailed by nearly everyone who sees him. His dogs are also celebrities.

Fromm is in Alaska from Germany looking for a lead dog for his team, and he inquires about D2, who is widely coveted because of his intelligence and determination. Buser laughs it off, as Fromm knew he would, because D2 is invaluable. A four-legged Buser, he looks over his shoulder while running lead, as if reviewing *his* troops, a habit other mushers would find reprehensible and try to correct, thereby ruining the dog. After arriving home in 1995, the injured D2 hid in his dog box for days and refused to look anyone in the eye. His spirits improved only when the team returned.

Buser says that D2's brother Dave is probably faster and a little more talented but not as well-known, showing that fame among dogs is as fickle as that among people. Dave does not usually start races in the lead because he sets too quick a pace, but the brothers work so well together that the temptation to run them in tandem cannot be denied. That was the plan for 1996, but injury before the race to D2 and during the race to Dave forced Buser to look among his young dogs for leadership. Those who emerged during the race, including the bright young leader, Blondie, present him with more, exciting possibilities for 1997, a changing of the guard.

Choosing a leader is no easier than breeding one. Susan Butcher, who is renowned for her dog care and training methods, which involve treating the dogs like members of her household, spayed and sold as a pet a young female named Bonnie after deciding she would not make the team. A working husky from birth, she found house life somewhat frightening and became alarmed at loud noises. The new owner tied her to a door and slammed it for four consecutive hours, having read in a dog-training book that she could thus desensitize the dog. Bonnie became so uncontrollable and destructive that the woman gave her back to Butcher, who discovered that she was an excellent lead dog. She is also extraordinarily shy of strangers because of that early encounter with human lunacy. Unfortunately, she is the last of her line, all of her littermates being dead.

Although Buser has "team" dogs who are good workers, like most successful mushers today, he prefers as many trained leaders as possible, should one or more falter. Traditionally, one leader runs at the front of the team, breaking trail, setting the pace, and executing the musher's commands to turn, speed up, slow down, walk at a snail's pace, stop. But even though most mushers have a primary leader, they will rotate that dog out of the lead during a long race to give it relief from the pressure, which is mentally and physically draining. They also run coleaders to balance the team. (Although teams can vary in size, the Iditarod now sets a maximum of sixteen dogs to start. They run in pairs along a gangline, also called a towline.) Still, it is the main leader who crosses the finish line first and achieves renown—Rick Swenson's Andy, Susan Butcher's Granite, Martin Buser's D2, Doug Swingley's Elmer. On the trail, a dog like that functions as the driver's alter ego.

Putting together a team of complementary talents is as challenging as choosing the proper leader, the closest thing in human athletics being the assemblage of an eight-man or -woman crew in rowing. Only in mushing, there are twice as many athletes involved, and they run in pairs, communicating in a language alien to the majority of people, including mushers. Most sprint racers want a whole team of intelligent, motivated dogs with a desire to win—leaders, in other words—and increasingly long-distance mushers look for the same. But because it is hard to assemble such a group, they choose as many leaders as they can find and supplement them with the strongest, fastest animals in their yard. In fact, many of those team dogs prove to be super athletes and even better sires and dams—the will of the leader being something that is apparently not inherited. Buser puts most of his effort into bringing along the least strong and motivated member of his team. No matter how great the team, there are always weaker dogs, he says, but if they perform to their full potential or beyond, they will not hold the sled back.

The smoothest-running teams are those on which the dogs have matched—closely similar—gaits. While a number of mushers focus almost obsessively on that, others believe that over the course of training dogs will grow accustomed to running with each other and balance their gaits. Buser says if dogs cannot trot at the speed he seeks—twelve to fourteen miles per hour—they do not race. The task then becomes one of excluding those who do not fit rather than concentrating on trying to find individuals whose habits of running fit an abstract mold.

The best individual talent does not always win a sled-dog race any more than the human team with the best talent prevails. The individuals must work together. The great dog or player has to inspire the lesser talents to excel while neither playing below his or her level nor performing a solo, although on occasion the great athlete can raise the level of everyone by force of will and ability. In sled-dog racing, the musher must come up with that mix, not only for the sixteen dogs with which he begins the race, but for the five (the minimum) with which he could end it and all combinations between.

Buser says he feels as good about the dogs born elsewhere, like Clifford, whom he raises into Happy Trails team members, as about those he breeds. After three tries, Wolfie, the heat loser who hails from Fort Yukon, one of coldest villages in Alaska, finished his first Iditarod in 1995, nursed and cajoled to Nome. (Wolfie was subsequently sold to another musher to make room for younger dogs.) Brought in to diversify the gene pool, the dogs do not always work out. When they do not, they are often sold to someone looking for a pet or a dog for recreational use, many of the nonracers being quite good for that.

"We don't breed dogs we don't want," Buser says. But sometimes the match is not right, or the dog simply lacks the physical ability to race at the top level. In fact, breeding is only part of what makes a super dog, the remainder coming from environmental and cultural factors, including the personality of the musher. Although breeding is uncertain and unpredictable no matter how close it is—say, mother to son—the environment is controllable. Humans can stimulate the puppy's development and socialization through early handling. Good nutrition can make a dog strong.

Most top mushers want well-socialized dogs on their team; fighters can wreak havoc. But that policy is not uniformly followed. In Finland, I mushed with a team of Siberian huskies used to entertain tourists—dogsleds not being an indigenous form of travel—and the dogs fought incessantly among themselves. Unlike Alaskan huskies,

Siberians have a reputation for fighting, but it is the mushers who con-
done the behavior and can stop it.

Of course, even the most socialized of dogs will fight when
stressed. During the Big Lake fire of June 1996, which burned nearly
eighty square miles of forest and threatened to engulf all homes in the
area, Chapoton evacuated with the boys, while Buser fought to save
their home and dogs. With a neighbor he ferried the huskies across Big
Lake using an island as a staging area so they could bring all away from
the approaching flames. On the island Milkcow and Clifford, freaked
by the fire and commotion, killed each other in a fight. The only other
casualties were two puppies who fell off the bank and drowned
because they could not get back to shore. Everyone else, and the home,
escaped unscathed, but the loss of the two big, hardworking dogs cast a
pall over the kennel.

Although training generally begins when puppies are six months to
a year old, it takes two years for a dog to reach maturity, and even
then, it might be another year or two before it joins a veteran long-
distance team. (Doug Swingley likes to hold his dogs back from racing
competitively until they are three years old.) Given the cost of feeding
a dog, it would be nice to have a test to determine whether it has the
talent and drive to make the grade, but as Susan Butcher discovered
that is not always possible. Some dogs, like some people, are late
bloomers.

As recently as fifteen years ago, it was commonplace among people
living in remote areas to cull dogs who failed to work out and
unwanted puppies. In many remote villages and homesteads, there was
not enough food for excess dogs and few people to whom they could
be sold or given. Some old-time mushers continue to do that, although
the practice is generally considered barbaric, especially since there is
high demand among the public for the dogs. The Humane Society of
the United States has repeatedly charged that culling is widespread in
the world of competitive mushing, but it has offered no proof of that.
Mushers and veterinarians I have interviewed, while admitting the
practice occurs, as it does among breeders of other working, show and
pet dogs, say that it is not prevalent. It is, however, true that respon-

sible mushers will put down a newborn puppy who is clearly defective and biters, who have no place in human society.

There were eighty dogs at Happy Trails when I visited in 1995, plus twenty belonging to a young businessman from Chicago, who had come to Big Lake to learn mushing and run the Iditarod. (He abandoned the sport before the 1996 race.) Buser generally has at least one kennel hand to help with feeding, grooming, and cleaning—excrement is removed almost as soon as it hits the ground. As in most sleddog kennels, each animal has its own box. It is attached to a pole in front with a chain long enough to allow it to circle the box, climb on top, where its food bowl is, go inside and lie down, visit with its neighbors without being able to engage them should tempers or love flare. Females in heat and those with puppies are kept in fenced runs.

Many dog lovers, unfamiliar with the arrangement of such kennels—some houndsmen also chain their dogs—think of staking dogs in front of their houses as cruel. It is far from that; in fact, at a good kennel, the huskies are better cared for than many beloved pets. They are groomed, fed, provided fresh water, worked, and given attention many times a day. They are staked because it is traditional to do so and because it is safe. They cannot wander off to be hit by a car, become lost, or get injured or stolen. Occasionally they run with their owners or dash through the yard after a workout. That said, some mushers do let their dogs run freely in confined areas, at least on occasion.

A walk through the yard reveals a wide range of personalities and phenotypes, from the lop-ear, short-coated houndy huskies to those with a more traditional husky look. Lafite, a shorthaired black-and-white hound, demands to be hugged and then picked up by anyone passing near. Her father, Milkcow, a blue-eyed dog with a distinctive black-and-white, husky-style coat, watches strangers with interest and suspicion from atop his dog box. Clifford, the dollar dog, looks like the friendly and beloved neighborhood mutt. D2, Dave, and their brothers are among the dogs with a more traditional husky look, while blue-eyed Primus has a greyhound look, Hillary is a short-coated white dog and Blondie is in the heat pen.

"Do you want to hear me howl with them?" Buser asks after an evening feeding, a smile on his face. Almost before hearing my answer, he tilts his head back and, starting low, raises his pitch in a long howl. The dogs join in twos and threes until the entire yard is harmonized. After about a minute, they quit, a full orchestral stop.

The dogs howl, like other huskies, after meals, at dusk, when excited, and when barking alone will not suffice. If a dog breaks free from his chain and goes on an unauthorized dash through the yard, his mates bark and howl loudly enough to summon the dead, or at least Buser or a kennel hand to restore order. Similarly, they report when the puppies begin to move around their pens. When it is time to run, even in front of the four-wheel all-terrain vehicle used in the off-season, they bark, yelp, and howl, straining at their harnesses as they are hooked up. They are ready to run and will take off in frenzy if allowed to, but they are trained to vary their pace on command, even dropping to a slow walk to pick their way over bad terrain or thin ice. Buser knows each dog's personality and habits intimately, can tell at a glance who is off his or her stride mentally or physically, who is slacking off, who working well. Each dog will log 2,000 practice miles during the off-season; the best and most healthy will race.

In harness, they are a line of fluid energy. They are grace and power in motion, reaching with their forelegs, driving with their hindquarters, always forward. Yet their backs remain so level it seems you could rest a full glass of water on them and it would not spill. That efficiency and smoothness show that they are transferring their power to pulling.

Even those who do not work out are eager to return home. Several years ago, a couple considering the purchase of Brother, a respectable nonteam dog, took him one hundred miles north for a trial run. While they were stopped for a break, he escaped the dog box on their truck and vanished. Concerned for the dog, Buser took food up the highway and left it at houses, asking the people to feed Brother if he came their way. His handler at the time, Chapoton's nephew, regularly drove north looking for the lost dog, and one day, not far from Big Lake, he climbed out of the truck and without much expectation called Brother's name. The prodigal dog dashed across the road and leaped into his arms, having found his way home. (Brother ended up with the same couple and flourished as a member of their team.)

"I have a hard time convincing visitors that not all kennels are like Happy Trails," says Buser as we take a final tour around the yard. There are other mushers, like Susan Butcher, Jeff King, and Doug Swingley, who maintain kennels that are clean and full of high-spirited, well-cared-for huskies. But there are also kennels that have a veil of unhappiness hanging over them. The dogs are not exactly abused; they are just not happy. The facilities are a bit shabby. The owners do not have the attention to detail, the love of order, and the concern for their animals that mark Happy Trails.

In the fall, Buser begins the process of selecting his team for the upcoming season, seeking a balance of old and young dogs. Since first coming to Alaska, he has become a veteran on the Iditarod trail. "I hear these newcomers look over and say, 'There's old Martin over there.' It gets me fired up." Close to forty, he is actually the same age as most of the top mushers in the sport, but to those mushers just starting on the long trail to Nome, he is a close to a legend.

Iditarod: The Controversy

In 1994, Susan Butcher lost a dog, HC, 230 miles into the race to what was diagnosed later as exertional myopathy, a relatively rare condition in which a breakdown of muscle tissue floods the body with proteins and enzymes that can cause death from kidney failure or heart attack. The tragedy nearly drove Butcher from the race. She had lost dogs before when a moose rampaged through her team, but HC's death had the most profound repercussions.

The Humane Society of the United States, which bills itself as the largest animal-protection organization in the world—with 3.5 million members and constituents (a vague word meaning basically anyone on the HSUS direct-mail list)—announced that it was opposing the race on the grounds that it was bringing injury and death to dogs in the name of entertainment. David Wills, HSUS vice president for investigations, leveled the charge on ABC's TV show *Good Morning America* right after the race, thereby guaranteeing a wide audience. (In the fall of 1995, Wills was dismissed from HSUS while under investigation for financial improprieties and sexual harassment. Suits and countersuits followed.) Ironically, Butcher had used her considerable influence to gain Wills a seat on the Iditarod's animal-care committee in an attempt to prevent his organization from opposing the race by teaching him and its constituents that every effort was being made to ensure the health of the canine competitors.

Enraged by what it viewed as a major betrayal, the Iditarod Trail Committee, the race's governing board, expelled Wills from its animal-care committee and campaigned to rally medical and popular support. But the HSUS charge took its toll. In September 1995, Timberland, the manufacturer of shoes and sportswear, announced that it would not renew its contract to provide close to $360,000 a year as a major corporate sponsor of the race, which it had been since 1985. Instead, it said it would donate $50,000 to an organization called PRIDE (Providing Responsible Information on a Dog's Environment), founded in 1993 to promote the humane treatment of dogs. The money was to go to animal care and medical testing in the 1996 race. Following that running, Iams, the pet-food company and the sole remaining major corporate sponsor, declined to renew its $150,000-a-year contract.

The Iditarod Trail Committee found sponsorship among state companies, but its luster was dimmed by a campaign founded on false statements, misinterpreted medical information, and manipulation of the media, and, as far as most mushers are concerned, deception. Merritt Clifton, editor of *Animal People*, a newsletter devoted to animal-rights issues, called the HSUS effort against the Iditarod "a bullshit campaign." He observed that the Iditarod is one of the best-supervised races in the world and should be held up as "a model."

My conversation with Clifton occurred after an article I wrote on the controversy appeared in the March 1995 issue of the *Atlantic Monthly*, while I was investigating why so many veterinarians and other animal-welfare activists I had interviewed had spoken badly of HSUS. Primarily, they felt that the organization took on many issues purely for their publicity value, regardless of the facts of the case;

subtly misrepresented itself in its fund-raising efforts by leading contributors to believe they were donating to local humane societies for animal rescue, when in fact those groups received no money from HSUS; and frequently sought to gain credit for the work of smaller, less well funded organizations. On the other hand, since its founding in 1954 in a dispute with the American Humane Association over the use of dogs from animal shelters in biomedical research—it was common for institutions to buy from them—HSUS has worked to end that practice, conducted important investigations of puppy mills, moved forcefully against dog fights, and provided valuable research on dog bites and other behavioral problems. It received high marks in its formative years for its programs that promoted companion animals and advised animal shelters.

Unfortunately, in its campaign against the Iditarod, HSUS has provided neither sound research nor compelling evidence to support its chief claim that dogs are being run to death for human entertainment. That failure has led many observers, including me, to conclude that the campaign is intended more to aggrandize HSUS at the expense of the Iditarod than to help the huskies.

The simple fact is that for years after its founding in 1973 the Iditarod as an entity and many of its participants held a cavalier attitude toward their dogs, albeit one with deep roots in the Arctic. Whips were used to drive dogs. Starvation and beatings were common punishments. If after all of the abuse, the dog failed to perform its function, it was killed. If it dropped in harness or in the dog yard, it was replaced. Dogs were bountiful and expendable. Before 1990, when records were started, probably more than one hundred dogs died during the race. Since then, twenty-four have perished from moose attack, broken necks, collisions with snowmobiles, heart failure, an exploded liver, and sled-dog myopathy, the name applied to a cluster of conditions including exertional myopathy. Hundreds of dogs have dropped out owing to sore feet, sprains, fractures, and exhaustion. Occurring in a race with an average of around 1,200 starters, those casualties represent a significant figure, and for that reason have long drawn the attention of animal-rights activists.

In 1992, the Humane Society of the United States, seeing a chance for good works and publicity, began to monitor the race, and the Iditarod Trail Committee named a tough new chief veterinarian, Karin Schmidt of Anchorage. Only one dog died that year, the lowest number on record, but for what were officially called financial and political reasons, Schmidt's contract was not renewed. The grapevine held that the old-timers were annoyed at her insistence on dog care.

In 1993, six dogs died. ABC television decided not to renew its contract to broadcast the event, and Dodge became the first major corporate sponsor to drop its support. Seeking to stanch the defections, the Iditarod Trail Committee rehired Schmidt and established an animal-care committee, which included David Wills of HSUS. Wills proclaimed that his sole interest lay in eliminating unnecessary dog deaths, not protecting the Iditarod. In 1994, he proved the latter half of that statement.

Citing a report on HC by pathologists of the Tufts University School of Veterinary Medicine, Wills claimed that she was a victim of exertional myopathy and that all previously unexplained deaths in the Iditarod resulted from the same condition. Furthermore, he said that the nature of the race—and the ultramarathon Yukon Quest—was responsible. Shorter races, he told me during several telephone interviews, did not cause deaths from exertional myopathy. Wills also charged that mushers frequently culled unwanted animals.

Taken at their face value, the charges and implicit threat of a boycott of their products by enraged animal-rights advocates were sufficient to frighten many corporate sponsors, who publicly gave other explanations for their decision. For example, Timberland said it wanted to redirect its promotional dollars. The media have no such excuse, since their reporters and research departments could have investigated the charges but, with few exceptions, including the *Boston Globe*, chose simply to repeat them.

Responding with bombast and an attitude that said, "Fuck you, if you don't like us," the old-line mushers who hold sway on the Iditarod Trail Committee did not help their cause. They succeeded only in shutting out the voices of their colleagues who devote substantial time to the well-being of their dogs. Nonetheless, for the 1995 running, the committee implemented several rule changes including a reduction from twenty to sixteen dogs per team to start and from seven to five to finish. HSUS had long claimed that the reduction in team size would slow the race down, and the committee apparently agreed. But two dogs died, one from unknown causes and the other when a team was caught in a severe storm on the Bering coast that nearly killed the musher as well. And the mushers proved that fewer dogs slowed nothing down: Doug Swingley shattered Martin Buser's record, and in 1996 Jeff King won in the second-fastest time, over a bad course. Within a few years, the nine-day barrier will probably fall: perhaps the reduction in team size means mushers can spend less time on dog care and more on racing.

For 1996, Rule 18 was adopted, mandating that any musher losing a dog for other than unavoidable external reasons, like an accident, had to leave the trail. Ironically, when the new rule was applied to five-time champion Rick Swenson just over 200 miles into the race, it raised such a cry of protest from Alaskans and other mushing devotees that following the race, the Iditarod Trail Committee voted to scratch it from the books. Swenson's dog Ariel, the only fatality, had died suddenly after the team ran through open water on a section of the trail that should have been, and subsequently was, closed. Apparently, Ariel fell and became tangled in her lead during the crossing. She was asphyxiated before Swenson could free her. Clearly anyone abusing his or her dogs must be ordered out of the race, but to suspend someone who has lost a dog in a freak accident or without knowing the reason—and it is often difficult to tell even with a necropsy—is perceived by the mushers and many fans as unduly harsh. In repealing Rule 18, the Iditarod Trail Committee also "reinstated" Swenson.

The battle continues on two fronts: medical and public relations (call them fact and perception). Ironically, the mushers hold the medical high ground but have thus far been unable to use that advantage to change perception, in large measure because of HSUS's access to the press from its Washington headquarters and the media savvy of its staff. It must also be said, however, that the Iditarod Trail Committee has in the past shown an astonishing insensitivity to the legitimate concerns of the press and public, which cannot be explained by provincialism. For example, the death of the dog early in the 1995 race was not disclosed until after it was finished, leading to charges of a cover-up. (In fact, the failure to inform resulted from ignorance of the need to be proactive.) In 1996, organizers were much more open, a change that must endure.

Medically, it is clear that an unknown number of dogs, including HC, have died of what veterinarians are now calling sled-dog myopathy, which can range from simply "tying-up," the equivalent of a bad case of cramps, to sudden death from a catastrophic breakdown of muscle tissue. The suspicion of those veterinarians most familiar with sled dogs is that the afflicted have a predisposing condition—hypothyroidism, for example—and that some lines of dogs might be more affected than others. Whatever its causes, sled-dog myopathy can strike a dog out for a recreational run as easily as one competing in a sprint or ultramarathon. Distance is not the determining factor; exercise is. But one cannot stop a dog from running or exercising, which is what dogs do, without imperiling their health and forcing them to lead a boring, unsatisfactory life.

HSUS has refused to recognize the changes that have occurred in the past fifteen years, when a new group of mushers achieved success with dogs they cared for and trained and pampered when necessary. Rick Swenson, Susan Butcher, Jeff King, Doug Swingley, and Martin Buser own more than half the victories and the fastest times in the Iditarod, and their success has probably done more than pressure from animal-rights groups to change the attitude of mushers toward their dogs, success spawning more imitators than failure. Mushers have realized that although they might force their dogs to pull the sled, they cannot compel them to run hard or to win. The animals themselves must want to do that. The human competitors have also begun to recognize that the mental attitude, physical health, overall conditioning, and nutrition of the dog are as important as its breeding.

Buser, who openly discusses his grief over the death of his lead dog Stafford in the 1989 Iditarod and believes his colleagues should reveal their own feelings so the public will understand the bond between them and their dogs, says that HSUS became involved just at the time that many of the people who committed "atrocities" against their dogs were leaving the sport, having gotten too old to continue or realized that they would never be competitive. In this view, David Wills and his colleagues simply misread history and the direction the race and dog care in general were taking. They were more interested in publicity and fund-raising at the expense of the race.

The Iditarod is by design a grueling test of humans and dogs across rough country. Accidents happen, injuries occur—both can result in death. No one who is sane looks forward to that happenstance. To minimize the chance for unnecessary deaths, the Iditarod Trail Committee must tighten its eligibility requirements to exclude inexperienced mushers and those who rent or buy whole teams on the eve of the event, and institutionalize a sound policy of prerace screening of all dogs for potential fatal defects. Beyond that, it should undertake an active program to educate people about the race and the sport of mushing in general by putting forward its top competitors.

A number of reformers have suggested that the Iditarod be converted into a true stage race, like the Alpirod and several new events in this country, in which competitors would race over a prescribed distance each day, then break to rest themselves and their dogs. The musher with the best cumulative time would win. Underlying this suggestion is the notion that the dogs would be rested, but in fact the dogs are asked to run harder in each stage, which has its own victor while also contributing to the final result. The Iditarod, on the other hand, rewards a consistent and slower pace.

Until research is conducted to determine why dogs are dying, the question of which side is correct will remain moot. HSUS and other animal-rights groups should work with the Iditarod Trail Committee to sponsor a comprehensive medical study of the Alaskan husky and the causes of sled-dog myopathy. Traditionally, such groups have eschewed sponsoring research, as has the American Kennel Club, but no organization claiming to have the welfare of animals at heart can responsibly ignore the value of scientific studies. Without facts, charges

remain public relations ploys designed to intimidate corporate supporters and change public opinion. They have nothing to do with the
welfare of the animals.

Humans and Dogs

At the heart of the HSUS charges against the Iditarod lies a misunderstanding of the unique relationship between dogs and humans as
profound as that of the people who routinely abuse their animals.
Both HSUS and abusers share the attitude that the dog is a servant or
slave to humans, a disposable creature. The difference is that HSUS
and other animal-rights activists project their bias onto people using
dogs for any purpose identified as entertainment, while the dog
abusers cast the dark shadow of their maltreatment onto all other dog
owners.

Lost in the charges and ad hominem attacks is the fact that among
mushers, as among other people who work and live with dogs, are
individuals who possess an uncanny ability to understand their animals, "to get inside the minds of their dogs," as they put it, to understand what they are thinking, feeling, saying. George Attla, Martin
Buser, Susan Butcher, Gareth Wright, and other successful mushers
possess that quality, as do a number of trainers and handlers of other
types of dogs. They read subtle shifts in the way a dog moves, its
overall demeanor, its vocalizations, the angle of its tail and ears, the
look in its eye to determine its physical and mental state. Then they
talk to it in a way it understands.

Susan Butcher wants first and foremost to establish a bond
with each of her dogs. "I have a strong understanding of what dogs
are thinking," she says. "I've learned their language and get into
their heads."

George Attla, the greatest sprint racer to date, says, "By reading dogs you can tell how the person behind the sled is, what kind
of person they are to their dogs. Body language is easy to read. Even
a picture will tell you what the team is thinking by the position
of its ears. I can read the same thing by looking at the reactions

of dogs to the musher's tone of voice. You learn to read dog language. There aren't a whole lot of people who have a talent for dogs."

"We wear many hats when taking care of our dogs and racing them," says Buser, who is widely respected for the time he spends educating people about the sport he loves—and the athletes, who deserve the credit. "Most of all we are custodians. My dogs speak to me, and I understand what they are saying, but other people can't usually do that and so it's hard for them to understand. After they come and see us, they understand that there is a bond that we won't break."

Chapter Eight

BY LAND, SEA, AND AIR

Breeding and Training

Although from any perspective the question of breeding presents a conundrum, certain truths appear irrefutable: that various types of dogs have distinctive styles of working and enhanced talents for running, stalking, herding, retrieving, swimming, tracking by sight or scent; *and* that individual dogs of all breeds, except those physically unable, can be found who are capable of performing those acts, to a degree, if they are trained. These particular types—be they racing huskies, sight and scent hounds, stockdogs, pointers, or retrievers—are products of selective breeding for function and form, albeit in a way different from that celebrated in the show ring.

Form for a working dog refers to locomotion, agility, strength, bite; for a show dog, good looks. Mate two dogs who look like pointers but have never really pointed, and you probably will end up with a litter of dogs who look like pointers but do not reliably freeze when they encounter prey. But breed two scruffy-looking mutts who come to a screeching halt whenever their noses encounter another animal and stare, waiting for it to move, and you have a good chance of getting at least a couple of puppies with the same disposition. They might look like street curs, but they will point and probably do other things as well. In other words, the look does not make the dog—something that many of us have never learned.

While the breeds, or subgroups, into which these animals are narrowly divided are often arbitrarily based on the irrelevancy of coat characteristics or ear shape, the general types more appropriately reflect broader behavioral and phenotypic eccentricities. Insofar as the dogs are employed at tasks for which they ostensibly were bred, their styles of work reinforce our notions of breed specialities. On the other hand, when we watch them performing in a different arena—for example, chasing a Frisbee or detecting scents—we realize how much they have in common in terms of their innate canine drives.

"The general principle," J. P. Scott and John L. Fuller wrote more than thirty years ago in *Genetics and the Social Behavior of the Dog*, "is that many breeds have a wider range of adaptability than is ordinarily recognized, and that the scope of adaptability may be much narrower in some breeds than in others." They believed, as a rule, that breeds showed combinations of special characteristics that allowed them to perform in a specific fashion, among them a proclivity in the retrievers and bird dogs to accept "inhibitory training." But the degree to which any of those traits were inherited varied greatly, even with inbreeding.

I view the various behaviors available to the generic dog as colors on a spectrum. In certain breeds, several primary colors carry precedence over others, but in each individual in that breed, these colors are altered in tone, hue, brightness, intensity, and even shade when mixed with other colors that are basic to dogs. The result is a portrait in flesh, blood, and bone. As with scent dogs, the behavioral differences between breeds are often less pronounced than those between individuals within breeds. Dogs from different breeds can themselves bear more remarkable similarities than those of the same breed—except for morphological characteristics, which explains why people traditionally select for those attributes.

Pointers freeze and sometimes raise a leg when they encounter game, which happens to be normal behavior for a canid stalking prey. Although some will retrieve—another natural predatory behavior— most are trained not to. Hunting setters and Brittanies also freeze in a point, sometimes with a raised leg. Working spaniels flush, pause ("hup"), and retrieve. Hunted on dry land, retrievers will point, flush, and do what retrievers are supposed to do. All rely on their eyes and noses to guide them. All must be trained to perform the specialized task for which they ostensibly were bred—suspending their stalk for an indefinite period. I say ostensibly because we do not know precisely what behavioral characteristics are involved in that long pause.

A number of books and experts claim, for example, that bird dogs point only for birds or feathers on ladies' hats at the show ring. It is, they say, genetically programmed. But, in fact, pointers and other gundogs start pointing rats and just about any other creature they can see and smell from about ten weeks of age, if not before. The trainer has to focus their attention on birds and condition their inclination to freeze when they encounter a particular animal. Scott and Fuller observed that any dog can be trained to be a setter provided it has a good nose and a desire to hunt birds, and the same can be said of pointers. The original setter, after all, was trained to lie down after detecting a covey of partridges until a net was pulled over its head and around the birds.

By that definition, basenjis, who hunt that way for the Pygmy, are setters. A border collie frozen and showing eye at Canadian geese littering a golf course or park with their excrement is "set" or "pointing," depending on one's interpretation. Then it rushes and flushes the geese, driving them into the air. Is the dog a setter, a spaniel, or a herding dog? I have seen a number of "pointing" and "herding" Dalmatians, including one I owned who would stand frozen over a flower for twenty minutes inhaling its scent. My parents' Dalmatian points squirrels, birds, and our Catahoulas. In Scandinavia, the spitz is used to point and flush birds. Montague Stevens, a rancher in New Mexico at the turn of the century, had a bloodhound who pointed stray sheep when it found them.

Then there is a man who claims absolutely to have developed pointing Labradors, and another who has an inbred line of "turkey dogs." The Lab puppies are guaranteed to hold a point at seven weeks of age, not a great distinction given that many pups of different breeds will do the same. At seven weeks, Marlow's daughter would hold a point for ten seconds; I suppose she could be called a pointing Catahoula catch dog. Any dog who stalks, freezes, and has a nose can be trained to point turkey. Probably what the creator of this line had were dogs who looked like his notion of a turkey hunter and to whom he responded accordingly. They learned according to his expectations. Their success reinforced his belief that he was breeding turkey dogs rather than causing him to realize that he had become skilled at training them. Nonetheless, there are buyers for these fabrications.

In a fundamental sense, pointing and setting are hunting behaviors that fall under the heading of what we might call "passive alert," which many detection dogs are trained to perform. Smell, or see, the object of your desire and freeze, pointing at it with your nose, body, and leg. Among gundogs, those taking readily to the training and seeming to gravitate to birds are called "birdy" and biddable. Pointing and setting also require that dogs stare intently at their prey, the way border collies do; thus, they can be said to have "eye," just like their herding cousins.

Breeding fixes particular traits and establishes a higher probability for certain complex behaviors to manifest themselves in a stronger than normal fashion. It does not preprogram a dog for birds or any other specific prey. That is the role of training, which is nothing more than the human adopting the role of adult wolves in educating the puppy into the culture of the pack. Bird-dog trainers have more stories than they can count of people who drive in with their pet pointer, spaniel, setter, or retriever in a fancy four-wheel-drive vehicle complaining that their dog won't do what it was born to and suggesting that it must be genetically deficient. During the ensuing conversation, they admit that they have not really attempted to train it. They expected that it would turn on at the start of bird season, the way their vehicle starts right up. Worse, they might have followed a book or article and decided that the way to get it to point quail was to tie a quail wing around its neck, so it could live with it day and night. That is analogous to tying an open book around a baby's neck and assuming it will learn to read. Although yard training—the basic commands of sit, stay, heel, come—can begin at an early age, as long as it is made enjoyable, many people believe that more complicated lessons should not begin until the dog is nearly a year old, with some waiting until it is two and others starting at six to nine months if they feel the animal is mature enough.

The same books and experts who talk about the innate affinity of pointers for birds maintain that retrievers are born with an inability to kill the object of their quest and a need to swim. They are said to be possessed of inhibited prey drive, meaning they will not follow through on an attack to dispatch and dissect their quarry. They are arrested at a point in their wolfish development where their idea of adult behavior is playing with objects—balls, dead birds, lures, sticks—until they drop.

Like many notions about dogs, this one has some basis in human observation of canine behavior, and it is often trotted out as evidence that the gundogs are more refined—call them civilized or neotenic— than "primitive" breeds, like the basenji and Catahoula, or the "wolfish" breeds, like the German shepherd and border collie. A number of experts claim that further proving the Labrador's or pointer's neoteny is its sociability toward people and other dogs. Indeed, both appear as a rule to be weak in intraspecies and inter-species aggressiveness. Like hounds and Alaskan huskies, they are bred to get along with other animals—except those they are hunting.

The assessments are true within limits. Hunting dogs are by their natures not pacifists. Nor are they always model citizens. I have encountered Labs and golden retrievers, another putatively docile breed, who attack other dogs without warning. Pointers can be as testy as any other breed, and many Chesapeake Bay retrievers back down from no person or animal, which does not mean they are fighters. They are hardheaded, a trait excused by people who say, "They were bred to sit in a skiff all day and protect a hunter's decoys." It is nice to make up stories to explain generalizations about breed behavior, but not useful. The old histories said the dogs were developed to fetch hundreds of ducks a day out of the Chesapeake Bay, so presumably they have been revised to reflect a reassessment of the breed's character. Given that the style of hunting at the time of the Chesapeake's devel-opment more nearly approximated mass slaughter than leaving decoys in a skiff, I prefer the original accounts.

Trainers of Labradors and Chesapeakes, as well as the various upland hunters, report that young dogs have to be taught not to attack and kill cats, rabbits, and wounded birds if they move. I have seen young pointers snap at birds that flush under their noises, and receive a stern reprimand from the human handler for doing so. Good hunting spaniels will pounce on a bird that stays on the ground rather than flushing, and some of them will kill it unless, like the retrievers, they are trained not to do so. Occasionally, spaniels or pointers with high prey drive will want to go after—herd—a moving infant or sheep. (Hounds, who are also said to be "object players," will jump and kill game that either fails to run or leaps from its tree or den into their midst.) Humans want to arrest the predation in order to kill the game themselves, of course, so they are constantly selecting for a dog who can be trained not to execute the attack that begins with a stalk or complete the meal after fetching it home. Thus, as with any dogs, one of the first and most useful commands is "No" or "Back off."

Beyond the attacks, there is the phenomenon common in retrieving breeds of the hard mouth, meaning the dog bites down too hard, killing the game it is supposed to bring back alive. Many trainers cure a hard mouth by driving nails into the object being retrieved in training so that when the dog chomps down it is pricked. Of course, the preference is a human one. Charles Darwin in *The Descent of Man* reported on a retriever who, when presented with the seemingly impossible task of retrieving two wounded ducks, killed one, so it could not swim off, brought the living one to the hunter, and then returned for the dead one. Darwin took the act as one of intelligence. A Labrador trainer I presented with the case said that the dog had simply violated its training.

For gundogs, as for every other type, good breeding will often fade before improper handling. Many years ago, I adopted a German short-haired pointer who had spent his first six months in a small, chain-link kennel in the country north of Baltimore. When I took Strider, he was a bundle of energy, undisciplined, unschooled even in the rudiments of obedience. He just loved to run, retrieve, and chase dogs in heat, once climbing over an eight-foot-high chain-link fence in a veterinarian's clinic to mount the bitch in the kennel next to his, and on the last day of his life, escaping the house on a snowy morning in Kansas and traveling five miles before meeting not the object of his desire but a car.

With so much drive, Strider should have been a great hunter, but he was, I learned, gun-shy. He hid from firecrackers and all other explosive noises. He did not destroy things or try to escape as some dogs will, tearing through fences and doors; he just hid under my arm or the bed. After much work, he learned to come reluctantly when I called, as if expecting to be hit—the same person who kept him in a pen the first six months of his life had clearly struck him for not coming, which guaranteed he would not, and fired guns around him to condition him to the sound. He was probably broken of any desire to point at the same time.

But when Strider was retrieving a stick, ball, or Frisbee on land or in the water, he was focused. He would leap out of the car window to get to the lake where he and Max, the big Chesapeake, swam. He dove off rocks with a drop of ten feet into fast-moving water, his legs already in motion. No match for Max, Strider was nonetheless a better swimmer than many retrievers I have seen. In fact, although willing to grant that retrievers inherit an affinity for the water—probably a lack of fear—I am not convinced that it is very strong.

All dogs seem to swim instinctively in that their flailing rapidly settles into a paddle that keeps them afloat and moving forward, but not all are at ease in the water, no matter their desire to retrieve or breeding. At age eight, our female leopard dog, Clio, who had learned to swim as a puppy but subsequently dabbled only in freshwater and never enjoyed breaking surf, waded into a lake behind my parents' house and set to work retrieving sticks with far more precision than a female Chesapeake we once owned, who was bred from "hunting" stock—inbred I now suspect. For all her grace in calm water, Clio lacks the fixation that Max had on getting wet and his eagerness to meet even rough surf or rapids head-on. On the other hand, although he swims proficiently, Marlow is not at home in the water and, in fact, treats the entire concept with disdain. Like people, dogs must learn to swim and then be encouraged to follow their desire, but if they do not care for the activity, no amount of training will convert them.

One of the more fascinating attempts to determine the genetic component of specific behavior occurred more than fifty years ago and involved the Dalmatian, a pointer and herder who had gained notoriety as a coach hound. Chosen to accompany coaches and carriages because of its striking looks, running ability, and seeming fearlessness around horses, the Dalmatian became so popular in its new role that it was declared to be a hippophiliac—a lover of horses—much the way other dogs are said to be born with sheep on the brain. (Dalmatians have also been skinned and turned into fur coats in some parts of the world.) There are dogs of many breeds, just as there are people, who love horses, but there is no proof that the feeling is inherited. More likely, the dogs just learn that hanging around horses gives them a chance to run and hunt.

Nonetheless, in February 1940, two Harvard University biochemists, Clyde E. Keeler and Harry C. Trimble, published a curious item in the *Journal of Heredity* about coach dogs and their renowned hippophilia. Keeler and Trimble were given access to the records of a large kennel that for a quarter of a century had bred and trained Dalmatian coach hounds, as they were known. Training started at six months and basically involved yoking the juvenile to an experienced dog until it understood that it was to run with the coach. After that it was taken off the tether and allowed to seek its own position relative to the horse and carriage—the best from the standpoint of the coachmen being anywhere from under the front axle to the horse's rear legs and the worst being behind the carriage. The scientists found that mating dogs who preferred the forward position produced puppies who preferred the forward position, whereas mixing good and bad dogs produced decidedly poor puppies who ran well back of the horses. Breeding bad to bad was a disaster: at least two of those puppies were "man-shy" or timid.

The results suggested to Keeler and Trimble that the distinctive preferences trained Dalmatians showed for where they ran behind horses were being selected for genetically. But because they recognized the impossibility of that, they attempted to determine what traits were being passed on that influenced the decision. They concluded that the position Dalmatian coach hounds selected was the result of the interplay of "inherited tendencies capable of training" and their level of fearfulness. All breed "specialities" represent unique combinations of common talents and tendencies, such as sociability, trainability, fearfulness, aggression in its various guises, agility, strength, speed, and overall size.

The case of the Dalmatian underscores the need to speak as precisely as possible about behavior, environment, nutrition, and genetics, a task made difficult by the imprecision of the language available to us and limited knowledge of canine genetics. Compounding the problem is the habit of many people involved with dogs to emphasize breeding at the expense of all other factors. Too often, talk of the genetics of behavior resembles a theological disquisition on predestination, with genes substituting for God, more than an inquiry into the nature of the organism under consideration.

Humans with their deep bias about what particular dogs are born for will deny it, but the dogs who excel at Frisbee are also retrievers at heart. They are border collies, Australian shepherds, whippets, mixed-breed cattle dogs, mutts—fast and agile. Labradors can do the routines too, and a few, including mixes, have made it into the finals over the years, but as a rule they lack the speed and agility needed to compete at the top level. A sixty- or seventy-pound Lab is also too heavy for most people to handle in the series of close-order drills and body vaults that win competitions. When we take dogs, define them by what they do, and breed them for those talents, regardless of their pedigree, we end up with some interesting animals—and if the breeding is pursued in narrow enough fashion, new breeds. Thus, an enterprising person could create a Frisbee breed: light, fast, agile, leaping retrievers.

More than a few purists will be annoyed at that thought. They complain when someone uses border collies to haze geese off golf courses, as is now done in many areas where they have become pests and their excrement an unpleasant hazard; to chase a Frisbee; or to hunt turkey, as a gentleman in Virginia reportedly does. Among dedicated bird and duck hunters are notorious snobs known to become aggrieved when someone hunts over what they perceive to be the wrong dog. At times the distinctions have a sound basis: pointers are the dog of choice for hunting quail in the South, for example, because their short coats remain free of cockleburs after a day in the field and keep them cool. But choosing to hunt exclusively over them is a matter of human culture.

Charles Fergus describes the situation in *A Rough-Shooting Dog* (1991), an account of his decision to hunt grouse with a springer spaniel (from a field-trial line) rather than a setter. To the old hands in western Pennsylvania, Fergus was a heretic, although his dog Jenny did beautifully on grouse, woodcock, pheasant, and ducks. There are also Labs who learn to flush upland birds as well as any spaniel, not to mention retrieving pointers. Citizens of industrialized countries, we are raised to believe in specialization as the highest achievement—be it in a profession, academe, on the athletic field— and we expect our dogs to follow our lead. So we invent for them degrees of expertise and emphasize those, narrowing our own focus as much as theirs. We pay lip service to the Renaissance man, the Super-woman, the generalist, but there is always an undertone to the praise, a refrain saying, "Yes, but if he, she, or it would *only* concentrate on one thing . . ."

Specialization is so far advanced in dogdom that even among working lines there are divisions between trial and hunting or herding dogs. Whereas not too many years ago field trials were merely a way to keep a dog employed in the off-season, they have become ends in themselves. Trial dogs, be they pointers, retrievers, spaniels, setters, herders, or hounds, tend as a rule to be possessed of high energy, drive, and speed. Some of the trials are timed events with scores awarded for the number of animals treed or flushed, while others simply require precise execution of prescribed tasks. Intensely trained and drilled, the dogs work close to their handler, taking direction from him or her.

Working dogs must be more independent. Situations on the hunt, the ranch, or farm are considerably more complicated and subtle than those in a trial, where the goal is to make everything uniform so the dogs can be measured against each other or against a standard of behavior—for example, whether a retriever can follow a beeline for a duck on the ground one hundred yards away and bring it back with minimal human direction. A super trial dog, trained to point one tamed bird at a time, might forget entirely what to do when in the field on a hunt it encounters a covey of wild quail intent on scattering to all points of the compass. Or it might face pheasants whose idea of fun is to keep moving along the ground, forcing it either to hold point over empty space or to engage in a kind of moving point, which its handler has worked to discourage.

Whether in trials or more outlandish competitions, people are finding ways to preserve the drives and talents of dogs, indeed to improve upon them, even though the so-called traditional uses are fading. The trend is not new—setters, spaniels, retrievers, and even pointers existed before shotguns were invented and then made that transition—but it is more broadly based. Labradors provide an intriguing case in point. Known as the essential retriever, they also have worked as sled dogs, stockdogs, detection dogs, and guide dogs—for all their specialization showing themselves to be excellent generalists when they are bred for working ability not the fancy.

Not surprisingly, I wanted to watch these all-purpose dogs in the field and check in on retrievers of a different sort—the mismatched band of quirky animals who chase the flying disc. Like the other dogs I have seen, these live, regardless of the qualities we assign to them, to be dogs—running, hunting, moving through the world of their senses.

Birdy

The plantations around Thomasville, Georgia, and Monticello, Florida, were created in the decades following the War Between the States when wealthy northerners fled south for the winter in an effort to lessen the strain on their respiratory systems, weakened by asthma, consumption, the grime and cold of their industrial North. They sought the curative airs of the southern piney woods, and finding the land cheap and birds abundant, they bought thousands of acres each and established quail-hunting preserves. Call them carpetbaggers of a benign sort; the locals welcomed them and their money as long as they came for visits and did not import too many alien ideas.

In the process of building their plantations, they preserved stands of longleaf pine from the woodsman's saws and maintained unbroken stretches of habitat for their beloved quail and any number of other birds and mammals. It is beautiful country at the southern end of the Appalachians, a land of overarching live oak, pine, Spanish moss, cypress domes, palms, redbuds, dogwood, wisteria, wire grass, azaleas, and magnolias. Under a bright sun, the shadows are so deep as to appear impenetrable. The clay soil offers multiple shades of red. Driving down some of the unpaved roads, you almost seem to be passing into a time out of time.

In this land, the shotguns have two barrels—side by side or over-under—in 20 or 28 gauge. People shoot pump guns and semi-automatics, just as they chase birds using Jeeps. But that is definitely the path of those the novelist J. P. Donleavy calls the "bootless and unhorsed," the new rich who lack all appreciation of the aesthetic of quail hunting and do not bother to learn. They also fire on farmed and released birds as a matter of choice.

Traditionalists follow their pointers on horseback, with horse-drawn wagons loaded with Labradors and handlers bringing up the rear. The pointers work in shifts, locate and point quail, wait. When the shooters arrive, they dismount, approach on foot, flush, and fire. The pointers are leashed, while the Labs are sent on the retrieve, returning birds to the handlers, not the shooters. At the end of the hunt, someone ends up with several excellent meals. There is a ritual to the hunt, a culture surrounding it that involves, as much as the actual shooting, the dogs, horses, wagons, shotguns, and movement through the country. Now as frequently southerners as northerners the hunters are white and generally wealthy men and women, the trainers white country men, the handlers black men. It is an adaptation of a style of hunting developed in England in the nineteenth century and imported to the United States by wealthy sportsmen in the 1920s.

The pointers—technically American lines of English pointers—are energetic, short-coated animals usually kenneled when not afield, although some find their way into the house. They are white with liver, black, or even lemon spots, generally small and graceful, gentle in appearance, fleet afoot. Show dogs are larger and slower and far less interesting in their personality than these eager speed merchants.

The Labradors are hunting stock, varying in size from thirty to ninety pounds, in color from black, which predominates, to a light red-orange that matches some of the clay and is called yellow although it does not match the standard written by the fancy. The red dogs—sometimes called deadgrass by Lab people—are in high favor for hunting because they blend with marsh grass that has died back. They are lithe and leggy, tall and rangy, short and stolid. A little thirty pounder looks more like a large feist than her half brother, a solid, long-legged eighty pounder. Often you have to look twice to make sure you are seeing a "Lab."

Like most working dogs, they are selected for their drive, their biddability, and their intelligence. Most of them would be thrown out of the show ring if their owners ever deigned to take them there. A person who wanted a real dog would feel comfortable taking them home, and many of these Labs double as pets, staying in the house, sleeping on the bed, serving as companions for adults and children. In fact, a number of trainers argue that the best dogs are raised in the house, where they learn not just to respond to commands but to behave. They are not, however, layabouts. They need their exercise to flourish and so would not make good pets for someone wanting a dog to lounge around the kitchen all day growing fat and neurotic.

In February and early March, toward the end of the quail season, this plantation country—and neighboring Alabama—play host to a gathering of serious amateur and professional trainers of pointers and retrievers who compete in hunting and field trials intended to show off their dogs and, as important, their skills.

"There's nothing natural about what we're asking these dogs to do here," says Greg Oyer from Tremont, Illinois, who is regarded by many of the plantation owners as one of the top gundog trainers in the country. Professorial in appearance, with a slight middle-aged spread, a neatly trimmed beard, glasses, and deliberative demeanor, he is the man called in to solve problems. Specializing in retrievers and pointers now, he has also worked with hounds and stockdogs. He is a dog person, gentle and calm in his approach to the animal, willing to work with what is available. He is also unafraid to voice his opinion about dogs and training, even if it seems to run counter to prevailing wisdom.

This first weekend in March 1996, Oyer was participating in a hunting trial, a charity event for Ducks Unlimited held on Borderline Plantation, nestled appropriately enough on the Florida-Georgia border. It was his first competition in sixteen years, and he was entered because his friends had twisted his arm and, not coincidentally, he had a nice dog he wanted to test. Hunting trials were started as an alternative to field trials to keep the gundogs in shape during the off-season without the pressure of the more formalized competition, the custom having been to kennel the dog—literally or metaphorically—when the shotgun was put up and not even give it much in the way of exercise until just before hunting season opened again. Not surprisingly, the dogs grew rusty. They would not completely forget what to do, but they would not dive off the mark like champions either.

Field trials originated as tests of a dog's hunting or retrieving skills but over the years have evolved into a much more intense, abstracted game. Each part of the dog's performance is scored, including its style of work. Precision is the rule, as it retrieves, usually dead birds or ducks, over distances that can reach 400 yards. Points are deducted if the handler must direct the dog along its course, which should be a straight line, and if it hesitates or anticipates commands. Because field trials, like military exercises, require such precise training and handling, lines of dogs have been developed to compete in them. Although they can hunt, they usually are too intense by nature to sit still in a blind and too handler conscious by training to think for themselves, a prerequisite in hunting. They are bred for high prey drive and the toughness to handle the compulsory training they are put through to compete at the top level. Built for speed, they are more leggy and lighter than their show-world cousins. Because field trials are usually held in warm weather and the dogs move at high speed, many of them have single coats, rather than the double coat common to the traditional Labrador—a necessity for a dog working in cold water. With such high stakes, people interested in field trials often start training their dogs intensively well before they are a year old, even though that age is traditionally considered too young.

Many competitors in hunting trials think that field trials are too much about human competition and ego, a working version of the show ring, if you will. More than a few, like Oyer, say that the hunting trials are following the same path. Among professionals, the gap in the level of training for field and hunting trials has narrowed in recent years, but the hunters retain a looser attitude. Usually, the dogs simply pass or fail, whereas in field trials they are ranked. The American Kennel Club sponsors most of the major field (and a number of hunting) trials, but the majority of hunting events are held under the aegis of the United Kennel Club or the American Field in Chicago. Despite the increasing emphasis on competition, many participants still care the most about fairness and testing the abilities of their animals.

At the Ducks Unlimited benefit hunt, the top dogs were also ranked according to their performance in five tests covering three days and involving retrieves across different terrain and through water. In addition to the open class, which drew the professionals and top amateurs, there were categories for amateur trainers—meaning that they did it purely as sport—for dogs of different levels of expertise, from the novice to the accomplished; and for children training and handling their dogs. The amateur class followed a sequence like the open, while the lesser classes competed generally on one day, testing primarily the dog's ability to retrieve by land and water. Because it was a benefit, the judges for each class maintained a friendly, low-key demeanor intended to move dogs along rather than flunk them, as happens in other competitions, where if you miss the cut you are out.

The first dog in the novice class, for example, a nice-looking male black Labrador owned and handled by a young man from

Alabama who, like his dog, was participating in his first trial, showed interest neither in the duck he was sent to retrieve nor in a training lure. He even ignored his tennis ball. Perplexed, the judge asked, "This dog has had a duck in his mouth, hasn't he?" The chagrined handler whispered, "yes," as they walked across the stubble in an attempt to interest the dog in taking something into his mouth, to no avail. In the open class, a dog missed a retrieve on the first day while during the second test a beautiful swimmer passed within two feet of the duck he was pursuing and kept going, finally picking up a different bird thirty yards away.

Other dogs, of course, waltzed through their drills with varying degrees of coordination and speed. Ducks were launched from large slingshots with enough arc for the dogs to mark their flight and landing while a shotgun was fired. The dogs were expected to retrieve them by land and in a separate test from the water on command from their handler. Until receiving it, they sat by his side. Breaking early was cause for disqualification. On other tests, the dogs were sent to fetch a duck that had been laid on the ground out of their field of view. They followed the directions of their handlers, turning to face them on hearing a whistle, then pursuing the direction they indicated with their arms and bodies. The dog who held the most direct line and required the least guidance was deemed the best at that task. Wind direction, the rough cut of the stubble in the field, the layout of the course—all affected their performance.

The tests became increasingly difficult as the skill level of the dogs and handlers increased, so that in the open class dogs were expected to engage in multiple retrieves that took them, if they followed a straight line, over land, through water, and over land again. It seems easy, but a surprising number of dogs once they hit the water turned and stayed in until whistled out rather than hold their line through it and back onto land. Once on land, they tended to stay dry rather than cut through water. It was, as if having struck a channel and a medium, they could do nothing but follow it, like a ship on autopilot. "It's the way they're trained," Oyer said. "They haven't worked on that."

• • •

Oyer was running Percy, a nearly six-year-old, sixty-seven-pound, squarely built black male, who worked with speed and dedication that delighted the judges and took a few seasoned competitors by surprise. The new old hand was someone they had not reckoned with. Many of them had come with three or four dogs for the open and several more young animals for the beginning events. In the business of breeding and training, success contributed to their reputations and profits.

I had met Oyer and Percy the night before the opening of the competition at a cocktail party, introduced by Edwin Richardson, a dedicated bird hunter and Labrador man who had taken an interest in my desire to see humans and dogs working together and doubtless some pity on the fact that I was not a hunter. Calling himself "as dumb as a dog," Oyer took me out in the chill drizzle from a late-winter cold front to meet his "reclamation project." Percy bounded from his crate in the truck to investigate the grounds, his tail flying high. "You wouldn't believe what this dog has had done to him," Oyer said. "He's had cattle prods stuck up his ass. He's been beaten and whipped. He's been shocked. He was a field-trial dog who one day just quit performing. He was a mass of Jell-O from the pressure the handler had put on him. I got him for almost nothing and turned him into a happy hunting retriever. He's a great dog. We're just going to have a good time and see how he does."

Oyer was being polite when he said Percy could not take the pressure. That kind of abusive training is an extreme form of the compulsory practices that are too common in field trials, Schutzhund, and other canine competitions demanding strict obedience, not to mention hunting itself. It is the way Strider was trained before I adopted him. People have called it discipline, correction, and more recently negative reinforcement, a misnomer. They have learned to treat dogs this way not only from their parents and friends but also from reputable books and trainers claiming to have a direct line on the best method. By any name, compulsory training is designed to get fast results and to weed out dogs who cannot take the "pressure." When they quit, or suffer the canine equivalent of a nervous breakdown, they are disposed of—delivered into the hands of people like Oyer if they are lucky, killed if they are not.

People who train dogs with those methods claim that it is necessary to correct faults promptly and efficiently, that there is no other way to accomplish their goal. That is a cover-up for ignorance and, too often, sadism. They want control and fast results, nothing more. Although their fellow trainers will seldom criticize them publicly, a careful observer can spot them by the cowed way their dogs respond to commands or ignore them while acting as though expecting a shock or lash. Or they find a trembling mass like Percy. The practices persist because they do sometimes succeed in producing dogs who can garner awards and because nothing reinforces human behavior more than ego gratification.

Dogs who perform well are beautiful to watch. During a hunting test, they make a beeline on one command across one hundred or more yards of obstacle-strewn field to fetch an object they cannot see; they hit the water, legs churning, and swim for their distant prey while, returning, they pause to mark the fall of another duck, craning their necks out of the water. After each cast, they deliver the duck to their handler, then are sent out again. Oyer observed that teaching a dog to run in a straight line on a cast is one of the hardest things to do because its inclination is to quarter the field, seeking scent. Indeed, the wet grounds, soggy ducks, and shifting winds wreak as much havoc with the dogs on blind retrieves as the rows of tall stubble, which tend to drive them off course as they cross on the diagonal. But when that beauty and precision are achieved through brutality, they are tainted. The trainer has turned a dog into an automaton.

In Fairbanks, Alaska, one August day in 1995—at last count there were six dogs per person in Fairbanks, one of the highest ratios in the world—I watched a man train his dog for an upcoming field trial. They were walking along a road through Creamer Field, a local dairy farm converted into a park and wildlife refuge. Sandhill cranes preparing for their flight south foraged in a mowed field. Hot-air balloons hovered over the hills. It was a beautiful summer day, and the man, wearing a fashionable outdoor vest and carrying a remote unit for a shock collar, moved his sleek black Lab through its paces with a series of jolts. He threw three lures out and commanded the dog to retrieve them, sending a shock each time it showed the slightest hesitation. If the dog performed well, it received no praise or affection. It was supposed to do that, after all. When it screwed up—zap. Man and dog presented one of the most joyless twosomes I have seen in recent years.

Robert Milner, owner of Wildrose Kennel in Grand Junction, Tennessee, author of a book and eighty-minute video on retriever training, says simply, "If you can't train a dog without a shock collar, you can't train a dog with one." He imports British Labs as bloodstock because he believes them to be more trainable. More significant, perhaps, trainers in England do not employ shock collars, believing them unnecessary and cruel. Americans not only demand quicker results but also are intent on ranking everything according to their ideal of perfection, without actually considering the dog's performance. Those habits have led Milner, like Oyer and other trainers, to forsake the trials.

In Oyer's opinion, the problem lies with the human, not the shock collar, which judiciously used can be a useful tool in training some dogs who work far afield and have bad habits. It certainly is more humane and productive than chasing the dog down and trying to deliver a late punishment. But too often it is turned into an instrument of torture by people who find themselves in constant need of upping the volume, raising the level of correction because they are not teaching the dog anything. They are driving it with fear, not motivating it with reward. The dogs themselves often learn to ignore the pain or to forget all they supposedly know during competition, when it is not on. (Recognizing that, many trainers will put a fake electric collar on the dog for some sessions so that it will not cue on when it is liable to a shock.)

It is not necessary to train dogs in that fashion, and the best trainers do not. They learn to deal with the personality and temperament of their dogs, to select animals with a high prey drive, intelligence (but not too much, most of them say), and biddability. They want to see a dog perform with joy. That is the way Percy dashed through the hunting trial, because that is the way Oyer trains his dogs. He does so through "teaching, repetition, and training," a recipe that can apply to getting a dog to do nearly anything within its physical ability. Show the dog what you expect, train it to perform, rewarding its success, and practice. It sounds simpler than it is because dogs, being dogs, do not think or act the way we expect or desire.

"I don't usually buy puppies," Oyer said. "When I do I let my kids pick them out, and invariably they choose the runts. But kids are great with puppies. They play with them and keep them stimulated. They do the yard training, housebreaking them, teaching them to come and sit. They socialize them, in other words, and that's the most important thing you can do for a puppy. Then at about eight months or a year, you can begin to put pressure on them to perform." By that he means that they can begin to learn to retrieve or point, depending on their task in life.

Oyer retrained Percy when he was four years old. Now he is a hunter, pointing and retrieving on command. He is fit and high-spirited; indeed, all the several hundred dogs in attendance were well conditioned and possessed of abundant, if controlled, energy— hunting Labradors must sit for long periods in a blind or wagon, then explode into action. But only a few work with Percy's elan. "The ideal would be to train every dog without the collars and other accoutrements, using maybe a long cord and clip, but that is time-consuming," Oyer explained. "The shock collar gives immediate control over a dog operating at some distance, which for field and hunting trials is what you need. That is true if you're running a kennel, too. You have to train a number of dogs for working."

There are people who train dogs successfully without the use of electric collars or more traditional tools of punishment: whips, sticks, and bottle caps pinched into the inside of the ear. They work intensively with their dog and attempt to keep the volume and frequency of correction low, their goal being to build on the dog's innate talents and interests by reinforcing good behavior. They operate within a different culture than the old-style trainers of bird dogs and retrievers, whose methods doubtless will vanish when more people win with more positive techniques.

Without changing my mind about electric shock collars, which I think should be used only to correct the most outrageous behavior when all else fails, Oyer demonstrated the proper use of a collar on Anne, a two-year-old pointer he had brought south to train. She was an eager dog, so quick she could nearly grab from the air a bird that flushed in front of her, a trick for which she received a jolt of electricity equivalent to a mild shock. Otherwise, Oyer employed the lowest intensity to get her attention, not an easy task for a dog with so much energy that she ran in every direction when let out for the drill. For the trainer, the key is to exercise patience and not rely on the collar to alleviate his or her frustration or to train the dog. It is important to address the offense immediately and just as promptly and more powerfully to reward good behavior. (Ideally, the object fetched is the reward so that the behavior becomes self-reinforcing.)

Oyer said: "An old black handler told me once when I was getting aggravated with a dog who didn't seem to learn anything, 'Greg, you needs to put the dog away, sit down on an oak stump and think about this.' He was right. You can't let your frustration control how you treat the dog. You have to break down what it is you want the dog to do and work on one thing at a time. So the most important thing to teach a Lab is 'Sit.' For a pointer it's 'Whoa.' Both really are to focus the dog. The Lab has to learn to mark and retrieve when you send it. The pointer you want to hold its point. The pointer has to see, hear, smell, point, tolerate a gunshot, honor another dog's point—that is, not . . . run over to it."

At the hunting trial, Percy sprinted through his first event, a land retrieve of five ducks: the first, a bird shot for him to fetch; the second, a long blind retrieve of a dead bird; the third and fourth simulated kills, one behind the other; and the fifth a longer blind retrieve. Then, with darkness closing in, Oyer decided to wait for the next morning to run a sequence of land and water courses. Buddy, a young reddish-yellow Lab from Louisiana, raced through that test near day's end. Although he largely avoided the water on his returns, he did not hesitate over even the most difficult task.

The next morning, Percy ran as nearly the last dog, again racing through the course and taking the final retrieve, a duck thrown into a pond while he was bringing another back to Oyer, without missing a stride. He was the only dog of the day to handle that difficult test cleanly. In fact, his performance with those five birds was so outstanding that he received a round of applause, even from the judges. His only mistake was ignoring a whistle to enter the water and swim a duck back. It was a command to please the judges, but Percy, eager to return his prize, kept running. You could see him thinking, Why bother? I can move faster on land.

Watching Percy and the other dogs, I was intrigued by how they kept track of the birds. During the first half of the event, for example, they had to mark three ducks thrown in sequence in an arc one-hundred yards away. I remarked to Oyer that I have often observed that dogs appear to have a well-developed ability to remember where things are, even days later. They have a geographic memory, he suggested, which is also associative, so that they place objects in a complex web of sights, sounds, and smells. Vague though the notion sounds, it explains how they locate not only objects but also themselves even after traveling thousands of miles by car. Remember how well a dog responds when you make the turn for a frequently visited house that is still ten miles away, and think about the cues he is reading through the window on the air coming through the car's vents. We actually navigate in much the same fashion, by landmarks and signposts. The dog just incorporates more scents and sounds.

The next day, in the final event, Percy needed direction from Oyer to get the second of two ducks that fell close to each other during a test employing ducks shot for each dog. By one-tenth of a point, he finished second in the overall standings to Super Sue, a nice yellow Lab, who worked more deliberately but made fewer mistakes—the goal on the hunt being to bring back the bird. "I'm pleased," Oyer said. "He missed that second bird because I hadn't worked on the problem with him in practice."

As I watched the long retrieves, I found myself wondering why the dogs were not trained, like sheepdogs, simply to move according to the signal from the whistle; why, rather, they were taught to spin around when they heard it blown, sit, and look for a waving arm, a dancing human, whose direction they were then to follow. No one could answer, until Edwin Richardson explained that thirty years ago they were trained in sheepdog fashion because the first man to work with the field-trial Labs was a border collie handler from Scotland. Sometime in the intervening years the custom changed, probably because humans had success with the different approach, which is better suited to training with an electric collar. The whistle is blown, a shock is delivered and released only after the dog turns for instructions.

Ironically, the dogs would work better if they stayed focused on their prize and, like the sheepdogs, changed their course according to the duration of the whistle or sequence of blasts. They would be able to keep an eye on the line they were being directed to follow. They would also avoid the error many made at one time or another of anticipating the whistle. Uncertain of the location of their quarry, they would spin and sit, looking for direction, a clever maneuver that nonetheless cost them points because they are supposed to respond only to commands. That is a curiosity about nearly all trials; the dogs can be penalized for exhibiting initiative by finding shortcuts or anticipating commands, which they clearly do in part to speed their task. Some doubtless seek to avoid the shock of the collar that exists in their mind.

Like most dog trainers, Oyer believes that it is possible to breed—to a degree—for intelligence and drive, or will, without which the dog, no matter its other attributes, can never be great. Dogs lacking the will to excel can do quite well. They can retrieve or pass hunting tests, the way many of the dogs on display at the Ducks Unlimited trial did. They are nice dogs and even memorable in their way, but the great dog has something extra. "I bought one of those kits to test your dog's sense of smell," Oyer says, "and I found that the ones with the best nose weren't usually the best pointers. They lacked that will and drive."

The battle over the relative merits of training and breeding will continue for years to come. Oyer himself believes that training accounts for as much as 90 percent of what the dog becomes and that the good owner never gives up on a dog—he or she just figures out a way to deal with its eccentricities. Studies conducted since the 1960s have confirmed that hunting traits like pointing and retrieving are inheritable, but no one knows to what degree, partly because they are complex and have not yet been properly broken down and defined.

The studies have shown, however, that the best trial dogs do not necessarily produce top dogs, a finding consistent with those from other fields and one just now being studied. The notion flies counter to a dominant strain in breeding and Western eugenic thought—that the best performers will duplicate themselves with a little extra. It is likely that the dog with great will is too stressed to be a prolific stud or dam. It might also be the case that what we call will is not heritable directly.

But it is clear that one can breed dogs who consistently perform the way dogs should by selecting against fear, or timidity, for prey drive and sociability. Because many of those traits seem to derive more from the dam than the sire, especially fearfulness, it is likely that certain genetic predispositions are amplified in the hours and weeks immediately after birth. Looking at the result of those influences some weeks later, we assume they are genetic, although in fact we cannot distinguish clearly between what is inherited, what is caused by events before and immediately after birth, and what is learned from the mother. The relative undetectability of paternal genetic influence suggests, however, that probably early environment is more important in the dog's subsequent development than many people suspect.

It is also clear that the extremely compulsory methods of training employed for field trials and Schutzhund can break down any number of excellent dogs who do not have the imperviousness to pain that allows them to withstand human punishment. No one knows how many dogs succeed at the field-trial game, as its participants know it, but anecdotal evidence suggests that they might represent no more than 20 percent of the total and possibly less. Many people believe that the failures are due to poor breeding, but it is more likely that the majority of them result from human actions that work against the nature of the dog.

After Percy made his first run of the competition, Greg Oyer and I climbed in his truck and went to look at pointers. "I hope you don't mind my taste in music," he said, turning down the stereo that was playing Beethoven's Sixth Symphony.

"No," I said. "It's not what I expected to hear, though, on a cold damp morning on the Georgia-Florida line."

"My mother was a trained musician who fell in love with my dad, a German-American carpenter in central Illinois. But she played this music for me all the time. I think it's one reason I can get along with the people who own these plantations. I can talk about something other than dogs."

For a number of years, Oyer managed the Borderline Plantation of Sally Sullivan, who is known for never "washing out" her Labradors. He also trained dogs and designed a large pond system for hunting trials. His music and comments reminded me of the cultural divide at work throughout much of the dog world. Here the trainers are working-class, often rednecks as they are called in these parts, rough country men, like the Big Cypress cowboys, whose idea of training dogs is often as hard as the way they were raised, whose jokes are about the size of their penises. (The operative word here is, as always, "often," because not all of them follow that course.)

At the trials, as noted earlier, the professionals compete in the open class, along with a few top amateurs who want to test their dogs. At least in quail country, those amateurs are frequently the owners of the plantations and kennels, some of whom might even employ professional trainers to work with the dogs they then handle. The socio-economic and cultural gap is apparent in the types of vehicles—Jeeps and Volvos on one side, pickup trucks on the other—the clothes, the language, and demeanor. For the amateurs, the trials are sport; for the professionals, they represent a chance to claim supremacy for a dog, a kennel, a method.

"There's not much new in dog training," Oyer said. "It's just that if you name something, you claim it, so you'll hear guys describing some new technique they've invented." Fame leads to business and puppy sales—it's a simple equation.

Oyer is not so simple. A classical music–loving man, dumb as a dog, and smart as any trainer in the business, a man who can design a pond, talk elegiacally about Cooper's hawks zipping through a stand of pine at thirty miles an hour after quail, praise the old longleaf pine and wire grass found here. That ability to watch the world and the dogs, to figure out what the animals are really doing, sets him in the class of top trainers in whatever field.

Having achieved success with his reclamation project, he says he might wait another sixteen years before running another hunting trial. He loves training and hunting over dogs. He admires dogs performing to their peak ability, but he does not cotton much to the human posturing and ego that course through the "sport" like a nasty undercurrent. When that becomes dominant, the dogs are forgotten.

Disc Drive

A retriever waits for the bird or duck to land before fetching it back. A superior Frisbee dog, on the other hand, runs up behind the rotating disc and with a well-timed leap snags it from the air—higher points being awarded for distance and midair catches in a weighted scoring system. A spotted little dog just eighteen months old, Coda is mixed Australian shepherd, Australian cattle dog, and Catahoula leopard dog. Possessed of blinding speed and agility, she races up behind the Frisbee, leaps and bats it forward, then grabs it when she hits ground, losing points for missing the flying catch but putting on a spectacular show. Bred to herd cattle, she is a Frisbee dog. She is not a champion, yet.

Cisco is not either, but with Lourdes Edlin the strikingly handsome border collie took first runner-up at the 1995 Friskies Canine Frisbee Disc World Championship (renamed for 1996 the Alpo Canine Frisbee Disc World Championship, as part of the game called corporate sponsorship) on the Mall in Washington, D.C.—the highest finish ever for a first-time finalist. They are chosen in a series of regional competitions that are like major field trials, only of an urban sort. In addition to traditionalists, who find them sacrilegious, many animal-rights activists object on the grounds that dogs vaulting off their owners for Frisbees will hurt themselves for nothing more than human entertainment.

The vault, in which the dog uses its trainer as a springboard, is dangerous, because having achieved a height of five feet or more, the dog is often off balance, its hind legs twisted when it hits ground. Even when injuries do not occur, the repeated impacts take their toll on hips, elbows, and spines. Organizers of the event publicly discourage "excessive" vaulting while continuing to award high marks for flair, which the act epitomizes. Thus, even though many top players minimize vaulting to protect themselves and their dogs, the complaints have an undeniable validity and cast a shadow, as does what competitors perceive to be inconsistent judging at the regional level, on a sport otherwise noteworthy for its emphasis on good treatment and behavior of dogs. Unfortunately, audiences and television cameras love the high-flying, acrobatic catches that made Ashley Whippet winner of the first three competitions, 1975–77, and the mixed breed Soarin' Sam champion in 1993–95.

Looking beyond the correctable human problems, I see dogs who love the chase as much as the people who choreograph their routines and work on their throws. Without question, a dog has to want to play, has to possess the desire to track down the Frisbee, to dance and catch a flipped disc, to perform any of hundreds of intricate maneuvers while keeping its eye fixed and mouth ready to catch. Not all dogs can catch a ball, much less a spinning disc, as anyone who has tried to turn his or her pet into a center fielder can attest. But those who learn have a game they can play for years.

On college campuses and in parks almost from the day Whammo introduced the mass-produced plastic flying saucer, people have thrown it to their dogs for the sheer pleasure of watching them race for the leaping catch. It was more aesthetic than a ball, it seemed, more in keeping with the spirit of the 1960s and 1970s—a countercultural answer to the precision of field trials, the blood of hunting, the sterility of the show ring. The activity was democratic and noncompetitive, just a dog playing catch with its people. In all likelihood, because the disc is slow moving and somewhat erratic in flight, it more nearly resembles prey than a ball, which explains why dogs like to chase it. They are hunting; we are playing catch.

From those playground throws evolved the Ashley Whippet Invitational, named for the first recognized canine Frisbee champion. That was 1975. Owned by Alex Stein of Hudson, Ohio, Ashley Whippet was featured in football halftime shows—Frisbee dogs are now only slightly less common than marching bands and dancing women in hot pants and halter tops—television, and film. A documentary, *Floating Free*, garnered no small amount of fame and an Academy Award nomination for the flying whippet. Ashley's popularity brought attention to the sport, which gained sponsorship from Friskies PetCare Company—pet food producers being major sponsors of canine competitions, seeing them as a way to promote their products.

I went to the Southeastern Regional Friskies Canine Frisbee Disc Championship in Orlando on May 20, 1995, to watch Edlin and Cisco in their quest for the national title and to observe the novice dogs who were there. Whereas at the world championships only the best dogs appear, the regionals are open to local participants and so draw a fair sampling of dogdom—from the flashy border collies and Australian shepherds so much in vogue to deliberate crosses like Coda, accidents like the Labrador–pit bull cross rescued from a pound, the little terriers, and the lackadaisical greyhound, who trotted faster than most of the competitors ran but was largely indifferent to catching and retrieving. Rocket, a young Aussie in his first competition, left the field thirty seconds into his ninety-second routine. He started to chase down a thrown Frisbee and then kept right on going past the low rope marking the field, into the crowd and beyond, his master in hot pursuit. When he caught the stage-frightened dog and gave him a hug, the crowd applauded.

Reflecting its roots, the Frisbee competition resembles a picnic, a morning outing with the dogs. Emphasis is placed on sociability. Participants show up with their pavilions, lawn chairs, water buckets, and dog pens if they use them. Unlike hunters and field trialers, they do not keep their dogs in boxes on the pickup truck; in fact, pickup trucks are noticeably absent. Spectators are families and young couples, often with their dogs in toe, who line the field or stand in the shade, this being central Florida in late spring, a time when heat and humidity dictate that dogs not be left in cars, heatstroke being a constant danger. Ill-mannered dogs are booted from the grounds.

Competitors are generally in their twenties and thirties, one of the significant exceptions being Bob Evans, winner of the Midwest Regional who had come to Orlando as an observer. In his early sixties, Evans first took up Frisbee throwing in 1988 as something to do with his dog and himself. By 1995, he had traveled to the world finals three consecutive years. Video camera in hand, Evans explained that he used an Australian shepherd because the dogs in general accelerate more quickly than border collies and are more devoted to making the catch. "If a border collie misses the first time," he said, "he'll let it go."

Compared with the prescribed drills of obedience work or field trials, Frisbee competitions are a mixture of anarchism and authoritarianism. Each competitor has ninety seconds to perform a "freeflight" routine choreographed to music he or she has selected (usually a rock 'n' roll song) and using up to five Frisbees. The women seem to opt for dance tunes, the men for heavy metal—grace versus power. At the end, the judges have their say. Each contestant is awarded a score based on perceived difficulty, artistic merit, and the number of successful catches the dog makes. A pass of the Frisbee from hand to mouth does not count as a catch, nor does a Frisbee plucked from the ground. The maneuver must begin or end with the disc in flight to receive points. Those rules place a high emphasis on short throws and acrobatic catches. After the first round, usually eight finalists are named. They start with blank score sheets.

In the final round, scores for catch and retrieval, in which the competitor has a minute to complete as many throws with one Frisbee as he or she can make from behind an end line, are added to those for a new freeflight performance—generally the same drill as the one used in qualifying. Points are awarded for distance and successful catches, with those made in midair receiving a bonus. Competitors debate whether to go for distance and higher scores on each throw or a higher number of short throws, the necessary path for those with slower dogs and weaker arms. The world championship uses a longer field and different scoring system than community and regional events for reasons that remain obscure.

The world distance record for a canine Frisbee catch was set on October 12, 1994, when a speed merchant named Cheyenne Ashley Whippet raced 130 yards to make a leaping catch on a disc thrown by Mark Mohar. The little dog was clocked at thirty-five miles an hour. Such a throw in the world championship would earn the team the maximum of 3.5 points awarded to any flying catch more than forty yards from the line and guarantee that they would lose because the time involved in the catch and retrieval would not permit more than two throws.

There were some fine and amusing dogs among the thirty-three who started in Orlando: Sergeant Stratosphere, an Australian cattle dog wearing a red bandanna who liked to bat the Frisbee back to his owner, Max MacAlister; Sparky, a smooth-coated fox terrier, who resembled a head on legs; Jet, an Australian shepherd with great athleticism, who carried his owner, Wade Matthews, to best-novice-team honors; Carolina Kisha, a big Lab who was a marvel at the midrange throws; Chancey, Sandy Seward's little Cairn terrier mutt who took best-small-dog honors and liked to chase a rolling disc; Radical Rush, a powerful border collie who with Steven Heeter of Centerville, Georgia, was first runner-up in the 1994 world championship.

• • •

At the end of the throws, Radical Rush and Heeter held a half-point lead over Cisco and Edlin, who by her own admission is unable to achieve the distance that men can, especially a large man like Heeter. She is lithe and athletic, graceful in her movements, but lacking in upper-body strength. The freeflight, representing a replay of the morning routine, was to settle everything.

Radical Rush and Heeter performed well to heavy-metal music and properly dropped what sounded like "Seig Heils" at the beginning of the tape in the qualifying round (the Nazi salutes being part of the song). Those may have biased my observations, but in general their routine was one based on unspectacular maneuvers solidly performed, to pile up points, with a few high vaults for emphasis. They were prac-ticed, and Radical Rush, as manifest in the distance flight, was in out-standing physical condition—fast and coordinated. But they pounded through their routine like soldiers.

Smiling, moving with grace and precision, Edlin danced through a drill that saw Cisco standing on his hind legs, like a bear, catch-ing Frisbee after Frisbee, performing acrobatic, if not particularly high flying, vaults. Their performance was bolder than the other team in that they risked more difficult catches. Whereas in the open-ing round they hit a few rough spots, the final time through, they had none.

Most of the observers, including their fellow competitors, thought that Cisco and Edlin had dominated the freeflight with their polished, flawless, graceful routine and therefore would overcome that half-point deficit in the final tally. But the judges chose the Georgians first, Edlin and Cisco second, Donna Schoech and Coda third. They just missed out on a trip to Washington.

As long as the judging is done by officials of the organization who also manage the event, there will, I suspect, be these margins of error in determining the top few places. The situation is worse than in figure skating, diving, or gymnastics because the judges do not post their marks at the end of each performance nor are degrees of difficulty assigned to each move. (The judges determine the difficulty of each routine and assign it a score.) Competitors have no sense of how they have been scored or will be scored. At the world finals, a greater professionalism reigns, perhaps because the expenses of the competitors are paid and, in a sense, the world is watching. It is also true that wherever one goes in dogdom, even at hunting trials where whether a dog trees, points, or retrieves game should be incontrovertible, there are disputes over scoring. Or there are charges of favoritism. The arguments might be unavoidable, but I suspect they more likely arise when a sport begins to outgrow its "clubby" origins and to draw people from a wider circle who demand fairness.

I do not mean with these observations to tar the Frisbee competitions. Watching the variety of dogs and people playing with the flying disc of my youth is a delight. The sport itself is ideal for dogs in urban and suburban places where space is at a premium. It is far more interesting than fly ball, the tag-team competition in which a charging dog hits a board that shoots a tennis ball into its mouth, then races back across a line for another dog to take off. The event is popular on the show circuit, as something even mutts can do. I would like to see the Frisbee competition expand and become more evenhanded without losing its picniclike atmosphere.

For the world finals, Edlin worked on new stunts, including one in which she did a handstand with the Frisbee between her ankles. Cisco was to leap and grab it. During the first practice session, he missed the Frisbee and grabbed her ankle. She yelled in pain, and Cisco stopped the routine. "I had to take him back to the beginning," she said. "He's the most sensitive dog I've ever had." He learned the drill and performed it flawlessly in Washington.

Chosen because he was a product of outcrossing and had a high prey drive, which Edlin saw on a videotape when he was six weeks old, Cisco looks bigger than his forty pounds. He acts that way as well. From the time he was eight weeks old, Edlin began training him to the Frisbee. Contrary to the advice of training pamphlets, she let him chew on the discs, to "build his prey drive." When he performed well, he received praise and a Frisbee as his reward, the way some dogs are given food. In short, the Frisbee became the object of his desire and his reward. Even when he was trained to hit the sleeve in Schutzhund and to herd sheep, he had the Frisbee—rather than the traditional tennis ball—as his reinforcer.

Cisco ranks as one of the smartest and best-trained dogs I have met. He is also always busy. When not working with Edlin, he spends hours in her pool, swimming laps. After that workout, he is calm and collected.

Cisco, like Percy, is a super dog, one of those animals who comes along periodically and makes everyone sit up and take notice. But he is that way as much by virtue of superior training and his will as by his inheritance. And Edlin knows that. She has not bred him, seeking a Cisco clone. Rather, to find his ultimate successor, she turned to an Australian shepherd, taking a six-week-old puppy produced of an accidental fusion of show and working lines, making him, according to the genetic superstition that rules so much of dogdom, suspect in both worlds. That pup, named Skylar, was a dominant, bold little character, so full of himself that Edlin thought she would have to work to tone down rather than build up his prey drive. She thought the Aussie would be a little stronger, faster off the mark, and more athletic than the border collie.

Watching Cisco and Edlin is a delight. Listening to her talk about selecting and training him and her other dogs is illuminating. She searched four years for a Frisbee dog, through animal shelters and from breeders, testing temperament and above all their drive. When she decided to purchase a puppy, she interviewed breeders about their practices because she wanted an outcrossed dog. Most told her they did not line breed, but when she checked the pedigrees on their dogs, she discovered otherwise.

"I was amazed when I started looking," she says, "at how many were breeding grandfather to granddaughter and other types of close line breeding even when they said they weren't. I had to look hard for outcrossed dogs, but that's what I wanted." Border collies were too often showing up with hip, elbow, and eye problems, and the majority of those were the result of poor breeding. Like most people in the dog world, Edlin believes the problem arises from ignorance. Sometimes, however, the ignorance seems willful.

In December 1995, Edlin, Cisco, and Skylar, along with another

Frisbee team—John Misita and his mixed-breed CJ—from Fort Lauderdale, started a two-year tour with the circus. (Competing in the 1996 Southeast regional in his hometown, Misita, on leave from the circus, finished first, just ahead of Coda and Donna Schoech.) "I have problems with some of the uses they put animals to," Edlin says. "I hate the bear tricks. But it's a chance to see the world and learn from other animal trainers."

꧁ৼ꧂ *Chapter Nine* ꧁ৼ꧂

DOGS FOR PEOPLE

Guides

Eve McNanamy wants me to see Rory's tail, a finely feathered red banner of happiness wagging upright as he works. She had a friend photograph that tail as they walked through a mall and sent the pictures to the Seeing Eye Foundation in Morristown, New Jersey, where Rory was trained—twice. His first owner had him for three years before having to give him up after his wife developed an allergy to dogs. He was renamed and retrained from left to right hand to accommodate McNanamy, who after six dogs in some forty years could no longer take the strain on her left arm, the traditional working side for a guide dog.

Rory not only accepted his new name but also performed the canine equivalent of a person learning to use the opposite hand, not adequately but superbly. Joining McNanamy, a clinical psychologist in Miami, in 1991, he was with her when a fire damaged her office building, when Hurricane Andrew ripped off the roof on its rampage across southern Dade County in 1992, and when a photographer took the portrait that hangs in the Historical Museum of Southern Florida, in a display honoring one hundred women who have made an impact on South Florida.

Rory is McNanamy's seventh guide dog, all from the Seeing Eye. The oldest and most widely recognized of the fifteen organizations devoted to breeding and raising guide dogs for the blind in the United States, it controls information about itself and protects its name, a registered trademark, as vigorously as some kennel owners protect their bloodlines. For years, it has insisted to the public and writers that See-ing Eye dogs are *its* animals, often bred, always trained and assigned through its school. Generically, the animals are "guide dogs," the first of what has become a growing number of service or working dogs who help people with disabilities, be they seeing, hearing, or neuromuscular. (Guide Dogs for the Blind is the best known of these schools on the West Coast, with others located throughout the country.)

Dorothy Harrison Eustis established the foundation in 1929 to breed German shepherds in Switzerland for use as guide dogs in the United States. She believed that overbreeding for the show ring had ruined American bloodlines, a situation even truer in 1996. But now German shepherds are not the only dogs employed, and many guide-dog programs breed and train their own animals, emphasizing physical and temperamental soundness. According to canine geneticist Eldin Leighton, the guide-dog kennel he supervises has achieved remarkable success in reducing the incidence of hip dysplasia in its German shep-herds through rigorous selection, based on the soundness not just of the individual but also of its littermates and near relatives on its sire's and dam's sides—just as the Orthopedic Foundation for Animals recommends. Not surprisingly, the German shepherds re-sulting from those efforts lack the down-sloping hindquarters prized in the show ring. Their back legs run straight down from under their croups (rumps). The results parallel those achieved by other rigorous breeders.

Eustis's interest grew out of watching blind World War I veterans being led by dogs—perhaps not ironically the same type of animals that had excelled on the battlefield. There was nothing new in the behavior: the sixteenth-century French essayist Michel de Montaigne marveled at the talents of the guide dogs he encountered in Paris. "I have seen them, along the trench of a town, forsake a plain and even path," he wrote, "and take a worse, only to keep their masters further from the ditch." They also knew which homeowners would give their charges alms and so stopped regularly at the proper address, like a delivery person making rounds. They were experts at picking their way through people, horses, carts, past the pitfalls of the city's streets. Sometimes those dogs were barbets, the curly-coated all-purpose dog of the period believed to be the forebear of the poodle; often they were just dogs.

The quality of thought and concern for their charges that Montaigne celebrated distinguishes the best guide dogs today, only, as extensions of their owners, they experience the full stress of modern life, a terrain perhaps more sanitary but far more dangerous than any faced before. Cars with quiet modern mufflers, which are sometimes difficult for the dogs to hear at a distance, and the universal right turn on a red traffic light mean that no intersection provides even the promise of clear passage. Drivers career around sharp corners without pausing to check for pedestrians or obstacles. Cities, towns, shopping malls, even stores are crowded with people concerned with little beyond following their eyes to the next bright counter. They cut and weave, without regard to who is walking near them. The fear and reality of crime that keep sighted citizens locked in their homes present even greater threats to blind people and their dogs. Stairs, elevators, and, despite a raft of laws giving them free passage, restaurateurs, shopkeepers, and even hospital officials who refuse entry to service dogs make life a challenge. Even normal walks are not without their demands, as the human must keep track of clues like numbers of blocks traversed or flights of stairs climbed or turns made in order to direct the dog toward their destination.

To appreciate the physical demands placed on a guide dog and the discipline with which it meets them, you have to watch one take its human down a flight of stairs. Most dogs charge down, working their feet fast enough to keep up with the pull of gravity; a few never overcome their timidity and either inch their way down, pausing frequently, or engage in a slow-motion dive. Schutzhund, search-and-rescue, and police dogs are trained to walk up and down a ramp with slightly raised bars for footing. Although difficult, it is short. A guide dog has no luxury. At the top of the flight, it waits for its owner to position himself or herself, foot to the edge of the first step, free hand on a rail. Then, on command, the dog walks, one step at a time, matching its pace to that of its handler, which can be slow and tentative or, like that of Eve McNanamy, confident and measured. Even her pace is slow for a dog, who must keep its weight well back on its haunches. You can see and feel its muscles straining, the pressure placed on its body, its concentration. A dog with bad hips will break down; one prone to impatience will crack under the pressure.

Over the years, the traditional modern dog of choice for guide work, the German shepherd, has been joined by Labradors, boxers, golden retrievers, and most recently golden retriever–Labrador crosses. The shift to goldens and crosses between them and Labs reflects the changing demographics of blindness. More often now, those needing guide dogs are older, suffering from adult-onset diabetes, whereas before they were young people blinded by accident or childhood disease. Older people often want a dog with less drive, or energy, than many German shepherds or Labs. According to surveys of guide-dog kennels in Australia, the United Kingdom, and the United States, breeding for the primary qualities wanted in a guide dog—for good temperament and trainability and against fearfulness, which is the primary cause of failure—appears successful, although to what degree is not yet clear.

Puppies from kennels devoted to guide and assistance dogs are sent out to families at seven weeks of age so they will bond with humans, become thoroughly socialized, and receive basic obedience training. The families expose them to a variety of experiences and environments—giving the sort of rich early education every dog should have. At fifteen to eighteen months, they return to the school for training. Although success rates vary between kennels and breedings, overall approximately 50 percent of the dogs brought in for training as guide dogs fail to work out. Most of those are in high demand as pets, for obedience, scent work, even field trials, but they lack the temperament, concentration, or physical stamina to lead a person through life. As the saying goes, the dogs must be smart, but not too smart, so that they stay focused on their work and do not wander off looking for something to do. If they have an active owner, they too must be active. If they have a more sedentary owner, they must adapt to that.

More significant, all of them are trained to "intelligent disobedience," to decide, in other words, when to ignore a command to cross a street or proceed in a certain direction. A story circulates from several sources of a woman in Florida who following a heavy rain urged her guide dog to cross the street. The dog refused repeatedly, despite the woman's certainty that there were no cars and her firm commands. Finally, she returned home and told her husband. He drove her and the dog to the intersection to find, parked in the middle, a ten-foot alligator.

In other cases, the dog might decide not to cross because of an obstacle or an oncoming car. Such behavior in an obedience dog would bring a stern correction. But in the world of the blind, where people are literally putting their lives in the paws of their dogs, it is essential. There might be stronger interspecies bonds than those between a blind person and his or her dog, but they would be hard to imagine. When they take to each other—and, as with human relationships, not all matches are equally strong—they form an inseparable unit.

People and the dogs selected for them train together, even if the person has worked with guide dogs before. With their quirks and personalities, they are all different, and it never hurts the handler to brush up on his or her own behavior. Consistency in commands and treatment is the order of the day, precision in movements the rule. But beyond the basics, the best schools take their dogs and clients through drills that resemble their own circumstances: tough stairs, small elevators, crowded shopping malls, classrooms, busy streets.

The complex dance steps take time to master. "When they first get out of those schools, they're all over the place," a veterinarian who treats several guide dogs told me. With everything in the dog's life new, consistent handling is all the more important. To cite one of the greatest truisms about dogs: the people who perform best with a dog are the ones who are steady and try to understand what it is doing, who know when to encourage it, correct it, and let it have its lead.

"I don't like living without a dog, moving without a dog," McNanamy says during a conversation in her office in the fall of 1995. Tall, ramrod straight in her bearing, and thoughtful in her speech, McNanamy wants me to understand the importance of the dog in her life. "The dog has been a part of me all my adult life. I've cried each time I've lost a dog. The first time I went back after losing a dog, the director was a man who had raised German shepherds and he said,

'We will always train another dog for you.' And he told me that I was fortunate and even though blind there was not much I'd been deprived of. The greatest deprivation for me is not to have a dog. You become part of what the animal is, and it becomes part of you."

The first blind person in the state of Florida to receive her teacher's certificate and among the first women to earn a Ph.D. in psychology, McNanamy has overcome obstacles with determination, good humor, intelligence, the help of friends and her dogs—four German shepherds and three goldens. She received her first dog, a German shepherd, when she was sixteen, blind from retinitis pigmentosa. It was a liberating experience.

"The first time I held onto the harness I felt I was flying," she says. "You learn to absolutely trust the dog."

In the 1950s, the state of New Jersey, which she called home, did not allow blind people to become teachers, and so, having graduated in the top 5 percent of her high school class, McNanamy moved to Florida and enrolled at the University of Miami where she earned her degree in secondary education and teaching certificate. By then she and her dog had already starred in a film that played as a short in movie theaters worldwide and educated the public about guide dogs. It featured, she says, a girl in three-inch heels and her dog telling their story.

After teaching at Miami Senior High School, she went back to the University of Miami to work on a master's degree in psychology and stayed for her Ph.D., which she received in 1966. Dog in hand, she then started on a path that led her ultimately to become one of the first women in the area to go into private practice as a clinical psychologist.

McNanamy remembers the feel and personality, the eccentricities of each dog. Not all are created equal, she will tell you. Like people, they vary in their intelligence, their desire, their temperament, their ability to accommodate to the lifestyle of their partner. Some shepherds, for example, like a routine and become upset if called upon to jump into a strange car in the middle of the night and speed off to an emergency. It is a habit of mind that makes them good guardians, but not always the best guide dogs for people with irregular hours. One of her shepherds, her third dog, was too smart, McNanamy recalls, and became bored with a desk job.

In 1979, she switched to a golden retriever, believing the breed presented a friendlier visage toward patients and also would be calmer and more adaptable to her hectic schedule. All guide dogs must possess "retrieve drive" in order to learn to pick up dropped keys, wallets, purses, or other objects. Blessed with retrieving instinct to spare, McNanamy's first golden, Andy, developed his own variation on the training. Walking through the department store in the mall across from her office, he would grab objects stocked at mouth level without breaking stride and carry them out if not stopped. The behavior ulti-mately led to his "arrest" as a compulsive shoplifter.

Andy's successor, Samson, had some difficulty with the stress of the job and developed diabetes, which self-corrected when he retired in 1991. Fair or not, we all play favorites with our dogs, finding in one attributes that set it apart from the others we have owned. That animal possesses a unique personality and combination of talents that resonate in our imagination. Rory, who succeeded Samson, occupies the posi-tion of number-one dog in Eve McNanamy's pantheon. "When I was a little girl, my father went to a nearby town and saw a man there who had a red dog, and so my father told me that when I was old enough I would have a red dog with long hair." Rory, she believes, is that dog.

"They're not all the same," she says. "You can't generalize. I was just lucky this time. A golden angel came to be with me. We are a unit. You train to become coordinated. It's like a dancing partner. He loves to be with me."

He even plays a role in her clinical practice as a bridge to children, many of whom are frightened or withdrawn, and he also remains calm through the loud, emotional arguments that sometimes accompany family therapy sessions. But Rory, a guide dog from birth, is a therapy dog by avocation. McNanamy believes that not only his presence but also her blindness contribute to her professional effectiveness.

For five years the lives of Eve McNanamy and Rory have been linked by more than the harness he wears while working. Theirs was, she says, an instant bond. She recognizes the truism that dogs often bond more closely to their second owner, in part to compensate for their sense of abandonment. But something more is clearly at work with these two. "Rory has never had a leash correction in his life," she says, a sign of remarkable understanding. They are devoted to each other in a way that boosts the spirits of both. When she had to go into the hospital a few years ago, Rory fell into a depression until he came to stay with her in the hospital. When she leaves him at home, he howls. "He wants to find me," she says. "The bond is such that the dog can't exist without me. He wails, calling."

Service Dogs

Around A.D. 800, the citizens of Geel, Belgium, were urged by their leaders to take handicapped people and their dogs into their homes and give them aid. Additional references are scarce until Montaigne's essay seven centuries later, but it is logical to assume, given the dog's talents, that it was serving as a guide for blind people long before then, in many different places. Indeed, a leashed dog pulls unless trained to do otherwise, and it has a strong inclination to follow the same route every time out—unless distracted. Human acceptance of the dog as leader is another matter, requiring a leap of faith, which for people unfamiliar with animals or from cultures and families devaluing them is often difficult.

In nineteenth-century France, guide dogs for the blind were classed with guardians of the flock, home, and business as "useful" dogs, to be taxed at a lower rate than pets or "luxury" dogs. In a fit of bureaucratic inanity, dogs who alerted their deaf owners when someone came to their door were rated as pets because they did not technically guide or guard. The significant point is that people were using dogs as hearing aids and probably had been for some time. Like guide dogs, but more invisibly, they operated in a realm that seldom received public discussion—that of the physically disabled. When people employed them as aids, they apparently did so on their own initiative, with dogs they, a friend, or relative had trained.

The ancient Greeks promoted horseback riding to lift the morale of terminally ill people, a prescription that persists in more dilute form today. Horses are used in therapy, but the soothing horseback ride generally became "getting out"—for a ride in the car. In Europe and England, physicians began using dogs and other animals in the eighteenth century to treat mentally ill patients. Enlightened though those efforts were at a time when mental illness was commonly treated with torture, exorcism, or neglect, they did not spawn any widespread movement. Dogs in therapy remained an oddity.

The tremendous casualties of World War I and "scientific" training methods spawned by that conflict accelerated development of guide-dog programs. Their success in turn inspired new ways of employing dogs, which took root after World War II and blossomed in the mid-1970s. That explosion of interest coincided with the beginnings of the large-scale shift from compulsory, often brutal training methods to those emphasizing positive reinforcement. Abuse continues to occur, but men, and the few women, who engage in it are finding themselves—I would like to call them a minority, but they are not—with unhappy dogs who are not performing at the same level as those of their enlightened competition.

In the 1950s and 1960s, Boris Levinson, followed by Samuel and Elizabeth Corson, conducted pioneering work in the United States in the use of pets, especially dogs, in therapy for children and adolescents. In *Pet-Oriented Child Psychology* (1969), Levinson argued that pets could act as "stabilizers" in "acute family crises," such as divorce, illness, job loss, and accidents. Working with his mixed breed, Jingles, Levinson showed that pet therapy could be effective with "the young nonverbal child, the inhibited, the autistic, the withdrawn, the obsessive compulsive and the culturally disadvantaged child. It is not too effective with organic, acting out, character disorders and extremely bright children who can verbalize."

Pets break down the wall of solitude among children, helping those who are disturbed obtain physical contact "without the painfully embroiling emotional entanglements that the child already knows accompany emotional involvement with humans," Levinson wrote. Schooled in Freudianism, Levinson also argued that dogs embodied the id and anal fantasies. "Dreams and fantasies involving horses and dogs reveal penis envy in women," he said. "Men, on the other hand, while they have a lot to do with dogs, rarely imbue their pets with phallic significance." A quarter of a century after the fact, such interpretations seem outdated, but the point is that dogs and other animals help certain people come out of their shells of isolation, which in turn means they are more receptive to therapy. They also provide comfort for children—and adults—stressed by illness, family breakup, death, a move, or job loss.

Levinson found that children raised with pets were more cautious around strange animals and less fearful of animals in general, meaning they had developed a balanced approach to unknown creatures. Those children who feared animals tended to be unhappy at home and displace that unhappiness onto the animal. Frequently, they learned the phobia from their parents, the way a puppy learns fear from its dam. Moreover, Levinson emphatically refuted a notion popularized by the Nobel Prize–winning ethologist Konrad Lorenz that children were inherently gentle with animals and, therefore, along with their mothers, the agents of domestication. Rather, Levinson said, children had to learn not to hurt animals. Having jury-rigged a little suction-capped dart gun to fire pins and chased the family cat around the house one fine morning when I was four, I can attest to that.

When Levinson first reported on his work at the 1961 convention of the American Psychological Association, he received responses ranging from applause to open ridicule. Even many therapists who used pets, he wrote in *Pet-Oriented Child Psychology*, considered them part of "play therapy" or symbols, not as useful tools in their own right. Although the particulars of his interpretations have changed over the years, his fundamental insight into the value of pets in treating mental illness has been confirmed time and time again. The profession has just been slow in employing them, in no small measure because of the varying responses practitioners themselves have toward dogs.

Similar skepticism greeted initial reports in 1980 on research by a graduate student at the University of Maryland, Erika Friedmann, showing that heart attack victims had a better chance of surviving a year or more if they had a pet than if they did not. Building on that, researchers began to show that people's blood pressure dropped and their heart rates slowed when they stroked a dog. Subsequently, the Baker Medical Research Institute in Melbourne, Australia, found that triglyceride and cholesterol levels, as well as blood pressure, were lower in pet owners, regardless of other risk factors, like smoking and diet. Men, it was found, could often interact much more easily with dogs than with humans. More prone to high blood pressure and coronary heart disease, they seemed to benefit more than women from the connection, although for both men and women the benefits of pet ownership were substantial after the loss of their spouse.

The pet serves as a bridge to a life suddenly interrupted and buffers the surviving spouse from the decline in health that often accompanies loss of a partner. A woman I know recounts how after her husband of nearly fifty years died, their Rhodesian Ridgeback, who had been devoted to him, transferred his allegiance to her. "I could do anything with him," she says, "but no one else could touch him. He was my friend." For many people in this woman's situation, the dog provides more solace and protection than family or friends. It is always present and forever giving. When her Ridgeback died, she received a German shepherd as a gift from friends wanting to alleviate her grief, and although she appreciates the dog, she does not share any special bond with it, a common state for people who are given dogs as opposed to selecting their own.

For young and old, dogs provide a reason to get out of the house and take a walk. They also serve as a means of meeting neighbors who otherwise would remain anonymous. Walk a dog around your neighborhood or local park enough, and you will get to know other owners. That is a simple truth. Disabled people often find that a dog breaks down barriers that exist between them and others, providing an opening for conversation. Dogs and other pets often help foster children adjust to their new environment. Dogs rely on their own judgments; they do not care about a person's past or reputation among other people.

Research conducted over the past several decades has resoundingly refuted the presumption, still common in many circles, that dog owners are less social than nonpet owners. In fact, the opposite appears true. Walking the dog is but one of the indicators of that. Children raised with animals appear to learn to read human body language better than those without pets, and they gain, on the whole, a better understanding of human behavior, which in certain respects is not much different from that of their dogs, despite the intellectual sheen laid over it. Generally, children with pets are *more* social than those without.

In some quarters, the findings about the benefits of pet ownership were greeted with the same disdain that met those documenting the healthiness of daily exercise; after all, real men never eat quiche or work out and die a miserable death on their way to the office, their ties knotted, their shoes shined, their health insurance up to date. Unreal men opt for life—dogs, exercise, culture, a little love. Real women, of course, do not sweat for labor or play, and they absolutely cannot run marathons. They might handle dogs, but only in the show ring.

The findings also added fuel to a movement to bring dogs as assistants in therapy into hospitals and nursing homes and to train assistance dogs for people with hearing impairments, paralysis, and other disabilities. The same training methods emphasizing positive reinforcement that were being applied to detection dogs and guide dogs were turned to this task with remarkable results. In fact, positive reinforcement is the only method that can work in many cases. People with limited use of their hands cannot hold a leash or reach a dog to deliver a correction. Nor can they hand out food rewards. Often they cannot shout. All of those factors mean the dog must be trained to voice commands, often based on changes in pitch: a low "No" like a growl; higher, lilting tones for commands and praise.

In 1975, Canine Companions for Independence was founded to provide service dogs for people who were not blind. Linda Hines and Leo Bustard, a veterinarian from Washington State University, founded the Delta Society two years later to promote the health benefits of companion animals. Whereas Canine Companions for Independence, like the top guide-dog schools, breeds, certifies, trains, and places dogs with people in need, the Delta Society conducts an ambitious program of advocacy, education, information, referral, and research. It also sponsors a Pet Partners Program, which certifies people and their animals—dogs, cats, birds, and assorted other creatures—for visiting nursing homes, hospitals, schools, prisons, and other facilities where humans are confined voluntarily or involuntarily, for engaging in "animal-assisted activities" and "animal-assisted therapy."

As the term implies, animal-assisted activities are informal affairs—visits primarily—to bring a spot of nature to the lives of people frequently abandoned to their loneliness. Alan Beck and Aaron Katcher report in their 1983 book, *Between Pets and People*, on an elderly man in a nursing home who spoke for the first time in twenty-six years upon seeing a dog brought there for a visit. For many people, an animal is not only easier to converse with than another human—after all, it appears to give its undivided attention, especially if being petted, and is nonjudgmental—but also evocative in many cases of a more robust, satisfying time. They begin talking to the dog directly and then to its handler, often about animals they have known, loved, and lost.

Just as the handler of a detection dog has a dramatic effect on its success rate, so apparently does the handler of an assistance dog. More significant, the dog sets its handler at ease on a visit to a nursing home, so that she or he can more easily talk with the patients. Barriers of isolation are not erected solely by the people who are alone.

In prisons, the presence of animals seems to lessen violence among inmates, while caring for them provides work that is emotionally and physically satisfying. Animals allow prisoners, no less than other people, to care for something outside themselves. From some penal institutions come reports of prisoners who spoil the dogs and other animals, lavishing attention on them that they probably never received or devoted to their own families. Inmates at a Texas prison were said to have pampered a black, flop-eared wolf-Lab cross who, like many of them, was deemed unfit for proper society. Project Pooch, a Delta Society program at the MacLaren School for juvenile offenders in Oregon, involves the student inmates in obedience training dogs rescued from a local animal shelter. The reclaimed dogs are then sent to people needing animal companionship. The training addresses behavioral problems, which are among the primary reasons that dogs adopted from shelters are frequently returned or abandoned. Not coincidentally, the children learn to discipline themselves as well.

As the term suggests, animal-assisted therapy employs animals in the treatment process. Their contributions to treating certain psychiatric patients are well documented. Less well known is their value to certain head-trauma patients who often need help performing basic tasks. Owners of therapy animals receive initial training, which is designed in part to teach them how to train their dogs, and are certified by the Delta Society once they have completed all tests. They must be recertified every two years.

The 1990 Americans with Disabilities Act mandates that dogs trained to help individuals with disabilities—be it to lead them if blind, alert them to sounds, pull their wheelchairs, brace them, retrieve dropped items, open doors, anticipate epileptic seizures, or serve them in whatever way—be admitted to public places, offices, transportation, and businesses. The owner need not provide proof of training or certification papers, which in the absence of national standards, do not exist. That significant achievement underscores the progress that has been made over the past two decades not only in recognizing the needs and rights of disabled individuals but also in training and distribution of service dogs.

The growing use of those dogs has created a nationwide demand that local entrepreneurs have moved to fill. They compete for foundation and other support, and, although their intentions might be good and they might train some excellent dogs, their ambitions sometimes exceed their talent. They also compete for dogs, many of whom come from breed rescue clubs or animal shelters.

The Delta Society, which like Seeing Eye and Canine Companions for Independence has registered its name as a way of keeping it from being used by imitators, also operates the National Service Dog Center to help people with disabilities find the trained dog they need. A person wanting such a dog is best advised to work through a group providing dogs who meet standards established by the Delta Society or a similar group. Canine Companions for Independence and various organizations belonging to the National Council of Guide Dog Schools also provide certified dogs.

Whether through these or another body, rigorous national standards need to be developed for the training of service and assistance dogs, just as they must be for detection dogs. Certification need not be a government program; rather, it can take the form of the Red Cross swimming and lifesaving classes that lead to water safety–instructor certification for those trained in advanced lifesaving techniques. Often swimming pools and summer camps require their lifeguards to have completed that course. To fill their tanks with air, scuba divers must produce proof of their certification. We should expect no less of dogs since a poorly trained one can set back years of good works.

Despite the overwhelming evidence attesting to the advantages of pet ownership for the elderly, disabled, lonely, and troubled, our society makes it most difficult for them to have animals. The woman with the Rhodesian Ridgeback, now in her midseventies, maintains a house she considers too large and burdensome just so she can keep a dog, most condominiums and apartments in South Florida, as well as in this country in general, being inhospitable to pets. Yet the elderly and people living alone are the very ones who benefit most from having dogs in their lives.

Many people with AIDS also have difficulty caring for their pets as the disease progresses. These people and others with suppressed immune systems, from chemotherapy and other causes, must exercise some caution when around pets because they are at greater risk to zoonoses—diseases or parasites contracted from another species. Worms, including tapeworms carried by fleas, are an obvious problem, as are Lyme disease, carried by deer ticks, and various bacterial and fungal infections.

Statistics on pet ownership provide some insight into the problems elderly people have in keeping pets. According to figures compiled by Andrew Rowan, director of the Center for Animals and Public Policy at the Tufts University School of Veterinary Medicine, dog ownership declined slightly in the United States during the early 1990s due to oversaturation of the market and then plateaued. In other countries, and perhaps in the United States, although the records are difficult to compile, overall declines ran parallel to an increase in families with multiple dogs. Part of that drop appears related to a fall in birthrate and the number of families with children, although fully 80 percent of them had dogs, compared with 40 percent for young adults and 20 to 25 percent for senior citizens. Whether those numbers are changing in the waning years of the millennium, as the number of children has again increased in the baby boom's baby boomlet, is hard to determine. Certainly, there appears to be renewed interest in dogs and in dog ownership.

Clinics run by local Humane Societies and other groups have helped alleviate some of the financial problems faced by those on fixed incomes by offering low-cost inoculations, spaying, and neutering of pets to prevent unwelcome breedings. But pet ownership remains difficult for the least wealthy, the elderly, and the most needy. Kit Jenkins, director of community education at the Humane Society of Greater Miami, says that in Atlanta, where she worked before moving south, the Humane Society's clinic inoculated the dogs of homeless people for minimal charge. Among the clients was an old gent with a mixed-breed Australian shepherd who had been his constant companion and protector for years on the street. When Jenkins met the man, he was regularly chewing food for the dog, who had grown old with him and lost its teeth. Loyalty works both ways.

Failed Contracts

Local Humane Societies are not subsidiaries of the Humane Society of the United States; in fact, they frequently accuse it of suggesting in its fund-raising material that it is related to local groups in order to entice individuals to donate directly to it. Local groups rely heavily on those benefactors, so if their money goes elsewhere, the animals needing shelter lose. Local animal-welfare groups are the ones who establish clinics, provide rescue work, and often perform the unwelcome task of culling unwanted animals. Although the number of those euthanized in the United States has dropped by 85 percent during the past decade, it still amounts to 2.4 million dogs—out of some 3 to 4 million taken in each year. In all but a handful of shelters, men and women who have devoted their lives to animal welfare find themselves in the unwanted role of executioner. The slaughter wears many of them down emotionally and psychologically, leaving them with a rough and troubled edge, an understandable fanaticism regarding the poor treatment of animals.

The numbers are far lower than they were in 1987 when euthanasia was the fate of an estimated 17 million animals. The San Francisco Society for the Prevention of Cruelty to Animals proclaims that it has euthanized no healthy dog or cat since March 1994. Other shelters have experienced dramatic declines as the numbers of spayed and neutered dogs and cats have risen around the country—by some estimates, more than 65 percent of dogs and 85 percent of cats that are owned have been altered—and the census of stray dogs has plummeted from 30 percent in the late 1960s to 2 percent in the 1990s. Increasingly, vasectomy is an option for male dogs, and, perhaps, forms of birth control other than spaying—removal of the ovaries—will become viable for females, thereby preventing the hormonal changes and weight gain that so often accompany the procedure.

As people have moved to exercise more rigorous control over their pets' reproduction, so have they, as we have seen, changed their approach to dog training and upbringing. The result is that people are less likely to abandon a dog with a behavioral or health problem than attempt to cure it. In one sense, they take greater responsibility for the animal they have brought into their lives; in another, they recognize, especially if it is purebred, that it is too valuable to treat badly.

Andrew Rowan believes the difference is also due to a change in attitude, from considering the dog a "stimulus reaction machine," like Pavlov's salivating experimental subject, to granting it intelligence, volition, and feelings, the way many eighteenth- and nineteenth-century naturalists did. Nature films widely distributed on television, such as the specials of the National Geographic Society and the long-running program *Wild Kingdom*, have greatly expanded the public's awareness, as has the work of researchers like Jane Goodall with chimpanzees and Dian Fossey with gorillas. Farley Mowat's fictional *Never Cry Wolf* (1963) brought those wild canids home. Barry Lopez's *Of Wolves and Men* (1978) popularized the work of a number of researchers on wolves, especially that of David Mech, with the U.S. Fish and Wildlife Service, considered the dean of wolf researchers. Lopez's best-seller furthered a radical reinterpretation in the popular imagination of the wolf's place in the world. Except in isolated pockets, where people choose to remain fearful and ignorant, the wolf is no longer seen as a man-eating embodiment of the devil; rather, it is viewed as a highly intelligent, social predator at the top of the food chain.

The films and television programs especially gave a wide audience a firsthand look at animals in their element. The view was a select one, to be sure, focusing on their nobility, their intelligence and ingenuity. Predator and prey were presented as locked in a necessary cycle of life and death, with the more brutal aspects of hunting often cut away. Sanitized though they were—even occasionally anthropomorphic— the portraits served to substitute for the time-honored Western metaphor of the great chain of being, with man as master of the world, the concept of a supple web of life, in which humans are inextricably woven. They also clearly showed that much of what we take as innate behavior is, in fact, learned.

On film, we watch how cheetah cubs playing with prey have no idea how to kill or digest it until their mother shows them, and even then they must practice. We observe that in packs of wolves or African wild dogs, there are individuals who excel at hunting and others who rarely bring down their own meal. We see a full range of personalities and behaviors. I even recall a nearly lame, lop-eared African wild dog who made it through at least one year of life, helped by its sound packmates. The diversity of behavior and the knowledge that much of it is learned among wild animals make us realize that the same is true of dogs.

Within the literature on dogs, the change is also due to new training and attitudes reflected especially in popular writings as diverse as the dog stories of the late James Herriot and Elizabeth Marshall Thomas's *The Hidden Life of Dogs* (1993). Thomas was widely criticized in dog circles for allowing a husky featured in that book to roam the streets of Cambridge, Massachusetts, and her conclusion that all dogs want is to be with each other seems overstated to many observers, given that even her rambling male always came home. But she contributed to a deeper understanding of the animal nature of the dog, as well as its innate intelligence and character.

Positive though that change has been, the growing popularity since the early 1990s of genetic determinism has threatened its accomplishments. Blaming genes is equivalent to saying that the organism by its nature is good, savage, intelligent, dumb—whatever attribute one wishes to assign it. Environmental and social factors contributing to its personality are ignored. Thus, a wolf preying on sheep and cattle can be condemned as bad and executed, as if it should know or care about the human-defined difference between an elk and a cow. Although people who understand genetics know better, there is a growing public willingness to believe that bad acts reflect a bad nature, and, therefore, both must be squashed. The corollary holds that good breeding is by definition superior.

The success of no-kill shelters in San Francisco and other areas is due in part to a divorcement of adoption and humane care, offered through the local Society for the Prevention of Cruelty to Animals (SPCA) or Humane Society, and animal control, a branch of local government. For decades, animal-welfare groups ran animal-control facilities throughout the country, putting them in the position of deciding which animals would live and which would die. They also asked supporters to pay for the removal and euthanasia of surplus animals. During the 1990s, animal-welfare groups have moved out of the animal-control business, properly forcing local governments to take on that responsibility if they did not do so already. So, although animal-welfare groups can rightly boast about their success in adoption, the sad fact remains that dogs who find new homes represent at most 40 percent of those eligible, some 1.6 million dogs, and most of them are puppies.

No matter who does it, euthanasia remains a daily and thankless task. The animal-control facility in Dade County, Florida, funded by income from dog-licensing fees—cats do not require licenses—and no general tax dollars, is a warehouse of death, a place animals are taken to die if their owners do not claim them or they are not lucky enough to be adopted. Its funding means that responsible dog owners are paying to kill the discards of irresponsible owners. Whether these facilities will ever see the day when only animals with terminal illness are euthanized remains an open question.

Merritt Clifton, editor of *Animal People*, observes that the success of no-kill shelters, led by the North Shore Animal League on Long Island, has spawned demand for facilities devoted to caring for unadoptable animals. Those care-for-life facilities house hundreds of dogs, preferably in large areas, yet to date, failure has marred their promise, as some animal collectors stockpile and mistreat animals they are supposed to nurture. Clifton proposes a national "accrediting-and-helping association, to set appropriate standards for each type of no-kill, including not only humane outposts, high-volume adoption, and care-for-life, but also non-sheltered fostering groups." The goal is to make sure that the protectors of unwanted animals do not by omission and commission become their exploiters.

By any measure, adoption has changed radically since the early 1960s when I was a child in Winter Park. The *Uncle Walt Show*, a late-afternoon local television program on which groups of children would appear, usually on someone's birthday, to be interviewed by Uncle Walt—"What do you want to be when you grow up?"—and watch cartoons or *Little Rascals* clips, would occasionally feature a dog from the local Humane Society in need of adoption. One day, the show featured a puppy purportedly a cross between a German shepherd and a Lab. He was brown, with prick ears and a black muzzle. Wanting a dog to replace our Dalmatian, Spot, who had been put down when unable to control himself after repeated strokes, I suggested we look at the dog. We brought him home and the next day rushed him near death to the vet. He was so severely infested with hook worms that he needed a blood transfusion. He was eight weeks old. Saved, he was named Lucky.

Lucky turned out to have a sizable amount of basset hound in him. As the Italians say, he was *il cane mista*, a "mixed-up dog." With the body of a shepherd and the legs of a basset hound, hardly the large dog we had expected. He was nice and somewhat dumb, a state I always attributed to his worm infestation and near death. Fortunately, most animal shelters now treat puppies and dogs before they release them. In fact, some more rigorously screen people wanting a pet than do breeders.

Animal welfare, or protection, tends to concern itself with the well-being of the animals in human care. Its adherents traditionally have sought to end animal suffering, especially when its source is human. Animal rights involves granting legal and moral standing to animals. Accustomed to "rights" movements and arguments, most Americans call the whole cluster of philosophies and groups "animal rights." Although there is overlap—many in both camps oppose the use of animals for profit and entertainment, for example—they are not the same. People in the animal-rights movement are, for clear reasons, frequently, if not exclusively, vegetarians, opposed to the consumption of any animal flesh. More significant, they tend to oppose the killing of animals for any reason. While not a posture to be maligned, it is clearly not one that most people want to follow. More than a few animal-rights activists oppose the very concept of pet ownership or domestication, judging it tantamount to slavery.

For philosophical reasons, many animal-rights activists and animal-welfare proponents denounce all selective breeding. They would rather see dogs breed themselves back to the "ur-dog"—the universal mutt—and do whatever dogs do naturally without excessive training. No one is certain what such an animal looks like, although it is imaginatively taken to be a dingo in the South and husky in the North. Of course there are several basic types within the broader division between large and small, but no matter. The scheme falters for an even more fundamental reason: its failure to recognize that the dog does not exist outside the human cultural context. Selective breeding is not the problem with dogs; poor breeding and irresponsible ownership are. Training and working dogs does them less harm than doing nothing with them.

Dogs, it is clear, chose humans as much as humans chose them. We just have not fulfilled our end of the contract, as Kit Jenkins says: "When we domesticated certain species we entered a contract, saying, 'We're going to change you so you can provide things for us, but we're going to provide for you, too.' Somewhere along the line, we broke that contract and are now throwing animals back to the wild [onto the streets] and expecting them to fend for themselves."

People at the end of the twentieth century have no monopoly on conscience. For as long as there have been dogs, individuals have treated them with respect and demanded that others do the same. If their voices did not find their way very often into print, it is in part because they were a minority crying against customs that were wasteful of humans and beasts and, in part, because animals were so common-place that they received attention only when they performed out-standing feats or were outrageously abused.

The modern animal-welfare movement has its roots in the late eighteenth and early nineteenth centuries when naturalists, artists, and thinkers began to attribute consciousness, intellect, and emotion to animals, suggesting that they were not so different from humans after all. Charles Darwin and his followers came from that school of thought and contributed to it.

In 1824, the Royal Society for the Prevention of Cruelty to Animals was founded in London to improve the lot of horses and other domestic animals and to end such spectacles as dogfights. In 1854, it successfully lobbied Parliament to ban the use of dogs for transport. Combined with a tax on dogs, which made the animals cost money they could no longer help earn, the ban caused the slaughter of thousands of working dogs across England. The RSPCA presented evidence that the dogs were abused, and many were, but just as many were treated with as much and possibly more respect than people showed each other.

The RSPCA drive was motivated not only by a legitimate concern for animal welfare in general but also by the belief of its predominately urban middle-class supporters that dogs belonging to the working class were, by definition, mistreated. In other countries, dogs continued to pull carts—not to mention sleds—through World War I, when they helped bring munitions across the mountains. Only with the spread of motorized vehicles and bicycles to all corners of the world has their use as beasts of burden diminished to almost nothing.

The humane movement took off in the 1870s in England and the

United States, where the American SPCA and Massachusetts SPCA were founded respectively in New York in 1866 and Boston in 1868. The American Humane Association was established in 1877. These groups tended to support animal protection and antivivisection. AHA was also concerned with the welfare of children, there being then and now a direct correlation between the abuse of children, women, and animals.

Animal protection fell into eclipse between the World Wars—due to the Great Depression and widespread behaviorist view of the dog as a jumble of conditioned responses—to rise with renewed vigor following World War II. Growth in pet ownership, shifts in theories of behavior and learning, the civil-rights, women's, and child-protection movements, all of which reflected a drive for greater equality in society, helped strengthen the move to improve animal welfare. Andrew Rowan found that the number of animal-protection groups increased steadily between 1950 and 1980, when it exploded. Membership went from the tens of thousands to the millions. The movement itself began to concentrate on animal rights as well as such issues as welfare and treatment.

According to Rowan and other observers, publication in 1975 of *Animal Liberation* by Peter Singer provided an intellectual foundation for expansion of the movement. Singer argued that because all animals experience pain, the suffering inflicted on them for medical and scientific research as well as in breeding, raising, and slaughtering them on factory farms for food is morally and ethically indefensible. Singer's argument is straightforward, intelligent, and powerful: animals deserve the same consideration as people. Formation of People for the Ethical Treatment of Animals in 1979, which today has more than 300,000 members, ushered in a new phase of militant direct action, especially against research laboratories and the fur industry. Other organizations have joined the fray.

Many people with working dogs—be they guide dogs, service dogs, racing huskies, hunting dogs, detection dogs, or Frisbee dogs—have felt the disapproval of one or more animal-rights groups. My attitude has always been that if the dog, or other animal, is not compelled to do something that brings it pain or suffering, there is nothing inherently wrong with the activity. Thus, I am no fan of animal testing, except in the rare cases where it is essential to perfect a vaccine that is of overwhelming importance to humans, and no alternatives exist. Most research does not fit that bill. I also support completely efforts to end the grotesqueries of factory farming, a related but different issue.

For the same reason, as I have made clear, I do not find anything inherently wrong with sled-dog racing, hunting, Frisbee, or detection work. Each case must be measured separately. As long as animal-rights groups condemn those activities, and by implication the people engaged in them, they will create ill will among those who could be their allies and leave themselves open to charges, often correct, that they are opposed to all uses of dogs. Those who believe that should make their position clear at the start, so people can judge the philosophy behind their arguments. At times, as with the Iditarod, groups like the Humane Society of the United States seem more interested in the publicity and income to be generated from a campaign than in helping to alleviate animal suffering. They sponsor no studies or research to support their claims and regularly overstate problems, tarring everyone in the process. Those are the tactics of publicity hounds and fund-raisers, who because of the peculiarities of American interest-group politics are often mistaken for advocates.

Perhaps the greatest achievements of the animal-rights movement are the reduction—and one hopes the ultimate elimination—of animals used in unnecessary research and the transformation of many animal shelters from institutions for killing to adoption centers. Along with that has come the great expansion in training those dogs as companions and working animals. Through direct action and legislation, animal-rights people have also put pressure on various groups to improve their treatment of animals. Those accomplishments coincide with a trend among dog owners, even those with working dogs, to treat them more humanely, breed them more responsibly, and train them using more positive methods.

The lot of animals in many industrialized countries may have improved dramatically, but it is not idyllic for many of them. Although more easily attacked, institutional abuses, like the use of animals in research or factory farming, are easier to change than those of individuals. Longtime workers at humane shelters witness daily that terrible underbelly of pet ownership. Collars put on puppies are not removed for months, so that the dog literally grows around it the way scar tissue forms around an unremoved splinter. Maggots, pus, and blood form a seal around the collar that constricts the dog's breathing and must be surgically removed. Often such animals are physically neglected as well—malnourished, alternately abused and ignored. Dogs are abandoned on streets or tied up in yards and left when people move away. Many times people will move from a home or apartment and leave several dogs and cats inside. As they weaken and become sick in their own excrement, they kill and eat each other. Cats and dogs are stolen and used as training bait for fighting dogs or sold to research laboratories. Dogs are shot for target practice.

Even people who want to do good sometimes make a botch of things. A man or woman collecting strays ends up with so many animals that he or she can no longer afford to feed, walk, or care for them. They turn the house into a putrid dog yard. A story, perhaps apocryphal, tells of a woman in New Jersey who had more than thirty malnourished dogs in her house when local animal-control officers raided after numerous complaints. She was told by the court that she could keep no more than three animals. She soon had thirty or more, and again her house was raided. She was sent for treatment to a mental institution, diagnosed as being lonely and depressed, and told by her doctor to get a dog.

Rescue

Gracie was one and a half years old when Kit Jenkins found her. "I can predict what her [human] father looked like," Jenkins says. "He smoked a pipe, drove a Jeep, and was thin. I know that because after all these years she responds to men who look like that as if she should know them, and she perks up when she hears a Jeep. She wasn't abused. I don't know why he gave her up."

Gracie lies on her bed while we talk, feigning sleep as dogs who are alert but want to seem uninterested are wont to do. At one point Jenkins calls her to have her strut her stuff, then thinks better of it, saying there is no reason to have her perform tricks for tricks' sake. Gracie is a whippet, descendant of the workingman's racing ratter of the nineteenth century and the late-twentieth-century show dog who whelps only with difficulty—"that's why whippets are so rare; they're hard to breed." Although a member of a breed adjudged by experts one of the least intelligent and difficult to train, she was the Delta Society's activity dog of the year, honored at a ceremony in New York. At a party afterward, she achieved a modicum of notoriety when she refused to kiss the host because "he had been drinking." Call Gracie a temperance dog.

Gracie gained her award for her work with autistic children and her ability to move into a hospital and go up to people, by name, lay her head or paw on their bed, or touch them on command. "She knows over 450 phrases and remembers names," Jenkins says. "She knows to go to people by name." Those are not exaggerations. They are documented.

Along with her abandonment, Gracie faced another obstacle on her way to success as an activity-assistance dog. Soon after beginning training, she was picked up and shaken by a German shepherd, intent on harming, if not killing, her. The experience left her traumatized, afraid to be around large dogs. Not content to let Gracie's fear rule her, Jenkins hit upon the idea of desensitizing her by training her with the German shepherd club in Atlanta.

Give the Dog a Treat

A different way of thinking about dog training that emphasized positive reinforcement and behavior modification began to emerge from marine mammal training and human psychological research in the 1960s, picking up speed in the 1970s and 1980s as its graduates began winning competitions and excelling in detection work. In addition to success, the rising cost of dogs contributed to the trend: few people want to harm or ruin an animal worth $1,000 or more. As one husky trainer in New England told me, "We were working on positive reinforcement in the education of children during the 1960s and then coming home and kicking our dogs, so we decided we had to treat dogs like they were children." They fenced five acres and pulled the stakes on the dog yard, then they set out to enrich the environment of the dogs and to train them using only positive reinforcement.

The new school of trainers would teach a dog to retrieve keys or a phone with the same ease a hunter would teach it to retrieve a bird. The behavior is the same, the object is different. Or they would teach a dog to stand, legs locked, while its paralyzed master braced himself against it to move in and out of his wheelchair. That requires a big, strong dog, but teaching it to freeze for a human is not much different from teaching it to set when encountering a covey of quail.

The key was not to use force but to change "the level of motivation," to make the dog want to do something for a reward, be it food, praise, a tennis ball, Frisbee, or rag. Commands were to be crisp and clear, free of ambiguity and threat. They were a way of telling the dog directly what to do and then rewarding it for doing so. Correction was kept to a minimum and issued when the bad behavior occurred; thus, a firm "No," accompanied if necessary by a rattled can or key ring. For greater offenses a shake might be in order, according to some schools, but you had to deliver it immediately. The proponents of shock collars welcomed them for that reason while missing the general point.

Training based on shaping and rewarding good behavior, on leading rather than commanding the dog required a new metaphor. People began to speak of the dog as a companion and to seek a word less freighted than "owner" to describe their relationship. Like many people, I prefer to think of myself as the custodian or guardian of my dogs. I have a responsibility to provide medical care, food, shelter, and certain instruction on how to get along in the world, and legally, I own them. But morally, I do not.

It is necessary, however, to let the dogs know that the humans are the boss—the pack leader, as it were—and so from an early age, our Catahoulas learned that we can and will pick them up, tell them to do something and expect that they will do it, and, in general, assert our dominance over them. Some trainers teach the "alpha roll" as a way for people to do that, believing it mimics what the top wolf does to subordinates who misbehave. They get down on the ground and literally roll the dog over into a defenseless, submissive position. Started early, they argue, it need not and should not become a battle; rather, it can be something the dog does as a way to get a belly rub. Too often, thought, the "alpha roll" becomes a physical contest, and so it is best not done at all. I hear more than a few trainers scream; indeed, there are times when it is necessary to inform the dog who is boss, but if you have to do it repeatedly and with force, you have not socialized or trained the animal well from the start.

Neither training nor discipline should turn into a struggle with the dog. If either does, something is wrong. To avoid difficulties of that sort, many trainers and dog books advise people not to stare their dogs in the eye, arguing that such behavior hints at dominance challenges and predation. You're telling your dog, they say, that you are going to eat it or beat it. That is the prevailing wisdom, and it is reinforced through discussions of the border collie's management of sheep with its eye and the wolf's way of focusing on its prey. But not all eye contact has to be a challenge. I would not have a dog I could not look in the eye, and virtually all of the people I have met who are good with dogs are the same way. Staring into a dog's eyes, no less than a person's, is a way to get and focus its attention and to communicate with it.

To repeat: the keys to training a dog, no matter whether it is a worker or a pet, are consistency in approach and rewards for proper behavior. Commands that are issued in mushing, herding, Schutzhund, and hunting are different not because the dogs understand them better but because of human traditions that are passed down through the generations. Susan Butcher has commented that when she moved to Alaska, she was giving her sled dogs commands she had developed on her own—"Turn right" and "Turn left," for example—rather than the customary "Gee" and "Haw." Hers worked fine, but she changed to follow custom. The point is that good training involves teaching the dog to associate certain words or phrases, intonations, and inflections with actions it is to take. In that way, "Yes" muttered in a deep, warning tone can mean "No," just as a dog called all manner of foul names in a pleasant, rising voice will wag its tail in agreement. Most dogs are eager to please; it is the trainer's job to allow them to do so.

Its practitioners speak of "shaping behavior" through positive reinforcement as "new," citing Karen Pryor's popular *Don't Shoot the Dog* (1995), a practicum on behavior modification (not dog training), as their inspiration. Insofar as increasing numbers of people are applying the techniques with broad success, they are new, but from a historical perspective, the trend more nearly approximates a growing popularization of an approach to dog training that has been around for some time—probably as long as dogs. In the late nineteenth century, Montague Stevens used food reinforcement to train a pack of grizzly bear–hunting dogs, including bloodhounds, a pit bull terrier, fox terrier, Russian wolfhounds, Great Dane, and crosses between a "bobtailed sheepdog" (what the old English sheepdog should be) and bloodhound. That crossbred dog was a "slow trailer" trained to track the hounds who otherwise would outrun Stevens, making it difficult for him to find them when they had tired the bear.

Stevens describes in *Meet Mr. Grizzly* (1943) how he trained his dogs using jerky as a reward and yoking younger hounds either to more experienced ones or to the Great Dane, who always ran near him. "I always demanded strict obedience," he says, "but obedience without fear. As to beating them, I always held that if there were no other way of making a hound obey than to beat him, I didn't want him." Stevens taught his dogs tricks to instill obedience, keeping them busy and active.

An Englishman living on a ranch in western New Mexico, Stevens developed his training methods in part to compensate for the loss of an arm in a hunting accident when he was young. He was considered an eccentric—at best—by his neighbors and other hunters whose idea of training was praise with a whip and a boot. When they encountered Stevens on the trail, they would marvel at his dogs before growing resentful that their own abused animals wanted to leave their side and follow him.

Nearly a century later, the same differences in approach are found throughout dogdom. Many hunters and other dog owners train their dogs with abuse, which they call discipline, and then wonder why the animals refuse to perform. Or they get rid of the dog when one day it turns on them. After feeding his dog a steak dinner, a man I know took his six-year-old out and shot it because it had snapped at him when he tried to pull it from a bitch it wanted to mount. Anyone who has been around dogs and people for any length of time has heard countless stories of that type: a "beloved" animal had to be shot because of human stupidity.

Sadly, Stevens's hounds died one day almost immediately after feeding on a cattle carcass that a rancher had laced with poison in an effort to destroy wolves and coyotes. He had habitually allowed them to feast on fallen game while on the trail because, he figured, that was the dog's habit.

Dog-training manuals abound, and most of them are poor to incomprehensible in the eyes of trainers and animal behaviorists. Some offer wrong advice about swatting dogs with rolled-up newspapers when caught in some bad behavior or rubbing their noses in their excrement when, as puppies, they soil the house. A number of obedience classes involve what is appropriately called the "circle jerk," where students with their new dogs are placed in a circle and taught to yank hard on their choke collars by way of correction. It works with some tough, hardheaded dogs, but even with them it is unnecessary and with more sensitive animals it is counterproductive. It can also damage the dog's trachea.

Arguably, the best books are *Good Owners, Great Dogs* (1992) by Brian Kilcommons and Sarah Wilson, which is comprehensive and clearly written; *How to Teach a New Dog Old Tricks* (1991), by Ian Dunbar, founder of the Sirius Puppy Training Program; and *How to Raise a Puppy You Can Live With* (1992), by Clarice Rutherford and David H. Neil, experts on puppies. These books and good obedience classes teach people how to teach their dogs, their primary lessons being that there are no shortcuts, that learning should always be enjoyable and end on a positive note, that it should not extend the dog to the point of exhaustion, that corrections should be immediate, precise, and then end. People must remain consistent and fair, while thinking about what they are doing.

The same applies in housebreaking puppies, a process easier for some dogs and, apparently, some breeds than others. Our Catahoulas were never trained to newspaper, a common ploy. Rather, we made it a point to take them out after they ate, after they woke up from a nap or night's sleep, after they finished playing. We praised them when they relieved themselves outside, and we trained them through repetition and reinforcement to go to the door when they had to do so. Most dogs hate to foul their den site, so housebreaking should not be a difficult problem for attentive people and normal dogs.

A simple issue, housebreaking leads to the abandonment of many dogs, as does teething, when puppies are apt to turn their attention to anything chewable, including chairs, shoes, tables. If they are trained from the start to understand what is chewable in terms of toys and not left alone for long periods with the run of the house or apartment, destructive chewing—usually the result of separation anxiety or boredom—should not become a problem. For many working people, those are big ifs.

Arguably, if a person is at work eight to ten hours a day and the puppy is unattended during that whole time, he or she might well run into problems. It is not healthy to spend every waking hour with your pet, but it is essential that dogs have regular guidance and attention while puppies. They can learn no other way. Dog-walking services can alleviate some of the problem, as can farming the puppy out to a trainer, but both are expensive options. Some people use training crates, a practice fraught with as much controversy as any other in dogdom. On the one hand, a number of veterinarians and animal behaviorists argue that the dog is not by nature a denning animal and, therefore, the very concept of the crate as the dog's "den" is mistaken. On the other hand, there are those who say that a dog must be acclimated to the crate so it can travel and because it provides a sense of private space for the growing animal.

When our Catahoulas were puppies, we bought crates and locked them in a few nights, then stopped. We left the crates in the room for them to use as beds, but kept the doors open. We did so because the puppies were the same age and enjoyed each other's company and because I did not like the thought of locking them up—my own peculiarity. We retired the crates completely after a few months but would use them sparingly for puppies in the future. A major problem with crates is that people make them places of punishment when their dog misbehaves. Or they warehouse the dogs in them for eight or more hours at a stretch—a poor idea.

A number of breeders have told me that they disapprove of raising puppies together because they bond to each other rather than the human. We have not found that so, and the advantage is that they keep each other company when left at home. Although our puppies also played together for hours, now that they are nearly ten years old, they are content to conserve their energy for their long walks and poking around the house and yard. When a puppy is taken from its litter at seven or eight weeks of age and brought to a strange home, it is in a real sense alone, torn from its siblings and mother. It is incumbent on the people—and most do—to provide it with a new family, not to coddle it but to give it a sense of belonging. Teaching it how to come, sit, lie down, stay, and retrieve a ball or sock while it is young by making a game of the activities will produce a much better behaved animal.

These are far from simple bromides. Up to one-third of all puppies bought in the United States in any given year end up in a new home or more commonly in animal shelters. Countless more fail to make it through their second birthdays. By some estimates, as many as one-quarter of those who are abandoned have severel behavioral problems, leaving three-quarters with no apparent reason other than they are no longer desired. The puppy cannot be housebroken, the lament goes; it chews on things; it does not mind; it bites; it barks. There is an inclination among animal behaviorists not to blame the owner for the misdeeds of their dogs, and in some cases the animal is bad—miswired, deficient, the way a psychopath or sociopath is. In others, the dog and people are mismatched, and no amount of training will make them compatible. But often, the dog's ignorance has found its match in that of the owners, who have not taken the time to learn what to do with the puppy or how to train it.

It is easy to see how that can happen once or twice, but when people do it repeatedly, there is little excuse. The dog suffers, as do the people. Increasingly, some of those dogs are finding new employment and fulfillment in the hands of skilled trainers. Veterinary behaviorists are becoming more successful at treating various aggression-related problems and separation anxiety with medication, including the anti-depressant Prozac, and exercises intended to desensitize and recondition the dog. They have also found that the new high-fat, high-protein diets provide dogs who do not get much exercise with too much energy—an association of diet with activity that the Navajo made long ago. Cut the richness of the diet, and the animal tends to become calmer. Persuading owners to stop encouraging undirected, unconstrained aggression in their dogs also helps. Although far from universally successful, these efforts at behavior modification represent a significant attempt to save dogs and people.

Chapter Ten

BRINGING IT ALL BACK HOME

The Perfect Dog

Othello was sitting erect and alert in the aisle when Phoebe Stanton entered the hall to deliver her lecture on the history of art one day in the fall of 1970. Gray-haired, somewhat rumpled in her appearance, she was a favorite of undergraduates, tough-minded but generous, a superior professor, a woman known to take in stray dogs. Her class drew crowds because, well, introductory art history courses were renowned throughout the land as "guts," easy marks, especially when taken with a pass-fail option. Premedical students enrolled to fulfill degree requirements and prove to medical schools that they knew more than science. At Johns Hopkins University, the introductory course was Stanton's domain, and in it she conveyed the emotion, aesthetics, and intelligence of art in all its forms. Catching sight of Othello that morning, she turned to exclaim, "He's the perfect dog."

Othello, a.k.a. Otis and a half dozen other monikers to which he happily answered during his life, was reportedly a cross between a shepherd and collie, but to my eyes he always looked to be something else. Today, I would call him a cur and say we need a lot more like him. Weighing in at around sixty-five pounds, with brown eyes, he sported a rough, short, reddish brown coat, with a black mouth, dark ears, a small white blaze on his barrel chest, black and white at the tip of his tail, dewclaws front and back. He had powerful shoulders and sound, muscular hindquarters. His proportions were that of the classic dog; his demeanor beyond reproach. His drive and energy inexhaustible.

A gift from Daryl Smiley to her boyfriend, David Byer, Otis was walking in anti-Vietnam War demonstrations and attending classes at Hopkins from the time he was eight weeks old. Raised in a house of men and women, he never lacked attention or training, learning to sit, heel, come, stay, shake, speak in no time. His rewards were praise, attention, occasional snacks, and sticks. Otis had several passions in life: being with David or Daryl, fetching sticks, running along when Daryl went horseback riding, swimming, riding in the car, and sitting through classes. In short, he lived the way his people did.

He became feverishly excited when people played stick with him, retrieving beautifully for hours, which meant relays of throws. To instigate play, he would bring whoever was with him the largest stick he could find, plop it down at his feet, and bark—to make sure he was understood. He preferred long retrieves of multiple sticks in the water. Over the years we were students, other dogs came into the house, including a Dalmatian I received for Christmas, Sebastian—a.k.a. the Pig, for his love of eating and piglike noises—but, like many Dalmatians, he suffered chronic dermatitis and epilepsy, which brought his demise at age five. Othello was the star, one of those rare animals, "the perfect dog."

What he had besides his innate drive and looks was a rich environment, attention, training, love. He was exposed from the time he arrived in David's life to experiences few people have. He was always stimulated, even when tearing the mail out of the postman's hand as he tried to slide it through the slot in our front door or barking at people in uniform—stunts he learned on his own. David and Daryl trained him well; equally important, he learned just by living with people and doing things with them.

Dogs like Othello stick in one's mind and also prove that mutts or mixed breeds are as fine in all respects as those who have pedigrees. In any number of responsible books devoted to selecting the "perfect puppy," experts caution against mongrels. You don't know what you're getting with a mixed breed, they write, even adding that with a purebred dog you do. They explain that most crosses are accidental, that without knowing the dam and sire, you'll end up with a dog like Lucky—a big dog on dwarf legs or worse.

They are far more wrong than right. Most people who deliberately cross dogs are attempting to bring forth certain qualities—call them habits of work they cannot find in available pure breeds. Even in accidental breedings, the sire is often known or strongly suspected. That said, it is possible for a litter to have several sires—even among pure breeds—and for bitches in heat to escape for a rendezvous with a local Lothario, dogs being indiscriminate fornicators. In any of those cases, the results might be dogs like Lucky, but that is probably not common, and even those mutts have their charm. On the plus side, crossbred dogs tend to benefit from what biologists call hybrid vigor: they are healthier in mind and body than their inbred cousins. They are seldom worse except, perhaps, in looks, and even then they can as easily be more beautiful.

The most interesting dogs I have seen in recent years have been the Alaskan huskies, the crossbred curs of the Big Cypress, the Basketmaker dogs of the Navajo, Cisco the border collie, the little cowdog Coda, and Percy the hunting Lab. Among that group, only the Lab was registered, although Cisco is now probably eligible for the AKC stud book. I like them because they were bred and raised to be just dogs. They were judged by what they did and by their functional conformation, not what they were supposed to look like or be in the abstract, yet nearly all were intriguing and some were exceptional.

Tell a musher like Martin Buser that one of his eight-month-old puppies looks great, and he thanks you, then responds that the test will be whether it arrives in Nome at the front of a sled. Comment on the spirit and apparent intelligence of one of Jeff McDaniel's young curs, and he will respond that he has high hopes for the dog but will not know anything until it meets its first cow and probably not until it encounters its first irate cow with a calf in tow. A good-looking dog to them is one who moves efficiently—with whatever combination of grace, speed, power, coordination, and good sense are needed for the task at hand. A dog working against itself because of physical disability or lacking stamina is not going to last. It certainly is not going to be allowed to breed in their kennels.

Those dogs are not all perfect, nor are they clones—as nearly identical as they could be. The only reason to want to clone a dog, after all, is fear that one as good or better will not come along. That concern has no genetic base; the best dogs, horses, or humans when mated with other top animals, or with their own siblings, do not as a rule produce offspring that matches or surpasses them. If they did, we would not be looking for the next Secretariat or Citation, the second coming of that great pointer from thirty years ago. People with exceptional sled dogs or hounds or guard dogs would always have them. That they do not should, after all these years, tell even the most devoted eugenicist that the super dog (human, or other animal) results from favorable environmental circumstances, hybrid vigor—genetic variability—and that intangible, apparently uninheritable quality called will, rather than from a narrowing of possibilities.

The puppy's personality is formed through a unique combination that no one has yet been able to decipher or reproduce but that includes everything from the genetic makeup of the parents, the way the puppy's own body and brain develop, the health of the mother, the stresses to which she was subjected during pregnancy, her diet, the puppy's birth experience and neonatal care, its level of stimulation by its mother, littermates, and human "parents," the food it eats after it is weaned, and traumas it suffers or avoids. Clearly, its genetic blueprint establishes parameters of behavior, as well as size, shape, mental ability, and overall health, but beyond that the variables begin to weigh in. What that puppy becomes is then largely a matter of the training and encouragement it receives as well as its own desire. People interested in working dogs usually look for those with physical talent and drive, but if they are wise, they also know how to take a dog with abundant desire and moderate physical abilities or the reverse and make it better.

Martin Buser says that a good musher, like a good coach, always concentrates on the weakest member of his team, meaning the one with the least ability. Help that dog reach and exceed its potential, and you will have created an environment in which even the best in the team can flourish. Meanwhile, the putative weak link might just be an excellent breeder or a stabilizing influence among the other dogs. Susan Butcher had a dog like that. Always the last chosen for the team, he nonetheless was always in Nome at the end of the Iditarod. That he was a great friend to the lead dog Granite and a better sire than the star made him all the more valuable.

Buser's advice applies equally to pets, to the dogs most of us bring into our homes as companions and guardians. They represent the vast majority of dogs in the world. In the United States and other industrialized countries, many of them occupy homes and apartments in cities and suburbs where they are not permitted to run freely, where the level of exercise they receive is often as slight as that of their owners. Dogs and people are subject to ordinances mandating fences and leashes, "pooper scoopers," which breeds are acceptable, licenses, inoculations, insurance, and a certain, very basic level of humane treatment.

The regulations grow in direct proportion to the tension between the majority of nondog owners and the minority who have them, especially to the perceived dangers of dogs. Until rabies vaccines were developed, those fears focused on disease; now they relate to fatal attacks on humans and other animals, defilement of vanishing urban green spaces, and parasites transmitted from dogs to people. Undeniably, people who do not properly supervise their dogs contribute to the tension, but even if all dogs owners were model citizens and their animals perfect pets, the problem would persist. There are many people who hate and fear animals, and in this country they hold considerable power.

That fear is reinforced by the recurring story about the adult whose beloved dog kills a child, perhaps her own, and then grieves that it must be put down. Like the rabies scares of the nineteenth century and the pit bull mania of the 1980s, that story, repeated several times a year in all major media, conveys the message that people with dogs have skewed values, that they place the welfare of a deadly killer above that of a child. Not surprisingly, it finds echoes in reports about people who attempt to help an "incorrigible" killer escape the death penalty and work to save from execution cougars, wolves, or bears that kill humans. It is bad enough that so many people live in fear of other animals; it is worse when they turn that fear into public policy.

In May 1996, a flap over unleashed dogs in Central Park spilled into national consciousness when an item appeared in the *New York*

Times describing how dog owners were ticketed in record numbers during the first months of the year for letting their dogs run free. Facing fines of up to one hundred dollars, several miscreants vehemently protested to park police ticketing them and were arrested. Following the report, the *Times* ran an op-ed piece by Elizabeth Marshall Thomas extolling off-leash walking and the attitudes toward dogs in many European countries, where they are welcome in most public facilities and businesses, including restaurants. Scores of letters applauding and condemning her poured into the paper, which on May 6 printed an editorial observing that New York City Parks Department officials had made clear that they were not enforcing the ban on unleashed dogs between the hours of 9 P.M. and 9 A.M. It was an attempt to strike a compromise on a contentious issue.

In principle I agree fully with Thomas and her allies. I believe absolutely that dogs need to run and have always taken mine for exercise in parks, on campuses, the beach—wherever there is open space. I consider attempts by civic authorities to ban them to be unfair, misguided, and discriminatory; that is actually the polite way to describe my reaction. I have fond memories of encountering dogs and their owners in parks and restaurants in France, Italy, and England, not to mention many parks and college campuses in this country. (I have also noted with amusement the annual article from a new American correspondent in Paris complaining of dog excrement on the streets and sidewalks.) In short, I consider a landscape without dogs to be barren, but too many community and state parks, including Florida's, ban them or severely restrict their mobility, in the process keeping people from enjoying the pleasures of dog ownership and, not coincidentally, getting exercise for themselves and their animals. Even national parks refuse admission to dogs, arguing that they bother wildlife and people, defile campsites. (Some national forests and isolated monuments are better.) But I have encountered far more problems with irresponsible humans while camping or hiking than with dogs.

Thus, the Central Park affair is really a manifestation of a larger problem: the conflict between those of us with dogs and those without. Often the gap appears unbridgeable, with dog owners forced to engage in criminal activity to exercise their dogs or adjusting their schedules to avoid conflict. I walk early in the morning for precisely that reason. I would much rather go out when it is light, but that is not always practical in dog-unfriendly South Florida. And this area is not unique in that regard, nor are the attacks directed only at pets. Initiatives to ban hunting with hounds have their roots in the same mentality, which says that dogs are bad for civilized life. In fact, dogs are central to civilization, our chief aides in domestication of other species, fellow hunters, and, more important, companions. Without dogs, our lives would be poorer.

The debate over the roots and meaning of the relationship between humans and dogs will rage for as long as we coexist. Psychologists and anthropologists will argue with a formidable array of opinion disguised as "data" that this relationship is little more than social parasitism perpetuated because we humans respond to warm furry creatures and that we have made our dogs perpetually juvenile, neotenic creatures who do tricks for their dinner. Others will assert that sharing food, furniture, beds, sometimes even clothing with a dog is a sign of deviancy or social maladjustment. Or they will proclaim dogs surrogate children and dismiss people who own them as misfits.

Following the view common through the nineteenth century, many people call the dog a slave. It must obey, after all, and it has no choice in how it will live, breed, feed itself, or even die. Insofar as the dog becomes what we name it, they are correct. A more expansive attitude considers that the dog's dependency on humans is similar to that of a child, and while it was long common to treat children as virtual slaves to their parents—and still is in many parts of the world—a more enlightened stance holds that children are humans with rights. We are responsible for shaping their behavior but not dictating their lives.

Yet even that analogy has its limits, for dogs are no more children than slaves. They have their own integrity and needs, which we have an obligation to meet, although many dog owners refuse to recognize their responsibility. Dogs have been with us for some 15,000 years because they, like we, have benefited from the union. To come up with a proper understanding of the relationship, we must start there. When we do, we begin to see that individual and societal treatment cannot be easily categorized in terms of human relationships, even when it appears to resemble them.

As they always have, individuals develop abnormal relationships with their dogs, or cats, treating them like people, using them as shields from human contact. Dogs have suckled on women's teats throughout the world, been coddled, pampered, eaten, abused, treated like royalty, heroes, slaves, and agents of evil. James Thurber is perhaps better remembered for his dog stories and cartoons than anything else he produced, and he is not alone among those who have celebrated and made light of their canine companions. The artist William Wegman is the best known of a number of artists who have achieved considerable fame portraying dogs in familiar, human guises. His weimaraners have posed in a variety of costumes to illustrate types of people or fairy tales. They are not much different from the bicycle-riding poodle in the circus, dressed in its sequins and lace.

Just as frequently, owners ignore their dogs, expecting them to fend for themselves intellectually and emotionally. A large number of those animals end up confined to basements, garages, or yards, un-trained and largely unwanted. Such a fate is little better than assignment to a pound and much worse than return to the breeder, who will probably find them good homes. Far better off in dog terms are the vast number of pariah, or ownerless, and feral dogs roaming the countryside and towns of many parts of the world. Although their lives are often short, they at least have the company of other dogs.

The best dogs are those who add depth to our lives, be it as workers, aides to our mobility, guardians, or, especially, companions. I believe that Homo erectus began to associate with wolves more than 300,000 years ago out of a desire to connect with another being, and our direct forebears followed suit. Humans found in the wolf a creature whose path constantly crossed theirs, whose family structure, methods of hunting, and prey were remarkably like their own. So they studied the wolf and shared food with it. Out of that curiosity and caring that represent the best aspects of human nature, they took in strays and puppies who became first their friends and then their helpers. Those of us who know and rely on dogs do so because, like people throughout the ages, we cannot conceive of not having them with us.

Over the years, I have met doctors, lawyers, business executives, writers, artists, laborers, housewives, homeless people, retirees who describe their dogs—be it large or small—as their best friends. Cliché though the phrase has become, freighted though it is with enough cultural baggage to break a strong dog's back, it nonetheless refers to an emotional condition that seems quite normal to me. The dog walks with them, attends them while they work, garden, or sit reading—usually by knocking closed the book or magazine and demanding to be petted. It helps them through depression and loneliness. Even if they do not count on it to work for them, many of the men and women I have met amuse themselves and the dog by training it. Just as significant, the dog demands nothing more than food, exercise, attention. It is as unambiguous in its desire and devotion as any being can be. At its core, the relationship between human and dog is an uncluttered one involving two distinct animals who just happen to understand each other at a basic level. That more than a few people end up preferring dogs to humans can come as no surprise.

A high-ranking executive with a Fortune 500 company retired in the mid-1980s, while in his midfifties, at the same time his son brought a female rat terrier puppy into the house. Through a variety of circumstances, the former executive became the owner and caretaker of Chelsea, who learned from the time she was a puppy to ride in the basket of a bicycle, to accompany him on walks, recognize people by name, find and retrieve hidden balls, open wrapped gifts without harming them, and a number of other "tricks." Each morning they walk together in a nearby park. She sits with the family at dinner—not begging or eating from the table, just watching. Chelsea never had a formal obedience lesson in her life. She learned because her owner taught her through repetition and reinforcement in the form of praise, the reward of a ball, perhaps a piece of food, and because she is eager to exercise her abundant energy.

For children, the bond is often greater. Many of the outstanding memoirs of dogs, including Farley Mowat's *The Dog Who Wouldn't Be*

(1957), and Willie Morris's *My Dog Skip* (1995), are about dogs the authors had as boys. The dogs were attentive, protective friends and amusing companions. As long as people have recorded narratives, they have written about the great loyalty of dogs, describing animals who have sacrificed their lives for their masters, pined away after the death of their human companions, protected especially their child wards when they have become lost or been threatened, prevented rapes and other physical attacks, broken free of restraint to dig from the grave their own still-living puppies. Not infrequently, the guardians are strays who appear as if from nowhere to succor a lost child or warn someone of danger. It is finally those stories of dogs, I think, that bind many of us together. We can laugh and cry while talking about them in ways that are difficult otherwise. The dog opens doors to other worlds and to our own; all we have to do is follow it through, whether to hunt, travel fast and far, or just knock around matters little.

Down the Road

People who get on best with their dogs treat them with respect and attempt in dealing with them to understand what they are seeing or feeling, while not forgetting that they are the leader. The task requires empathy and a desire to look at the world from the dog's perspective, to imagine how it views its circumstances. That is a difficult task, given the dog's physical approach to the world, its acute sense of smell, its superior hearing, and its different seeing—good at low light levels and motion, poor at distance, color, and depth. Yet professional and amateur trainers, individuals who work or race their dogs find that taking this imaginative step allows them to better deal with their animals, to perceive not just their own human inconsistencies but also each dog's motivations and concerns. Why has it regressed? Why does it stubbornly refuse to obey? Am I giving mixed signals? Is it challenging my authority? Why does it seem sluggish and unmotivated when I know it has the ability to work hard?

Intelligent animals, dogs will challenge authority especially when they are young, refusing commands, taking shortcuts, behaving in a seemingly erratic fashion. Rather than throw them away, beat them into submission, or give up and allow them to rule the house, the successful trainer—whether an amateur or professional—works through their stunts and refusals by looking at their cause. Those who take the time often end up with a superior dog; those who don't have a disobedient hardhead.

I have talked about the problems dogs face when they are poorly bred, socialized, or treated. Although I wish none of them had to deal with any of those disadvantages—since they are all of human design—I know that they are resilient enough often to excel despite them. Thus, a dog with genetic defects, like our Clio with her nonexistent hips, can live a fruitful life if she has the will, the care, the circumstances, and more than a little luck. She, for example, is not expected to hunt cattle or hogs, which surely would have broken her down in short order, bringing chronic pain and lameness. A dog like Percy who quits working for one person because he or she is too overbearing and abusive in his or her treatment may turn into a champion for someone else.

Since the end of the 1980s, the number and skill of animal behaviorists have increased dramatically, as has their success in treating many of the mental and emotional disorders afflicting dogs today. Aggression and separation anxiety represent the major reasons owners part with their dogs, yet in many cases, conditioning, training, and medication can "cure" them. The chief difficulty for the owner of a problem dog is finding someone who can help. Most cities have freelance animal behaviorists—usually dog trainers—who for a fee will come to your house, evaluate, and then train your dog. Eight of the nation's twenty-seven veterinary schools now have clinics devoted to behavioral problems, and an increasing number of veterinarians are taking an interest in the problem, although some rely too heavily on medication. There are also approximately thirty applied animal behaviorists specializing in pets with at least a master's degree in ethology.

Early in 1995, I received a call late at night from friends whose soft-coated wheaten terrier, bought as a puppy from a reputable breeder 2,000 miles from their home, had taken to biting their young children and growling at the mother. Was the dog somehow flawed genetically, they wanted to know, or was its problem behavioral? A trainer who billed himself as an expert in behavior modification came to the house and proclaimed the dog fine, saying it needed more consistent handling and the children needed to learn to give it space. Whether his advice would have worked, no one can say. He was not engaged; the dog continued to bite. My friends finally returned it to the breeder and requested their money back. She initially refused, arguing that they had not properly socialized and trained the dog. A few weeks later, news arrived that the breeder had put the dog down after it bit her child. She subsequently honored her guarantee.

Whether the terrier belonged in a home with small children in the first place is not relevant at this point, although arguably it did not, nor is the question of whether the dog was poorly bred or turned into a demon through inconsistent handling. A miniature poodle my friends bought to replace the terrier has done quite well, and the first dog's subsequent death made it impossible to determine whether its behavior was indeed correctable. Nonetheless, it is clear that the trainer in this case made a snap judgment, as did the breeder, that failed to take into account the actual dynamic in the household and the character of the puppy. The trainer who had no credentials or skill in animal behavior, established that he could gain its attention and exert some control over it—which anyone with experience should be able to do with almost any dog—and said he would undertake the project for around seventy-five dollars an hour spread over eight visits. This man has a local reputation for going into people's homes and training problem animals, but among trainers, he is not considered a person with great sensitivity or knowledge. Rather, he is looked upon as someone who saw a need and set out to meet it.

In a field that is still relatively young and requires no licensing, the man is the norm. Consumers wanting to do more than rely on uncertain recommendations or dialing names picked at random from the yellow pages should call their veterinarian, local obedience clubs, Humane Society, or the nearest veterinary school for the name of veterinarians interested in behavioral problems or a consultation with the school's behavioral laboratory. Veterinary behaviorists are certified through the American College of Veterinary Behaviorists; professional ethologists specializing in dogs and cats through the Animal Behavior Society. The Association of Pet Behavior Counsellors, based in England, also certifies professionals.

A qualified behaviorist might have looked at the soft-coated wheaten terrier, studied it in relation to the family, especially the children, talked to the owners, then made a diagnosis, prescribed a regimen involving behavior modification and possibly drugs, monitored the progress of humans and canine, and revised the diagnosis. Although the end result might have been the same, the dog might also have responded favorably and become a model citizen. Many owners, for example, allow puppies to bite on their hands and arms during play because they assume it knows no better and must be handled gently. In fact, it must be taught that people are not prey while its drive is directed toward desired objects. At the same time, children must learn not to taunt young dogs with food and when to leave them alone.

But that same qualified behaviorist might have looked at the situation and promptly recommended that my friends find a new home for their dog, calculating that they could not provide it with the kind of training and structured life it needed to thrive. The terrier and its adoptive family were due for a divorce before the dog's innate aggressiveness dominated its being. The behaviorist would have eased that blow by observing that some dogs and some people just do not get along, and the better part of rationality is admitting the mistake, finding a new home for the dog, and moving on. The breeder, who should not have sold a terrier, a type of dog with a predisposition toward heightened aggression, to a family with young children, should have taken the puppy back on the first sign of trouble and refunded the purchase price.

I am not a dog trainer by inclination, although I like to have trained dogs. I teach them to come when called by making a game of it, to sit, to heel—after a fashion—and also to listen to what I am saying. Traditional trainers will blanch at the thought because they want the dog to respond to crisp, clear commands, but we have always talked to our dogs in complete sentences, and they understand with some frequency. Other people report the same phenomenon. Whether the dogs understand the words as well as the intonation, I cannot say, but they certainly learn what is meant, largely through observation and association. After all, they study us and our moods more closely in some ways than we observe theirs, learning in the process when it is time to walk or ride in the car or go on a trip to an enjoyable place or to the kennel or veterinarian's office. They respond to our emotional states, just as they expect us to understand their needs—for attention, exercise, food, play. Clio, for example, tells us when she wants to play with a concealed tennis ball by sitting in front of the furniture that hides it, heaving her belly and quietly chirping.

Everyone who has ever been associated with a dog has numerous stories of its stupid and sublime tricks, its eccentricities, loyalty, lunacy, brains or lack thereof—the way we all do of any other being who has shared our lives for any period of time. The great variety in dogdom parallels our own. The attributes we associate with dogs, be they positive or negative, are reflections of our attitudes toward ourselves. Our ancestors came together because of those similarities, and we should celebrate them rather than attempt to force our best friend into becoming a projection of what we expect it to be.

A dog in motion, driving over the land or through the water with its powerful legs, alert to the wind and animals around it, delighting in its ability to move, is a beautiful sight. At such times, whether it is hunting game, running down a Frisbee, pulling a sled, or simply gamboling, it is fulfilling its nature and drawing us into an often ignored part of our own. It is just a dog then, and as long as we remember that, we will do fine by the animals that have stood by us all these millennia, moving with us from the forest and savanna to the farm, town, city, and suburbs. The transition requires a great deal of people and more of dogs. We have sometimes forced our putative best friend into shapes and sizes that defy nature; we have robbed it of its physical and mental vitality to suit our notions of beauty and nature; we have deprived it of the right to breed naturally.

Traditionally, we also have given it a chance to flourish, to continue to use its talents to their fullest, and now we must redouble our efforts. In addition to our working dogs, we must strive to produce companions with physical and temperamental soundness, with intelligence, trainability, drive, and sociability. After all, those are the traits that first attracted us to dogs, which we have too often ignored in our quest to make the dog in our own image. But we can correct that error and reinvigorate the animal and our relationship. We already have the knowledge to make remarkable progress in that direction, and with proper support for research into genetics and behavior, we can do more. Refusal to do so is fair neither to dogs nor to ourselves. All that we need is the sort of will we seek in our dogs.

APPENDIX

Finding a Dog

Many people who love dogs have a habit of collecting them. They take in young dogs whose owners have despaired of ever training them, pick up strays, travel far and wide seeking the type of puppy they want, often relying on a wide circle of friends in the community of dog enthusiasts, maintain their own kennels. When buying dogs, they may examine videotapes and have a puppy shipped directly to them by a breeder whose reputation is solid and who stands behind the health of his or her animals, but as a general rule they want to see what they are getting firsthand. Some trainers prefer dealing with older dogs, finding the whole process of raising and housebreaking puppies time-consuming, while others believe the best dogs are those they raise themselves. Not all of their choices are correct, but with experience they learn the type of dog they prefer in terms of structure, temperament, and drive. In short, they develop a way of evaluating dogs.

Following the advice of a woman who once told me that two dogs were quite sufficient because "you only have two hands" and lacking the space and energy to handle more, I do not collect dogs. But over the years, I have adopted dogs close to a year old, raised puppies, had dogs die young, put them down because of illness, and kept one dog who was so miswired her life was hell. I have rescued dogs from the shelter, from owners who mistreated them, from the jaws of death. I have bought puppies from home breeders and through other people. I have met wonderful dogs who wandered into people's lives off the street and high-priced show dogs with the personality of burned oatmeal. I have talked to scores of people about choosing dogs and read most of the literature, and I can say that there is no magic formula for selecting a "perfect puppy" despite a number of books designed for just that purpose.

Still, the books exist because the question that concerns many of us revolves less around our relationship to dogs than how to find the proper animal for our lives and circumstances. The best among them build their arguments around a few basic tips that can help even the first-time dog owner improve the odds of selecting a healthy puppy who with proper training, socialization, and exercise becomes a vital member of the household. But before undertaking the search, first-time owners or those without a preconceived notion should ask themselves why they want a dog, whether for protection, for companionship, for participating in field trials or some other event. Then they should consider whether they are already attached to a particular type or breed suited for that task.

Those without a clear preference are better off attending obedience club meetings or the events that interest them; reading several dog books, especially those that talk honestly about potential health and behavioral problems; talking to veterinarians, breeders, dog owners, trainers, and judges of obedience and field trials. Magazines devoted to virtually every type of dog can be found, and many of them have articles that can provide names of people to contact about particular breeds and lines. (Like books, the magazines should be approached with the attitude that much of what they say represents received wisdom and opinion.) Local search-and-rescue teams and police canine trainers can also be good sources. From those interviews more names will arise of breeders and handlers and of types of dogs that might be suited to the individual's circumstances.

It is important to remember that despite claims that border collies or Australian shepherds or Mississippi mud hounds are the smartest dogs in the world, no breed of dog is perfect, free of genetic and behavioral problems, superior in every regard. Some dogs who are robust and intelligent in, say, obedience work may be incapable of solving a problem without guidance. Dogs with keen noses, independence, and great associative skills might have no desire to heel on a leash or do other simple obedience work. They just want to run after whatever that nose is smelling. But that does not mean that they cannot be trained to do things quite well. Within every breed and line, dogs will vary markedly in temperament, soundness, and ability. A poorly bred border collie can be destructive, stupid, with no eye, bad hips, weak elbows. A well-bred German shepherd can be unsurpassed in beauty and working ability. A poor environment and improper socialization can turn even the best-bred dog into a terror.

That said, a few observations and tips are worth remembering. These are provisional. I once had a call from a woman who had read similar advice in my *Atlantic Monthly* article, confirmed it with independent experts, and followed the recommendations to the letter. She found a breeder of dual show and obedience champion golden retrievers certified by the Orthopedic Foundation for Animals to be free of dysplasia for three generations, paid in the neighborhood of $600 for a puppy—a fair price—and ended up with a dysplastic, monorchid dog with eye and skin problems. It is a temptation in such cases to observe that breeding is an inexact art, and drop the matter, but I agree with the woman that there is a deeper problem, relating to AKC-registerable dogs and their multiple ailments.

On the other hand, I selected a Catahoula puppy for a friend, and they have formed quite a happy union. Of course, in that case, the sire was our dog, the dam belonged to another friend who was in the whelping box at the delivery and never stopped interacting with the puppies. Gina and I observed them off and on from the time they were young, and we kept the puppy with us between her seventh and ninth weeks. She is well socialized, bright, and healthy. Our friend's stimulation of the puppies from the time they were born accounts, I believe, for their success more than any other single factor and certainly was crucial in overcoming the pronounced fearfulness of the dam. Studies have repeatedly shown that early handling, actually a form of benign stress, helps the brain develop more fully and quickly than just leaving the puppies to see a human when it is feeding time for Mom.

As a preface to these recommendations, I add the caution that in buying a dog one must seek out people who are producing animals that can and do perform physically, who discuss openly with you the health problems facing their breed in general and their line in particular. Find people who are not engaged in close line breeding and recognize that without genetic screening, which is available for only a few ailments in a limited number of breeds, one can never know for certain the soundness of the offspring. You do, however, increase the odds of obtaining a good puppy by dealing with breeders who maintain diversity in their gene pool. Study their pedigrees, observe their dogs over several visits. Do not listen to the pontifications of someone whose knowledge falls far short of your own, no matter their intentions. Ask questions.

Investigating Catahoulas, Jeff McDaniel called a breeder who had placed an ad in the breeders directory of the National Association of Louisiana Catahoulas (NALC), the largest registry for the leopard curs, saying he had cowdogs. When McDaniel asked whether he worked his cows with dogs and horses, the breeder told him never. He worked his cows with trucks. He simply raised his dogs for competing in NALC events. Needless to say, the man was engaging in misleading advertising.

Here, then, are a few suggestions for those looking for a puppy.

• Unless wedded to a giant or toy breed, avoid extremes in size and appearance—the mutants. The giant breeds are short-lived by their nature and subject to an inordinate number of ailments, while the toys tend to be fragile and sickly. Short-nosed, brachycephalic breeds, including bulldogs, boxers, and bull terriers, have respiratory and whelping problems. The achondroplasic, or dwarf, breeds, including basset hounds and dachshunds, often have leg and spinal problems. Dogs bred for excessive coats and other extremes in appearance have too many problems to enumerate, including an overall lack of intelligence or innate ability. The few exceptions to this rule involve the unspoiled terrier breeds, like the Jack Russell, jagdterriers, and rat terriers, and the equally fine feist, although these dogs are suitable for apartment life only if thoroughly socialized, well trained, and regularly exercised. Feists are available primarily in the South. Although the Jack Russell has gained notoriety for the movie *The Mask* and television series *Frazier*, which has brought an unwelcome increase in its numbers, it, like the other working terriers, is relatively rare.

• For overall intelligence and versatility, look to the herding, hunting, and working dogs—retrievers, pointers, and some hounds; stockdogs, including border collies, Australian and English shepherds, Australian kelpies, Catahoula leopard dogs, curs; the terriers listed above. If you are in a cold climate, consider an Alaskan husky from a reputable musher; those lacking the speed to race are sometimes available. Bred for work, these dogs require an hour or more of exercise a day—not just a stroll on a leash—whether they live in an apartment or have access to a fenced yard. In other words, they need something to do with themselves. A poorly conditioned animal becomes bored, destructive, and sickly.

• Having settled on a likely breed or two, seek reputable breeders in your area who are producing dogs for their abilities and temperament, not for appearance alone. You may have already located several breeders through your early research; if not, go back and talk to veterinarians, breed club members, trainers, and people who have the kind of dog you like. The best way to find top breeders is through word of mouth because many of them do not advertise. Some dog people refuse to deal with anyone who advertises in the newspaper or magazines, dismissing them as either commercial breeders or amateurs. Others treat them with caution while recognizing that there are successful breeders in both groups. In terms of publications, *Dog World* and the specialty magazines provide a place to start. If the dogs are AKC-registerable, make sure they are competing successfully in performance events and not just the show ring. You can also track down the associations that register the less well-known dogs and obtain lists of breeders from them, but you should treat these dogs with the same caution as AKC breeds.

• Visit the breeders even if they do not have puppies immediately available. Talk to them about your needs and desires and see whether they believe they are producing dogs that match. When asked for a designer dog—say a blue merle Australian shepherd with one blue and one brown eye—the best breeders will send you away without even the name of their worst enemy. The best breeder will ask you as many questions as you ask her and refer you to another excellent breeder if she thinks you are serious and she will not have any puppies for some months because of her breeding schedules. If you like her, you might decide to wait.

• When you go to see a litter, take another person, preferably a friend who is familiar with dogs. Ask to see the dam, as well as the sire and grandparents, if possible. If the sire is not available, find out why and ask about him. These animals give you a hint of how the grown puppy will appear and behave. Observe the puppy who interests you for as long as possible, to see how it interacts with people and its littermates. Then watch it alone to judge its level of inquisitiveness, activity, aggression, fearfulness. Check the sire and dam for the same attributes, especially fear. Several books now available offer tests that cover these areas, the majority of them attempting to measure: retrieve (prey) drive, aggression, timidity (fearfulness), reactions to strange noises, sight, and touch. The breeder should willingly fill you in on many of these characteristics, as should your friend. Thus, you have several opinions to collate. Most people simply seek dogs who are not overly aggressive and not fearful or timid around strangers and new stimuli. The puppy should be at least six and preferably seven or eight weeks old and have received one round of shots already. If it is nine to fourteen weeks old, you need to proceed with caution. If older than fourteen weeks, stay away unless you know it has been well stimulated and socialized. The puppy can be excellent if the breeder has spent time with it.

• The breeder should have discussed the known genetic defects afflicting his or her breed and line before you get around to negotiating a price. If the breeder does not, even on direct inquiry, you should go somewhere else. The breeder should offer proof of sound hips and clear eyes for generations. It is most important for you to be informed about potential problems and to receive straightforward answers from the breeder. If you do not, find a new breeder. Remember, buying a dog is a business transaction affecting real lives. It is illogical to spend less time on it than starting a family or buying a car.

• Often only the most popular AKC breeds are available locally; sometimes you can find a litter of a rare breed rising in popularity, but little else that is different. If you are fixed on a particular breed and on finding the best dog available, you should be willing to travel, wait, and pay. If you want a trained protection dog, you will have to deal with a local trainer, so be certain that you have interviewed him or her and checked with other trainers in the area for independent assessments of the person's abilities, remembering that the dog world is filled with professional jealousy and respect. A number of trainers will help you find and train dogs, usually for a fee. If you are confident of the breeder and your own ability to judge a dog based on a videotape, you might go on and have a puppy shipped to you. But you have to be careful.

• In general, if you are after a pet, you are better off changing to a different breed if unable to find suitable specimens of your first choice within easy driving distance.

• Make sure in buying a dog from any source that you are given the proper registration material (if it is a purebred) and a guarantee specifying that you can take the dog to a veterinarian for examination and if the dog is found defective, it will be replaced or your money refunded. In fact, the guarantee should extend until the dog's hips can be certified at two years of age (a quick way to end the breeding of dysplastic dogs.) Most guarantees are of shorter duration; the best ensure that you can have a replacement puppy without returning the one you have or return it for your money back. A growing number of states—including, Florida, California, New York, New Jersey, and Massachusetts—are requiring such money-back guarantees for genetic defects in puppies, and some mandate reimbursement for medical expenses, but enforcement is erratic and usually only commercial breeders are covered. A "restricted transfer" holds that the buyer will not breed the dog until it is certified free of hip dysplasia and/or other ailments. If it does not obtain certification, the breeder will replace it for free. No puppies from uncertified dogs will be registered.

• Do *not* buy a puppy from a pet store or commercial breeder.

• Look for interesting crossbred dogs or mongrels. Although the practice is anathema to the fancy, people regularly crossbreed dogs to cure defects or simply to create a hybrid more healthy and vigorous than either pedigreed parent. For working northern dogs, the Alaskan husky is best; for southern dogs, I like the feists and curs, although you have to proceed with caution when dealing with the Catahoula.

• Besides deliberate crosses, there are accidental mixes. Those mutts can be more healthy, even-tempered, intelligent, and enjoyable than purebred dogs. In picking a mongrel, you should exercise as much caution as with a purebred. Remember that without knowing what kinds of dogs the parents are, it is nearly impossible to guess what the mature dog will look like.

• Local animal shelters often have adoption programs, but sometimes they are so restrictive in determining where they will place their animals that it is easier to buy a purebred dog. Also, animals from shelters are more prone to have serious behavioral problems.

• If you are unable or unwilling to raise a puppy—and people who work are often in this category—you might consider an older dog. In addition to animal shelters, many local breed clubs sponsor rescue programs for abandoned purebred and, occasionally, other dogs, and some dog tracks have greyhounds too slow or too old for racing who can be adopted. Otherwise, they are destroyed.

• Always be prepared to walk away from the cute puppy who seems dying to hitch its life to yours. A dog is a serious commitment. If you do not feel right about that commitment to a particular dog, leave it. You can always change your mind and heart, but it is essential to listen to them from the start.

• Occasionally, you may run into a friend or acquaintance who has bred his or her pet, who just happens to be your favorite dog, and has handled the puppies from birth. You have watched them grow and decide to buy one. Sometimes those dogs are very nice and quite bright, but you should still clarify the parentage and terms of sale.

• If you do end up with a dog, take it immediately to the vet for a checkup and whatever inoculations it needs. If despite all your research, you have not thought about training, ask the vet how to contact a good trainer who emphasizes positive reinforcement and shaping of behavior. While your puppy is growing, investigate training classes. For experienced dog owners, they may be unnecessary, but for beginners they can help with socialization of the dog and education of people, who usually need the most help. Before you enroll, visit a class, talk to the teacher. If you see him stringing dogs up by their leashes, bopping them under the chin, yelling at canine and human students as if they were stupid, save your money and find another instructor. If the person teaching the class has never heard of the type dog you have, find another class. Remember, there are trainers who make dogs do things, and there are trainers who educate people to teach their dogs. You want the latter.

SELECTED
BIBLIOGRAPHY

BOOKS

American Kennel Club. *The Complete Dog Book*. 17th ed. New York: Howell, 1989.

Anderson, R. S., ed. *Nutrition and Behaviour in Dogs and Cats: Proceedings of the First Nordic Symposium on Small Animal Veterinary Medicine, Oslo, September 15–18, 1982*. Oxford: Pergamon Press, 1984.

Beck, Alan, and Katcher, Aaron. *Between Pets and People*. New York: Putnam, 1983.

Brown, David E., ed. *The Wolf in the Southwest: The Making of an Endangered Species*. Tucson: University of Arizona Press, 1983.

Caius, Johannes. *A Treatise of Englishe Dogges*. 1576. Reprint. Amsterdam: Theatrum Orbis Terrarum; New York: Da Capo Press, 1969.

Chapman, Samuel G. *Police Dogs in North America*. Springfield, Ill.: Charles C. Thomas, 1990.

Clutton-Brock, Juliet. *Domesticated Animals from Early Times*. Austin: University of Texas Press, 1981.

Corbett, Laurie. *The Dingo in Australia and Asia*. New York: Cornell University Press, 1995.

Coren, Stanley. *The Intelligence of Dogs: Canine Consciousness and Capabilities*. New York: Free Press, 1994.

Darwin, Charles. *The Descent of Man, and Selection in Relation to Sex*. London: John Murray, 1871.

———. *On the Origin of Species*. London: John Murray, 1859.

———. *The Voyage of the Beagle*. London: P.F. Collier and Son, 1839.

DeVoto, Bernard, ed. *The Journals of Lewis and Clark*. Boston: Houghton Mifflin, 1953.

Dodman, Nicholas H. *The Dog Who Loved Too Much: Tales, Treatments, and the Psychology of Dogs*. New York: Bantam Books, 1996.

d'Orbigny, Alcide Dessalines. *Voyage dans l'Amerique Meridionale.* Paris: Pitois-Levrault, ca. 1826.

Dunbar, Ian. *How to Teach a New Dog Old Tricks.* Oakland: James & Kenneth, 1991.

English, Douglas. *Friends of Mankind: A Study of Our Domestic Animals.* New York: E. P. Dutton, 1924.

Fergus, Charles. *A Rough-Shooting Dog: The First Season of a Hunting Spaniel.* New York: Lyons and Burford, 1991.

Flamholtz, Cathy J. *A Celebration of Rare Breeds.* Ft. Payne, Ala: OTR Publications, 1986.

Fogle, Bruce. *The Dog's Mind.* London: Stephen Greene Press, 1990.

————. *The Encyclopedia of the Dog.* London and New York: Dorling Kindersley, 1995.

Fox, Michael W. *The Dog: Its Domestication and Behavior.* Malabar, Fla: Robert E. Krieger, 1987.

Frank, Harry, ed. *Man and Wolf: Advances, Issues, and Problems in Captive Wolf Research.* Dordrecht, The Netherlands: W. Junk, 1987.

Hart, Benjamin L., and Hart, Lynette A. *The Perfect Puppy: How to Choose Your Dog by Its Behavior.* New York: W. H. Freeman, 1988.

Hearne, Vicki. *Adam's Task: Calling Animals by Name.* New York: Alfred A. Knopf, 1986.

Kete, Kathleen. *The Beast in the Boudoir: Petkeeping in Nineteenth-Century Paris.* Berkeley: University of California Press, 1995.

Kilcommons, Brian, and Wilson, Sarah. *Good Owners, Great Dogs: A Training Manual For Humans and Their Canine Companions.* New York: Warner Books, 1992.

Lee, Richard B., and DeVore, Irven, eds. *Man the Hunter.* Chicago: Alden, 1968.

Levinson, Boris M. *Pet-Oriented Child Psychology.* Springfield, Ill: Charles C. Thomas, 1969.

Lopez, Barry. *Of Wolves and Men.* New York: Charles Scribner's Sons, 1978.

Lorenz, Konrad. *Man Meets Dog.* Baltimore: Penguin, 1964.

Manwood, John. *A Treatise and Discourse of the Lawes of the Forest.* 1598. Reprint. London and New York: Garland, 1978.

Mech, L. David. *The Wolf: The Ecology and Behavior of an Endangered Species.* Minneapolis: University of Minnesota Press, 1981.

Milner, Robert. *Retriever Training for the Duck Hunter.* Long Beach, Calif.: Safari Press, 1993.

Montaigne, Michel de. "Apology for Raimond de Sebonde." In *The Essays of Michel de Montaigne*, trans. Charles Cotton, ed. W. Carew Hazlitt. New York: A. L. Burt, 1892.

Morris, Willie. *My Dog Skip.* New York: Vintage Books, 1995.

Mowat, Farley. *The Dog Who Wouldn't Be.* Boston: Little, Brown, 1957.

————. *Never Cry Wolf.* Boston: Little, Brown, 1963.

Olsen, Stanley J. *Origins of the Domestic Dog: The Fossil Record.* Tucson: University of Arizona Press, 1985.

Pitcher, George. *The Dogs Who Came to Stay.* New York: Dutton, 1995.

Pryor, Karen. *Don't Shoot the Dog: The New Art of Teaching and Training.* New York: Bantam Books, 1985.

Pugnetti, Gino. *Simon & Schuster's Guide to Dogs.* Edited by Elizabeth Meriwether Schuler. New York: Simon and Schuster, 1980.

Rindos, David. *The Origins of Agriculture: An Evolutionary Perspective.* Orlando: Academic Press, 1984.

Ritvo, Harriet. *The Animal Estate: The English and Other Creatures in the Victorian Age.* Cambridge: Harvard University Press, 1987.

Rosenblum, Robert. *The Dog in Art: From Rococo to Post-Modernism.* New York: Harry N. Abrams, 1988.

Rutherford, Clarice, and Neil, David H. *How to Raise a Puppy You Can Live With.* Loveland, Colo.: Alpine Publications, 1992.

Scott, J. P., and Fuller, John L. *Genetics and the Social Behavior of the Dog.* Chicago: University of Chicago Press, 1965.

Serpell, James. *In the Company of Animals: A Study of Human-Animal Relationships.* Oxford: Basil Blackwell, 1986.

————, ed. *The Domestic Dog: Its Evolution, Behaviour, and Interaction with People.* Cambridge: Cambridge University Press, 1995.

Shook, Larry. *The Puppy Report: An Indispensable Guide to Finding a Healthy, Lovable Dog.* New York: Lyons & Burford, 1992.

Singer, Peter. *Animal Liberation: A New Ethics for Our Treatment of Animals.* New York: New York Review of Books, 1975.

Stanley, Steven M. *Macroevolution: Pattern and Process.* New York: Freeman, 1979.

Stephens, John Richard. *The Dog Lovers' Companion.* Rocklin, Calif.: Prima Publishing, 1992.

Stevens, Montague. *Meet Mr. Grizzly.* 1943. Reprint. Silver City, N. Mex.: High-Lonesome Books, 1990.

Stockard, Charles. *The Genetic and Endocrinic Basis for Differences in Form and Behavior.* The American Anatomical Memoirs, no. 19. Philadelphia: Press of the Wistar Institute of Anatomy and Biology, 1941.

Thomas, Elizabeth Marshall. *The Hidden Life of Dogs.* Boston: Houghton Mifflin, 1993.

Tuan, Yi-Fu. *Dominance and Affection: The Making of Pets.* New Haven: Yale University Press, 1984.

Varner, John Grier, and Varner, Jeannette Johnson. *Dogs of the Conquest.* Norman: University of Oklahoma Press, 1983.

Wentworth, Edward N. *America's Sheep Trails.* Ames, Iowa: Iowa State College Press, 1948.

Yamazaki, Tetsu. *Legacy of the Dog: The Ultimate Illustrated Guide to Over 200 Breeds.* San Francisco: Chronicle Books, 1995.

Zeuner, Frederick E. *A History of Domesticated Animals.* New York: Harper and Row, 1963.

DOCUMENTS ISSUED BY GOVERNMENT AND PRIVATE ORGANIZATIONS

Alpo 1996 Canine Frisbee Disc Championships. "1996 Guidelines & Competition Schedule."

Corley, E. A., and Keller, G. G. *Hip Dysplasia: A Guide for Dog Breeders and Owners.* Columbia, MO: Orthopedic Foundation for Animals, 1989. Pamphlet.

Friskies 1995 Canine Frisbee Disc Championships. "1995 Guidelines & Competition Schedule."

Green, Jeffrey S., ed. *Protecting Livestock from Coyotes: A Synopsis of the Research of the Agricultural Research Service.* Dubois, Idaho: USDA-Agricultural Research Service, U.S. Sheep Experiment Station, 1987.

Natural History of the Dog. Pittsburgh: Carnegie Museum of Natural History, n.d. Exhibition booklet.

Rowan, Andrew N., and Loew, Franklin M., with Weer, Joan C. *The Animal Research Controversy: Protest, Process, and Public Policy.* Boston: Center for Animals and Public Policy, Tufts University School of Veterinary Medicine, 1995.

Transcript of proceeding before the Honorable William M. Hoeveler, U.S. District Judge, at Miami, Florida, May 31, 1989. Case Number: 89-771-CIV-Hoeveler.

United Kennel Club. "U.K.C. Pit Rules." Revised October 1, 1940. Reprinted in the pamphlet *Combat Rules*, by Sharon and Raymond Holt, June 1975.

U.S. Department of Agriculture, Animal and Plant Health Inspection Service, Regulatory Enforcement and Animal Care. *Animal Welfare: List of Licensed Dealers.* Washington, D.C. Printed annually.

U.S. Department of Agriculture, National Agricultural Statistics Service. *Sheep and Goat Predator Loss.* Washington, D.C., 1995.

ARTICLES

Belyaev, D. K. "Destabilizing Selection as a Factor in Domestication." *Journal of Heredity* 70 (1979): 301–8.

Black, Hal, and Green, Jeffrey S. "Navajo Use of Mixed-Breed Dogs for Management of Predators." *Journal of Range Management* 38, no. 1 (1985): 11–15.

Boitani, L., and Ciucci, P. "Comparative Social Ecology of Feral Dogs and Wolves." *Ethology Ecology and Evolution* 7 (1995): 49–72.

Canemaker, John. "An American Icon Scampers in for a Makeover." *New York Times*, April 6, 1995.

Clutton-Brock, Juliet. "Origins of the Dog: Domestication and Early History." In James Serpell, ed., *The Domestic Dog: Its Evolution, Behaviour, and Interaction with People.* Cambridge: Cambridge University Press, 1995.

Coppinger, Lorna, and Coppinger, Raymond. "Livestock-Guarding Dogs That Wear Sheep's Clothing." *Smithsonian*, April 1982.

———. "So Firm a Friendship." *Natural History*, March 1980.

Coppinger, Raymond, and Schneider, Richard. "Evolution of Working Dogs." In Serpell, ed., *The Domestic Dog.*

Daniels, Thomas J. "Down in the Dumps." *Natural History*, April 1988.

Davis, Donald, and Stotik, Jeffrey. "Feist or Fiction?: The Squirrel Dog of the Southern Mountains." *Journal of Popular Culture* 26, no. 3 (1992): 193–201.

Derr, Mark. "Common Scents." *Scientific American*, September 1995.

———. "Growing Bigger Coyotes." *Audubon*, November–December 1994.

———. "Marathon Mutts." *Natural History*, March 1996.

———. "The Perilous Iditarod." *Atlantic Monthly*, March 1995.

———. "The Politics of Dogs." *Atlantic Monthly,* March 1990.

Finn, Robin. "One Last Call of the Mild: Champion Akita Ready for Another Round." *New York Times*, February 13, 1995.

Frank, Harry, and Frank, Martha G. "The University of Michigan Canine Information-Processing Project (1979–1981)." In Harry Frank, ed., *Man and Wolf: Advances, Issues, and Problems in Captive Wolf Research.* Dordrecht, The Netherlands: W. Junk, 1987.

Gordon, Gregory. "High Price of Pedigrees." *Detroit News*, March 4, 5, and 6, 1990. A three-part series.

Gotteli, D., Sillero-Zubiri, C., Applebaum, G. D., Roy, M. S., Girman,

D. J., Garcia-Moreno, J., Ostrander, E. A., and Wayne, R. K. "Molecular Genetics of the Most Endangered Canid: The Ethiopian Wolf *Canis simensis*." *Molecular Ecology* 3 (1994): 301–12.

Gottlieb, Alma. "Dog: Ally or Traitor? Mythology, Cosmology, and Society Among the Beng of Ivory Coast." *American Ethnologist* 13 (1968): 477–88.

Gould, Stephen Jay. "Mickey Mouse Meets Konrad Lorenz." *Natural History*, May 1979.

Green, Jeffrey S., and Woodruff, Roger A. "Breed Comparisons and Characteristics of Use of Livestock-Guarding Dogs." *Journal of Range Management* 41, no. 3 (1988): 249–50.

———. "The Use of Eurasian Dogs to Protect Sheep from Predators in North America: A Summary of Research at the U.S. Sheep Experiment Station." In D. J. Decker, ed., *Proceedings of the First Eastern Wildlife Damage Control Conference*. Ithaca, N.Y., 1983, pp. 119–24.

Hart, Lynette A. "Dogs as Human Companions: A Review of the Relationship." In Serpell, ed., *The Domestic Dog*.

Hawk, H. W., Conley, H. H., and Kiddy, C. A. "Estrus-Related Odors in Milk Detected by Trained Dogs." *Journal of Dairy Science* 67, no. 2 (1984): 392–97.

Jackson, Virginia. "Domestic Pets in New Urban Areas." *Australian Planner* 31, no. 3 (1994): 148–52.

Jolly, Simon E., and Jolly, Lorraine M. "Environmental Influences on the Ability of Captive Dingoes to Find Meat Baits." *Journal of Wildlife Management* 56, no. 3 (1992): 448–52.

———. "Pen and Field Tests of Odor Attractants for the Dingo." *Journal of Wildlife Management* 56, no. 3 (1992): 452–56.

Keeler, Clyde E., and Trimble, Harry C. "Inheritance of Position Preference in Coach Dogs." *Journal of Heredity* 31 (1940): 51–54.

Kiddy, C. A., Mitchell, D. S., and Hawk, H. W. "Estrus-Related Odors in Body Fluids of Dairy Cows." *Journal of Dairy Science* 67, no. 2 (1984): 388–91.

Klein, Richard. "The Power of Pets," *New Republic*, July 10, 1995.

Kopas, Leslie. "Last Days of the Tahltan Bear Dog." *Dogs of the North*, (Alaska Geographic) 14, no. 1 (1987).

Leibetseder, J. "Nutritional Management in Heart Disease and Diabetes." In R. S. Anderson, ed., *Nutrition and Behaviour in Dogs and Cats: Proceedings of the First Nordic Symposium on Small Animal Veterinary Medicine, Oslo, September 15–18, 1982*. Oxford: Pergamon Press, 1984.

Lemonick, Michael D. "A Terrible Beauty." *Time*, December 12, 1994.

Lockwood, Randall. "The Ethology and Epidemiology of Canine Aggression." In Serpell, ed., *The Domestic Dog*.

Morey, Darcy. "The Early Evolution of the Domestic Dog." *American Scientist* 82 (July–August 1994): 336–47.

Nieves, Evelyn. "Agency Fails to Protect Pets, Critics Say." *New York Times*, February 5, 1996.

Orlean, Susan. "Profile: Show Dog." *New Yorker*, February 20 & 27, 1995.

Owren, T. "Communication with the Dog When Training." In R. S. Anderson, ed., *Nutrition and Behaviour in Dogs and Cats*.

Podberscek, Anthony L. "Dogs on a Tightrope: The Position of the Dog in British Society as Influenced by Press Reports on Dog Attacks (1988 to 1992)." *Anthrozoos* 7, no. 4 (1994): 232–41.

Poling, Eric. "Right Hand Man." *Cattleman*, May 1973.

Powers, William K., and Powers, Marla N. "Putting on the Dog." *Natural History*, February 1986.

"Prepare for Post-Pet Overpopulation." *Animal People*, September 1995.

Puttnam, Clare. "Can Police Dogs Really Sniff Out Criminals?" *New Scientist*, September 14, 1991.

Scott, J. P. "The Social Behavior of Dogs and Wolves: An Illustration of Sociobiological Systematics." *Annals of the New York Academy of Sciences* 51 (November 7, 1950): art. 6.

Serpell, James, and Jagoe, J. A. "Early Experience and the Development of Behaviour." In Serpell, ed., *The Domestic Dog*.

Vines, Gail. "Science Goes to the Dogs." *New Scientist*, October 29, 1987.

Washburn, Sherwood L., and Lancaster, C. S. "The Evolution of Hunting." In Richard B. Lee and Irven DeVore, eds., *Man the Hunter*. Chicago: Alden, 1968.

Wayne, Robert K. "Cranial Morphology of Domestic and Wild Canids: The Influence of Development on Morphological Change." *Evolution* 40, no. 2 (1986): 243–61.

———. "Molecular Evolution of the Dog Family." *Trends in Genetics* 9 (1993): 218–24.

Willis, M. B. "Genetic Aspects of Dog Behaviour with Particular Reference to Working Ability." In Serpell, ed., *The Domestic Dog*.

Zimen, Erik. "Ontogeny of Approach and Flight Behavior in Wolves, Poodles, and Wolf-Poodle Hybrids." In Harry Frank, ed., *Man and Wolf*.

PERIODICALS

Animal People
Anthrozoos (The Delta Society)
Bloodlines (United Kennel Club)
Dog Fancy
Dog World
Full Cry
Gazette (American Kennel Club)
HSUS News (Humane Society of the United States)
Hunting Retriever
Sports Afield

INDEX